# THE FIRST FILM MAKERS

D.W. Griffith directing Lillian Gish in a scene in *Way Down East* (1920)

# THE FIRST FILM MAKERS

*Richard Dyer MacCann*

THE SCARECROW PRESS, INC.
Metuchen, New Jersey & London

*in association with*

IMAGE & IDEA, INC.
Iowa City, Iowa

1989

*Other Books by Richard Dyer MacCann*

Hollywood in Transition (1962)
Film and Society (1964)
Film: A Montage of Theories (1966)
The People's Films (1973)
The New Film Index (1975)
    (with Edward S. Perry)
Cinema Examined (1982)
    (with Jack C. Ellis)
The First Tycoons (1987)

*In Preparation:*

The Stars Appear
The Comedians
Films of the 1920s

*Film/Video Works:*

Degas: Master of Motion (1960)
How to Build a Freeway (1965)
How to Look at Freeways (1965)
Murder at Best (1981)
The Quiet Channel series (1983)
American Movies: The First 30 Years (1984)
A New York Boy Comes to Iowa (1988)

**Library of Congress Cataloging-in-Publication Data**

MacCann, Richard Dyer.
    The first film makers / Richard Dyer MacCann.
        p.    cm. — (American movies)
    Includes bibliographical references.
    ISBN 0-8108-2229-6. — ISBN 0-8108-2230-X (pbk.)
    1. Motion pictures — United States — History. 2. Motion
picture
producers and directors — United States — Biography. I.
Title.
II. Series.
PN1993.5.U6M186        1989
384.8'0973—dc20                                      89-10870

# Contents

viii  Acknowledgments

xi  Preface

1  Introduction. *D. W. Griffith's American Dream.*

27  Chapter 1. *The Earliest Days.*

    31  Terry Ramsaye. The Story Picture Is Born.

    36  Fred Balshofer and Arthur Miller.
        Going Into the Film Business.

    41  Robert Hamilton Ball.
        Shakespeare by Vitagraph (1908-1911).

    46  Theodore Huff. Hollywood's Predecessor:
        Fort Lee, N.J.

    50  Anthony Slide. Alice Guy Blaché.

    56  Kevin Brownlow. Allan Dwan.

61  Chapter 2. *Ince and Hart.*

    66  Terry Ramsaye. The Discovery of California.

    69  Steven Higgins. Thomas H. Ince.

    72  W. E. Wing. Tom Ince of Inceville.

    75  William K. Everson. *The Italian.*

    77  Diane Koszarski. C. Gardner Sullivan

    82  Jean Mitry. The Concreteness of Ince's Films.

    92  William S. Hart. Working for Ince.

100   Moving Picture World. *The Bargain.*

102   Bruce Firestone. A Man Named Sioux.

107   Joe Franklin. *Hell's Hinges.*

109   Thomas H. Ince. The Challenge
for the Motion Picture Producer.


**115   Chapter 3. *Griffith.***

118   D. W. Griffith. My First Real Battles With Life.

123   Arthur Knight. The Father of Film Technique.

126   Karl Brown. The Great D. W.

130   Tom Gunning. Weaving a Narrative.

137   Frank Woods. Deliberation and Repose.

139   Lewis Jacobs. Griffith Leaves Biograph.

147   Lillian Gish. Planning *The Birth of a Nation.*

150   Arthur Knight. *The Birth of a Nation.*

152   Karl Brown. The Proof of the Pudding.

160   Francis Hackett. Brotherly Love.

164   Rolfe Cobleigh. A Propaganda Film.

169   Thomas Cripps. The Year of *The Birth of a Nation.*

171   Joseph Henabery. *Intolerance.*

175   Russell Merritt. *Intolerance.*

179   Sergei Eisenstein. Dickens, Griffith, and the Film Today.

186   Alan Casty. Griffith and the Expressiveness of Editing.

191   Blake Lucas. Infinite Shadings of Human Emotion.

197   Arthur Lennig. An Unconventional Masterpiece.

202   Richard Schickel. *Way Down East:*
Finances and Responses.

210   James R. Quirk. An Open Letter to D.W. Griffith.

212   Blake Lucas. *Lady of the Pavements.*

216   Eileen Bowser. *Isn't Life Wonderful.*

218 Chapter 4. *Stroheim.*

231    Erich von Stroheim. The Seamy Side of Directing.

233    Herman G. Weinberg. Stroheim's Pictorial Art.

237    S. J. Perelman. Vintage Swine.

242    A. R. Fulton. Naturalism:
       From *McTeague* to *Greed.*

249    Joel W. Finler. Reassessment:
       Stroheim as Stylist and Myth Maker.

255    Arthur Lennig. *The Wedding March.*

259    Gavin Lambert. Stroheim:
       He Didn't Really Belong to America.


263 **Appendices.**

263    A. Richard Corliss. Writing in Silence.

267    B. Extant Films of Thomas H. Ince.

274    C. D.W. Griffith's Feature Films.

280    D. Erich von Stroheim's Feature Films.

285    E. Twenty Notable Directors.

288    F. Bibliography.


303 **Index**

# Acknowledgments

It is with special appreciation that I acknowledge the kindness of Lillian Gish in reading my introductory chapter about D.W. Griffith. My gratitude also to Richard Schickel, Eileen Bowser, Ron Mottram, and Arthur Lennig, who read the same material. Professor Lennig checked the introduction to the chapter on Stroheim as well, and saved me from several errors. My thanks to Charles O'Brien for suggesting the offbeat S.J. Perelman piece about *Foolish Wives*.

Steven Higgins read the Ince/Hart introduction and gave encouraging advice. He also directed me to the printed version of the Ince memoirs in *Exhibitors Herald*. It was Ursula Hardt who first called my attention to the draft of the Ince manuscript (deposited at the Museum of Modern Art) which she found on microfilm in the University of Iowa library while doing her research on Erich Pommer.

I am most grateful for the skill, care, and patience of Helen Lemley at Iowa City's Technigraphics, who was the typesetter for the book, and her assistant on the paste-up process, Jennifer Sayers.

For the rest, I should somehow express my general debt to all those observers of events who have gone before, from Terry Ramsaye to Kevin Brownlow. All of them, with their varying viewpoints, have worked at the task of telling some part of the truth, and so have the authors of differing critical opinions, which equally deserve their place in a book of this kind.

—R.D.M.

Acknowledgment is made of the following permissions to use material from copyrighted works:

Excerpts from "The Story Picture Is Born" and "The Discovery of California" from *A Million and One Nights* by Terry Ramsaye. Copyright (c) 1925, 1956 by Simon & Schuster. Reprinted by permission of Simon & Schuster Inc.

Excerpt from "The Early Film Companies Crescent and Bison" (herein titled "Going Into the Film Business") from *One Reel a Week* by Fred Balshofer and Arthur Miller. Copyright (c) 1967 The Regents of the University of California.

Excerpt from "Shakespeare by Vitagraph, 1908-1911," from *Shakespeare on Silent Film,* by Robert Hamilton Ball. Copyright (c) Robert Hamilton Ball, 1968. Published by Theatre Arts Books. Reprinted by permission of Routledge, Chapman, and Hall Inc.

"Hollywood's Predecessor: Fort Lee, N.J.," by Theodore Huff, in *Films in Review*, February 1951.

Excerpts from "Alice Guy Blaché," in *Early Women Directors*, by Anthony Slide. Copyright (c) 1977 by Anthony Slide. Reprinted with author's permission.

Excerpt from "Allan Dwan" by Kevin Brownlow and "Intolerance" by

# Preface

I hope some of my readers are acquainted with the preceding volume, *The First Tycoons*, which tells the story of the founders of the studios in the silent era. There they will find in the somewhat reclusive guise of "Appendix A" an "author's note" about the purposes of this planned series of five books, "American Movies: The First Thirty Years."

Among other things, my note suggested that an anthology or reader is more relevant for film study than the smooth gray pages of the academic textbook tradition. Because it makes use of some of the raw materials of history — anecdotal, personal, contradictory — a collection of eye-witness accounts, memoirs, historical judgments, and critical reviews is a suitable way to reflect the turbulent actions and reactions of movie-making. Statistics and surviving "documents" are also important for the traditional historian, but they rarely convey color or feeling, and they often tell lies, just as memoirs do.

The entire story cannot ever be told in any kind of history. There is no way the richly varied events of Griffith's career, for example, can be conveyed adequately in any short account. What is attempted in this volume, as in the others, is a selective file of information about representative as well as "important" films and film makers of the period, and some of the controversies about them. Sometimes it is possible to build, with these intriguing fragments, the cumulative illusion of a connected narrative — of what it was like to be there.

This is less achievable, perhaps, in the case of the film makers than for the executives, stars, or comedians of the silent era. On the one hand, the directorial autobiographies we have are sketchy, at best — awkward (Hart), stodgy (Ince), incomplete (Griffith), or nonexistent (Stroheim). On the other hand, directors' lives after a certain point tend to be connected closely with their works, and as students we are often more interested in works than in lives. Hence this volume offers more critical analysis than the others.

The most notable among critical views offered here — and one of the landmark auteur studies of all time — is Jean Mitry's estimate of Thomas Ince. Evidently written in the early 1920s, and recently published in France (1965), its translation first appeared in *Cinema Journal* in 1983. It is doubly valuable when read together with Ince's own little-known manifesto, his emphatic advocacy of the realist impulse in film.

The invigorating insights of Eisenstein's response to Griffith remain valuable today, even in condensation, and Mitry has also provided us with occasional helpful contrasts between Ince and Griffith. But the reservoir of Griffith criticism — including the early fanfares of Rotha and Jacobs in the 1930s — is not as large or as adequate as it might be.

The brief, somewhat excessive encomiums by James Agee in 1948, in both *Time* and the *Nation*, were more historical than critical, based on hazy memories of "permanent images" and Griffith's personal qualities. Significantly, he urged the need for a deeper and broader comparative criticism of rare works which are today more available. Andrew Sarris in 1968 put Griffith in his Pantheon, but again his three pages were more like an agenda for future study. Among his usual brief baffling indirections there were some wise words about Griffith's natural landscapes, classical acting, and expressive editing, as well as paradoxical references to his "stark simplicity" and "extraordinary complexity and depth."

More recent probes have either centered on a kind of respectful revisionism, inspired in part by Bazin — as in the very useful work of Dorr, Cadbury, and Lucas — or a drive to apply some form of specialized theory, as in some of the pieces in the special issue (edited by Altman) of *Quarterly Review of Film Studies.* My own view is that the most fruitful approach in future will be along the straight lines of the Barry/Bowser monograph and the Schickel biography — taking up the films one by one and searching for significance by watching primarily what the characters say and do to each other.

Certainly a massive close inspection of all the early one-reelers remains as a challenging and instructive experience for, say, a young film maker/critic who wants to develop a fresh approach by looking at all those early films as experiments with content as well as form. The task might well center on the elusive quality of poetic realism identified by so many writers, including Mitry, Sarris and Agee.


I am myself guilty of some gray textbookish pages in this volume. In the attempt to be fair to Stroheim, whose works I don't particularly admire, I got involved in arguing out a rather extensive analysis of his works and his philosophy, as the first of several major directors who, I believe, brought certain attitudes with them from European backgrounds. I did not find myself becoming more sympathetic, but some readers may judge my interpretation worthy of attention, after so many years in which critics have taken for granted that Stroheim represents some kind of ill-defined aesthetic innovation but is really interesting primarily as a victim of Hollywood's business practices.

For Griffith, too, I have expanded the number of selections and the scope of my introductory writing beyond the original intent. This extraordinary man deserves far more attention than he has been getting in film history books and courses. My contribution here, if any, is not in trying to negotiate (as others have) the slippery slopes of visual art or narrative development, but in calling attention to Griffith's rather steady optimistic view of life, which I believe stemmed not only from his own experiences in reaching fame and fortune but also from basic American attitudes related to the invigorating myth of the historical frontier.

If (as I suggested in brief outline at the end of the author's note in the first volume) Hollywood and the visual communications industries were about to become the vital new frontier of the 20th century, then the protagonists of this volume can be seen as pioneers and innovators following a pattern of individualism drawn from the American experience as well as from the romantic tradition of personal creative talent in poetry and art.

I don't propose to do more than introduce this notion here. But it may be worthwhile to point out that the auteur approach, which I think is the inevitable framework for anyone who seriously examines the career of Griffith, always needs modification in real-life terms. Hence the necessity for sketching in some kind of background, as I have tried to do, to show the collective obligations and personal interactions which affected the art of D.W. Griffith — his backers, his associates, his performers. He accomplished many things by himself, but the individual who is a creative contributor to society also draws stimulus and support from others.

— R.D.M.

D.W. Griffith (about 1916)

# Introduction

# D. W. Griffith's American Dream

*He was a born general. His voice was a voice of command. It was resonant, deep, and full.* — Lillian Gish*.

Like Charlie Chaplin and Mary Pickford — like Lillian Gish, who later remembered his "voice of command" — D. W. Griffith became famous and successful only after years of privation and struggle.

For Griffith, the dim vistas of self-help in the American way of life always seemed hopeful. He was ambitious and hardworking. The American dream was supposed to reward these qualities. He found himself drawn to the stage, and his ambition was lofty: he was going to be America's Shakespeare. Then there were the years of insecurity on the road, winning and losing jobs as an actor. Through all the menial work and nights of hunger in between, he held to his dignity, his faith in his talent. When he sold a poem to *Leslie's* magazine, it was the greatest day of his life. When he sold a play and it was produced in Washington, it was proof he was on his way. Then the play failed. Griffith eventually had to humiliate himself by accepting a five-dollar-a-day job as an actor in motion pictures.

In this state of discouragement and abasement, he found himself, much to his surprise, coming into happy synchronization with the new technological apparatus that was preparing to

*"Conversation with Lillian Gish," *Sight and Sound*, Winter 1957-58.

take over show business. In due time he discovered that the moving image projected on a screen was to be his art, his livelihood, his mark in history. Instead of being compared to some famous playwright or poet, D. W. Griffith would become an original, a man with whom others are compared.

Griffith was for ten years renowned as the world's greatest motion picture director. Believing, like his father before him, that he was descended from Welsh kings, he moved among heads of state with the assurance of a Southern cavalier. He was only a parvenu, of course, despite a heritage that included some prosperous and landed forebears. He was bitterly conscious of humble beginnings in Louisville, where he had to quit school to go to work. But from 1915 to 1925 he was making and spending vast sums of money won simply by his skill as an artist and as a dynamic organizer. It was no mean thing to become for a time independent of Hollywood and own a studio of one's own at Mamaroneck, N.Y. In America, the talented could vie with the well-born for public attention and approval. This was the essence of the democratic way of life as he understood it, and Griffith knew that he had "made it" as certainly as Adolph Zukor or Marcus Loew.

The rewards of rugged individualism, and the rise to professional and financial success, are not often stressed in latter-day studies of Griffith. Different questions of a critical nature are usually raised: How many technical innovations was he responsible for? Was he primarily a pioneer or did he also leave us enduring works of art? Did his curve of achievement go into decline in the 1920s? Yet no one who studies his career closely can fail to notice Griffith's pride in his own success, linked in his films with a burning consciousness of the contrasting deprivations of poverty and temptations of wealth.

A memory he held at the end of his life (and shared with a Kentucky journalist in a half-begun autobiography in 1938) tells us of a desperate adventure in cross-country one-night stands. The show closed in Minneapolis, and he rode freight cars to Chicago, where he spent his "last nickel" on a beer and the free lunch that went with it. Heading for Louisville and home, he was forced off the train. In a nearby village he "found a Dutch baker who was just opening his shop in the early morning light." Letting him warm himself beside the bake oven, the baker gave him enough stale doughnuts to get him home.

Whatever the enlargements bestowed upon this memory by someone who had written and directed nearly 500 films, the combined atmosphere of adventure and despair seem authentic enough as a source for Griffith's personal sense of struggle and achievement. There is no reason to doubt that he did sleep in flop houses in New York City and that he shoveled concrete and iron ore when he needed money for food, lodging and travel.

At any rate, once he had made the transition from Louisville to New York, from theater to film, and from acting to directing, Griffith embarked urgently on the familiar American path, determined to get ahead. A tall, gangling man, Lincolnesque both in height and in what he always felt were rather unprepossessing features, he was full of unquenchable ambition and energy.

He was an outsider five ways — a poor young actor from the South, engaged in the lowbrow business of making movies. Cautiously using only his stage name (Lawrence Griffith) he nevertheless set out, as he did for the rest of his life, to work carefully and enthusiastically on the project of shaping as perfectly as possible whatever came to hand. He wanted to make money, but more than that, he wanted to be somebody, to become a leading character. As he became aware of the technical aspects of film making, he determined to be an inventor, to do new things first. And by the time he left Biograph in 1913, he could, with considerable credibility, put an ad in the *New York Dramatic Mirror* describing himself as "Producer of all great Biograph successes, revolutionizing Motion Picture drama and founding the modern technique of the art."

He learned from his cameraman, Billy Bitzer, what a camera could do, then turned around and persuaded Bitzer to do radical things, like natural-source lighting or cutting figures off at the waist, or showing just their faces, or on the contrary, showing them far away. He knew what Edwin S. Porter had done, of course, since he had worked for him as an actor, and to some extent he knew the work of his French, Scandinavian, and Italian contemporaries.

Always he was interested in the best way to present the dramatic story he had in hand. He was the first master of parallel editing: in climactic chase scenes for many of his early suspense stories, the shots would switch back and forth between pursuer and pursued, and often to a rescuer pursuing the pursuer. The shots would become shorter as the chase went on, thus adding excitement and tension to the finale. They called it the "switchback" and the "Griffith last-minute rescue."

He developed in almost every direction the possibilities of the cinematic form, working partly with the aesthetic aspects, but more characteristically with the dramatic elements. Although in the earliest days he urged quick movement on the actors because the bosses wanted as much story as possible in one reel, he soon developed more self-confidence in his story-telling, leaning on the values of character and seeking variations in pace. He won from Frank Woods (reviewer for the *Dramatic Mirror* who would later join Biograph's scenario department) an accolade for the naturalness of his performers, for their "deliberation and repose." Griffith had learned on the road, as Karl Brown remarked, that giving audiences what they want meant "making them laugh, making them cry, and making them wait."[1]

## His Subjects

What kinds of stories did he choose? His range was wide, and Robert Henderson, who has chronicled the Biograph days, makes only tentative classifications, like "contemporary romance," "farce," "child-centered melodrama," and so on. In 1909 alone he made 141 one-reel pictures, of which only 22 were romances, and 53 were melodramas. Alan Casty is certainly justified in claiming that Griffith loved to look back to the melodramatic plots of the 19th century. At the same time, he was responsible in that year for 41 comedies — a form we don't think of as especially comfortable for him. Of course Mack Sennett was part of the early stock company, and so was Mary Pickford. They made their contributions to the lighter side.

Among other things, D. W. Griffith established the audience appeal of action and suspense. On the other hand, he loved to draw on literary sources like Dickens, Poe, and Browning. Nostalgic stories of farm and small town life gave him special pleasure: *A Romance of Happy Valley* and *True Heart Susie,* (both 1919) are two of his features given high praise by recent critics. Yet he was also drawn to panoramas of history. Always there was the epic impulse: *The Birth of a Nation* was intended to shake up the movie industry and overwhelm the public, and the Babylon set for *Intolerance* was the greatest ever built up to that time. Five years later, in 1921, Griffith took on the French

1. Karl Brown, *Adventures With D.W. Griffith*, (1973) p. 61.

revolution, in *Orphans of the Storm*, and in 1924 he used a play he had once written about 1776 and called it *America*. Almost always, even inside the epics, there were intimate stories of individual lives. Almost always he was bent on teaching some sort of lesson; his themes of social conscience were many and varied. In all these respects he influenced American movies from that day to this.[2]

It is unfortunate that Griffith's enthusiasm for history was not rooted in either scholarly depth or breadth of experience. He was something of a reader, to be sure: as a youth he had worked in a bookstore. He was proud of his meticulous tableaus — Lincoln signing a document, for example, and the reconstruction of Ford's theater for the scene of the assassination. Such moments were heavily researched for external details, as they were by Cecil B. DeMille in later years. But Griffith was not one to weigh conflicting views and make fine distinctions. Note what he says on the teaching of history: an article he wrote for a magazine called *The Editor* in 1915 and reprinted in Harry Geduld's anthology, *Focus on D. W. Griffith.*

> The time will come, and in less than ten years . . . when the children in the public schools will be taught practically everything by moving pictures. Certainly they will never be obliged to read history again. . .
>
> Imagine a public library of the near future, for instance. There will be long rows of boxes or pillars, properly classified and indexed, of course. At each box a push button and before each box a seat. Suppose you wish to "read up" on a certain episode in Napoleon's life. Instead of consulting all the authorities, wading laboriously through a host of books, and ending bewildered, without a clear idea of exactly what did happen and confused at every point by conflicting opinions about what did happen, you will merely seat yourself at a properly adjusted window, in a scientifically prepared room, press the button, and actually see what happened.
>
> There will be no opinions expressed. You will merely be present at the making of history. All the work of writing, revising, collating, and reproducing will have been carefully attended to by a corps of recognized experts, and you will have received a vivid and complete expression.

Here is a sudden insight into the engaging simplicity of Griffith's mind. Of course it is a benevolent vision of libraries and classrooms served by film makers, although he no doubt thought of the films as selective dramatizations, rather than documentaries. As a statement of faith, it is so extreme as to reveal its

2. "A film without a message is just a waste of time," he told his director of photography. G.W. Bitzer, *Billy Bitzer, His Story,* (1973) p. 89.

distance from the complexity of reality. It is a warning to all who might put too much trust today in "new media." An even more effective warning is the extraordinary motion picture Griffith himself had made. In *The Birth of a Nation* his yearning to present American history through film came to powerful and regrettable fruition.

When Griffith wanted to make a very long and impressive film to show what he could do (and to compete with imported epics like *Cabiria* which were coming in from France and Italy) he was reminded — evidently by Frank Woods, his scenario editor — that Thomas Dixon's novel and play *The Clansman* was already well known and successful.

Immediately his emotions were stirred. This was a story that powerfully justified the South during the Civil War and after. He could pour into it all his bitter memories of an impoverished childhood, all his fascination for the mythical "courtly" Southern way of life, as his Kentucky family and neighbors had described it to him. He could show the wrongs of the northern carpetbaggers and the former slaves they had tried, in some southern states, to put in power. The climax of the story would be the formation of the Ku Klux Klan — that original American terrorist organization formed to protect white interests and put the black race down again.

Of course a great deal of valid and ugly history about racial subjugation, before and after the war, would be suppressed in such an account. Fairness would not be the point. Griffith did make two gestures toward balance: he left out most of the language of hate in Dixon's novel (which was used only for the second half of the film), and he offered the audience the embarrassing presence of a few jolly black people, loyal to their southern masters.

If the magnificent war scenes were the climax of the first half, the Klan was certainly the high point of the second act. Karl Brown, youthful assistant cameraman, later recalled the reaction of the premiere audience in Los Angeles: "The cheers began to rise from all over that packed house. This was not a ride to save Little Sister but to avenge her death, and every soul in that audience was in the saddle with the clansmen."

Again at the end, "The audience didn't just sit there and applaud, but they stood up and cheered and yelled and stamped feet." The poet Vachel Lindsay made a more precise and disturbing observation. He called it a response to cinematic "crowd splendor" as epitomized in the Klan ride: "tossing like the sea," it represented a "whole Anglo-Saxon Niagara."[3]

*The Birth of a Nation* was unquestionably the greatest and most influential film ever made up to 1915. In it D. W. Griffith brought to bear everything he had learned of dramatic and cinematic art, and that was what made the message so powerful. But art is not innocent, and criticism is not confined to style. To treat this motion picture, in the classroom or anywhere else, simply as an expression of cinematic skills is to ignore the vital difference between those arts which are abstract (like music) or nontemporal (like painting), and those which, like literature and drama, act out human relationships and social implications. Film criticism that pretends to be "purely aesthetic" is vacuous as well as irresponsible. If art is blinding in its brilliance, this does not excuse but rather intensifies the deadly effects of violence and hatred.

What were those people in the audience in Los Angeles cheering and yelling about? Did they stand up and stamp and cheer because their critical judgment told them they had seen a great work of cinema? Or were they responding to the bold, naive appeal this movie made to underlying instincts of fear, ignorance, and racial superiority through the visual impact of that "Anglo-Saxon Niagara"? This is the *Birth of a Nation* problem, and we cannot avoid it if we honestly study film as a part of American life. Whether we call ourselves critics or historians, we cannot ignore the power of the motion picture for good and for evil.

If Griffith was riding high after *The Birth of a Nation* — prosperous and praised for his skill in a new medium — he had also committed a form of social libel by drama, a condemnation of a whole group in American society as barbarians and primitives.

There was a riot in Boston. A group of black people tried to buy tickets for the movie. Several hundred protesters rallied behind them. Two hundred policemen promptly appeared to prevent it. During the show someone threw a rotten egg at the screen, and stink bombs were dropped from the balcony. Showings were stopped for one day. In newspapers throughout the country the message of the film was attacked and Griffith's right to speak defended. Newly formed black groups — the Urban League and the National Association for the Advancement of Colored Peo-

3. Vachel Lindsay, *The Art of the Moving Picture*, (1922) p. 75.

ple — gained strength in confronting this inflammatory film. At different times and for different periods, *The Birth of a Nation* was banned in Chicago, Cleveland, St. Louis, Topeka, and San Antonio, and in the states of Ohio, Illinois, and Michigan. Censors made cuts in the film in New York, Boston, Dallas, Baltimore, and San Francisco. One of the first cuts was a fantastic tableau which showed the whole black population of the United States lined up at a harbor to be deported back to Africa. [4] Tom Dixon, author of *The Clansman*, told one editor that this deportation represented his main interest in writing the novel and encouraging the making of the film. [5]

What was Griffith's reaction to all this uproar? For the time being he remained the supremely confident movie magician. He never seemed to feel he was at fault in any way. He defended himself against every attack — and also helped make necessary cuts in the film. He issued a pamphlet stoutly claiming that the motion picture was a part of the free expression protected by the first amendment to the Constitution. (This rather persuasive position had just been contradicted by the Supreme Court in the Mutual Film case, not to be overturned until 1952.)

Then he turned to his own medium for further defense. He had already completed *The Mother and the Law*, a modern story of a boy falsely accused of murder. He took this modest film and combined it with a grand spectacle on the fall of Babylon, inflating both of them by intercutting two other stories in a historical extravaganza. He called the whole daring, innovative, rather indigestible concoction, *Intolerance*. He was busily attacking age-old prejudices, but not the racist barriers of the American North or South. Above all, he was attacking his critics. And with this rather unstable motivation, he brought forth a strange, violent picture intended to oppose hatred and violence.

Critics and academicians down through the years have looked at Griffith's creative intentions — especially his unique endeavor to intercut four different stories all the way through

4. Russell Merritt, "Dixon, Griffith, and the Southern Legend," in Richard Dyer MacCann and Jack C. Ellis (eds.) *Cinema Examined*, (1982) p. 183.

5. The title was changed from *The Clansman* to *The Birth of a Nation* after the Los Angeles premiere, evidently at Dixon's urging. "That was what the film was about," Robert Sklar suggests, "the creation of a new nation after years of struggle and division, a nation of Northern and Southern whites united." *Movie-Made America*, (1975) p. 58. But see advertisement on page 168: evidently *The Clansman* was the title as late as September 1915 in Los Angeles.

the film — and they have found *Intolerance* to be monumental, complicated, brilliant, and therefore exciting. Ordinary audiences have looked directly at the film and found it confusing and boring. Griffith himself later admitted that a single spectacle would have worked better. He recut the Babylonian and the modern stories separately and reissued them, but the total effort remained a financial failure.

Did D. W. Griffith go into a decline after *Intolerance?* This is the view of Lewis Jacobs in *The Rise of the American Film*, but it is a view bound to the aesthetic notion that montage is the highest form of cinematic art. His later films are simply different in purpose and therefore in style, and Blake Lucas has eloquently argued that "his more intimate and subtle works are often superior" because he sought to describe "the infinite shadings of human emotion and interaction."

It could also be proposed that Griffith simply closed the door for a while on his obsessive epic impulse — and on social controversy. He did make a grandiose film supporting the British cause in World War I, and he was exhilarated by the praise and honors heaped on him while he was in England and France. Then for quite a while he moved with confidence in a more comfortable range of subjects. His style tended to be more congruent with the simpler subjects he chose, more self-effacing, less flashy in terms of editing, with more long takes and continuity editing — more realistic, in fact, or at least ranging in the area between realism and romanticism where he was most at home.

In *True Heart Susie*, for example, Lillian Gish plays one of her most subtle roles, a farm girl who sells a cow so she can secretly support her childhood sweetheart through college. It takes her gawky neighbor (played by Robert Harron) a very long while to appreciate her, but there is finally a subdued and happy ending in this most rural of all possible worlds.

*Broken Blossoms* (1919) is another world altogether — the depressing atmosphere of the Limehouse district in London. A Chinese youth (played by Richard Barthelmess) comes to the violent Western world on an errand of mercy: to teach the peaceful ways of Buddha. He meets and loves a pitiful girl (Lillian Gish) who is in constant dread of being beaten to death by her father. He finally kills the father for doing exactly that, then kills himself — an ironic end to his mission.

A short, powerful film, *Broken Blossoms* stunned the critics. *Photoplay* called it "the first genuine tragedy of the movies." The public, too, surprised theater owners by supporting at the box-office the integrity of this film and its consistent mood, so perfectly achieved by the dim backgrounds and the tense, controlled performances of the two young actors.

*Broken Blossoms* is certainly the film which most clearly extends the Griffith range and persuades us of two things: He was an artist of the screen, and he was truly versatile. He was not merely an inventive pioneer to be studied for historical reasons. He was a creator of works of permanent value.

Another film also invalidates the theory of "decline"after *Intolerance*. *Way Down East* (1920) was enormously popular and profitable. It was a melodrama, one which had been touring the states since the turn of the century. A story of an innocent woman tricked into a fake marriage, pregnant, abandoned, mourning her dead child, wandering into the country — it is climaxed by a denunciation of her seducer, an expulsion from the household, and a rescue by the young son who loves her. The rescue takes place in a blizzard, and required Lillian Gish to ride a block of ice down the river.

It sounds both bizarre and banal, and critics then and since have often discounted the story as unworthy of a serious director's attention. But Griffith knew there were basic human values in it and he trusted his actress to bring them out. All the emotional high points are presented with intense conviction, and the love story, so long delayed, is heightened instead of overwhelmed by the hazardous chase on the ice.

The fascinating thing about this old-fashioned story is how modern its moral is. Of course Griffith takes the opportunity to put down the supercilious rich city people in the early scenes, but he also turns us against the farm folk, so ignorant and sanctimonious. We yearn to help this frail outcast woman, and when she is rescued, we realize it is not accomplished by her return to rural life, but by the younger generation.

Here is an early version of many similar situations in later Hollywood films (made by John Ford and others) in which our sympathy is with the sinner and not with the Pharisees of society. The melodrama of *Way Down East* not only looks back. It also looks forward and prepares the way for a time when women will be able to tell their own story and claim some kind of independence in a more sympathetic world. This is the secret of the film's appeal to audiences in the 1920s and the 1980s: we always know we are for Lillian and against the cruel condemnation of an unfeeling, outmoded moral code.

It is a curious and noteworthy fact that Griffith had already encouraged Lillian Gish in real life to direct one of the Dorothy Gish comedies he was responsible for as executive producer. Such a decision reflected good judgment as to his star's gifts and strengths. But it also was some kind of sign of an awkward move toward more liberal positions, socially if not politically. Griffith had tried in a small way to make up for the racism in *The Birth of a Nation* when he had a white Southern soldier kiss a dying black soldier in a film now lost, *The Greatest Thing in Life*. He had earlier shown rather consistent respect for native Americans in several early one-reelers that presented them as not only noble but exploited by the white man. He had made further points about prejudice, of course, with *Broken Blossoms*.

As usual, he didn't quite know what he was doing: he was not a literary man, an intellectual, or a trained historian. He was a dealer in myths and emotions, not theories and logic. But can we propose that Griffith was subconsciously trying in *Way Down East* to catch up with the world? It was a world which was barely beginning, long after reconstruction days, to value equality of rights almost as much as freedom for the strong to get ahead. Did he know that it was time to give up some of the cruder claims of Darwinism — perhaps even some of the traditions of caste, the old Southern proprieties he had always praised?

Although Griffith never found it possible to consider members of the black race equally entitled to power and position — and in that stubborn opinion was joined by many white Americans from that day to this — he nevertheless seemed to have a strong attachment to certain basic ideals of democracy. The poor and the underdogs were often his heroes. The selfish capitalist who managed momentarily to gain monopoly power in *A Corner in Wheat* fell to his death in his own grain bin. Rich dowagers who dabble in organized charity (in *Intolerance*) and wealthy ladies who lack sympathy for their poor, honest relations (in *Way Down East*) got harsh treatment at his hands.[6]

6. Sklar finds this emphasis especially in the later short films: "depicting the extremes of life, the extravagant ostentation of the rich and the daily struggle of the poor." *Op.cit.*, p.57.

During those early productive years when he felt so close to his audience — and was making two or three pictures a week — Griffith took up the conflict between rich and poor as often as he thought it was wise. Tom Gunning, in his analysis of parallel editing, finds carefully worked out visual contrasts of this sort in *The Song of the Shirt* (1908), *The Usurer* (1910), and *One Is Business, the Other Crime*. In 1911, along with the usual romantic triangles, costume pictures, Mexican stories, and civil war dramas, there was an outcropping of seven stories with slum backgrounds.

The last film Griffith was free to make on his own — before he gave up his independence to work on assignment for Paramount and United Artists — was a disturbing semi-documentary about the economic desolation of postwar Germany. *Isn't Life Wonderful* (1924) left its sad young couple, at the end, grateful just to be alive (as the title indicated), but near starvation after their precious hoard of potatoes is stolen.

This does not mean Griffith was any sort of political radical. The violent conflict between capital and labor in the modern story of *Intolerance* is supposed to have induced Lenin (according to Lillian Gish) to offer Griffith a position in charge of Soviet film production. Lenin certainly had the wrong man. Griffith's old aristocratic loyalties together with his developing democratic creed would have put him doubly at odds with the authoritarian system of leveling going on under the Communist regime. His inner conflict was the same one that has troubled Americans for so long, the dual Jeffersonian ideal which says everyone deserves an equal opportunity to participate and learn but the able and talented few deserve special rewards.

Rising from obscurity and poverty, Griffith drove toward fame and power as an individual. Yet in his films, he struggled with issues of class relations, economic hardship, unchecked personal domination, nationalism, and war. Even his gentlest romances often posed the question of a woman's role in family or in society. Like King Vidor in later years, he responded with earnest, untutored warmth to the currents of thought around him.

Richard Schickel has written a useful nonfiction film about Griffith and also an extraordinary 600-page biography — a richly textured chronological study exploring the mysteries of the man's personality, reviewing the content, style, and production of the films themselves, and assessing even his marvelously tangled financial affairs. Schickel regrets the "loss" of all those fine films which might have been made if Griffith had stuck to his best approach: the social realism of "urban poverty, the simple verities of rural life, contemporary problem dramas." This is a valid judgment and a suitable regret.[7]

Yet Griffith's genius lay partly in his eager willingness to respond to every challenge, from the earliest short films to the last potboilers for Adolph Zukor and Joseph Schenck in the 20s. The epic impulse, the civic duty of history, the lure of poetry — he wanted to do them all, and the sexy stories, too. He wanted to be a whole studio in himself. He was often an executive producer on the side — for Biograph, for Triangle, for Paramount.

Griffith was a true film author. From the point of view of 1960s *auteur* criticism, he certainly impressed his personal view of life on many films, from *The Birth of a Nation* to *Way Down East* and *Isn't Life Wonderful*. He was also an author in the historical sense: he chose most of his projects, did most of the writing himself (either in his head or under assumed names), and had total control over the making of almost all his films through final editing. He was continuously productive for 23 years and directed 26 features after *Intolerance*. As a creative artist, he was inventive and prolific, and his influence was greater than any other major American film director, because he was unquestionably the first.

His last picture was judged a failure, but the one before that, a sound picture based on the life of Abraham Lincoln (1930), was a simple, stirring, and beautiful work. He had 17 more years to live, and it was said that, unlike Cecil DeMille, he could no longer work because he had not "kept up with the times." This really meant that the times were no longer listening to his faith in a serene and generous America. As the Louisville theater director said when he first tried out as an actor: "You are too grand for us."

## His Backers

Novice historians are forever encountering the age-old controversy: is history caused by impersonal "forces" or by people? Eventually, most lovers of controversy find out that the only satisfactory answer is: both.

It is difficult to take seriously any theory of history which ignores personalities and reduces events to some kind of "scientific"

7. Richard Schickel, *D.W. Griffith: An American Life*, (1984) p. 185.

pattern. If we are writing history — rather than deterministic philosophy — and if we want to know what happened on Tuesday, we must be willing to deal with the rough texture of actual experience as expressed through human differences and individual effort.

Motion picture history, more than most subjects, makes this plain. As in other fields, the historian wants to know about leadership and human relationships and what people were like. But in movie history the unique traits of the works themselves are prime evidences of personal intention and invention.

What if we tried to withdraw from history the lives, the films, and the influence of D.W. Griffith and Charlie Chaplin? There would of course still be other silent movies and movie-makers to enjoy and examine — more than most people realize. But without these two creative and dominant personalities, Hollywood in the silent era would have been a decidedly different place and time.

This does not mean that the first thirty years of the movies depended solely on the personal wills of a few directors. We now know how absurd it is to stretch the valid historical study of authors into an *auteur* "theory." Such a romantic philosophy no more explains everything than does the opposite theory of determinism. It is too much a close-up view, leading to a blurred, egocentric version of what happened on Tuesday.

D.W. Griffith, all by himself, was undoubtedly a major "force" during the first thirty years of the American screen. This is attested by many of the directors who worked at the same time and often followed his lead. Yet without the collaboration and support of people under, around, and above him, Griffith could never have put his visions into effect. This is an aspect of his career not usually stressed in American film histories.

He was hired as a director in the first place (1908) in a moment of collaborative decision-making between Henry Norton Marvin, vice president and general manager of the American Mutoscope and Biograph Company, and his brother, Arthur Marvin, then acting as assistant cameraman to Billy Bitzer. Their vision of his gifts was tentative, but wise and practical. Five years later there was not enough wisdom at Biograph to measure Griffith's value.[8]

After Griffith had filled five years with an extraordinary and versatile record of activity — amounting to 458 films — he wanted his well-known skills to be rewarded with some form of stock interest in the company. If Biograph would not do that, then he would know they did not understand what he had done for them. He was tired of wrangling over every new technical device. He was frustrated over their constant reluctance to let him make even two-reel films. He wanted to present starring performers in feature-length films. He wanted, if he could, to be on his own.

All three of these ambitions were forbidden by the Patents Company trust. Biograph was a member of the trust and its president, Jeremiah Kennedy, was also president of the trust. Griffith had just directed in California a daring and costly four-reel picture, *Judith of Bethulia*. He returned to New York to confront a new coldness on the part of his bosses. From now on he was only to produce, not direct. Biograph was planning to ignore all the cinematic history he had made and copy Famous Players, using stage plays and stage actors.

It was clear that Griffith needed another, more far-seeing sponsor. Ironically enough, he decided to meet with Adolph Zukor, who had approached him in the past. He was offered $50,000 a year as director-general for Famous Players.

Zukor might have provided a secure base for feature film making. He seemed to be operating on his own without paying tribute to the trust. He had already presented the French picture *Queen Elizabeth* with Sarah Bernhardt in a legitimate theater and had just produced *The Count of Monte Cristo* with James O'Neill. But this was hardly Griffith's kind of film making. And he must have sensed that Zukor's approach might actually be based on the same sort of monopoly drive that kept Edison and Biograph and all the members of the trust in a groove of cautious sameness.

8. Linda Arvidson, *When the Movies Were Young*, (1925) p. 43. Arvidson, Griffith's wife, adds two elements of chance — or "fate" — involved in the Marvins' 1908 decision. The vacancy occurred because of the illness of "Old Man" George McCutcheon, who had hired Griffith in the first place as an actor. And it occurred just after the young couple had worried and fretted whether to leave town and join a stock company in Maine for the summer. "As sure as shooting," Arvidson wrote in 1925, if they had accepted the offer, "he would never have become the David W. Griffith of the movies." We may doubt the inevitability of that. Yet their choice, so unaware of the opportunity awaiting them, did make a difference.

The man who made Griffith's next move possible was Harry Aitken, whose production companies — Reliance in New York and Majestic in Los Angeles — released their films through Mutual. Aitken was president of Mutual as well, but he shared power there with John Freuler (who would later take control). Mutual looked prosperous. It was the company which would contract with Charlie Chaplin in 1916, and its motto was: "Mutual Movies Make Time Fly."

Majestic's offer was only $300 a week, or $15,600. But added to that would be participation in profits and some freedom to choose his subjects. Griffith was confident, after his experience with royalties at Biograph, that he could expect boxoffice response. In October 1913, he chose freedom and profit participation.

As so often happens in show business, there were problems he had not foreseen. Harry and Roy Aitken had a limited cash flow — it was brief and circular. What came in from the exchanges (including the busy European offices) had to go right out again to finance new films. And of course production had to move right along to supply the exchanges. Griffith plunged into supervising "potboilers" to help Aitken out, directing four himself.

His primary concern and his first independent feature, *The Birth of a Nation*, had to be financed through a series of heart-stopping last-minute arrangements.

In the first place, the Majestic board of directors refused to finance the film. Mutual (made up of some of the same people) was no better prospect. Harry and Roy reluctantly contributed a portion of their own salaries as executives in these companies in order to make up the $40,000 that would "get the picture started." Griffith only knew that "somehow" they were able to produce this amount and later $19,000 more. Thus he was served, as Roy later wrote, by "a couple of young men not many years out of the Wisconsin farmlands, and whose financial resources were already stretched perilously thin."[9]

Before long their mutual distrust was also stretched perilously thin. It was the old story of the artist versus the businessman. On the one hand (Harry Aitken said) Griffith seemed to have all his money spent before he got it. On the other hand (Griffith

9. Roy E. Aitken (with Al P. Nelson), *The Birth of a Nation Story*, (1965) p. 31.

said) Aitken didn't seem to understand how much money it took to create a great motion picture. The director began to seek out other sources of funds, without consulting the producer.[10] Later Aitken had to confront Griffith and ask him how much new money had been raised, to find out if he still had a majority interest. Soon he discovered that Griffith had even secured a copyright.

Yet all these tensions were momentarily eased. The Aitkens, like Griffith, loved what they were doing. They were united in wanting to astonish the world with one great film. So Epoch Producing Corporation (Harry Aitken, president, D.W. Griffith, vice president) took over copyright and distribution for *The Birth of a Nation*. Griffith had no original investment in the film, but he now bought some stock. Aitken kept control, and Thomas Dixon got what seems now an incredible 25 percent of the profits (instead of a flat $25,000) for the rights to his novel.[11]

After the premieres in New York and Los Angeles — customers were charged then and later $2.00 a ticket — the financial situation abruptly reversed. No longer trying to scrape up money,

10. Aitken, *op.cit.* p. 45. Among a number of names listed on the rolls at this point was William H. Clune (referred to as 'J.R.' by Roy Aitken), whose theater later became the premiere location for the film in Los Angeles. Lillian Gish puts dialogue to the scene, based on the theater man's pride in his orchestra. Griffith had invited Clune to watch a scene of Confederate soldiers marching up the street while a modest little band played "Dixie" on the set. "Think of how that tune would sound," he exclaimed, "if your orchestra played it!" And as they walked to the office afterward, the great film director sold one more little piece of his ever-more-costly action — for $5000 according to Aitken, for $15,000 according to Gish. (Gish, *The Movies, Mr. Griffith, and Me,* pp. 240-241.)

11. Aitken, *op.cit.* p. 49. All these overlapping proprietary rights have led to a variety of disputes and court cases in more recent years. Who had the right to show 16 millimeter prints (apart from the Museum of Modern Art prints, a gift from Griffith)? Or to strike new prints from an internegative? Or to sell or rent videocassettes? One group of claimants said they had been assigned rights by the D.W. Griffith Corporation, the estate of the last Mrs. Griffith, and by Dixon. The Aitken estate had conflicting claims. Blackhawk Films, of Davenport, Iowa, hired David Shepard to produce a new sound track and a tinted color version, based on a contract with Paul Killiam. Blackhawk then was taken over by Republic Pictures. It was a typical movie rights tangle, benefiting nobody, least of all the viewer. Finally, a decision in the U.S. Court of Appeals cut the Gordian knot and declared *The Birth of a Nation* to be in the public domain.

the Aitkens were now beseiged on every side by distributors offering large sums for "states rights."[12] It was certainly the greatest
hit in movie history up to that time. Possibly (if one corrects later
boxoffice receipts for inflation) the $5,000,000 the producers
received and the $50-60,000,000 taken in at the boxoffice nation-
wide made it the greatest hit of all time.[13]

Following the enormous success of their 12-reel film, Griffith
at once began planning another one of epic size. Aitken, for his
part, intended to expand his position as executive-in-charge. He
began planning a new distribution company, the Triangle Film
Corporation, and persuaded Griffith, Thomas Ince, and Mack
Sennett to join him. Supervising the works of other directors,
each of them set about supplying theaters with a movie every
week. Griffith produced at least ten films (most of which he
scripted under the name of Granville Warwick) during the time
he was giving his primary attention to preparing *Intolerance.*

The grandiose Triangle project lasted about two years, and
Aitken and Griffith became more and more estranged. At one
point, when Aitken allowed Mae Marsh to be hired away (by
Samuel Goldwyn), Griffith angrily wired his boss: "I would suggest that you attend to managing the Triangle which is conceded
to be the worst managed business in film history."[14] He could
not foresee how tangled his own finances would become in the
next few years.

Again he was in need of a sponsor. In 1917, he signed a contract with Adolph Zukor's Artcraft company. Again he was allowed much freedom of choice. But he also had to start right in again
as supervisor of other directors, especially on a comedy series

12. Roy Aitken reports (*op.cit.*, p. 58) that "Louis B. Mayer haunted our offices,
    offering to pay $50,000 ($25,000 down payment) with a fifty-fifty split on net
    profits after he got his original payment back. Mayer's partner was Daniel
    Stoneham, a wealthy Bostonian." They decided to sell Mayer the New England
    rights (which enabled him of course to make his first moves into production and
    later to become studio head of M-G-M). They withheld Boston and other major
    "road show" cities for themselves. Harry Sherman of Minneapolis got "the rights
    to sixteen western states, plus a fifty-fifty split on net profits." Clune and Grif-
    fith got California.
13. Schickel, *op.cit.*, p. 281.
14. Iris Barry and Eileen Bowser, *D.W. Griffith: American Film Master* (1965), p.
    49. This slender book, published by the Museum of Modern Art, was for years
    after its first publication in 1940, the only guide devoted specifically to the life
    and works of Griffith. With the fuller evaluations of the later films by Eileen
    Bowser, the 1965 edition is still the best brief introduction to his works.

starring Dorothy Gish. And he had to turn out some potboilers himself, two of them among his best work: *A Romance of Happy Valley*, and *True Heart Susie*.

All his life, Griffith tried to gain a position in which he would be in control of both production decisions and distribution income. The enormous costs of producing and exhibiting *Intolerance*, while they did not ruin him — according to Richard Schickel's examination of the books — kept him from ever getting far enough ahead to be secure. He held onto a kind of hand-to-mouth semi-independence for about ten years, from the time he started drawing profits from *The Birth of a Nation* in 1915 to his reemployment on a very short leash at Famous Players-Lasky in 1924 and United Artists in 1927. The Griffith history of affiliations goes something like this:

| | |
|---|---|
| *Edison Company (writer, actor)* | *1907* |
| *Biograph (actor, director)* | *1908* |
| *Majestic Film Company (Aitken)* | *1913* |
| *Triangle (Aitken)* | *1915* |
| *Artcraft (Zukor)* | *1917* |
| *First National (3 films)* | *1919* |
| *United Artists* | *1919* |
| *Famous Players-Lasky (Zukor)* | *1924* |
| *United Artists (Joseph Schenck)* | *1927* |

These affiliations do not take account of the corporations he set up to finance specific films, using different aspects of his name (D.W. Griffith Corporation, Wark Producing Corporation, etc.).

Schickel writes that a 1919 financial report indicates earnings on Griffith pictures at that time of $8,596,432, of which $3,445,346 belonged to his own corporation.[15] This was probably the last high point of his fortunes, but he was beginning the most hectic and complex time of his career in terms of obligations. It is hard to see how he could have kept track himself of all his transactions — bank loans on future projects and on past projects as collateral, public share offerings by his personal corporations, investment of his own salary, production advances from various motion picture companies, even loans on insurance policies.

His commitments at this time must have been bewildering to his associates. In 1919, while still under contract to Famous

15. Schickel, *op.cit.*, p. 418.

Players-Lasky (and Artcraft) Griffith joined with Mary Pickford, Charlie Chaplin, and Douglas Fairbanks in forming the United Artists Corporation. From this partnership, he could get returns of 80 percent (instead of the usual 70 percent) from his films. But he had to invest his own money in order to produce for United Artists release. So he turned around and contracted for three pictures with First National to help finance his UA pictures. (He had already bought back from Zukor the rights to *Broken Blossoms* in order to give it to UA.) And of course he was working all the time on his films for Zukor's Artcraft.

While it may be said that Griffith never found the sponsor who was just right for him, on balance his backers probably had more to complain of than he did. In terms of contract fees, he was treated as his fame deserved. Richard Schickel believes that Adolph Zukor had a soft spot in his heart for "the great D.W." Strangely enough, that commercially minded executive was instrumental in financing both *Broken Blossoms* and *Isn't Life Wonderful.* Joseph Schenck, too, who had become a full time executive manager for United Artists, was willing to pay Griffith, for his last production contract, $5000 a week and $1000 between pictures. By any overall reckoning he was a good deal luckier in his patrons than Mozart was.

## His Associates

During the early years of fame and fortune, Griffith also had the support and advice of cast, crew, and staff. They didn't constantly nudge the elbow of "the Master," but their words were often heeded. G.W. ("Billy") Bitzer, above all, was his intrepid, creative collaborator as director of photography.

Joseph Henabery gave Kevin Brownlow (in *The Parade's Gone By*) a number of instances of his consultation and criticism on research, performances, and even editing. Lillian Gish was a valued adviser. Frank Woods was Griffith's story editor for a long time. Albert Banzhaf was the in-house lawyer who took care of affairs in New York. Griffith's brother, who chose the name Albert Grey, was not so helpful, managing to mismanage some roadshows and other financial arrangements.

J.C. Epping, assigned by the agitated Aitken in October 1914 to watch and control expenditures on the west coast, continued as a loyal servitor in the film-maker's own entourage and on occasion actually loaned him production money. It was Epping, still a German citizen, who brought to Griffith's attention in 1924 the idea for a semi-documentary about his home country, which turned out to be, Eileen Bowser says, "the last great film." Griffith's high income year (1919) was the year the world emerged from World War I, a time of hope and relaxation for most people. For Griffith, it was a year when six features were released with his name on them. And it was the year he made his costly move to the east coast, buying a former estate (near Mamaroneck, N.Y.) of one of Standard Oil's millionaires. Here, in chilly grandeur, he could impress banks and distributors with his own studio.

And why not act the seigneur on spacious grounds, master of a studio as well as "master director"? Charlie Chaplin had built his own place two years before at LaBrea and Sunset in Los Angeles. Tom Ince for years was the master of vast acreage north of Santa Monica. Why shouldn't the most famous director in the world have a studio of his own? It became the staging area for *Way Down East,* and it contained the enormous sets for *Orphans of the Storm.* Yet the money he put into the studio at Mamaroneck was what he could have used over the next few years to maintain real independence in his production decisions.[16]

Always somewhat aloof, concentrating intensely on the project of perfecting his films, Griffith began at about this time to get less help from those he had once trusted for critical advice. Henabery had become a director. Some of the stars he had developed found they could make more money elsewhere — Mae Marsh for Goldwyn, Blanche Sweet for Lasky, Richard Barthelmess on his own. He let them go, convinced that he could always replace them.

There were other losses. Bobby Harron, a favorite performer who had worked up from office boy, died under circumstances suggesting suicide. Clarine Seymour, a new arrival, died before she could perform her role in *Way Down East.* Lillian Gish, who had brought him the idea of *Orphans of the Storm,* left shortly afterward.

The departure of Gish was more crucial than any other. Not long after the beginning of their director-actor relationship in 1912, he had discovered in her an unusual awareness of the cinematic

16. Schickel, *op.cit.,* p. 420.

process. She liked to stay around and watch even when she wasn't working. For *Intolerance,* she had little to do, playing only the symbolic "Eternal Mother" rocking a cradle between major sequences. But she says "he took me into his confidence as never before, talking over scenes before he filmed them, having me watch all the rushes, even accepting some of my ideas. He sent me to the darkroom to pick the best takes."[17]

With Lillian, Griffith shared not only a fascination with the medium but a commitment to its exalted role in human affairs. They agreed that at its best the motion picture could somehow uplift mankind, strengthen its humane values, and promote peace. Such a comradeship of ideas, together with a mutual work ethic of extraordinary tenacity, made them ideal partners in the difficult task of presenting movies as a respectable, responsible art.

That he was in love with her, Richard Schickel takes for granted. Griffith is supposed to have told Jim Hart, in those last years when he was preparing an autobiography, that for many years Lillian was "the only woman in my life."[18] This can be given more than one interpretation. She might have considered it a contribution to his life and his art to fill his need for companionship and warmth, however far that might go. Or she might quite easily have found ways to retain her independence, avoiding totally his undoubted sexual drives, while still giving him the artistic support and praise and inspiration he needed. After all, until later years, she never called him anything but "Mr. Griffith."

For Griffith himself it is harder to imagine celibacy for any extended period of time. In his life, as in his films, he evidently held to a distinction between sacred and profane love. Often in the films, the blonde, ethereal, and virginal heroine (Gish or Mae Marsh) would be pursued by a bullying villain, then rescued. In real life, the dark-haired Miriam Cooper (the elder sister in *The Birth of a Nation*) was pursued by Griffith in an embarrassing, if less menacing, scene. In his limousine at the end of a day of shooting, he reached for her but she resisted his kiss. [19] This was evidently not an isolated instance, though unusual in finding its way into a published memoir. In a 1911 letter to his estranged first wife (published after his divorce action in 1936) Griffith frank-

---

17. Lillian Gish, *The Movies, Mr. Griffith, and Me,* (1969) p. 177.
18. James Hart (ed.), *The Man Who Invented Hollywood: The Autobiography of D.W. Griffith* (1972), p. 7.
19. Miriam Cooper, *Dark Lady of the Silents,* (1973) p. 60.

ly confessed to having "many" women. He was better off, he said, "outside of marriage."[20]

Lillian Gish agreed with that. In 1969, she wrote, "Mr. Griffith was the least domestic person I ever knew. I couldn't imagine him married to anyone . . . He always looked uncomfortable in a house — out of place, caged in. The only surroundings in which he seemed comfortable were the studio, a hotel dining room, a lobby. He told me many times that he was trying to persuade his wife to divorce him. I secretly hoped that she would not; I felt sure that he would make an impossible husband were he to remarry."[21] And this passage occurs just after she has made the seemingly guileless remark: "I was in love with pictures and the man who created them — though not in the way Dorothy [Gish] loved Bobby [Harron]."

The man who created movies was a good deal more touchy about his movies than about his relationships with women. He was becoming more difficult to counsel with after the critical year of 1919. Lillian had already "learned to be more tactful" than her sister Dorothy (who always said precisely what she thought). If Lillian had a suggestion, she would preface it by saying, "Do you remember, Mr. Griffith, the other day you said . . ."[22]

Yet there were certain standards she felt compelled to defend. She became quite cross when Griffith told her (in *Way Down East*) to make up her face to "look pretty" just after her ordeal on the ice. During *Orphans of the Storm*, she disagreed with Griffith on the interpretation of a scene — and had her way — but could not convince him later that the picture was too long. No doubt Griffith saw her as claiming almost a proprietary interest in that spectacular film: she had urged him to choose it instead of the Faust story he had in mind. She knew quite well that Faust had never appealed to Americans, and she told him so. She also had the statistics on the popularity of the play called *The Two Orphans*.[23]

After *Orphans of the Storm* was released in 1922, he called her in to his office for what she thought would be plans for a new film. He announced instead that he couldn't afford any longer to pay her what she was worth: "You should go out on your own."

20. Schickel, *op.cit.*, p. 163.
21. Gish, *op.cit.*, p. 206.
22. Gish, *op.cit.*, p. 213.
23. Gish, *op.cit.*, pp. 235, 241-244.

She says she thought at once of "all the stars he had created and then sent on their way," even Mary Pickford, who had quarreled with him back in 1912 — the very year Lillian had joined Biograph. Her own association with the company and her acceptance of Griffith's direction had lasted ten years.[24]

"Perhaps he was tired of using me," she wrote in 1969, "or perhaps he thought I was becoming too independent." As Lillian well knew, there was also another woman.[25]

Griffith put Carol Dempster in twelve movies from 1919 to 1927, and most observers agree that her presence was not good for most of those movies. He apparently found in her someone who would respond easily to his advances. A certain coarseness now suited him, and came off well enough at the very last in *Isn't Life Wonderful*. But she never responded well to his direction, and by the time he returned to the west coast in 1927 her contract, too, was finally paid off and she shortly after retired into marriage in the east.

Some years afterward, Adela Rogers St. Johns, the screenwriter and fan magazine writer, saw Griffith sitting by himself in a dark corner of the Musso-Frank grill on Hollywood Boulevard. "It was late, we'd been to a picture up the way at the Egyptian Theater." She left her group and went over to speak to him. "I remembered him so vividly the opening night of *Birth of a Nation* at Clune's (now the Philharmonic) Auditorium. I remembered the wildly cheering throngs." Now he was a director without a job, without an audience. And "he needed a shave."

He said, "I never had a day's luck after Lillian left me."

Adela St. Johns was astonished. Everyone knew that Lillian had watched and waited while the plain but ambitious Carol Dempster, little by little, took her place. "But D.W.! Lillian didn't leave you! You chucked her out for that mediocre girl . . ."

And he said: "A man can be his own worst enemy, can he not?"[26]

Lillian Gish was D.W. Griffith's wisest, best informed, and most generous adviser — a balancing influence who kept him from some of his most tempting mistakes and excesses. She recognized all too well the pride and self-importance that so easily over-

24. Gish, *op.cit.*, p. 247.
25. Gish, *op.cit.*, p. 240.
26. Adela Rogers St. Johns, *Love, Laughter and Tears: My Hollywood Story* (1978), p. 75-76, 84.

whelms anyone who is successful in showbusiness. And this innocent, grandiloquent high school dropout who had somehow
managed, over the years, to show three of his films at the White
House — how could she help him when he would not be helped?[27]
In the long run, she was wiser and stronger than her idolized
director. She went on to other roles in film and theater, while
Griffith became less and less confident, more and more cynical.
He also became a compulsive gambler and, especially at the last,
a heavy drinker. From 1936 to 1947, he had the comfort of a new
wife, Evelyn Baldwin 35 years younger than he. But he was not, as
Lillian said, domestic. This, too, ended in divorce.

Griffith may not have thought that he ever had the perfect
helpmeet to carry him through all the creative crises of his life.
But he did have exactly that in Lillian Gish. He was wise enough
to keep her with him for ten years of high achievement. But the
strait gate and the narrow way were too restrictive for his busy
ego, striving as he was, year by year, to match his undoubted
gifts with adequate projects and huge sums of money.

Even Linda Arvidson, after years of separation, was willing
to offer him words of counsel in 1929-30: that he should make
films drawing on his own experience and on his love for America
and its history.[28] After he and Joe Schenck finally agreed to make
*Abraham Lincoln,* she wrote praising him for the decision.

It was a celebration of personal sacrifice, not of heroic bravado
— and of the constant struggle to attain harmony through a sense
of community — that these women held out to him as ideals for
his work. He embraced those ideals often in his films. But a self-
sufficient individualism, the need to be a great author, seemed
more noble, more truthful, and certainly more dramatic, to this
man who had come from nowhere to be a wonder of the world.

27. Because Thomas Dixon was a classmate at Johns Hopkins, Woodrow Wilson
granted a showing of *The Birth of a Nation* at the White House. Well known
as a defender of white supremacy in the South, Wilson watched the film with
intense interest and commented (at the halfway point? or after the ride of the
Klan?) that it was like watching "history written in lightning." He later had to
disclaim any official support for the film. The second White House occasion was
a showing, once again for Wilson, of the war propaganda film, *Hearts of the
World.* The third was *Orphans of the Storm,* when Warren G. Harding (who
"looked more like a President than Mr. Wilson") welcomed the Gish sisters with
open arms and called Lillian "darling." (Gish, *op.cit.,* p. 245).

28. Schickel, *op.cit.,* p. 546.

His last film, *The Struggle*, a confused attack on both Prohibition and alcoholism, was produced rather hastily with his own money. It met such a blast of critical rejection that it was never distributed. After that he faced years of idleness — this man who never had a home of his own and never had a vacation during his working life. For someone who had been used to issuing orders on the set to cameramen and actors — creating in his head from all that chaos a ribbon of enduring images — seventeen years of idleness could be a kind of hell on earth.

He traveled, he enjoyed celebrity status in his home state of Kentucky, he was given an honorary Academy Award (1936) — and a standing ovation — and a life membership in the Directors Guild (1938). He visited Hollywood sets with W.S. Van Dyke, his former assistant, and with Frank Capra. He was asked to be a production adviser for a movie Hal Roach was making. In 1940, the N.Y. Museum of Modern Art presented a retrospective of his films, and smaller showings were offered in later years at an art gallery in Hollywood and at the University of Southern California.

He faltered in discouragement at the last, and everything seemed harder than when he started in 1908. He had welcomed sound, and used it, but the first great master of the silent film told Ezra Goodman in his last interview: "The moving picture is beautiful: the moving of wind on beautiful trees is more beautiful than a painting. We have taken beauty and exchanged it for stilted voices. In my arrogant belief we have lost beauty." [29]

The beauty in his pictures has not been lost, nor the world view represented in them. Almost all of his feature films have been saved, and most of the early short ones. His works are no more outmoded, Andrew Sarris reminds us, than the plays of Aeschylus. James Agee called him a "great primitive poet," and the French film director Jean Renoir said "he had the naiveté of the authentic great man." [30] He was certainly one of the greatest innovative artists in history, comparable in America to Walt Whitman, George Gershwin, Frank Lloyd Wright.

29. Ezra Goodman, *The Fifty Year Decline and Fall of Hollywood*, (1961) p. 19 (paperback version). Goodman was *Time* magazine correspondent in Hollywood in the middle 1950s. He began his book with a depressing chapter describing Griffith in a room at the Hollywood Knickerbocker hotel in 1947, just before he died.
30. Sarris, *The American Cinema*, (1968) p. 50. Agee, *Agee on Film*, Volume I (1958) p. 314. Renoir, *My Life and My Films*, (1974) pp. 45-46.

# Chapter 1

# The Earliest Days

*The motion picture was now abreast of the dime novel.*
— Terry Ramsaye.

We are so well acquainted nowadays with film and video cameras that it's hard to imagine what it was like to make the very first movies. The earliest camera operators did what any new video owner might do today. They took pictures of the family and then went outdoors and looked for things that moved. Street scenes, ocean waves, and railroad trains were favorite subjects. The documentary impulse was there at the very beginning.

Then camera operators began to think about other subjects that would please a paying audience. And since the biggest audiences of the day were at the vaudeville houses, the next step was to bring before the camera the kind of acts to be seen in vaudeville — dances, magic shows, juggling.

Such films were shown starting in 1894 in individual peep-show "kinetoscopes," usually found in penny arcades. Later (when projection on a screen became possible) they appeared as a part of vaudeville programs, and still later in separate store-front "nickelodeons." By then it was clear that people would pay to see movies in theaters, and there began to be full time exhibitors, and after that, production companies.

Some of the documentary and theatrical subjects came from abroad. Louis and Auguste Lumière were noted for nonfiction — daily life films like *Workers Leaving the Lumière Factory* and *Feeding the Baby* (both 1895) — or news events like *Military*

*Review, Hungary* and *Flood at Lyons* (1896). Georges Méliès, on the other hand, was fascinated with the way stop-motion and dissolves could add movie magic to the magicians' illusions he performed on the stage. Becoming adept at these visual twists, he began to make longer films about imagined adventures like *A Trip to the Moon* (1902) and *The Palace of the Arabian Nights* (1905). Lumière travelogs and Méliès fantasies were widely seen — and sometimes imitated — in the U.S.

From the beginning there were comedies. In 1895 the Lumière joke film, *Teasing the Gardener*, set the pace for many practical joke pictures dear to the hearts of Americans. In the French film, a small boy doubles the hose and holds it, then releases the stream of water just as the gardener turns the nozzle around to inspect it. Among the kinetoscope items for 1895, produced by the Edison company, were *Drunks in the Snow, Husband and Stenographer, Boy and Fruit Peddler, Girls in a Dormitory*. By 1901 the Edison catalog included pre-Chaplin tramps in the Weary Willie and Happy Hooligan series.

There were lots of "dancing girls" — and lots of people who objected to such subjects. Terry Ramsaye, in his genial history of silent movies, *A Million and One Nights*, claims that a "staid and prim downtown financier member of the board" of the Biograph company complained that some of the pictures might be too revealing, from what he had heard. The arcade operator read him the record of pennies in the slot:

| | |
|---|---|
| *U.S. Battleship at Sea* | $0.25 |
| Joseph Jefferson in *Rip's Sleep* | $0.43 |
| *Ballet Dancer* | $1.05 |
| *Girl Climbing Apple Tree* | $3.65 |

Faced with this accounting, the stockholder is supposed to have agreed at once: "I think we had better have some more of the Girl-Climbing-Apple-Tree kind."

Our best record of the films of 1894 to 1912 has come down to us in a curious way. Nobody knew, in those early years, how to get copyright protection for their motion picture "publications." They did the best they could by sending in to the Library of Congress, as required of book publishers, a copy on paper of the "creative work" they wanted to protect. These coils of paper prints could not be shown on a screen. But they survived.

Most of the actual movies from those first eighteen years — that is, their nitrate negatives and prints — have since disappeared or disintegrated into highly inflammable dust. But their paper counterparts have been reclaimed. Sixty years after the first copyright (Edison's 1894 record of a sneeze by an obliging employee, Fred Ott) a program of restoration began. All those paper rolls were taken in hand by Kemp Niver, an industrial film maker who had an idea he could transfer them, one frame at a time, to 16 millimeter acetate safety film stock. His work was supported by grants from the Library of Congress and the Academy of Motion Picture Arts and Sciences. The project went on for ten years, plus two more for a catalog of synopses and credits.

These 3000 short films are now a treasure house for specialized historians to explore. They extend from the first Edison and Biograph experiments to the middle of Griffith's short films. They can tell us what the first film makers were doing — what their subjects were, what technical choices they made. In the first cinema Ph.D. dissertation at the University of Southern California (1961), Richard Sanderson asked those questions.

He went through a selected sample of 681 of the films reclaimed up to that time, finding, as one might expect, that the first camera movements appeared to develop because of necessity. A charging bull was the inspiration for what may have been the first panning shots (1898). This was not because of any danger to the cameraman. First there was "a series of jerks" to follow the action ("Lassoing Steer" and "Branding Cattle"). Then a month later, in "Bull Fight No. 2," a bull moved out of frame, but in a later shot the camera actually followed the bull's complete movement. Lewis Jacobs, in *The Rise of the American Film* (1939), found a comparable description of a bullfight in the 1901-02 Edison catalog. According to Sanderson, the idea was not picked up right away. Not till 1902-03 were there any further panning movements; then there were 18 examples.

Of course the "first time" for anything in history is almost always proved wrong by some new discovery of an older precedent. Dissolves, for example, are now well documented as familiar to audiences during projected slide shows before the turn of the century. And technical milestones, even if established, seldom relate to any dramatic or aesthetic advancements. The more important question is: do historical "firsts" tell us anything we really want to know? Do they announce to us the arrival of some liberating power in telling stories or representing human life?

For a long time it was assumed that one of the outstanding breakthroughs in cinematic editing was achieved by Edwin S. Porter in *The Life of an American Fireman*. But this little picture showing the rescue of a mother and child from a burning building was apparently not the "milestone" in film editing history we once thought it was. Here is the story as unfolded by Charles Musser in an article in *Cinema Journal* in 1979.

In 1944, the Museum of Modern Art came into possession of a print of the Porter film, completed in early 1903, but long considered "lost." The last half of the picture exhibited a remarkably sophisticated technique for building suspense, cutting back and forth six different times from outside the burning building to the room upstairs. It was some such version as this that was remembered by Terry Ramsaye, Lewis Jacobs, and later historians, all of whom had placed a big wreath on the brow of E. S. Porter as the veritable inventor of cross-cutting. Everything started here, they claimed, in one big moment of creation.

The only trouble was that nobody guessed there was a different version in the Library of Congress. When Porter's version, as deposited for copyright in 1903, was recopied from paper by Kemp Niver sometime after 1954, it caused a good deal of scholarly anguish. There was no cross-cutting — just a series of outdoor scenes, then all the actions inside the upstairs room. It was suspenseful, but not because of any new editing technique.

What to believe? Could Porter have sent in his rushes to the Library, not his final print? This may have happened later on, but scholars have figured out that it didn't happen during this period. And if Porter actually edited his film without any cross-cutting, this would explain another mystery. Why didn't he ever do such spectacular parallel editing again, even in *The Great Train Robbery*? He must never have known how to do it.

Musser speculates that some anonymous hand must have taken apart a surviving print of *The Life of an American Fireman* along about 1910 and recut it. Parallel editing was by then pretty familiar in movies, especially those made by D. W. Griffith. This doctored version must have been widely used, or else by the 1920s it was the only one remembered by historians.

The result of all this scholarly sleuthing, then, is that we are no longer willing to say who "invented" cross-cutting. We are more likely to say that it must have been a gradual development from the experience of various film workers. This kind of historical caution, based on facts we are fairly sure about, is more satisfactory for us as readers of history than to be worried over the removal of a wreath from the brow of Edwin S. Porter.

Porter still holds an important place in early film history as producer in charge of all Edison films (about 1900 to 1909) and director and photographer of many of them. He was also hired by Adolph Zukor (1912-15) as director general of Famous Players (the company that became Paramount Pictures) supervising or directing feature films. But the one film for which he will always be remembered is *The Great Train Robbery*. In this little thriller Porter did demonstrate, whether consciously or not, that individual shots, not complete theatrical scenes, are the essential elements of cinematic narrative. Soon D. W. Griffith would apply this principle in a rich array of motion pictures.

# TERRY RAMSAYE
# The Story Picture Is Born

*From 1922 to 1925, in* Photoplay Magazine, *there appeared a series of 36 articles by Terry Ramsaye on the history of the movies. Exhaustively researched, using documents and interviews, the series became the first important study of American movies, focusing primarily on early inventors, industry leaders, stars, and directors. From* A Million and One Nights, *(N.Y., Simon & Schuster, 1926), pages 414 to 419, here is Ramsaye, in his inimitable light-hearted style, trying to explain how Edwin S. Porter got involved in making the two films that contributed so much to the tradition of narrative film making.*

*Most historians would agree that* The Great Train Robbery *was a turning point in American movie history. It was not the first narrative or the first western, but because it was enormously popular and was shown repeatedly in nickelodeons for years, this 12-minute picture helped to make the whole idea of movie-going more acceptable. As a result, its action format was a permanent influence on American film style and content. The American audience evidently wanted something like this and they have continued to get it.*

'Twas the dark hour just before the dawn in the motion picture history in the early twentieth century. The film was again on the wane.

Men who were before long to become masters of millions won in the new art, were then running tent shows, furriers stores, haberdasheries, peep shows, pants pressing shops and loan offices.

The public was weary of pictures of prize fights, snatches of acrobatics, freaks and tricks on the screen. The picture had nothing new to say. What with the depressing effect of the patent wars, inhibiting initiative that might have come to freer minds, and the falling off of patronage, it appeared probable the films would disappear even from the screen of the vaudeville houses where they were used to mark the end of the show and clear the house.

There had been tiny, trivial efforts to use the screen to tell a story, exemplified by Cecil Hepworth's *Rescued by Rover*, the adventures of a little girl and a dog, photographed in London, and *The Burglar on the Roof* made by Blackton and Smith of Vitagraph. They were mere episodes.

Now in the Edison studios, where the art of the film was born, and also where it was best bulwarked against the distractions of the fight for existence, came the emergence of the narrative idea.

James H. White was in charge of Edison's "Kinetograph Department" and Edwin S. Porter, becoming a cameraman, was the chief fabricator of picture material. Between them evolved a five hundred foot subject entitled *The Life of an American Fireman.*

This picture was built up from the germinal thrill of the first fifty-foot subjects showing a fire department run. White cast himself for the lead in this picture. When W. E. Gilmore, general manager for Edison, screened the picture he ordered retakes to eliminate White, on the ground that it was subversive of corporation policy for an executive to be an actor. He did not state it in exactly those words.

*The Life of an American Fireman* portrayed the routine duties of a fire chief. The audience was taken the rounds of the firehouse and inspection with the chief. Then cutting in with an inspirational beginning of a new technique, came a scene showing a simple cottage, with a baby asleep in a crib, by a window with curtains fluttering close to the burning gas jet turned low. The curtains flicked into the flame and the fire crept up the window and licked along the window casings. The mother awakened in the smoke-filled room. Then the picture cut back to the fire house where the alarm tapped out a signal.

The firemen leaped to action, sliding down the brass poles from their dormitory into the engine house. The horses were hooked up in a flash, and with smoke and sparks flying the outfit thundered down the street.

Then the long arm of old John R. Coincidence, the perennial first aid to scenario writers ever since, reached out and got into the first motion picture drama. It was the fire chief's house.

The picture cut back to the baby's crib again, back to the frenzied mother in the swirling smoke. Then again to the rushing fire engine. Mark this: it was the grand staple situation of dire peril, with relief on the way, the formula that has made Griffith famous, or that Griffith has made famous, as you choose to view it. It was and is yet the greatest screen situation, of unfailing power. It may be the innocent man on the gallows with the pardon on the way; it may be the pursuing vengeance of the K.K.K.; it may be the maid in desperate conflict with the villain as the hero speeds towards the scene; but the bleached abstract barebones of the situation are the same.

In this ancient drama, *The Life of an American Fireman*, the chief arrived at last and leaping down rushed into the fire, emerging with his wife and child in his arms. Saved at last. The breathless race was over and the happy ending came in the closing close-up.

All this was crudely done measured in the light of our day. It was a gripping masterpiece then. It swept the motion picture industry.

Now Porter of Edison made a casual subject of no great screen importance that was to prove a stepping stone to an important extension of the story film idea. In the advertising department of the Delaware, Lackawanna & Western railroad was Wendell P. Colton, a young man with a highly successful advertising idea — the famous "Phoebe Snow," a mythical girl in white who rode on *The Road of Anthracite* without soiling her gowns, all to the rocking horse rhythm of accompanying jingles. Marie Murray, a photographer's model, was cast for a motion picture rendition of the Phoebe Snow role by Porter. The picture was made on the Lackawanna and Porter got on friendly terms with the officials of the railway. This was soon to prove valuable.

Not long thereafter Porter was talking of possible actors for some bit of a playlet with Billy Martinetti, acrobat, scene painter and handy man.

"I know a fellow that used to be in *The Great Train Robbery* on the road," suggested Martinetti.

Porter got a flash of an idea from the title. *The Great Train Robbery* was a stage production and was of no relation to the motion picture that resulted from this casual mention.

Porter went to work on the idea, writing a memorandum of the scenes of a simple story of a train hold-up, a pursuit, a dance hall episode, and an escape. This was a step a little farther into the creative realm than *The Life of an American Fireman* had been.

In the fall of 1903 Porter started *The Great Train Robbery*. He looked about for a cast. At this time the benches of Union Square, the rendezvous for variety actors and unappreciated Hamlets, were the hunting ground for Biograph, Edison and Vitagraph in the quest of performers. But this picture was a shade more exciting. It was necessary to have stunt actors. Frank Hanaway, an actor with experience in the U.S. cavalry, was induced to work in the picture because he could fall off a galloping horse without killing himself. George Barnes, a performer at Huber's Museum, a Fourteenth street variety house, was selected for the role of the robber.

At this juncture a vaudeville performer, with a sketch of his own to put on, appeared at the Edison studio casting about for a possible engagement. He was Max Aronson, who by the theatrical transmutation of names, had by this time become Max Anderson. It was not long after that he became G.M. Anderson by another stage in the process — the same who became world famous as Broncho Billy, which is another story.

"Can you ride, Anderson?"

"I was born on a horse and raised in Missouri," Anderson snapped back, in just that dashing western way. He had come on from St. Louis.

"Good," Porter decided. "You're a train robber in this picture."

Then Porter prevailed on the Lackawanna to loan him a special train. The train scenes were made near Paterson in New Jersey. As one of the thrills, the fireman, doubled by a dummy, was tossed from the train as it neared the high bridge on the Passaic river. The dummy fell on a trolley track below in front of a speeding car.

The emergency brakes screeched, and the car came to a violent stop, filled with fainting and screaming passengers. A riot followed when the unintended victims of the scene discovered the deception.

The riding scenes were made in the wilds of Essex County Park in New Jersey. Porter with his cast started from a livery stable in West Orange to ride to location. When the company arrived Max Anderson was missing. It was too late and too expensive to trouble about a missing star then. Porter doubled the part and went ahead. Essex Park resounded with rough riding and loud shooting.

In the evening when the horses were returned to the stable, Porter made inquiry about the missing Anderson.

"Lost a man somewhere along the line — did you see anything of him?"

"Oh, that guy — yep, the hoss throwed him about a block down the street and he led him back and took the next train back to New York."

So the legend runs of the first horse exploit of Broncho Billy. Anderson returned to appear in the train scenes only.

Marie Murray, the Phoebe Snow model, appeared in the dance hall scenes.

*The Great Train Robbery* vibrated with inserts and cutbacks in true photoplay fashion, and closed with a punch, consisting of a close-up of George Barnes as a robber pointing a revolver into the eye of the audience.

The picture was, for its day, the sort that the picture makers now would advertise to the public as "an epoch making achievement of the art of the motion picture" and to the exhibitors as "a box office knockout."

*The Great Train Robbery* went on its first runs at Huber's Museum, at the Eden Musee and at Hammerstein's. With the picture as their principal property, numerous exhibitors started with temporary store shows and traveling picture outfits. There was a new invasion of the back country with this thriller.

Porter swiftly followed this initial success with *The Great Bank Robbery* of like calibre.

The motion picture was now abreast of the dime novel.

# FRED BALSHOFER
# Going Into the Film Business

*In the same year D. W. Griffith started directing, Fred Balshofer discovered for himself the pleasures of film making. "The sale price of pictures at that time," he says, "was ten cents a foot." He thought it would interest audiences to see, among other things, the "shoot-the-chutes at Luna Park," and sure enough, he sold two 1000-foot rolls to Adam Kessel (who would later finance the films of Mack Sennett). Near the end of this charming story of youthful directorial enterprise, Balshofer introduces an eager 14-year-old, Arthur Miller, later to be one of the most accomplished of all Hollywood cinematographers.*

*Miller also collaborated with Balshofer on his reminiscences,* One Reel a Week *(Berkeley, University of California Press, 1967). Here are pages 17 to 22 of a chapter Balshofer wrote called "The Early Film Companies Crescent and Bison."*

In the spring of 1908 I began looking for a partner in order to form a company of my own to make moving pictures. I found the young man I was looking for in Herman Kolle. Although he knew nothing about making moving pictures, he was intrigued by the idea. His father owned Prospect Hall at 273 Prospect Avenue in South Brooklyn, New York. The hall had a good-sized dance floor, a balcony running around three sides of the place, and a stage at one end. Next to and in connection with the dance hall was an open air summer beer garden. On warm summer evenings neighborhood families would sit around at the separate tables, drink nickel schooners of beer, and watch second-rate vaudeville on a stage raised about seven feet above the ground. A screen rolled down from the arch over the stage and this was used to show movies. A song plugger sang popular tunes, accompanied by a piano, while the hand-colored lantern slides on the screen changed according to the lyrics of the song. There was only enough business to warrant opening on Saturday and Sunday evenings. If it rained, people would move into the dance hall and the show would continue there.

We used one corner of the summer garden for our open-air studio and, as in the early days of Lubin, daylight was our only source of light for photography. We arranged a tiny laboratory under the stage and bought a used Pathé field model camera that had seen better days. We also bought an old Powers projector head that had been converted into a step-printer (a device to print films frame by frame) with several rolls of perforated negative and positive film from Hans Schmidt, who ran a speakeasy-type movie equipment joint in the cellar of his house on Second Avenue in New York City.

Now we were ready to make moving pictures. We named our company the Crescent Film Company, and our trademark was a black crescent moon on a white background. Herman Obrock, the stage electrician at Prospect Hall who also ran the projecting machine in the evenings at the summer garden, spent a lot of time with us. He wanted to learn the business. He accompanied me to Coney Island the day I went there to photograph subjects I thought would make up a saleable reel. One subject was the shoot-the-chutes at Luna Park where a flat bottomed boat came down an incline through white bubbling water simulating rapids and made a big splash as it came to a stop in a large pool at the bottom, rather a spectacular scene. Another subject was the loop-the-loop on Surf Avenue. This was a wooden structure where an automobile gained enough speed as it came down a steep incline to make an upside-down loop with two passengers in the auto. I had just finished cranking when we were spotted by the bouncers and had to get out of there in a hurry.

We photographed scenes on the crowded Coney Island beach and scenes in Steeplechase Park. After shooting for two days, we ran out of film, so back we went to the summer garden to develop what we had photographed. This was the first film we developed in our little laboratory. Giving instructions to Kolle and Obrock, who helped, kept me hopping, and handling the heavy developing drums was by no means a one-man job. The next day I made nice, clean prints, rare in those days. When all the subjects were spliced together, there were two full reels of a thousand feet each.

Film exchange row was on Fourteenth Street in New York City, and with the reels under my arm, that's where I headed. First I called on the Empire Film Exchange, two doors west of Third Avenue on the south side of Fourteenth Street on the second floor. The exchange was owned by Adam Kessel and Charles Bauman. There was the usual counter where the operators from the nickelodeons brought back the reels of the program they had shown to exchange for other reels to make up their next program. Empire had a small office for the bosses and a still smaller screening room where they looked at pictures they might buy. Kessel and Bauman sat in the screening room with me as they watched the two reels I brought. We sat there in silence; the only sound was the clicking hum made by the projection machine. My apprehension grew. The lights were turned on but there was no discussion between the two men. Kessel seemed to be figuring everything out by himself. He turned, looked at me, and said, "If I buy five prints of each, will you give me an exclusive?" I replied I would have to think it over. "OK. We'll be outside. You take your time." The sale price of pictures at that time was ten cents a foot, so it was easy to figure a sale of this kind would give us a nice profit. I sat and stalled a little longer so I wouldn't appear too anxious. Then I went outside and agreed to the deal. Kessel asked me a few questions about my new company and said that he'd never heard of Crescent but that he would be interested in looking at the next pictures we made.

I promised to deliver the prints in a few days and left the place walking on air. When I told Kolle the news, he was elated too and immediately began talking about making moving pictures other than short subjects. Our next effort was a split reel. A split usually consisted of two separate comedies on one reel. We called one of our comedies *A Skate on Skates* and the other *Troublesome Baby*. Each was about three hundred and fifty feet in length. Our players could hardly be called actors as we used anyone we could pick up around the hall. The comedies didn't seem very funny to me, but they sold anyway.

Our little business was going along just fine when one pleasant afternoon a fellow came into the summer garden looking for me. He introduced himself as Al McCoy, said he represented the Edison Manufacturing Company, and wanted to see the camera we were using for making moving pictures. McCoy was a slim man of medium height in his mid-forties. I reminded him that he was trespassing on private property, and that if he didn't get out, I'd have him thrown out. I guess he believed I meant it for he left without making any trouble. McCoy didn't frighten me but I later noticed that Kolle was concerned. McCoy evidently never forgot our little encounter for it was his persistent spying and harassment that caused the Crescent Film Company to dissolve a few months later.

I had an idea that western pictures were what the exchanges wanted, but we were in no financial position to compete with some of the westerns being produced, many of which cost up to fifteen hundred dollars apiece. As a way out, it occurred to me to make a western with teen-age youngsters, so I asked Kolle if he could gather about eight or ten boys from the neighborhood who would like to play in such a picture. He said he'd see what he could do. I gave Kolle a written outline of the story, and within a couple of days he was rehearsing some boys in the gymnasium of Prospect Hall. The picture was titled *Young Heroes of the West*.

When the day came to shoot the picture, eight teen-agers gathered at the hall at eight o'clock in the morning. Some had their own costumes, while Kolle had rented others from an outfit that specialized in rentals for the masquerade balls that were popular in those days. All the boys had brought lunches and were a happy bunch of kids. I told them Kolle wasn't going to be there and introduced myself as the man who was going to make the picture. I took a good look around to be sure that Edison's private eye, McCoy, wasn't there spying, and then I carried the camera covered with a blanket while some of the boys grabbed the tripod and a leather case with some extra film magazines. We boarded a Fifth Avenue trolley car at the corner and headed for the location I had in mind, a golf course called Dyker Heights on 69th Street that was surrounded on three sides by wooded country, making it ideal for the background. Besides, it was quite secluded from prying eyes.

As we boarded the trolley, one youngster made it his business to sit beside me and began telling me about a Brownie box camera he used to make his own pictures. I gave yes and no answers to his questions about photography until he began interrogating me about the movie camera, still covered with a blanket, on the floor between my legs. I didn't know whether Kolle knew this lad or not, but I did know that McCoy would stop at nothing to find out what make of camera I was using. The boy followed one question with another. I sized him up and figured he was pretty smart for his age, about fourteen, and could be a spotter for McCoy.

When the trolley turned off Fifth Avenue onto 69th Street, we soon reached the golf course. We walked along the edge of the course until we found a good site among the trees. I started to set up the camera, but it was obvious the same lad was trying to get a look at it, so I quickly threw the blanket over the camera. Only when I was actually grinding a scene did the blanket come off. I watched the youngster all afternoon, becoming completely convinced that he was more than just one of the kids playing in the picture. Sure enough, when we went home in the trolley, there he was right beside me again, but the camera, as before, was covered with the blanket. This time he wanted to know how we developed the long strip of film we used in the movie camera. I told him if he wanted to see how it was done, he could come to the summer garden that evening and watch.

Obrock had enough experience by now so that the two of us could handle the developing, but as soon as I reached Prospect Hall I called Kolle and asked him to come over. I thought we were in trouble with McCoy and while we ate supper I told him of my suspicions.

Kolle didn't seem any more certain than I. We walked to the entrance of the garden, and there was the youngster waiting. The minute Kolle saw him, he began to laugh, for he thought that this was one of the funniest incidents he had ever experienced. Kolle told me he knew the youngster, who was one of the boys from the neighborhood.

We started to get ready in the laboratory, and the young fellow wanted to know if he could help. Now that I was sure he wasn't on McCoy's side, I gladly let him. At that time we used the drum system for developing the film, the same system we used when I was with Lubin. When we talked about making positive prints the next day, the kid wanted to know if he could be there to see how it was done. He reminded me so much of myself when I was about his age and had been stung by the photographic bug, I said he could join us. As I expected, he finally asked me for a job. In those days it was not uncommon for a boy of fourteen to start learning a trade. He told me that his name was Arthur Miller and that he lived about a block from the summer garden. Arthur wanted to learn all he could, he said, so he could be a cameraman, and it wasn't long before he was doing routine chores that made it easier for me when we were working in our tiny laboratory. Once he understood McCoy's business, he kept an eye open for him the same as the rest of us.

## ROBERT HAMILTON BALL
# Shakespeare by Vitagraph, 1908-1911

*As a professor of drama at Queens College, City University of New York, Robert Hamilton Ball invested twenty years of research in a unique contribution to film history. A trace is offered here of this gracefully written book,* Shakespeare on Silent Film *(N.Y., Theatre Arts Books, 1968) pages 38-40 and 45. Of course it was a curious anomaly that so many silent films were made based on works notable for their spoken poetry. Ball suggests that there was a need for respectability and for an author not protected by copyright, but also that Shakespeare's "variety of scenes fitted in well" with the cinema.*

*Most of the films no longer exist, but the author went to whatever sources he could find, including catalog descriptions, trade paper reviews, personal interviews, copyright lists, collections of still photographs. Here he gives us hard-won information about the Vitagraph studio way of working and about William Ranous, a director D. W. Griffith (according to his first wife, Linda Arvidson) considered worthy of admiration.*

And suddenly there was a march of Shakespeare on film. 1908 was the key year, 1908 through 1911 the period. The United States led the way; with somewhat different impulses, Italy and France joined the parade. In four years, not counting minor adaptations and petty pilferings, almost fifty new productions of Shakespeare were on the screens in America, England, and on the Continent. They included seventeen of Shakespeare's plays, seven of the tragedies, six of the comedies, two each of the dramatic romances and English histories. Most of them were in one reel, approximately a thousand feet of film; some spilled over into two; one anticipated the feature picture of a later era. Why were more Shakespeare films made in this period than in any comparable span later, more in 1908 than in any subsequent year?

There were no doubt cross-influences from one country to another. This was the period of the 'art film' in France and Italy and the stage-film in England. But these films with theatre actors, though they represent something pervasive in the air — and the air was inter-national — do not for the most part explain what lay behind the work and the choices of the studios in New York. The American films tended to get off the stage and go outdoors; they made little appeal to the intelligentsia; they did not employ known writers or name actors from the theatre — indeed, it was only gradually that companies revealed the identity of their mimers, and to movie audiences they were with a few exceptions merely familiar faces. In order to explain why there were ten American Shakespeare films in 1908, it is necessary to know what was happening in the United States.

By 1908 the story picture had become general. News items, local events, vaudeville skits, and comic episodes were no longer suffi-cient. For camera narratives, people were now writing scenarios as fast as they could but there were not enough. It was natural to borrow from literature and the stage, and surely Shakespeare himself would have approved. Moreover his variety of scenes fitted in well with new conceptions of scenario structure, with cutting and editing. For some years the major companies had been copyrighting their films in Washington, but for their scripts they went to whatever literary sources were handy or would be effective. Surely photographs could not be considered a means of plagiarism from written words, and no acknowledgments were necessary. But in 1907 the Kalem Com-pany produced a *Ben Hur*, and was promptly sued by its publisher, the producers of a stage version and the administrator of the estate of Lew Wallace's heir. Though the suit was not settled against Kalem until 1911, it had to be defended, and it frightened the major producers. One way of avoiding legal difficulties was to disguise their reconstructions, but another was to make use of authors not protected by copyright. Shakespeare was not concerned with rights and royalties.

An additional drive toward Shakespeare stemmed from the need for respectability. When the motion picture was an infant phenomenon, it impressed because it was a novelty and because it moved. Few cared what it said or implied. But narratives involve people, and people, conduct and morality. Favorite subjects were portrayals of crime, or risqué situations (at least according to the titles). There were sordid settings exemplifying a crude realism. The attraction of the *vulgus* could be maintained by vulgarity. In 1907 there were the first serious attacks from outraged society. The movies it was said in print, appealed to the baser passions, caused juvenile delinquency. Though the industry martialled its forces in reply, it knew the opposition had both power and justice on its side. It joined in 1909 in the formation of the National Board of Censorship of Motion Pictures, which later became the National Board of Review. Meanwhile no one could object to Shakespeare. It is ironic that someone did. In Chicago the police censor called the Vitagraph *Macbeth* 'worse than the bloodiest melodrama' and ordered the deletion of the stabbing of Duncan, the brandishing of a bloody dagger, and the duel between Macbeth and Macduff.

The enormous expansion of the industry in America invited the search for the untried.

The competition among companies was incessant. Much of it was quantitative, but it was also qualitative. The better the pictures, the better the profits. How could their films be improved? Well, Shakespeare was the best dramatist in the world, wasn't he? People spoke well of him. And finally, there were some concerned with the production of films who had read Shakespeare and acted in his plays. In at least two cases, they could urge, and even more important, act as directors of Shakespeare films.

One of those men was to come in 1908 into the Vitagraph company, the producer of the largest number of Shakespeare films ever made by one company: not counting a title-borrowing for an otherwise non-Shakespearean *Comedy of Errors*, ten of them within less than two years. An advertisement in the New York *Clipper* brought to the studio one William V. Ranous.

'Billy' Ranous had been in the theatre since childhood in a variety of capacities. He had done some acting in moving pictures made by the Edison company. If published theatre annals say little about him, he was obviously a man of wide experience, and a valuable acquisition for Vitagraph. Ranous was a theatre man; Blackton was not. Ranous had played Shakespeare, and probably also stage managed and directed some of Shakespeare's plays. It seems reasonable to suspect that now the time was ripe, he urged or supported Blackton in the decision to film Shakespeare at Vitagraph. In any case he directed most of the Shakespeare films made by the company and acted in some of them. When he left Vitagraph in the fall of 1909 to become the first director for the newly organized Imp, the Independent Motion Picture Company of Carl Laemmle, the number of Vitagraph's Shakespeare pictures dwindled.

Paul Panzer, later the villain of the famous serial, *The Perils of Pauline*, reminiscenced in 1917 about Shakespeare film production at Vitagraph and gives us a valuable picture of activity in the studio.

> 'And it was when we began work in Flatbush that we had our first salaried director — the late William V. Ranous. . . . He was a Shakespearean actor of the late Salvini school and a most capable man. Under his direction, Vitagraph produced *Macbeth, Richard the Third, Othello, Romeo and Juliet, King Lear* and other Shakespearean plays. They were all in one reel each. Those are the days that I remember best. We built our own scenery and props, and we certainly must have presented an incongruous sight, doing carpenter work and painting canvas while we were dressed in the costumes of Shakespeare's time. After we had built a set we threw saw, hammer and paint brush aside and stepped on to the stage and assumed the characters drawn by the immortal Bard.
>
> 'In this connection there is one thing that stands out with cameo clearness in my memory. There was a happy trio at the studio — a little girl named Florence Turner, a young man named Hector Dion and myself. Mr. Dion and I built our own frames for the scenery, and Miss Turner sewed the canvas together on a borrowed sewing machine. When all was ready, we three would tack the canvas on the frame. For these services we received the magnificent salary of $14 a week; but we got $3 a day extra when we played in pictures. As a memento of those times Mr. Blackton still has one of the rough battle axes that I made of wood for the production of *Macbeth*. . . .'

*Macbeth* was indeed the first of the plays to be filmed by Vitagraph; 835 feet long, it was released on April 17, 1908, and could be obtained 'beautifully tinted'. It contained at least seventeen sequences with the emphasis on the first part of the play. The witches are shown before an effectively atmospheric studio backdrop of gnarled trees;

they hail Macbeth and Banquo; Macbeth is informed that he is now
Thane of Cawdor; Duncan names Malcolm his heir; Lady Macbeth
receives her husband's letter; Duncan arrives at their castle; Macbeth
sees a supernatural dagger; Duncan is dispatched; his murder is
discovered; Banquo meets his death; his ghost appears at the feast;
Lady Macbeth sleepwalks; Birnam Wood comes to Dunsinane;
Macbeth is finally killed. There were other scenes too, but the rest
are difficult to identify.

It is necessary to warn the reader of the uncritical enthusiasm
displayed by trade papers, but the review in the London
*Kinematagraph and Lantern Weekly* of May 14 shows not only that
the Vitagraph *Macbeth* was almost immediately exhibited abroad
but also something further about the film.

> 'This firm are to be congratulated on the masterly way in which they have
> staged Shakespeare's tragedy. The famous play contains many situations
> which lend themselves admirably to effective treatment in picture form, and
> the company have made the most of them. Thus in the first scene, when the
> three 'Weird Sisters' prophesy that Macbeth shall be King we are shown him
> as in a vision, in the King's robes and crown. Another effective scene reveals
> Macbeth on his way to murder the King, the appearance of the dagger be-
> ing cleverly represented. Then in order are pictured the other famous scenes
> of the play, culminating in Macbeth's death at the hand of Malcolm[?]. . .
> Each scene is cleverly set, the costumes are accurate and the acting good and
> we shall be surprised if this does not prove one of the most successful of re-
> cent subjects.'

Two stills show Macbeth killing Duncan and Banquo's ghost at
the banquet, the latter confirming the hint of double exposure in the
review. Other details of the film are pointed out in the published
remarks of the unfortunate Police Lieutenant who censored it in
Chicago. He rules especially against its realism. It is difficult to have
much sympathy with censorship, but the point of view becomes
understandable.

> 'I am not taking issue with Shakespeare. As a writer he is far from reproach.
> But he never looked into the distance and saw that his plots were going to
> be interpreted for the five-cent theater.
>
> 'Shakespeare has a way of making gory things endurable, because there
> is so much of art and finish. But you can't reproduce that. The moving pic-
> ture people get a bunch of Broadway loafers in New York to go through the
> motions and interpret Shakespeare. . . .
>
> The stabbing scene in the play is not predominant. But in the picture show
> it is the feature. In the play the stabbing is forgotten in the other exciting and
> artful and artistic creations that divert the imagination. On the canvas you

see the dagger enter and come out and see the blood flow and the wound that's left.

'Shakespeare is art, but it's not adapted altogether for the 5-cent style of art.'


As far as one can gather, *Macbeth* was largely taken in the studio; for its next Shakespeare film, *Romeo and Juliet*, Vitagraph shot much of the action outdoors. The evidence is conclusive, for this is one of the films which has survived. In addition there are more stills to examine, and much more was published about it than for *Macbeth*. The balcony scenes for example, utilized a house near Fort Hamilton, Brooklyn. The duel between Romeo and Tybalt was fought on the paved terrace at the south end of the Boat Lake in Central Park, close by the tiered Bethesda Fountain surmounted by the winged Angel of the Waters. The figures on the fountain of Temperance, Purity, Health and Peace are perhaps only ironically suitable to the atmosphere of street fighting in Verona, but they were well in the background, and there is at least a tenuous appropriateness in that they, as well as the Angel, had been executed by the sculptress, Emma Stebbins, who at the time of their completion in 1865 was living in Rome in the home of Charlotte Cushman. The outdoor contestants were Paul Panzer as Romeo, and John G. Adolfi as Tybalt, both later with Warner Bros, the one as actor, the second as director. The Juliet of this film was Florence Lawrence. Others recognizable are Ranous as the apothecary — he also directed — Charles Kent as Capulet, Charles Chapman as Montague, William Shea as Peter, and Miss Carver as the Nurse. Josephine Atkinson, who the next year was to become Mrs. Panzer, had a bit part. *Romeo and Juliet* was 915 feet in length, could be had tinted, and was released on June 2, 1908.

THEODORE HUFF

# Hollywood's Predecessor: Fort Lee, N.J.

*This modest little piece, hidden away in* Films in Review *(February 1951, pages 17-21), bristles with facts about stars, producers, and directors of the teen years when most American movies were made, not in Hollywood, but in New Jersey. Students of today may be oriented by the fact that the Solax Studio was "near the present exit of the George Washington Bridge."*

*Theodore Huff was one of the earliest scholars of cinema in the U.S., author of a valuable biography of Charlie Chaplin (1951) and assistant professor at New York University, the College of the City of New York, and the University of Southern California.*

In the beginning most of the motion picture companies — Edison, Biograph, Vitagraph, Kalem et al — had their studios in New York City. At first they were on rooftops, then in converted ballrooms, stables, or lofts, and finally in the specially designed structures Edison built in the Bronx and Vitagraph built in Brooklyn.

When rural exteriors were needed, the companies went over to New Jersey, usually on the Fort Lee ferry at 125th street, especially after Sidney Olcott, then with the Kalem Co., discovered in 1907 that the picturesque woods and hilly roads of the Palisades near Coytesville and Fort Lee could be a convenient "wild west." Rambo's Hotel, in Coytesville, near the summer house of Maurice Barrymore, was used as a place to dress as well as for the exterior of a Western saloon. Alice Joyce and Robert Vignola (later a director of note) rode in many of the cowboy thrillers that Kalem staged in northern New Jersey.

From 1908 to 1912 D.W. Griffith used this terrain for location work, and Fort Lee and Englewood and their environs provided the exteriors for such of his little Biograph classics as *The Curtain Pole, The Lonely Villa, Pippa Passes, His Trust, The Battle* and *The New York Hat*. Mary Pickford, Arthur Johnson, Mack Sennett, Henry B. Walthall, Lionel Barrymore and the rest of the Griffith family were familiar sights. A favorite eating place for movie people was Cella's Park Hotel in Fort Lee.

In 1909 Mark Dintenfass, an associate of Carl Laemmle, built the first local studio near the Fort Lee-Coytesville line close to the edge of the Palisades. It became known as the Champion, after the brand of films made there for Laemmle's Universal (IMP) program. It was little more than a wooden platform roofed with sheets (to soften the sunlight when necessary). In 1911 the Eclair Company of France built a branch studio in Fort Lee. It was small but well equipped, was made of glass and resembled a green house.

But north Jersey's great period really began early in 1914, after the feature length picture had become well established. Jules Brulatour erected the Peerless studio off Linwood avenue, back of the Eclair, and within two years there were seven more large and well-equipped studios: the Willat, Solax, Paragon, Universal, Kalem, Ideal, and Lincoln. Most of them bordered on Main street in Fort Lee; a few were a mile or so away. Several laboratories were also built.

Fort Lee's greatest prosperity was from 1914 to 1919. Lewis J. Selznick, father of David Selznick, produced for the World Film Corporation, with William Brady as his director general, at the Peerless studio. In the period when the U.S. motion picture industry made 700 features a year, the World turned out one feature a week for five hectic years. A half a dozen pictures were often made on the main stage simultaneously. Sensational "society dramas" were favored and many of Brady's stage successes were screened. Lillian Russell made a version of her stage success *Wildfire*. Others who starred for World included: Clara Kimball Young, Alice Brady, Ethel Clayton, Kitty Gordon, Robert Warwick, Montague Love, Carlyle Blackwell, and Madge Evans (as a child). Among the many notables, largely from the New York stage, who appeared here were: Wilton Lackaye, Holbrook Blinn, Lenore Ulric, Vivian Martin, Lillian Lorraine, Florence Reed, Lowell Sherman, Fania Marinoff, Gail Kane, Warner Oland, Marie Dressler, Doris Kenyon, Milton Sills, Henry Hull and June Elvidge.

Most of the directors of World were French emigrés from the Pathé and Eclair studios in Europe. They included Albert Capellani, director of *Les Miserables*, one of the first features, and George Archainbaud, Emile Chautard and Maurice Tourneur. Elsewhere the French colony of Fort Lee included Francis Doublier, Herbert and Mme. Blaché, and Leonce Perret. A few miles down the river, in Jersey City, Louis Gasnier, an associate of Louis Feuillade, who had made the first serials in France, was making serials for Pathé with Pearl White. Clarence Brown started at World as an assistant to Tourneur, and Josef von Sternberg began as a cutter there.

Few World pictures are remembered today — the company was chiefly interested in vehicles for stars — but mention can be made of Tourneur's *The Wishing Ring* with Vivian Martin, of his *Trilby* with Clara Kimball Young and Wilton Lackaye; of Capellani's *Camille* with Miss Young, *Betsy Ross* with Alice Brady, and *Heart of a Hero* with Robert Warwick (as Nathan Hale).

Near the World studio, on the corner of Main and Linwood avenue, were the double stages built by "Doc" Willat. For a time the Willat studio was owned by Kessel and Bauman, who were also producers for the New York Motion Picture Co. Then it became one of the eastern branch studios of the great Triangle Co., under whose tenancy some Sennett comedies were made, including a few of the popular Fatty and Mabel series, starring Fatty Arbuckle and Mabel Normand. Douglas Fairbanks made the interiors there for *American Aristocracy,* one of his 1916 hits. The Willat was Fox's eastern studio for a few years, before his New York studio on Tenth avenue opened in 1920. William Farnum made his version of *Les Miserables* and other pictures at the Willat. Theda Bara, George Walsh, Virginia Pearson and other Fox stars worked there. Fox also took over the old Eclair studio for the production of Pearl White features and pictures starring Evelyn Nesbit Thaw.

Toward the west, down in a hollow on John street, the Paragon studio was erected in 1915. At the time it was the largest and most modern studio in the world. Its 200 foot-long stage was covered with glass. (Sunlight filtered through glass was the principal illumination at that time. When sunlight failed and at night — they worked day and night in those days — banks of the ghastly-hued Cooper Hewitt mercury lamps were used. Kleig arc lights for spots came later.) For a time the Paragon was part of the World, the eastern studio of Paramount-Artcraft. There, in 1916-17, Mary Pickford made *The Poor Little Rich Girl,* one of her greatest successes, under the direction of Maurice Tourneur. This French director, whose place in motion picture history has been either underestimated or forgotten, also made his version of *The Bluebird* at the Paragon, as well as *Prunella* with Marguerite Clarke. In these two films, Tourneur employed unusual lighting effects and stylized and impressionistic settings prior to the similar art work the Germans so strikingly exploited in the twenties. Among the stars who acted at the Paragon were Elsie Ferguson, Billie Burke, Thomas Meighan, Blanche Sweet and Norma Talmadge.

On the hill above the Paragon the Universal was built about the same time. Samuel Goldwyn took it over after a year or so of Laemmle ownership. In it, in 1917, Goldwyn produced his first picture on his own, *Polly of the Circus*, with Mae Marsh. His other stars included: Mabel Normand, Pauline Frederick, Geraldine Farrar, Madge Kennedy and Tom Moore. Among Goldwyn's directors were George Loane Tucker, Victor Schertzinger, and Arthur Hopkins. In line with the old Famous Players idea, Goldwyn hired stage celebrities, some of whom were past their prime or unequal to the demands of the camera. Among his disasters were *Thais* with Mary Garden; *The Eternal Magdalene* with Maxine Elliott; and *The Spreading Dawn* with Jane Cowl. The unpretentious comedies of Mabel Normand saved him from bankruptcy. One of Goldwyn's minor films in 1918 was *Thirty a Week* with Tom Moore and a newcomer — Tallulah Bankhead. After Goldwyn left, the Universal studio was used by the Selznick Co. from 1919 to 1922 for pictures starring Olive Thomas, Eugene O'Brien, Elaine Hammerstein, Owen Moore, Elsie Janis and Martha Mansfield.

The Solax studio was built by Herbert Blaché and Mme. Blaché, representatives of the French Gaumont Company, near the present exit of the George Washington Bridge. Olga Petrova, Ethel Barrymore and Nazimova acted in it in productions which the Blachés released through Metro. It burned down in the early twenties.

Why did the movies leave Fort Lee? Shortage of coal to heat the barn-like studios, the need to conserve electricity, and the shortage of labor during 1918 are some of the reasons given. Also the growing popularity of California. Goldwyn, for example, left in the summer of 1918 for California. Others followed. During the twenties there was sporadic production — perhaps 5% or less of what once had been.

# ANTHONY SLIDE
# Alice Guy Blaché

*This talented woman, both entrepreneur and artist, directed 400 short films in France and more than 300 in America (many of them in her own New Jersey studio) and after that 25 features. Anthony Slide, who has written a number of authoritative studies of the early silent years, says that perhaps a dozen of the Solax shorts survive in the Library of Congress. He has recently edited* The Memoirs of Alice Guy Blaché, *as translated by her daughter and daughter-in-law (Scarecrow Press, 1986). It is a life observed with wit and charm, taking due note of opposition to her career and constant attempts to deny her credit.*

*In his book,* Early Women Directors *(Cranbury, N.J., A.S. Barnes & Co., 1977) pages 15 to 35, Slide includes comments sent to him in a letter from a prominent silent screen actress, Olga Petrova, on Madame Blaché's quiet and considerate methods of directing. Note also the director's firm statement that "there is nothing connected with the staging of a motion picture that a woman cannot do as easily as a man."*

Alice Guy Blaché was a true pioneer of the cinema: Not only was she the screen's first woman director, she was one of the first directors. *Photoplay* (March, 1912) described her as "a striking example of the modern woman in business who is doing a man's work. She is doing successfully what men are trying to do. She is succeeding in a line of work in which hundreds of men have failed."[1]

This remarkable woman was born at Saint-Mandé on the outskirts of Paris, into a comfortable middle-class family, on July 1, 1875.[2] In the mid 1890's, she was hired as a secretary by the French film pioneer, Léon Gaumont. At this time Gaumont was primarily concerned with the manufacture of motion picture cameras and projectors; the actual production of films did not concern him greatly. It was possibly this lack of interest which led him, early in 1896, to allow his secretary, Alice Guy, to write, photograph and direct, with the help of a friend, Yvonne Mugnier-Serand, a short titled *La Fée aux choux (The Cabbage Fairy)*.

Gaumont was pleased with the short, and Alice Guy found filmmaking enjoyable. She was, therefore, raised from the typical

female occupation of secretary to the masculine one of film directing. Apparently, every motion picture produced by Gaumont until
1905 was directed by Alice Guy. In that year, needing additional
assistance, Alice Guy hired Ferdinand Zecca as a director, Victorin Jasset as an assistant and Louis Feuillade as a writer. In so
doing, it seems almost as if, with one mighty stroke, she had
created the entire early French film industry.

In 1905, Léon Gaumont marketed the "Chronophone," which
synchronized a projector with sound recorded on a wax cylinder.
Yet again, it fell to Alice Guy to pioneer "talking pictures," of
which she directed more than a hundred during 1906 and early
1907. Curiously, there appears to be doubt as to whether these
early experimental films were successful. Certainly, it was not
until December 27, 1910, that "Filmparlants" were demonstrated,
satisfactorily, to the Academie des Sciences in Paris, "when
Professor d'Arsonval had the unique pleasure of seeing and hearing
himself making a speech before that august body of Savants."
(Proceedings of the Royal Institution of Great Britain, May 10,
1912.)

Herbert Blaché-Bolton, a Londoner, had come to the Gaumont
studios to work as a cameraman, and to study French methods
of film production for the early British film entrepreneur, Colonel
Bromhead. Blaché-Bolton and Alice Guy fell in love, and became
engaged on Christmas Day, 1906. Early in 1907, Léon Gaumont
determined to open a New York office, and offered the position
as its head to Blaché-Bolton. He accepted, and married Alice Guy
only three days before they both sailed for the States.

The first thing the couple did on arrival in the United States
was to drop the "Bolton" part of their name. From henceforth,
they were to be known as Herbert and Alice Guy Blaché. For
a short time, Alice Guy Blaché settled down to the life of a
housewife; in 1908 she gave birth to a daughter, Simone. Then,
in 1910, she determined to return to film production.

On September 7, 1910, Alice Guy Blaché established the Solax
Company, with herself as president and director-in-chief. From 1910
through June, 1914, when Solax ceased to exist, Madame Blaché was
to supervise the direction of every one of Solax's three hundred or
so productions. The first, *A Child's Sacrifice*, was released on October
21, 1910, and featured "The Solax Kid" (Magda Foy).

Aside from Magda Foy, other players at Solax included Darwin
Karr (who joined the company in November, 1911), Vinnie Burns,

Marian Swayne, Blanche Cornwall, Claire Whitney, Billie Quirk, Lee Beggs, and Fraunie Fraunholz. The studios were at first located in Flushing, Long Island, but in September, 1912, new studios were completed at Fort Lee, New Jersey.

A description of Madame Blaché at the studio appeared in *Photoplay* magazine: "She quietly moves about the plant, unostentatiously and unobtrusively energetic. She carries with her an air of refinement and culture, and her dark, modest clothes bespeak and emphasize her dignity. This dignity, however, never borders on frigidity. She smiles encouragingly upon every one she meets. Her commands are executed to the letter with dispatch and efficiency, not because she is feared, but because she is liked. Although Madame has decided ideas, and at times will obstinately insist that they be carried out, she is always, too, willing to listen to suggestions. She is not a woman who is amenable to flattery. Unlike other women in business, she is really the first sometimes to see her own errors and will often, without resentment, admit the justice of criticism."[3]

In a letter to *Films in Review*, Frank Léon Smith recalled, "When I worked in the Pathé-Astra Studio in Jersey City her name [Alice Guy Blaché] was often spoken by my French bosses. They respected her, but, I think, also resented a woman succeeding as a writer, director, and producer of movies. One day I was sent to go over a script with a Pathé director working at Madame Blaché's glass-roofed Solax studio at Fort Lee. The big stage was empty at the time, and Madame Blaché was not there, but high on one wall, in letters two feet tall, was her mandate, 'Be Natural.' She had put this sign up for the guidance of the young and inept, self-conscious extras, and old pros (actors) addicted to stage tricks the camera could turn into farce, and it spoke to *me*, a confused young fellow — Her sign was amazing for those times, when the common phrase for acting in movies was 'posing for pictures.' "[4]

When Madame Blaché was otherwise engaged, her directorial duties were taken over by Edward Warren. Born in Boston in 1857, Warren joined Solax in the summer of 1911 after a lengthy stage career. He resigned from Solax in July of 1913 to direct a feature film on the Boy Scouts of America. From that point on, it was all downhill for Warren's career. By 1915, he was reduced to playing Douglas Fairbanks' valet in *The Lamb*. He died in Los Angeles on April 3, 1930.

It is difficult to determine exactly which films were directed by Warren and which by Madame Blaché. Certainly Blaché had overall supervision of all Solax productions. One of the first major releases of Solax, definitely directed by Alice Guy Blaché, was *The Violin Maker of Nuremberg* (released December 22, 1911). It was a tale of two apprentice violin-makers (Berkeley Barrington and Gladden James), who both loved their master's daughter (Blanche Cornwall). A violin-making competition is held to determine who will win the girl, but the better apprentice of the two, knowing that she really loves his rival, substitutes his violin for his competitor's. Of *The Violin Maker of Nuremberg, The Moving Picture World* (December 9, 1911) commented, "It is a story of tender sentiment told amid scenes of artistic quaintness. It carries a simple sentimental thread in a skillful manner that never descends to the commonplace, and, at the same time, holds the interest with its dignity and artistic charm." Incidentally, in a small role in this production, was Madame Blaché's daughter, Simone.

None of Madame Blaché's major Solax productions have survived, but some six one-reelers are preserved in the National Film Collection at the Library of Congress: *Greater Love Hath No Man* (released June 30, 1911), *The Detective's Dog* (released April 10, 1912), *Canned Harmony* (released October 9, 1912), *The Girl in the Armchair* (released December 13, 1912), *A House Divided* (released May 2, 1913) and *Matrimony's Speed Limit* (released June 11, 1913).

A viewing of these films reveals that Madame Blaché was demonstrating a remarkable sophistication in storytelling. *A Detective's Dog* is an amusing satire on early melodramas, with a dog racing to rescue its master, who is tied to a sawmill and about to be cut in half. In *A House Divided,* a married couple with domestic problems, of their own invention, adopt a policy of silence. *Matrimony's Speed Limit* is presumably based on the same David Belasco play, which was the source for Buster Keaton's *Seven Chances,* and involves a hero who must marry by a certain hour in order to come into an inheritance.

Solax productions by 1913 were released on an average of two-a-week. However, in October, 1913, Herbert Blaché founded Blaché Features — he had left the Gaumont organization a year earlier — and persuaded his wife to join him. Solax's last regular release was *The Rogues of Paris* on October 20, 1913. A few further films were released under the Solax label, but to all extents and purposes, Solax was no more. . . .

During its years of existence, approximately half of the productions of Blaché Features were directed by Madame Blaché. Blaché Features was followed by a new company, again promoted by

Herbert Blaché, The U.S. Amusement Company, which released through Art Dramas. Most of the productions of the U.S. Amusement Company were directed by Herbert Blaché. A few, including *The Adventurer*, based on the novel by Upton Sinclair, and released on February 15, 1917, were directed by Madame Blaché. It is interesting to note her reputation as witnessed by this review in *The Moving Picture World* of March 24, 1917: "This reviewer has yet to see a picture by Madame Blaché that was not sincerely and artistically directed and this, *The Adventurer*, one of her recent productions is no exception." . . .

In the summer of 1917, Madame Blaché found time from her directing chores to give a series of lectures at Columbia University on filmmaking.

Madame Blaché's last two films, both for Pathé release, were *The Great Adventure*, released on March 10, 1918 and *Tarnished Reputations*, released on March 14, 1920. The former was Bessie Love's first film for Pathé, and marked Flora Finch's return to the screen.

Madame Blaché was offered the direction of *Tarzan of the Apes*, but she declined that dubious honor. By 1922, she and her husband had separated, and Madame Blaché returned to France. In the late Twenties, she tried unsuccessfully to return to film production. She worked as a translator, and attempted, yet again unsuccessfully, to sell a book for children, which she had both authored and illustrated.

She lived in France, Belgium and the States with her daughter, who had become a secretary in the American Foreign Service. Eventually Madame Blaché suffered a stroke; she died in New Jersey — the state in which she had spent virtually all of her years of filmmaking — on March 24, 1968.

Herbert Blaché continued as a director until the end of the silent era. In the late Twenties, he remarried, and by the early Thirties, he and his new wife, Helen, were managing a shop in Hollywood. Herbert Blaché died in Santa Monica, California, on October 23, 1953.

In the July 11, 1914 issue of *The Moving Picture World*, Alice Guy Blaché wrote a piece on "Woman's Place in Photoplay Production." It seems more than fitting to end this chapter on her work by quoting from that article:

> . . . In the arts of acting, music and literature, woman has long held her place among the most successful workers, and when it is considered how vital-

ly all of these arts enter into the production of motion pictures one wonders why the names of scores of women are not found among the successful creators of photodrama offerings.

There is nothing connected with the staging of a motion picture that a woman cannot do as easily as a man, and there is no reason why she cannot completely master every technicality of the art. The technique of the drama has been mastered by so many women that it is considered as much her field as a man's and its adaptation to picture work in no way removes it from her sphere. The technique of motion picture photography like the technique of the drama is fitted to a woman's activities.[5]

NOTES

1. H. Z. Levine, "Madame Alice Blaché," *Photoplay* (March, 1912).
2. Most published sources list her year of birth as 1873, but Madame Blaché's daughter assures me it was 1875. — A.S.
3. H. Z. Levine, "Madame Alice Blaché," *Photoplay* (March, 1912).
4. Frank Léon Smith, Letter in *Films in Review* (April, 1964).
5. Alice Blaché, "Woman's Place in Photoplay Production," *The Moving Picture World* (July 11, 1914).

# KEVIN BROWNLOW
# Allan Dwan

*Believing that silent film makers contributed many works of art to our culture which have been foolishly forgotten and downgraded, Brownlow, a British film editor and director, set out on a search for survivors. His interviews and commentary appeared in a beautifully illustrated book (N.Y., Knopf, 1968) called* The Parade's Gone By. *Dwan, he suggests, may have been the most prolific director in history (pages 96-98, 100, 102, 104).*

Allan Dwan — ex-engineer, ex-inventor — was a man whose mechanical skill brought him into the industry and kept him at the head of it, a man with a strong dramatic sense whose clear and logical brain and rich sense of humor ensured for his pictures the highest standards of entertainment and craftsmanship.

Capability Dwan — the man you turned to in a crisis. Astonishingly resourceful, Dwan's training as an engineer gave him a rare knowledge. Like the hero of *A Connecticut Yankee in King Arthur's Court*, his firm grasp of practicalities made him an object of wonder among those less fortunately endowed.

One of the Big Six directors in the twenties, Dwan has survived them all; he has the longest record of any director in the business.

"I once tried to draw up a list of the pictures I'd done," said Dwan when I met him in Hollywood in 1964, "Someone sent me a list with eight hundred titles on it, and I tried to help him by adding on the rest. I got fourteen hundred and I had to give up. Just couldn't remember the others."

Unhappily, few of his pictures have survived, and a great career has been overlooked. But recently the young critics of *Cahiers du Cinema* rediscovered some of his talkies, and following their raves, *Film Culture* announced: "Dwan's career is still being mined for a possibly higher assay of gold to dross. Recent findings — *Silver Lode, Restless Breed, The River's Edge* — represent a virtual bonanza of hitherto unexplored classics. It may very well be that Dwan will turn out to be the last of the old masters."[1]

Allan Dwan was certainly one of the masters of the silent motion picture. He had to be; he made pictures so fast that anything less than mastery of the medium would have brought him early catastrophe.

When meeting such distinguished veterans as Dwan, preconceived ideas tend to make the actual encounter somewhat startling. Sparse facts, mixed with rumor and much supposition, had created for me a none-too-easy subject for an interview; I anticipated an elderly, rather fragile man, greatly embittered, impatient and short-tempered. For while the silent days were the peak years of his career, he has since kept himself in the background. "If you get your head above the mob," he has been quoted as saying, "they try to knock it off. If you stay down you last forever."[2]

The stout man with the breezy grin who opened the door was, I assumed, a friend or a business associate; he was too youthful to fit my image. But when he swept me through to a study, decorated with stills from *Robin Hood*, my illusion was dispelled. Any question of age seemed ludicrous; the undiminished enthusiasm, the vitality, and the hilarious sense of humor proved that Dwan as a person hadn't changed much. From this encounter alone I fully understood why people like Douglas Fairbanks and Gloria Swanson selected him as a favorite director.

Recalling the past was no effort; the anecdotes flowed in brisk profusion, as though we were talking between takes on a silent picture. The thick glasses he wore as protection from the studio lights have now become permanent — otherwise those who knew him then would notice little change. Scripts for current projects were piled high on his desk; and on the wall was an appreciation from the U.S. Marine Corps for *Sands of Iwo Jima* and a graduation certificate made out to Joseph Aloysius Dwan.

"That's a fine name to be known by." He grinned. "At school they used to say 'Aloysius to be a girl,' so I changed it to Allan.

"I went to work for the Peter Cooper-Hewitt company, and I developed the mercury-vapor arc for them — you know, the long tubes. In 1909 I fitted these mercury-vapor arcs in the postoffice in Chicago so that the men sorting the mail could work longer hours — it was a ghastly light, made you look mortified, but your eyes would last longer."

While he was fitting the mercury-vapor tubes, the attention of a passer-by was caught by the strange glare from the post-office basement. The man stopped, stared through the windows, and then walked down and asked for the person in charge. He introduced himself to Dwan as George K. Spoor and asked whether the lights would be suitable for photography.

"Yes,' said Dwan. "They ought to be very good."

Spoor, who was the *S* of the Essanay Company, Chicago,[3] placed an order for an experimental light. Dwan designed the first mercury-vapor arc bank, and the factory made up four, which he took to the studio.

"During this experimentation period, I watched what they were doing, and it kind of fascinated me — the silly pictures they were making under the lights. One day I asked them where they got their stories from.

" 'Well,' they said, 'We buy them from anybody.'

" 'What do you pay?'

" 'Oh — up to twenty-five dollars for good stories.'

"Well, I'd written a lot of stories for the magazine at university — *The Scholastic* at Notre Dame — so one day I brought over fifteen of them. They bought the lot."

They were so impressed, in fact, that they asked Dwan if he'd like to be their scenario editor — and they named a price far above anything a young engineer could earn. "I'll do both," said Dwan. "I'll supervise these lights *and* I'll be your scenario editor."

Two weeks later, most of the executives of Essanay left to form the American Film Manufacturing Company — and they persuaded Dwan to join them at twice his salary.

The new organization had a problem. Somewhere in California — no one knew quite where — was one of their companies. The supply of films had dried up and, despite frequent cables, so had the supply of information.

Dwan was asked to go and find out what had happened. He located them at San Juan Capistrano.

"They had no director because he was an alcoholic. He'd gone to Los Angeles on a binge and left the company flat. So I wired: 'Suggest you disband company — you have no director.' They wired back: 'You direct.' "

Faced with this sudden responsibility, Dwan called the actors together (among them was J. Warren Kerrigan) and announced: "Either I'm a director or you're out of work." Replied the actors: "You're the best damn director we ever saw!"

Dwan asked what a director was supposed to do. The actors took him out and showed him. "I found that was a very successful way to operate, and so I made that my policy. I just let the actors tell me what to do and I get along very well. I've been doing it now for fifty-five years — and they haven't caught me yet."

Dwan made three pictures a week for American Film — *and* took the weekend off. Of course, the pictures were only one-reelers — later they graduated to two-reelers, and by 1913 they had reached feature-length.

"In those days we had full control of our companies, with no interference from the producers, subproducers, supervisors, and front offices that came later. We did what we liked and we hired whoever we liked. That's how I got Marshall Neilan, Victor Fleming, and fellows like that into the business. It's unheard of today, to walk out and see somebody you like the looks of, and say, 'Come on, come and work with me.' He has to do an apprenticeship, join a union, pass all kinds of muster, and do four thousand other things — even then he can't get in."

The start of Allan Dwan's career coincided with that of D.W. Griffith; from the very beginning, Dwan took careful note of the delicate feelers Griffith was putting into the primitive void of motion-picture technique. As Griffith gained confidence, as his experiments left the field of speculation and became bold innovations, Dwan admits he became his god.

"I watched everything he did, and then I'd do it, in some form or another. I'd try to do it in another way — I'd try to do it better. And I'd try to invent something that *he'd* see. He finally sent for me and said he was sick of competing, and would I join him at Triangle?

"What fascinated me about Griffith? Well, I think his lack of long gesture, his simplicity, and his use of facial expression. He developed a strange new pantomime. I like pantomime anyway, but I don't like the extreme pantomime.

"Other actors exaggerated to make up for not having words. His players used short little gestures to get over their point — they were

much more realistic. And I saw Griffith was expressing vividly a lot
of things with very little effort.

"And then I liked the backlighting which his cameraman was using. I though it was great. Nobody else would use it — they thought
the sun should shine directly onto the person. I used to wonder how
he had the faces beautifully lit when the sun was behind them, and
then I went out to the studio one day and saw them using reflectors.
So we learned to use reflectors.

"That wasn't new, of course; professional photographers often used
reflectors in their portrait studios. But it was news to us. All we ever
did was to go out on the street and photograph the shot just as it was.
If there happened to be a shadow on the face, it stayed there. We
never thought of easing it off with a reflector.

"And then, of course, he taught us the close-up. He had a terrible
time with that. The theater managers almost canceled his pictures.
They couldn't understand how people were walking around without
legs. In the theater they were accustomed to seeing the whole body,
and what it was standing on. But to see a head moving around, cut
off at the neck, just wasn't acceptable. But I grabbed it immediately."

The question of who invented the close-up has long vexed film
historians. Close-shots can be found as early as 1896, but close-ups
were not in common use before Griffith's pictures. I asked Allan
Dwan if anyone predated him.

"Oh no, nobody ever did. Nobody living ever did. He was the first
person who ever dared put on a motion-picture screen anything but
a full-length picture."

"But surely," I persisted, "you pioneering directors did *something*
on your own?"

"We did. We did lots of things Griffith didn't do. But his
achievements are the real, vivid things."

Dwan paused for a moment, and then said, "It's hard to remember
and claim you were responsible for any one thing, but I was one of
the first to make full use of the moving camera."

While running shots were becoming a familiar part of picture
technique — the camera keeping pace with a moving vehicle — sustained traveling shots were a novelty. In *David Harum*, made in 1915
when Dwan was with Famous Players, the camera was mounted on
a Ford, and it tracked right down the main street of a town, following William H. Crane as he chatted with another character, as people greeted him, as he paused, talked, and continued walking. *David
Harum*, for most of its length, employs the simple, static technique
prevalent in 1915 but occasional camera mobility gave it the look

of a more mature silent film. And the opening is first-class cinema; iris-in to a masked close-up of a cup of coffee and a plate . . . the coffee is poured into a saucer, and the mask irises out to full frame. The camera then follows the saucer on its upward journey, to reveal a close-up of William H. Crane as David Harum. Then it pans across to reveal Kate Meeks as Aunt Polly. The smooth movement is interrupted by introductory titles, but the effect is still striking.

It would be a mistake, however, to give the impression that Dwan was obsessed by tricks of technique, and that his early experiments flowered into riotous camera movements and shattering montages. He just wasn't that kind of director. Warm and humorous, he had a great feeling for people — and his use of cinema was always subservient to the performances, to the story. He played around with every cinematic device, mastering each before discarding it in favor of absolute simplicity and a pure directness of style. . . .

"Artistic efficiency, that's Dwan!" declared Adela Rogers St. Johns — quoting him as saying, in 1920: "It's the most doggone fascinating game there is — directing motion pictures. It's a sense of power and a sense of creation in one. It's a gamble. Even if you know something about it, you're not so sure you know anything about it at all. The pictures that I have loved, that I thought were great, have been flivvers nine times out of ten. The ones that I sort of turned up my nose at went over with a bang.

"I am a businessman. I have a commercial mind. A man can make the most artistic picture ever filmed, but if it plays to empty houses it hasn't achieved a thing for Art or for Humanity. The great problem of the pictures is the welding of art and business. Waste is not artistic. Inefficiency is not artistic.

"Pictures must be made fast. If you muddle around with them, you lose your clear vision. You cannot hurry art, of course, but you can hurry commercial production. Get your art in hand before you start to produce and you'll save yourself a lot of time and trouble."[6]

NOTES

1. *Film Culture*, Spring 1963, p. 23.
2. Ralph Hancock and Letitia Fairbanks: *Douglas Fairbanks; The Fourth Musketeer* (New York: Holt; 1953), p. 186.
3. The A was G.M. ("Broncho Billy") Anderson.
6. *Photoplay*, Aug. 1920, p. 56.

# Chapter 2

# Ince and Hart

*The cogs of the big Ince machine oiled to the smallest
gear . . . this is the modern miracle.* — W. E. Wing.

Writers of early film history have traditionally focused on
D. W. Griffith, and with good reason. He is surely the dominant figure, by testimony of his contemporaries and by the
evidence of his films. He was credited as teacher by dozens of
direct successors and he made films on such a grand scale that
we are still in awe of their daring and their splendor.

At the same time a monopolizing trend has been at work, guided
first of all by the taste and wisdom of Iris Barry, critic and curator,
who chose in 1935 and after to emphasize Griffith's works more
than others for the film collection at the Museum of Modern Art.
She persuaded Griffith to give to the Museum his business papers
and prints of the films he controlled, allowing rental copies to
be made available for schools: a historic precedent for film study
in this country.

It was the right choice. It is sad that a choice had to be made.
Today we have almost all of Griffith's films. We have a much
smaller proportion of the films of Thomas Ince and other contemporary directors.

We lack further the perspective of a view in depth — all the
way down to the cheapest weekly output of momentary companies. Life, art, and literature in America are being studied
nowadays with a good deal more emphasis on the whole range

of production and of popular response. Film was and is a popular art. Perhaps more than any other art it requires a congruent breadth and depth of historical reporting. Yet this kind of study of the silent period will always be prevented, now, by the early dominance in film collections of star contributors like Griffith, Fairbanks, and Chaplin.

Only by a last-minute discovery were the features of Buster Keaton taken under the private protective care of Raymond Rohauer. The films of Mary Pickford were saved by the intercession of officials at the Library of Congress from destruction by her own hand. The discerning and vigorous efforts of David Shepard in searching out "lost" films for the American Film Institute during the late 1960s, and the subsequent deposit of the Paramount silent film collection, have made a significant difference. More may turn up in foreign archives. Yet so much has been lost forever, and we may have had our last chance for new findings which could affect our evaluations of film history.

The stately procession of world film histories by Arthur Knight, Gerald Mast, Jack Ellis, David Cook and other American writers have all depended in great degree for their American material on the earlier judgments of Iris Barry and of Lewis Jacobs, whose comprehensive social and critical chronicle of *The Rise of the American Film* (1939) is still an indispensable introduction to American film history. As always in the history of history writing, there is another generation, ready to offer contrary judgments — or denying that judgment is even possible. But the Griffith achievements do not need to be attenuated or made over into mere legends, in order for others to be given their due.

Partisans of the so-called gritty realism of Erich von Stroheim have naturally aligned themselves against the 'sentimentalism' of Griffith. There have been other 'rivals,' some of them noted in an interesting series of screenings prepared by Richard Koszarski for the Walker Art Center in Minneapolis in 1976. The program centered on three films directed by Maurice Tourneur, offering also recently recovered works by Frank Borzage and John Ford, as well as a Pickford drama by Marshall Neilan and a Fairbanks comedy by John Emerson. But there were four pictures which had been produced by Thomas Ince.

The stature of this director-producer-author has been enhanced in recent years, as American observers have noticed the praise heaped on him by certain French critics. As early as 1918, Louis

Delluc advanced his cause as a director by calling his work "lyrical," whereas Jean Mitry, a more analytical historian, has been at pains to contrast Griffith's "poetry" with Ince's clean-cut dramaturgy and expression of themes.

Ordinarily, for American critics, doubts might accrue from the fact that Ince became in time a historical prototype of the iron-fisted executive producer. He may have been the first person in the industry to insist on directors following to the letter every action and camera direction in the script he approved. His cost controls were legendary and his efficiency methods hardly conducive to the kinds of unchecked creative inspiration and uninhibited retakes that might be expected to result in works of unique art. Nevertheless, there has been a search for style in his films, and not only the early ones he directed but also the later ones which he influenced — by indirection — as producer and scenario editor.

Did his films reflect a personal "stamp?" William Everson proposes for Reginald Barker's *The Italian* (1915) both dramatic and photographic realism in presenting the hardships of an immigrant couple in New York City. Jean Mitry, recalling from his notes at the time several Ince films of social criticism, comments on the naturalness of the acting, and, in the westerns, on the use of concrete photographic detail to reflect and bridge the action. These features were all made by others after Ince began to stop directing in 1913.

From 1911 to 1913, according to Martin Sopocy's "tentative" list of U.S. archive holdings (May 1982), we have only 18 short films by Ince. These are hardly enough to judge for ourselves whether there is any notable contribution to style in Ince's own films. But total control over scripts does mean considerable control over style as well as substance. As more of Ince's works as producer become available on videotape for general viewers from archives like George Eastman House, UCLA, and the Library of Congress (and 15 Ince features are supposed to be at the Museum of Modern Art) scholars and critics can face the delicate task of sorting things out. Meanwhile we can be intrigued and perhaps persuaded by the attractive tapestry of arguments woven by Mitry, who is probably the nearest we have to an Aristotle of film history. He is convinced that there is great consistency in most of these films, and that none of Ince's directors afterward "achieved anything much above average."

Of the 80 Ince-supervised features that so far are known to have survived, nineteen are those starring William S. Hart. These are a more coherent group, and they belong less to Ince than to their star/director. Whether Hart or someone else gets screen credit as director, it is Hart's close personal supervision which is usually credited for any individuality in his westerns. He was certainly at odds with his producer a good part of the time.

They had met as struggling actors on Broadway. When Bill Hart got interested, some years later, in improving western movies, he called up the N.Y. Motion Picture Company and found out, to his surprise, that Tom Ince was in charge. The big boss was downbeat about westerns and offered him terms that were far from generous. Their chief quarrel, eventually, was over money, but there was also a temperamental difference.

Like many successful men, Ince rose to responsibility partly because of his very ambition, his focus on the values of position and success. Hart wasn't as much interested in achieving a position in society as in accomplishing projects. He had a vision of the way western films ought to be made, and every one he undertook became a kind of mission. Furthermore, Ince was more concerned with meeting budgets and schedules, whereas Hart was sensitive to the nuances of character traits and the interrelationship of landscape and story. Hart's love of animals is expressed in his writing about his dog and his horse, Fritz. Ince wasn't the sort to be sentimental over dumb creatures, and this even led to a special rift between them.

Here were two men who spent much of their lives interpreting the American scene, past and present. Both were self-made, starting from unpromising backgrounds, like Griffith, Pickford, Zukor, and Chaplin: Ince's parents were traveling actors and Hart's father a janitor and itinerant grist mill operator. Taken together, their scripts often dealt with problems of status and individualism in a free enterprise society, though Ince was more politically and socially liberal, and Hart more the nostalgic conservative. Yet they played out in their personal lives a kind of feudal or paternal relationship, in which Ince paid the wages and Hart discovered he was exploited.

Thomas H. Ince and William S. Hart foreshadowed the unhappy side of the familiar confrontation between producer and director. It was the more poignant, perhaps, because these two old friends did not realize they were playing out the conflicting roles for possibly the first time in Hollywood history. If Ince had been a little less insecure and tight-fisted, he might have given his star a looser rein, made better pictures, and lived longer. If Bill Hart had been a little less trusting to start with, and more temperamental over the long run, he might have made more movies and more money for Ince as well as for himself. As it was, his works were the center of the Ince achievement as long as they stayed together, and an enduring precedent for westerns to come.

They no doubt agreed on the main aspects of Hart's screen character. Ince would have approved the scripts, and the bridge between them often was Ince's favorite screenwriter, C. Gardner Sullivan. Hart played a strong, silent hero. His films were rugged, austere, full of the gritty sense of outdoor life under conditions of simplicity and hardship. The stories were sometimes depressing, even complex, though without much actual gunplay. Often Hart was a bad man at the start, an outlaw who is gradually reformed by the love of a woman. This pattern has influenced both movies and genre criticism ever since.

Did either Ince or Griffith think of each other in terms of rivalry? There can be little doubt of this, and it is probably confirmed by the fact that Ince is mentioned only once in the Lillian Gish memoirs. Richard Schickel suggests that Ince's five-reel *Battle of Gettysburg* in early 1913 spurred Griffith's work that same year on his own Civil War epic.

Ince's directing career began two years after Griffith's, but he was evidently not one of those like Allan Dwan and Cecil DeMille who openly proclaimed that they had learned 'everything' from the Master. As an actor, curiously enough, he took part in one Biograph film called *His New Lid,* in 1910, while Griffith was there, but this one-reeler, having something to do with a lost hat, was directed by Frank Powell. From 1915 to 1917, Ince was of course equally responsible with Griffith for providing features to Aitken's Triangle releasing company. By that time, they were both famous professionals, and if one was more of a cinematic inventor and poet and the other more of a hard-fisted supervisor of dramas with a gritty documentary flavor, that — they would probably say — is what makes movie history.

TERRY RAMSAYE
# The Discovery of California

*Like all "firsts" in history, the first movie made in California may not be a matter beyond dispute, but the Selig company seems to have the best claim. Note that the version of* The Count of Monte Cristo *referred to here is four years earlier than Adolph Zukor's feature film. No special reason is given for Selig's move, but Ramsaye says the N.Y. Motion Picture company went to California because of the guerrilla hostilities carried on by the Patents Company against independents in the East. Included was a company under Fred Balshofer, who has already told us of his encounter with an Edison spy.*

*As usual, Ramsaye brightens up his story of Tom Ince becoming a director with some invented dialogue and thus gets across his somewhat dim view of the Ince personality. The pages are 532-540 in* A Million and One Nights *(N.Y., Simon & Schuster, 1926).*

One day late in 1907 the first motion picture invaders detrained in Los Angeles. The party consisted of Francis Boggs, director for Selig, and Thomas Persons, who was cameraman, property man, business manager, assistant director and whatever else conditions required.

The immediate business of Boggs and Persons was the completion of a one reel version of *The Count of Monte Cristo*. The interior scenes had been made in the Chicago studio. Now, ignoring the little technical matter of an entire change of cast, the rest of the picture was to be made in California. . . .

January 30, 1908, Selig released *The Count of Monte Cristo* in one thousand feet, a full reel, the first big California feature. Meanwhile, Persons and Boggs set up a studio on a roof top in Main street in downtown Los Angeles. California production had begun.

The pressure of the Patents Company's attack on the Independents was a contributing factor to the development of motion picture geography in this period. Independent picture making activities in and about New York were beset by difficulties. Cameras vanished from under the noses of the guards. Mysterious chemical accidents happened in the laboratories, resulting in the loss of costly negatives. The fight was not confined to the courts.

A climax came with one of the New York Motion Picture's operations in the making of a big scene at Whitestone Landing, on Long Island. This impressive spectacle called for a total of twenty extra people, a vast army for that time. Just as the critical drama moment in the scene came, a riot broke out among the extras. Rocks and clubs and fists flew. It was a fight apparently over nothing. Nine of the extras fought together as a clan. When the dust of battle settled, they were found to be professional gunmen and gangsters. Some mysterious agency had sent them out to make a riot instead of a picture. Five of the actors went to the hospital out of that engagement.

What with the weather and such mishaps, Bauman and Kessel decided to transfer the operations of the N.Y.M.P. into the safe distance and sunshine of California. Fred Balshofer and a stock company, including J. Barney Sherry, Ethel Graham, Fred Gephart and Mona Darkfeather, were sent West to found a new studio. The first N.Y.M.P. plant was a defunct grocery store on the outskirts of Los Angeles.

Among the licensed film makers in the East, Griffith of Biograph led the way to California. In early January of 1910 the Griffith company went on a California excursion. The company included Henry Walthall, Mary Pickford, Owen Moore, Jack Pickford and Tony O'Sullivan.

In Los Angeles, Griffith rented a loft in which to store properties for his pictures, and engaged a vacant lot at Twelfth and Georgia streets for a studio. Tent dressing rooms were ranged around the edges. . . .

These California excursions of Biograph and seasonal trips of the various other concerns were without any consciousness of establishing a new seat of industry. All of their California plans and arrangements were temporary and transient. The motion picture was not yet ready to make an investment in California and its sunshine. Back of the studio operations and the art of picture-making, the business of the motion picture, officed in New York, was sitting in suspended judgment. It was not at all certain in the mind of any man in the motion picture business that it was a permanent institution. Newspapers, inspired considerably by jealous theatrical magnates, talked casually of the motion picture craze as one of the passing whims of the public.

Carl Laemmle's Independent Motion Picture Company, the "Imp," was struggling under patent prosecutions and injunction orders with a maze of plans for escape. . . .

In its squirmings against the Patents Company's injunctions the "Imp" first weighed plans to produce in California and at last determined to escape the jurisdiction of the United States courts entirely, by flight to Cuba.

The critical situation leading to this move was an aftermath of a second raid on the Biograph studios. The acquisition of Florence Lawrence, known as "the Biograph Girl," had proven most profitable. Now an emissary was sent downtown to see if "Little Mary," a rising screen favorite, could be lured away from Griffith. She was, of course, Miss Mary Pickford. The name of Pickford was unknown to the screen, but the girl herself, so often designated as *Mary* in Griffith's sub-titles, was known as "Little Mary" to all the motion picture world.

"Little Mary" was employed to work in "Imp" pictures at the amazing figure of $175 a week. Owen Moore, with whom Miss Pickford had played at Biograph, went along to "Imp." They were assigned to the stock company working under Thomas H. Ince, a newly appointed director.

Ince chanced into the pictures in the fall of 1910, when he arrived in New York at the end of a road show engagement, broke and "resting," as they say on Broadway. A street meeting with Joseph Smiley of the "Imp" stock led Ince to a day's work as a "heavy" at the Laemmle studio. Ince thereby earned his first five dollars in the films. In less than fifteen years the movies were to give him about a million.

Ince was born of a stage family and grew up in the life. As a youngster he appeared in many of the plays which took the road from New York, most notable among them perhaps being James A. Herne's production of *Shore Acres.* There was an interlude in his stage career one summer when Thomas H. Ince was a bus boy, carrying the dishes at Pitman Hall, a White Mountain resort. He took the ups and downs as they came, probably never dreaming of the ups that were to come. In the cast of *Hearts Courageous* at the Broadway theatre in New York, Ince met William S. Hart and struck up a friendship that was filled with potentialities of the future for both of them. . . .

But when Ince next encountered Smiley he was invited back to "Imp."

"You made a hit," Smiley informed him. "Go see Tom Cochrane — he likes your work."

By this time the shrewd young man Mr. Ince had made a discovery for himself. He was rather short and unheroic of proportions. He decided that he was not of the architecture of which stars of the screen would be made. He therefore decided that he would be a director.

Ince argued with Cochrane that, if he returned to "Imp," he should be given the first opening as a director. This was reluctantly agreed.

Then came the day when, overhearing a telephone conversation,

Ince discovered that a director had quit. He marched up to Cochrane. "That makes me a director," Ince announced.

Cochrane hesitated. Presumably he had not intended this development at all, but Ince was cocky and insistent.

"Yes, sure." A smile spread over Cochrane's face. He had to see it through. "You start now."

The actors of the "Imp" company had seemingly less enthusiasm for Ince as a director than Cochrane. The cast gave the new director the cold shoulder. Ince was annoyed with the amateurish high school girl scenarios available and resurrected a bit of verse, entitled *Little Nell's Tobacco*, for his first production. Hayward Mack, later a director, played the lead.

When the picture was completed, Carl Laemmle, accompanied by Mr. and Mrs. Ince, went down to Fourteenth street to see it in the "Imp" projection room. Throughout the screening of the picture Ince plied Laemmle with rapid conversation and expounded vigorously on the super-merit of the picture. It seems to have been a masterpiece that needed a good deal of boosting. Then, as it finished on the screen, Ince seized Laemmle by the arm and rushed him out of the room before any adverse comments from the rest of the audience could be overheard.

In this fashion Ince made himself a director.

## STEVEN HIGGINS
# Thomas H. Ince: American Film Maker

*For his Ph.D. at New York University, Steven Higgins offered as his dissertation what appears to be the first full-length study of* Thomas H. Ince: American Film Maker *(1988). During October of 1986, his program notes for the Museum of Modern Art Department of Film accompanied a retrospective showing of Ince films from seven different archives, public and private. His brief biography of Ince is from those notes.*

*Higgins is performing arts librarian for the university library at NYU. His M.A. in library science is from Columbia University. With three co-authors, he helped prepare a filmography of all D.W. Griffith's Biograph films for Scarecrow Press (1985). It is his considered judgment that Ince himself directed only one feature film,* The Battle of Gettysburg, *but that as many as 160 of Ince's productions (if only in fragmentary form) can be found in archives here and abroad.*

Thomas Ince came to motion pictures after a solid, if unexceptional career in the theater. He was born in Newport, Rhode Island on November 16, 1880, the second of three sons. His parents, John and Emma, were well-regarded character actors and light comics.

It is possible that Ince appeared onstage as early as 1889, but a small part in *Charley's Uncle* in May of 1894 is the first professional role that may be credited to him with certainty. Soon thereafter, he took on the part of Young Nat Berry in James A. Herne's *Shore Acres*, touring the eastern United States and Canada for two seasons, with the famous playwright himself in the lead. Working so intimately with Berne, the great American pioneer of theatrical realism, had a profound impact on Ince, both by his own written testimony, and by the testimony of his subsequent contributions to the development of a cinematic realism.

He married Elinor Kershaw, sister of musical star Willette Kershaw, in 1907 and, with the birth of their first son, the need for a reliable income became acute. His abilities as a writer, stage manager and performer led Ince to believe that his recent succession of light comic turns in vaudeville was a potential dead end, and a certain squandering of his talents. He was ready for a change and so, in the autumn of 1910, he turned to the movies. . . .

Ince did work briefly as an actor at Biograph and for Carl Laemmle's Imp Company, but he quickly saw that the only way to make a success of his new profession was to exercise control behind the camera; thus, as soon as the opportunity arose, he became a director for Imp, taking charge of the Mary Pickford unit. Within a year he moved to Adam Kessel and Charles O. Baumann's New York Motion Picture company, assigned to revive its ailing Bison releases. He set up shop in the Santa Ynez Canyon of California and, by 1913, had made "Inceville" a thriving studio.

In 1914 alone, New York Motion Picture employed over ten directors to turn out three two-reel films each week, as well as several feature-length releases — all under the strict personal control of Thomas H. Ince. He moved slowly but certainly into feature production, releasing one long film per month in addition to his regular schedule of two-reelers throughout 1915, until his studio was prepared to supply the newly-formed Triangle with a five-reeler each week. . . . By 1917 he could emerge from the debacle of Triangle unscathed and in complete control of a lucrative corporate entity — Thomas H. Ince Studios. If a filmmaker's success can be measured by his or her ability to meet and sustain artistic goals within the constraints of an uncertain marketplace, then by any reasonable account Ince was a conspicuous success.

With success came reliance upon formula. The irony of Ince's career is that, with the achievement of complete independence, his bold and innovative style showed signs of strain. He always prided himself on his ability to serve the public and its whims; thus, the late 'teens saw a succession of routine Ince pictures starring Charles Ray, Dorothy Dalton and Enid Bennett. He assured himself of further revenue by maintaining control over William S. Hart's releases, though in name only. Paramount/Artcraft, which distributed his productions, did little to prod Ince into more imaginative fare, for the ledger books showed clear profit on virtually every release. For the first time in his career, Ince allowed himself to be lulled into complacency, taking his audience and the bottom line for granted.

In the twenties, Thomas Ince sought new solutions as even the time-tested formulas failed him. Financial backing, though forthcoming, was harder to get and the number of films bearing the Ince name dwindled; in 1922, only three films came from the Ince studio, and one of them — *Lorna Doone* — was a Maurice Tourneur production. Having left Paramount, and with the demise of Associated Producers (a short-lived attempt at self-distribution with such other filmmakers as Tourneur, Allan Dwan, King Vidor, and Mack Sennett), Ince used several independent outlets to market his films.

He took more chances in production, varying his featured players and seeking out more interesting dramatic properties for filming (e.g., *Anna Christie, Human Wreckage*). Studio operations were scaled down to reflect a less ambitious production schedule and space was leased to independent producers during idle times. Finally, John Griffith Wray was appointed production manager of the studio, as Ince reorganized his staff and at last gave up the absolute control for which he had become notorious among his contemporaries. At his death, Thomas Ince was in the midst of filming *The Last Frontier*, a return to the epic western themes of his 101 Bisons, and was rumored to be in negotiation with William Randolph Hearst for management of Cosmopolitan Pictures.

When Thomas H. Ince died in November of 1924, after a party aboard Hearst's yacht, a pall of innuendo was cast over his entire career. Rumors of foul play immediately began to circulate around what was to have been a birthday celebration for the forty-four year old producer, and questions about the "mysterious" nature of his death — which was tragically premature, but natural nonetheless — haunt his memory to this day.

In his fourteen-year career as a film maker, Ince was responsible for the direction and/or production of almost 800 releases. His name is often invoked, but his work is largely unknown.

# W. E. WING
# Tom Ince of Inceville

*After early efforts by picture pioneers to seek new locations in New Jersey — and then the big leap to California — Ince was evidently the first to foresee the need to build a "back lot," where all sorts of foreign climes and city streets could be immediately at hand. His "system" as described here depended on domination of the beginning and ending processes of script writing and editing as much as it did on organizing production. In this, he was more emphatic than Griffith, who supervised many pictures other than his own, or even Jesse Lasky. As a model, Ince most resembles the future Darryl Zanuck.*

*Later he would have built for him a grandiose studio complex in Culver City for the features he was to contribute to Aitken's Triangle. Taken over by the Goldwyn company, this second "Inceville" was inherited by Metro-Goldwyn-Mayer. For two years after leaving Triangle in 1917, Ince worked on the old Biograph lot. Then he built for himself a third studio, also in Culver City, with a front entrance "an enlarged replica of Mount Vernon, home of George Washington." In the sound era, this production complex was taken over by David O. Selznick.*

*Our report appeared in Volume 70 of the* New York Dramatic Mirror, *December 24, 1913, page 34, and was reprinted in George Pratt's* Spellbound in Darkness *(Rochester, N.Y., University of Rochester, 1966/Boston, Mass., N.Y. Graphic Society, 1973).*

"For the love of Mike, boys, take a look and tell me if I have gone crazy!" cried Bob, who, in advance of the hunting party stood on an abrupt wall of a canyon and gazed into the depths with protruding eyes.

We hastened forward and gazed upon an unusual scene. For three days we had fought our way over that uncouth and unlovely range, missing out on two bucks and a beautiful doe in our efforts in deer hunting, side-stepping numerous bobcats and other playful denizens of the heights. Then, without warning, we brushed through the underbrush and looked down upon a Japanese village, beautiful in its planning and artistic in its dress. We assured Bob that we saw everything that his excited vision perceived, but he still was suspicious that the stuff he carried in his bottle was not treating him right.

We had to make a wide detour to reach the bottom of the mountain and encountered another shock. It was an Irish settlement, true to life. In our retreat down the gulch we ran the gamut of erratic emotions. For a bit of Switzerland, a peaceful Puritan settlement, and substantial colonies of various nations hastened our delusion that the Santa Ynez range had suddenly gone mad. Upon arriving at the peaceful Pacific we found the finishing touch. Weighted at anchor beyond the breakers we observed an ancient brigantine of grandfather's time, with cutlass-armed men swarming over the sides. To complete this mad-house medley a bunch of incoherent cowboys wrangled on the sands of the beach.

For fear that the gentle reader will believe this introduction written from a padded cell, I will explain that our hunting party merely had blundered upon Inceville, the remarkable mountain and seashore home of the Broncho and Kay Bee companies. The locations in the fastness of the wilds make a more fantastic appeal than is written here for each village is a permanent affair, the result of long and careful development on the part of Thomas H. Ince, Vice-President and Manager of New York Motion Picture Company. Nor did the wonders cease in the canyons as we saw them that day. In that two thousand acres of location Ince is raising stock galore as well as feed and garden truck on a wholesale scale.

Selecting this uncouth but striking coast range which lies above the city of Santa Monica, Ince established his first studio less than two years ago. He began with one little stage. Since that time he has extended construction throughout the mountains, each colony laid in its suitable and logical location. With more than seven hundred people on hand and an investment of $35,000 in buildings, Ince now is the proud manager of an organization as complete as a municipality. His shops construct everything from uniforms and furniture to houses. His cultivated lands feed the multitude. His range of locations travels in leaps and bounds from naval battles on the broad Pacific to the wild West, mountain life, Ireland and the Orient and in fact to every country save the extremely tropical. His first brigantine was the Fremont, a noted vessel in the days of the gold rush. A sister ship, almost a replica of the Fremont, has been secured and pirates once again ride the raging main.

To the writer the most striking feature of Inceville, aside from its wondrous array of foreign colonies was its system. Although housing an army of actors, directors and subordinates there is not a working hour lapses in which all the various companies are not at work producing results. We failed to see actors made up and dressed for their various roles, loafing about the stages or on locations; perturbed directors running here and there attempting to bring order out of the chaos, while locations waited and camera men idly smoked their cigarettes, waiting for the "next scene."

System with every-minute efficiency. "It can't be done," declare studio managers, "It is the character of the business that these rules cannot be applied strictly. There are delays; there always will be delays. They are unavoidable in picture making." These declarations I have heard, in reply to queries, in many studios. Therefore it would be advisable for Mr. Ince to patent his system and put it on the market.

With preparations laid out in detail from finished photoplays to the last prop, superintended by Mr. Ince himself, far in advance of action, each of the numerous directors on the job at Santa Ynez canyon is given his working script three weeks ahead of time. When the time arrives for putting on a picture, the costumes are on the hooks of the tailor shop; locations are ready, props are on hand and the producer has had much time in which to familiarize himself with the script. Filled with the theme and action, he goes out and, with the cogs of the big Ince machine oiled to the smallest gear and the entire plant running as smoothly as an automobile in the hands of a salesman, the picture travels from beginning to end without delays. To my mind this is the modern miracle.

Yet the work of the tireless Ince is not completed. More villages and ships are in store for the studio. More companies are being planned for the big things which the future holds. A fine club house, with billiards, pool, various other games and a dance hall, is coming soon. A motion-picture house for the further entertainment of employes evenings, is to be erected, while other free amusements are included in the plans. Ince is looking after the comfort of his employes with the same infinite care as that summoned to construct wonderful Inceville, where even the electricity for lights and machinery is generated from a private plant — remarkable Inceville of the Santa Ynez.

Tom Ince himself is a marvelous machine. A human dynamo, he travels a pace which few care to follow. From early morning, until 1 and 2 o'clock the following morning are his usual hours. Not only does he personally superintend the manufacturing, building and production of his mammoth studio, but he sits with Scenario Editor Richard Spencer many hours each week, hammering ideas into shape or building up chosen photoplays to the Broncho and Kay Bee standard. He also cuts the film turned out in the canyon to the tune of about 8,000 feet a week. The initiated will read these statements with doubting eyes, but they must stand as facts.

Ince is the "White Hope" of filmdom so far as physical and mental toil is concerned. He is built on the same plan physically. With a large head, shrewd countenance, stocky frame and muscled like the statue of an ancient gladiator, his physique has been able to withstand the terrible strain of the years. Despite the warning of fearful friends, he continues to grind on, his health seemingly unimpaired by his titanic task, which is measured largely by his remarkable success.

# WILLIAM K. EVERSON
## *The Italian*

> *This selection is taken from a chapter called "The Early Features," in* American Silent Film *(N.Y., Oxford University Press, 1978) pages 63-65. Everson begins the chapter: "Few periods in film history are as sparsely represented as those years between 1912 and* The Birth of a Nation *in 1915, when the feature-length film (of five reels or more) replaced the two-reeler as the staple program ingredient and restructured the art and the economics of film." He then shares with us descriptions of two films only recently rediscovered: Maurice Tourneur's* The Wishing Ring, *and this Ince film, which he finds partially documentary in style in its "picture of grinding poverty" among immigrant families.*
>
> *Professor Everson, as a teacher at New York University and the New School for Social Research, has shared with students and scholars his extensive personal film archive and has made many useful contributions to the film bookshelf, including* The Western *(with George Fenin, 1962) and* The Films of Hal Roach *(1970).*

. . . notable as an example of early naturalism — and a film that can in some ways be favorably compared with Erich von Stroheim's *Greed* (1924) — is Thomas Ince's *The Italian,* directed in 1914 by Reginald Barker (although Ince's fondness for assuming screen credit himself managed to deprive Barker of recognition for this remarkable film until much later).

*The Italian* is the story of a farm-worker who leaves his native soil to make good in America. Although confident that he will do so, he is under a certain amount of pressure. If he doesn't succeed within a year, the girl he loves (and who loves him) will be forced into marriage with another. This plot contrivance is, however, merely that — a contrivance, to inject suspense into the earlier sequences and to permit the luxury of picturesque farewells and subsequent cross-cuttings of the two lovers separated by thousands of miles of ocean. The early portion of the film is romantic in the extreme, with California countryside and missions substituting quite satisfactorily for the Italian equivalents. The canals in the Venice area of Hollywood are also pressed into service. In this "prologue,"

there is a great deal of smooth camera movement and many striking images, such as that of the lovers silhouetted at dusk on the side
of a hill. The immigrant's departure is also extremely well done, some
cunning editing and mobile camerawork managing to suggest quite
convincingly the departure of a ship loaded with immigrants.

The immigrant's destination is of course New York; but the slum
and ghetto areas where the bulk of the film then takes place were
actually shot in San Francisco, since Los Angeles' slums looked a
shade too prosperous to double for New York. The grime and the
disillusionment that the hero finds in "Little Italy" is depicted in a
grim and utterly realistic manner, suggesting that the perhaps excessive romanticism of the Italian scenes may well have been
deliberate for purposes of contrast. Although hardly finding the new
land the paradise he expected, the immigrant works hard as a boot-
black and saves his money. He also wins the (temporary) favor of
the local political boss, who uses him to win the votes of his "Wop
friends." The immigrant does manage to send for his fiancée, and
they are married.

The remainder of the film however, somewhat backtracks from
its traditional "Land of Opportunity" view of America to present an
unrelentingly grim picture of grinding poverty that must have been
disconcerting, to say the least, to the immigrants who formed a large
part of the film's contemporary audience. Things go badly for the
couple in New York, especially after the birth of a child. The child,
weak from malnutrition, is dying from that and related causes of
ghetto-living, including the heat: infant mortality from heat alone
ran high in New York's "Little Italy" at that time. Going out to buy
milk, the father is robbed of the little money he has. Searching for
his assailants, he finds them, begs for the return of the money, is
beaten — and then arrested by the police. While he is in prison, and
unable to get in touch with his wife, the baby dies. This middle portion of the film seems honest, touching, and incredibly realistic. The
beating in the street, though brief, has a savagery and a desperation
not encountered in films of that period, and director Reginald Barker
is adept at utilizing the naturalistic lighting of streets and alleys for
dramatic emphasis. When the husband is left unconscious in an alley,
his body is concealed by shadows, but his face is highlighted by a
shaft of light as the sun shines through slates and broken fences.

The final third of the film takes a novelettish turn (although only
in contrast with the controlled realism of the middle portions), and
the last scene is a disappointment. Perhaps for prestige purposes,
to suggest a major literary origin that the film did not in fact possess,
the story is told within the framework of noted actor George Beban,

resplendent in dressing gown and in a palatial home, sitting down to read the manuscript. (This also serves to stress the versatility of Beban in transferring from matinee idol image to that of the shabby Italian immigrant.) The last scene, however, is an intensely emotional wrap-up to the story, with the Italian by the grave of his child.


# DIANE KOSZARSKI
# C. Gardner Sullivan

*In the mid-1920s, Sullivan may have been the highest paid writer in Hollywood. With "more than 375 produced scenarios" he was certainly one of the most prolific of all screenwriters. Griffith may have depended only on notes, as Lillian Gish claims, especially in his earlier productions. Ince certainly didn't. Writers were much more important in the silent days than director-oriented histories would have us suppose.*

*This profile appeared in volume 26, devoted entirely to film writers, of the* Dictionary of Literary Biography *(Detroit, Gale Research Co., 1984), edited by Robert Morsberger, Stephen Lesser, and Randall Clark. Ms. Koszarski is the author of* The Complete Films of William S. Hart, *(1980).*


Charles Gardner Sullivan, who was raised in Saint Paul, Minnesota, began college studies at the University of Minnesota, but left before graduating and in 1907 took a position on the *Saint Paul Daily News.* He worked as a journalist in many major cities, including Chicago, Cleveland, and Philadelphia before settling in New York City, where he wrote a syndicated column for the *Evening Journal.*

In New York Sullivan sold a few sketches to the vaudeville circuit and began submitting stories to film producers in the metropolitan area. The first of his works to be filmed was *Her Polished Family,* a satire on the sensibilities of a recent college graduate, which the Edison Company bought and filmed in 1911. He continued to sell material for one-reelers to Edison and the Lubin Manufacturing Company, while studying the epic films — vigorous, occasionally morbid sagas of the Civil War hero, the vanishing red man, the intrepid pioneer — produced by the California studio of the New York Motion Picture Corp. By 1913 Sullivan had developed a similar "Indian-military thriller" and sold it to New York Motion Picture production head Thomas W. Ince for fifty dollars. Still employed by the *Evening Journal*, Sullivan began contributing regularly to Ince's company, and by 1914 it had produced more than sixty of his scenarios.

In 1914 Ince hired Sullivan to join his California writing staff. Sullivan and his wife were reluctant to leave the lively world of the big city for the unknown rewards of moviemaking in the hamlet of Santa Monica, California; but a handsome salary offer dissolved their resistance, and they found their new life much to their liking. Continuing to work under Ince's aegis, Sullivan wrote vivid stories that blended the narrative capacities of film with the craft of journalism. Ince insisted that each script include annotations for fully developed characterizations and dialogue, set and location breakdowns, and even advice on camera angles, gestures, and makeup.

At the Ince company, Sullivan soon gained an enviable reputation for his pungent stories. Used to short deadlines from his newspaper days and accustomed to seizing the human-interest angle in current topics, Sullivan supplied Ince with everything from bread-and-butter staples such as *In the Sage Brush Country* (1914) and *The Cup of Life* (1915) to big-budget specials such as *Civilization's Child* (1916) and *Peggy* (1916). His deadpan, sardonic humor illuminated genres as diverse as Westerns and drawing-room comedies. Sullivan's puritanical ethos was tempered by his appreciation of cosmopolitan virtues and his interest in Social Darwinism, and while working for Ince, Sullivan explored controversial topics — prostitution, drug addiction, adultery — confident that the visual element would fully portray what titles could only allude to.

Sullivan often observed filming on the studio lots in order to learn more about the process of filmmaking and the special talents of directors and actors that he might use in future stories. Among the directors working for Ince, Sullivan admired the work of Reginald Barker, Charles Miller, and Raymond West, and he designed many of his scripts for their production units. In addition, he liked writing for the newly popular cowboy star William S. Hart, who had joined the Ince company the same year as he had. After one of his earliest scripts for Hart, *The Passing of Two-Gun Hicks* (1914), impressed critics with its combination of action and complex characterizations Sullivan wrote many more stories in this vein for Hart, both two-reelers and features that not only brought windfall profits to Ince but also influenced the development of the American Western film by fixing in the public's imagination the character who could be both good and bad.

In 1915 Sullivan moved, under Ince's urging, to the five-reel feature, a format that was increasingly desirable for commercially released films. He wrote easily for the expanded length, using the additional reels to detail dramatic situations and character development more fully. Sullivan was especially good at concocting action-filled climax endings that did not rely too heavily on titles to explain them. Though much of his work, like that of all scenarists, was uncredited in the beginning, by the end of 1914 his name was being listed in trade advertisements as a gauge of reliable drama.

By mid-1915 Ince had allied the New York Motion Picture Corp. studio with the new Triangle Corporation, which would distribute the studio's feature films. Sullivan was made head of the scenario department and supervised the weekly programs of shorts and features that alternated in the Triangle schedule with material from Mack Sennett's Keystone studio and D.W. Griffith's group at Fine Arts. Sullivan's *The Iron Strain,* a contemporary discussion of marriage for money, starring Dustin Farnum, led the Triangle premiere bill at the Knickerbocker Theatre on 23 September 1915. He continued to write for the Ince coterie of actors at Triangle: juvenile Charles Ray, character actors Frank Keenan and Walter Edwards, leading man H.B. Warner, company vamp Louise Glaum, Ince protégée Dorothy Dalton, and William S. Hart. For actress Bessie Barriscale, the versatile Sullivan provided a wide variety of parts ranging from sprightly girl, society matron, country miss, urban working woman — a range that gave full play to Barriscale's intelligence and feminine vitality. One afternoon, after completing her demanding role as a kept woman in *The Payment* (1916), she asked Sullivan to write her a less taxing part. The next morning the obliging author handed her *Plain Jane* (1916), a script he had written the night before. The tale of a love-struck slavey in a college town, *Plain Jane* was as popular with filmgoers as was *The Payment.* By the second year of his association with Triangle, Sullivan was assisting Ince with administrative duties and in 1917 wrote relatively little. In the summer of 1917 Ince left Triangle and secured a new contract as a producer with Adolph Zukor, taking many of his stars and staff, including Sullivan, with him to Paramount.

At Paramount, Sullivan worked with several well-known star-director teams, including Lambert Hillyer and William S. Hart, Jerome Storm and Enid Bennett, Victor Schertzinger and Charles Ray, William Neill and Dorothy Dalton, Fred Niblo and Louise

Glaum. By the end of 1919, Zukor was pressuring Thomas Ince productions to move, and Ince left to form Associated Producers with
longtime colleagues J. Parker Read, Jr., Allan Dwan, Mack Sennett,
Marshall Neilan, and others. He was unable to persuade Sullivan
to join them because Sullivan was more interested in forming an independent company with other scenarists such as Monte Katterjohn.
But in the end he became a free-lance writer, finding a ready market
for his plays with Ince's group and with old collaborators still at work
on the Paramount lot.

In the early 1920's Sullivan worked closely with directors John
Griffith Wray and Fred Niblo under Ince's auspices, and in 1923 and
1924 Joseph M. Schenck commissioned him to adapt several popular
Broadway plays as vehicles for the Talmadge sisters. During the same
period, Ince continued to assign Sullivan projects for his actors, including *Dynamite Smith* (1924), Charles Ray's comeback film; the
narcotics-exploitation drama *Human Wreckage* (1923) with Mrs.
Wallace Reid; and *Wandering Husbands* (1924), a light sex comedy
for Lila Lee and Margaret Livingston. Sullivan reportedly earned
$150,000 in 1924, and this was rumored to be the highest pay for
a writer at that time.

Sullivan was in the midst of his first independent production,
*Cheap Kisses* (1924), a comedy-melodrama about the nouveau-riche,
to be directed by John Ince, when Thomas Ince died suddenly on
19 November 1924. Sullivan's association with that shrewd and
dynamic producer had been felicitous for both men, and although
he continued in a productive, professional capacity at the top levels
of the film business, Sullivan would not establish such a fruitful
partnership with his subsequent collaborators. During the next year
he worked with old acquaintances Ralph and John Ince (the brothers
of Thomas Ince), John W. Considine, Jr., and William S. Hart in
preparing adaptations and special projects and wrote one more independent film, *If Marriage Fails* (1925), a sensationalist divorce
drama.

With *Three Faces East* (1926) Sullivan began his alliance with Cecil
B. De Mille, one of the few remaining independent producers of
stature in an increasingly studio-dominated industry. As was the
custom with De Mille, Sullivan worked with a round table of writers
in adapting magazine stories and popular plays. Sullivan, who in
the past had written his scenarios alone, shifted to administrative
duties and for the next two years worked primarily as supervisor
for directors William K. Howard, Rupert Julian, Paul Sloane, and
Donald Crisp on such films as *Her Man O'War* (1926), *The Clinging Vine* (1926), *Gigolo* (1926), *Corporal Kate* (1926). *White Gold*
(1927), *Yankee Clipper* (1927), *Vanity* (1927), *The Fighting Eagle*

(1927), and *Turkish Delight* (1927). During this period Sullivan worked as a scenarist on *Bachelor Brides* collaborating with Garrett Ford.

The last silent films crafted by the longtime master of the form were released in 1928. He titled Raoul Walsh's scenario for *Sadie Thompson*, starring Gloria Swanson, and composed a romantic fantasy about the Russian revolution, *Tempest*, to feature John Barrymore. For Joseph Schenck he prepared a treatment of Guy de Maupassant's *Boule de Suif*. Entitled *The Woman Disputed* (1928), the film was directed by Henry King and benefited from the music and sound effects added for the new sound-market.

During the early sound period Sullivan wrote two adaptations of Broadway plays: For Schenck he collaborated with author-director Roland West on a grim gangster film, *Alibi* (1929), and for producer Joseph Kennedy he wrote the scenario *The Locked Door* (1929), a remake of a 1921 melodrama about murder and blackmail in high society.

In a filmmaking period constrained by the relative immobility of both the camera and the microphone and by the cautious reliance on proven dialogue from Broadway plays, Sullivan again assumed duties as a script supervisor, this time for Universal in 1930 and 1931. He moved to M-G-M in late 1931 and continued there through 1933, working along with other staff writers to adapt the stream of bestsellers and hit plays sought by the studios as story sources. His most significant project during this period was an adaptation of Eugene O'Neill's *Strange Interlude* (1932), which he wrote with Bess Meredyth. After his contract expired in 1933, Sullivan returned to free-lancing, working with old friends such as John W. Considine, Jr., and Cecil B. De Mille on selected projects.

The "dean of silent screenwriting," as *Variety* called him, retired in 1940 after writing more than 375 produced scenarios to enjoy the company of his wife and four children. He died at home on 5 September 1965.

REFERENCES:

Harry C. Carr, "What next?" *Photoplay* (March 1917): 60-63, 146; Interview with Bessie Barriscale, *New York Telegraph*, 1 October 1916;

Carolyn Lowrey, *The First 100 Noted Men and Women of the Screen* (New York: Moffat, Yard, 1920), pp. 176-177;

Obituary for C. Gardner Sullivan, *Variety*, 8 September 1965, p. 69;

Scott O'Dell, *Representative Photoplays Analyzed* (Hollywood: Palmer Institute of Authorship, 1924), pp. 91-103, 164-165, 274-280.

JEAN MITRY
# The Concreteness of Ince's Films

*Championing Ince as against Griffith was very much the fashion for a time in France. Maurice Bardèche and Robert Brasillach, in one of the earliest film histories (translated by Iris Barry, 1938) gave him only four pages but traced some of the admiring responses that forecast a continuing fondness for the American western on the part of French critics. Louis Delluc compared Ince to Rodin and Aeschylus. Jean Cocteau saw a "masterpiece" in a battle of "naked bodies slippery with blood." The film historian Georges Sadoul, in his Dictionary of Film Makers, said Ince "turned the western into art." And picking up a Delluc suggestion that the future of film would lie in celebrating a "simplified humanity," Bardèche and Brasillach proposed the notion that "in a dramatic film the actors are only part of the mise en scène and that inanimate objects" in Ince films take on their "proper role."*

*After such panegyrics, tending of course toward formal abstraction, it is reassuring to follow the exacting analysis and humanistic argument of Jean Mitry, with its corollary emphasis on the content of the films. He cares very much about the visual values, but places them in the context of the story. He notes in the westerns the direct comment achieved, for example, by a horse that moves off alone or a dipper of water representing a refusal to give help. He speaks of a tragedy "condensed into a single image" and sometimes an over-all mood of "somber and desperate idealism." Nevertheless, he feels, the images are not stretched into some kind of symbolism, as in Griffith, but rather are concrete expressions serving the needs of the drama.*

*Translated by Martin Sopocy with Paul Attalah, this is an admirably brisk "English adaptation of three complete sections of Mitry's monograph on Ince printed in the·Anthologie du Cinéma, November 9, 1965," one of the few translations from Mitry available. It appeared in Cinema Journal, Winter 1983, pages 2 to 25, under the title "Thomas H. Ince: His Esthetic, His Films, His Legacy." We have had to condense somewhat and omit detailed translators' notes and three pages by Mitry dealing with specific directors. Sopocy's archive film list is Appendix B, page 267.*

*His death in January 1988 at the age of 84 deprived us of a great human being and a meticulous scholar who, like Aristotle, insisted that historical observation must precede theory.*

*If D.W. Griffith can be called the earliest poet of an art whose basic syntax he elaborated, then Ince can be said to be its earliest dramatist.*

Unlike Griffith, staging for Ince was a secondary concern and consequently his personal touch is to be found elsewhere. It would thus be incorrect to speak of his "style" if indeed style subsists more in a work's outward form than in its spirit. It would, however, be quite legitimate to speak of an esthetic, of a certain concept of what a movie is which runs throughout his films, making them so many diverse instances of a single underlying intention.

His primary concern was to establish an equilibrium between form and content, between the means of expression and the dramatic exigencies of the theme, imposing on the latter values and requirements similar to those of classic dramaturgy.

While careful to distinguish the formal attributes of theatrical construction from those of filmic construction, Ince nevertheless came to form a bridge, however shaky and precarious, between two apparently antithetic art forms which, through a reversal of their respective means, had too often been confused on the screen.

In other words, in addition to taking full advantage of the possibility of shooting anywhere which had freed him from theatrical staging, Ince drew upon dramaturgy for a construction which avoids every semblance of theatrical representation.

His work, which can be seen as complementing Griffith's, seems thus a kind of "dramatization" of the real by means of a certain way of representing reality.

Griffith almost by need created a language which allowed him to express himself to the full measure of his genius. If at the beginning of his career his themes were simplistic and rudimentary, they were so only to the same extent as were the forms he had to work with. As he continued to enlarge these forms he gradually heightened his tone and expressed — at least until his apogee in 1919 — ideas of increasing ambitiousness, his weakness being his oversimplified and rather old-fashioned ideas, a weakness attributable as much to the straightening of an ungrown medium as it was to the receptive capacities of his audience at that time. Nevertheless precisely because he was still shaping his own language, it tended, by very reason of its newness, to fall short of the ideas for whose expression he had brought it into being. With the possible exception of *Broken Blossoms* and *True Heart Susie,* his two most polished works, the richest and most complex of his films, not excluding *The Birth of a Nation* and *Intolerance,* suffer from the lack of a steady balance between form and content. Splendid as they are, those great wobbling structures are often unable to contend with the mighty subjects they were supposed to be expressing.

Availing himself of Griffith's discoveries and content to apply them with discrimination, Ince proceeded, as it were, from the opposite direction. Accepting acquired form and uninterested in perfecting it, he valued the means at his disposal only for what they allowed him to express clearly through the sole resource of the moving image. . . .

The challenge was in letting the story unfold with enough freedom to give the audience the impression that it was watching a document taken directly from life — an "image," at very least, of real life — rather than a dramatic contrivance with a predictable ending. While giving the film its indispensable structure, it was important to lose none of the advantages of cinema, none of its ability to capture life "in the very heart of life."

But since psychological development was desirable only to the extent that it made the motivations of the characters comprehensible, and since analysis was out of the question, Ince chose to apply his efforts to stripping the facts down to their bare essentials. He concentrated the action around a few dramatic mainsprings, leaving in shadow — ambiguous or suggested by a few sufficient hints — the background events and the dragging moments, mercilessly cutting away anything that would impede the forward thrust of the action. By this means he achieved extreme leanness, but also, perforce, excessive oversimplification in his social dramas. . . .

The whole of his output can be divided into historical propaganda films (Custer's Last Fight, The Battle of Gettysburg), thesis films (The Painted Soul, The Moral Fabric, Those Who Pay), comedy dramas (Peggy, Plain Jane, Paddy O'Hara), and Westerns in which he established concepts and patterns that would culminate in the films of William S. Hart.

His personal work can strictly be said to comprise only the first two of those categories.

In The Wrath of the Gods (1914) action was for the first time paralleled with a natural phenomenon (a volcano's eruption) which stood in for it, simplistically but very effectively, as its outsize symbolic projection: a husband kills his unfaithful wife and then commits ritual suicide while the oncoming cataclysm steadily sweeps all before it, destroying the city of Sakurajima.

This device, which became so identified with Ince, of intercutting a natural phenomenon into a dramatic event, was somewhat later to be adopted by Griffith in Way Down East in the sequence of the break up of the ice. The construction of these Ince films seems no less deliberated than that systematic arousal of the audience which Eisenstein described as the mounting of attractions; in any case they are the earliest instances on record of the kind of parallel editing the latter would eventually define in his essay "Nature is Not Indifferent."

*The Battle of Gettysburg* (1914) is a big spectacular fresco. Griffith was then preparing *The Birth of a Nation.* Ince wanted to try his own hand at a broad canvas, even though his temperament was not especially suited to the epic form. Even so, thanks to a sensitive feeling for the life of crowds, thanks to breakneck pacing, to a narrative thrust which is at first held back and then released on a downward course of gathering speed, the film's rhythm at times transforms it into something that all but equals Griffith. In it Ince consistently employs the measured power, the chastened line and the directness he had already evinced in *Custer's Last Fight* (1912). It is without a doubt his grandest achievement.

His most violent, however was *The Typhoon* (1914). This was simply an emotional drama whose governing sentiment might be described as a deviant variety of classical passion. Yet the forward motion of the narrative, together with the headstrong nature of the characters, made for a visual schematization which, without prejudice to the film's psychology, powerfully reinforced its action. The somewhat banal turns of plot, while serving no other purpose, portray a morality and a psychology that is unabashedly stunted: it is not hard to see in it a forecast of Naziism. The drama revolves around such mainsprings as the victimizing of the innocent, the grim will to become the tool of a narrow nationalism, the contempt for weakness and the destruction of anyone who lets himself succumb to it (which can all the more easily happen if he begins by feeling contempt for it). Cecil B. De Mille's success *The Cheat*, released some fifteen months later, was little more than a melodramatic elaboration of the same ideas, a rehash of techniques — cutting, lighting, acting style — that Ince had already used.

*The Despoiler* (1915) and *Civilization* (1916) are anti-German propaganda films. The first deals with atrocities to prisoners: "In the Near East a German colonel hands over to the Kurdish troops under his command a convent of Catholic nuns to slake their lust upon. As it happens, his own daughter has taken refuge in the cloister. Raped by the chief of the Kurds, she kills him, but the colonel, enranged when this is reported to him, orders the execution of the girl who did it. The order is carried out, whereupon the colonel receives word that his daughter is hiding among the nuns. He has a search made for her and learns, too late, that she is the very one whose execution he had ordered."

An arbitrary and conventional tale, to be sure. Yet thanks to precise and economical plot development, it has impact. With some truth it could be called a *psychological Grand Guignol*.

With *Civilization* Ince tried to uplift his tone to the level of *philosophical Grand Guignol*. The philosophy, alas, is nothing to rave about, purveyed as it is through a rudimentary symbolism which cheapens it and at moments lends it to ridicule. Thanks to the device still prevalent at the time of "picturing" literary symbols and of "representing" metaphysical entities, this film, which created a furor when it was first released, is one of the most badly dated of the Ince films.

Gardner Sullivan's theme might have breathed life into a work conceived as a fable in which the tragedy was transposed into the realm of fantasy. As it is, fancy is superimposed on a realist framework which cannot support it: the image of the Nazarene looms large in the foreground of the universal conflict. Crucifixions are juxtaposed with tanks and cannons. Entering the remains of Count Ferdinand, who was killed while torpedoing a luxury liner, the reincarnated Christ proceeds to preach peace to the German people, tries to get the Kaiser to see reason, etc.

It must be emphasized, however, that the naivete of this symbolism was peculiar neither to Ince nor to the cinema in which he was working. Indeed, just as it did here, that cinema often made use of an outmoded pictorial art which the middlebrow culture of the day still considered the last word in artistic expression. It was nothing worse than a lapse into those stock ideas which often define an era. We have only to glance at the newspapers, the occasional poetry produced by the favorite versifers of the epoch, and at the official painting and statuary of 1914!

A realism whose intentions were less grandiose and less grandiloquent would have been more moving, and would certainly have given rise to a more durable piece of work, for there are numerous moments where the film is redeemed by its visual power, and never more so than when it is not trying to preach or convince but just to describe, to reveal in all its horror a reality whose meaning is itself. Yet despite its breathless rhythm and the broad sweep of its scenes of spectacle — such as the sinking of an ocean liner — one must still look to its details to see the style of its maker: "Only an artist," wrote Colette, "could have composed those groupings, such as the one of the stricken mother pressing her three children to her while there files before them an off-camera army the shadows of whose spiked helmets and slanted bayonets rake their trembling knees."

Among his films of social criticism, *The Painted Soul* (1915) was one of the first to successfully develop its argument within a visually cinematic form. Careful lighting, the authenticity of the settings and especially the naturalness of its actors gave it a particular truth. It concerned a young painter who falls in love with a girl he picked up in a bar. She becomes his model and, tired of a life on the streets, tries to live down her past. But the young man's upright family oppose their union and the girl returns to her old life. Free living arrangements were still so far in the future that they could not be countenanced by the official morality of the day, which condemned them as an affront to virtue. The subject may well seem trite and melodramatic to us now, but in their films Ince and Sullivan regularly castigated middle-class narrow-mindedness and hypocrisy, just as, in films like *The Hateful God* (1914), they pilloried puritanism and religious bigotry.

*The Sons of Toil* (1915) defended the right of laborers to take collective action against exploitive employers.

*The Moral Fabric* (1916) developed the argument that advocates of the new morality are wont to put their theories into practice only to the extent that they serve their passions and self-interests. As soon as they themselves might be threatened by the emancipation they preach, they raise an outcry and take refuge behind respect for the usages of modern civilization and for established principles.

*The Sorrows of Love* (1916) strove to assert the rights of women and young girls in a man's world where they are often victims of their trust and credulity.

*The Corner* (1916) compared and contrasted the deeds of an unscrupulous financier with a jobless man jailed for stealing food to feed his family.

*Those Who Pay* (1917) insisted on the rights of abandoned mothers and of natural children vis-a-vis society. And so on. . . .

In his Westerns he stays away from conflicts between men of different social backgrounds, or their opposition to laws which oppress them — situations in which nuances are unavoidable — but rather he establishes individual characters in some brief, violent, savage drama highlighting their relationship to their geographical and social environments and exalting raw but powerful feelings by means of the exemplifying act. . . .

It may be said that instead of the prefabricated moral intentions of the thesis films, we find something here which was not *intended* exactly but which gradually emerges in the course of these films, a thing of which the author is fully aware and *which his composition takes into account* but which has not been artificially contrived. It is in this way that a dimension of aliveness, that immediate and palpable truth which is a part of his intentions but which is denied his other films, appears in these in all its power and in all its novel splendor.

It is, for instance, a stream flashing in the sunlight at the bottom of a quiet and majestic valley, while on its banks, a little way off, we *know* that two men are struggling, locked in mortal combat. After the fight, whose outcome is carefully kept from us, the horse of one of them moves off alone. There hangs from its trailing saddle a drinking gourd, a revolver jutting from a half-open holster — and the bag of gold which caused the fatal struggle.

Some of these films — the finest of them — contain a sort of somber and desperate idealism. All feelings are laid bare; it is drama reduced to stark savagery, senseless tragedy, life given a vigorous shake so that its most tempting fruits can be gathered but yielding only uselessness and extinction.

Of William S. Hart's earliest Westerns, the most impressive are *The Passing of Two-Gun Hicks* (1914) and *The Taking of Luke McVane* (1915), both directed by Hart assisted by Clifford S. Smith, and both based on stories by Bret Harte.

The first tells the story of the leader of a gang of outlaws who rides down from the mountains with his men. They hold up a stage coach, shoot up a small town, rob its saloon, commit rape on its girls, and leave as unopposed as they came, going on to an extended raid on the ranches of the vicinity. The Hart character — we'll call him Rio Jim — brings away the memory of a woman, the wife of the town drunkard, who gave herself to him in part to save her husband and in part to put a stop to the pillage of the town.

The second already has the earmarks of some poetic short story. "Rio Jim, this time a tough gambler, is taken with a dance-hall girl. He comes to her aid when she is molested by some drunken Mexicans. Surprised and touched by this unexpected bit of chivalry, she offers him the rose she wears over her breast. Then, during a card game, a man cheats. A fight ensues and Rio Jim shoots him. With the girl's help he makes a getaway but, feeling guilty of no crime, he doubles back and waits for the sheriff in his office. The latter comes and places him under arrest. The two of them set off on horseback for the next town, where the sheriff must hand him over to the authorities. As they cross the desert they are attacked by Indians. Both defend their lives dearly. The next day the two men are found dead. Rio Jim is smiling, the rose entwined in his fingers."

These sketches inevitably culminated in *The Aryan* (1916), the first masterpiece of its type:

"Rio Jim, a frontiersman, is on his way home with a money-belt full of gold dust. In the first saloon in the first little town he comes to, he is sized up as an easy mark by some cardsharps. A female decoy plays up to the guileless man of the prairies, gets him drunk and persuades him to gamble. Waking the next morning with a hangover, Rio Jim discovers that he has been victimized and at the same moment learns of the death of his mother, the news of which had been kept from him the night before in order to get him to the roulette table. Blind with rage, he dashes to the room of the girl who has duped him, kills her lover, gives her a beating and then, throwing her across his saddle, spurs his horse and gallops into the desert.

"The years pass. Rio Jim, who has reduced the former casino belle to working as his slave, has nurtured in his simple and hasty heart a distrust not only of women but of the entire white race. Now the leader of a gang of racially mixed outlaws, he preys upon the wagon trains of the white settlers and lives by robbing and spreading havoc.

"One day, the leader of a wagon train of immigrants and gold seekers which has lost its way comes to him and appeals for help and protection. Nursing his grudge, Rio Jim refuses to help his blood brothers, denying them water for their children and taking the women captive in order to hand them over to his brutish men. But one girl, hardly more than a child, dares to come all alone to the outlaw camp and plead for her companions. At first, the leader repulses her, ridicules her, refuses to be swayed. But the girl is not discouraged. She persists, appealing to the bad man in the name of his own race and of simple humanity. Rio Jim, surrounded as he is by cutthroats, suddenly realizes where his duty lies. At the risk of his own life, he rescues the women, provisions the wagon train and personally leads it back to the right road. Then, rejecting their thanks but with a last goodbye, the frontiersman rides back to the desert alone."

It is easy to see how cleverly the authors have turned everything to account in this tale. There are innumerable touches which suddenly acquire a tragic meaning, such as the water bucket from which Rio Jim drinks with a dipper in the scene where he refuses to help the thirsting wagon train. The girl's glance, the glittering water, Rio Jim's manner, these together compose a tragedy condensed into a single image with the water in the foreground. At each moment some similar detail is registered and enriches the impressionistic synthesis of an *essentially descriptive* gesture.

*The Coward* (1915) is one of the Civil War stories. Frank, son of a Southern colonel, enlists against his will. On sentry duty he is seized with panic, deserts his post and flees to his parents' home. The colonel, despite his advanced age, goes off to take his son's place in order to eradicate the dishonor incurred by his behavior. The advancing Union army arrives, however, and sets up its headquarters in Frank's house. Through a series of lucky circumstances Frank succeeds in laying hands on the Union battle plan. At the risk of his life he brings it through the Union lines to the field headquarters of the Confederates who, that same day, use it to score an important victory.

Obviously, the theme itself is not strikingly original, but the feelings delineated in it are extraordinarily understated, except those of the old colonel, which finally become irritating. The important thing is the manner in which the characters behave, the truth with which the incidents are present, the *factual* authenticity of a story which is plausible, albeit conventional and arbitrary. In short, it is not the anecdote that matters but its presentation. And from that standpoint it is masterly. . . .

In reviewing Ince's work as a whole there is one point that is particularly important for evaluating his legacy and his originality. In an Ince film the telling detail is never insisted on as it is in Griffith. The close up which isolates a detail in order to extract nothing but its value as a transitory *sign* can be used effectively only in the epic or in subjective analysis, in any situation, in fact, which tends more or less to transfigure reality symbolically. Ince, by contrast, never loses his objectivity. In an Ince film, when it comes to emphasizing acts rather than ideas, he uses *what things say in themselves* rather than *what they are made to say*. The telling detail is grasped within the totality it forms a part of. It gets emphasis only from the special placement it is given.

Which is not to say that, in his view of it, the signifier is identical with the thing signified; but merely that the meaning is inherent in the things themselves and that he "dislodges" it from them spontaneously. To put it plainly, Ince does not *signify*, he *expresses*.

Indeed, "signification" gives rise to concepts, not to things; ideas signify, things express. So, with Ince, when any object acquires the value of a sign it is always that of an immediately perceivable concrete reality understood within the limits of the narrative itself. The symbol never transcends the apparent facts of the case. It may rise to the level of concept only insofar as the empirical world of the drama can justify its doing so.

It has long been established that filmic signification — unlike that of verbal expression — is not based on convention. It is fleeting, constantly differentiating, but always and necessarily *implicational*. It attaches to a detail (usually isolated), returns it to the work in its entirety, and operates through discrimination and assimilation (i.e. the eyeglasses in *Potemkin*).

In this case, the concrete fact will give rise to an *idea* which somehow transcends the presented act or object. It follows, then, that "signification" is basic to a type of language which seeks to magnify or aggrandize events: the language of epic, the language of Griffith and Eisenstein.

"Expression," on the other hand, is usually part of a flow, a continuum. It particularizes things as themselves, transcending their immediate sense only to enhance the drama of which they form a part. In *this* case, their implication is always concrete; they are things concerning things, actions concerning actions, facts concerning facts, but never things, actions or facts concerning ideas.

When William S. Hart drinks from the dipper in front of the young girl whom he is refusing to help, the meaning that attaches to the act does not go beyond the exact one which was motivating his behavior at that instant, a bit of behavior which sums up and expresses it. Instead of constantly moving, as the epic does, from the particular to the general, we stay within what particularizes a unique and carefully defined drama. Nothing outstrips the concrete fact. The concept is inherent in the things themselves; they are characterized but never transcended.

Which, in a nutshell, is the language of the short story teller, if not the novelist. Whatever lyricism accrues to it consists of just such facts or their immediate repercussions, not of any ethical or metaphysical extrapolation.

With Ince, then, film veers decisively away from *theatricality* as it does also from theatrical *construction* of drama. Rejecting the dramatic construction that goes with stage production, he uses a kind of construction more in tune with filmic expression. In this sense he can be called the true founder of cinematic dramaturgy. . . .

Unfortunately, when speaking of the clarity and conciseness of Thomas Ince's films, one must do so from memory. To speak personally, I have not been able to see again any of the films of which I have written here (and whose negatives were scattered when the Triangle Company was dissolved). The last time I saw *The Aryan* was in 1925. I was quite young then and cannot say to what extent that work may have aged. But happily some negatives were recovered in the past ten years and I was fortunate enough to see for the first time, in Germany two years ago, an excellent print of *The Coward*, which Reginald Barker directed, with Charles Ray in the leading role. If one keeps in mind the kind of thing that was being done in 1915, it is an extraordinary film which might have been produced at the end of the silent era and which has dated no more than, say, *The Wind* or *Sunrise*, except for such features as the sometimes broad overplaying of Frank Keenan. It is as beautiful as *Broken Blossoms* and of such starkness that, even if Ince's place in the history of forms and of a new language's means of expression is, in all truth, less than Griffith's, it still places him on a par with the latter in the history of art. Alongside the manifest authenticity of its finest sequences, certain Italian neo-realist works of the 1950s seem like mere fustian. The discovery of this film in 1963 was a momentous event for me. It is possibly Thomas Ince's masterpiece (yet how many of his other films would have to be seen before one could say for certain!). The least that can be said of it, however, is that if it lacks the brio, the flight, the epic power of *The Birth of a Nation*, it is infinitely more limpid, and in any case much closer to us now and to contemporary cinema.

# WILLIAM S. HART
# Working for Ince

*No more a real cowboy by experience than was Bronco Billy Anderson or Tom Mix, Bill Hart had at least traveled a lot in the west while his father was hunting for jobs, and he clung to a naturalistic image of the west as he felt he had observed it. Born in 1870, he was already an actor at 19, but not till ten years later did he get roles of some importance in such plays as* The Squaw Man, The Virginian, *and* Ben Hur. *He and Ince met during a Broadway show, as Ramsaye reminds us, then met again in the manner described below.*

*My Life East and West, Hart's autobiography (Boston, Houghton Mifflin, 1929) is absorbing in its homespun charm, but it is not neatly organized. (Our extracts are from pages 198-202, 208, 209-213, 235, 240-244.) In that, and in his feeling for animals, Hart reveals the difference between his more creative temperament and his "old friend," businessman Tom Ince. Hart loved to guess what his dog and his horse were thinking, and was emotional enough to report that Annie, when the Harts left for California, "threw her apron up over her head and cried." But he took a long time to figure out what Ince was doing to him, and when he did, he took it hard.*

*There was nothing glamorous about this long-faced, gloomy-looking man in his late forties, but from about 1914 to 1921, he was one of the most popular actors ever to appear on the American screen.*

While playing in Cleveland, I attended a picture show. I saw a Western picture. It was awful! I talked with the manager of the theater and he told me it was one of the best Westerns he had ever had. None of the impossibilities or libels on the West meant anything to him — it was drawing the crowds. The fact that the sheriff was dressed and characterized as a sort of cross between a Wisconsin woodchopper and a Gloucester fisherman was unknown to him. I did not seek to enlighten him. I was seeking information. In fact, I was so sure that I had made a big discovery that I was frightened that some one would read my mind and find it out.

Here were reproductions of the Old West being seriously presented to the public — in almost a burlesque manner — and they were successful. It made me tremble to think of it. I was an actor and I knew the West. The opportunity that I had been waiting for years to come was knocking at my door.

Hundreds of ideas seemed to rush in from every direction. They assumed form. It was engendered — the die was cast. Rise or fall, sink or swim, I had to bend every endeavor to get a chance to make Western motion pictures. Usually when stirred by ambition I would become afraid. But surely this could not be the valor of ignorance. I had been waiting for years for the right thing, and now the right thing had come! I was a part of the West — it was my boyhood home — it was in my blood. The very love I bore it made me know its ways. I had a thorough training as an actor. I was considered the outstanding portrayer of Western roles on the American stage.

It was the big opportunity that a most high Power, chance, or fixed law, had schooled me for. It had been many years in coming, but it was here. And I would go through hell on three pints of water before I would acknowledge defeat.

The remainder of the season I visited all picture shows wherever possible. During the summer at Westport and on trips to New York, I did the same. I talked to my actor friends in The Lambs Club who were working every day playing Western parts in pictures being made over in Jersey. I was secretive. I told them nothing of my great plans. When it came time for *The Trail of the Lonesome Pine* to open again, my reluctance to take an engagement before trying my pet scheme caused me to raise my salary to one hundred and seventy-five dollars a week. While waiting for their answer, I met an actor who was going to California to work in Western pictures.

*The Trail of the Lonesome Pine* was going to California. I was frightened! They might refuse to give me the part on account of the raise in salary. I was on the point of writing them that I would go for *any salary*, when they wrote me O.K.

The finger of Fate was pointing in the right direction. Fortunately, we came West immediately after opening, or I believe I should have gone nutty. At San Francisco I learned that all the principal studios were in Los Angeles; that the principal companies making Westerns were the Universal Picture Corporation in Hollywood, and the New York Motion Picture Company in conjunction with the 101 Ranch at Santa Monica.

When we reached Los Angeles, while a friend was registering for me, I went into a telephone booth, called up the New York Motion Picture Company and asked for Joe Miller. A man who said his name was Brooks answered, and said that Mr. Miller was not there, but that he represented him.

I then said, 'I am an actor and I want to see about making some Western pictures.'

He replied: 'Mr. Miller only owns the stock and the cowboy end of the company. If you want to see about acting, call up Thomas H. Ince — he is manager of the picture company.'

I did so.

'Hello, Tom.'

'Hello, Bill.'

The next day Tom called and took me out to the old camp. I was enraptured and told him so. The very primitiveness of the whole life out there, the cowboys and the Indians, staggered me. I loved it. They had everything to make Western pictures. The West was right there!

I told Tom of my hopes, of my plans. I told him everything.

'Bill,' he said, 'it's a damn shame, but you're too late! The country has been flooded with Western pictures. They are the cheapest pictures to make and every company out here has made them. You simply cannot sell a Western picture at any price. They are a drug on the market.'

And to prove his statement, he showed me all the sets they were photographing on. The scenes were all laid in Ireland.

'But, Tom,' I cried, 'this means everything on earth to me. It is the one big opportunity of my life. Why all these cowboys? Why all these Indians?'

'Bill,' he said, 'it's a contract. Kessell and Bauman, the owners of this company, have a contract with the 101 Show that has another year to run.'

'Fine,' I said. 'Let me make some Western pictures and use these people.'

'Bill,' he said, 'I know you; I know, if there was any possible chance that you could put it over, but it just can't be done. I made a picture when I came out here, a Western picture, *Custer's Last Fight*, and I had all these Indians and cowboys. It was a fine picture, but it didn't sell.'

I looked at him, and he answered, 'Sure, Bill, I used the story you told me — that is why I'm telling you this — to show you that it won't go, that it cannot be done.'

I didn't have any more to say. We walked all round the camp. When we were leaving, I talked in Sioux to some of the Indians, and Tom was so astonished. He walked back and said to a young Indian: 'What did he say?'

The Indian just smiled and would not answer, until I told him in Sioux to do so, and then he replied, truthfully, that I had said that I was going away from here, but that I wanted to stay here.

I was late leaving (they had to hold the curtain at the theater for me), but just as Tom was putting me in his car he said: 'Bill, if you want to come out next spring and take a chance, I'll give you seventy-five dollars a week to cover your expenses and direct you in a picture myself.'

'Tom,' I replied, 'I'll be here as soon as we close.'. . .


I liked my work in *The Bargain* and *On the Midnight Stage*, and I told Tom I would like to stay if he would give me a year's contract. He said that he couldn't: that the company was taking big chances on these two pictures; that he would not make any more.

'Bill,' he said, 'why don't you take up directing? That is where the money is. I will give you a year's contract as a director at one hundred and twenty-five dollars a week.'

I replied: 'No, Tom. I have devoted too many years to acting to quit now. If I am to fail, I'll fail as an actor! Besides, I have no ambition to become a director.'

'Well, Bill,' he said, 'I'm sorry, but that is the best offer I can make and the best advice I can give you.'

I said: 'All right, Tom. I'm sorry. You know if I don't get back to New York now I'm likely to lose a season's work. I hope the company don't lose any money on these two pictures, because I know I talked you into making them. If they blame you, just tell 'em it's all my fault.'

At seven o'clock the next morning, September 1st, Cal Hoffner, who had charge of the automobiles, drove me and my trunk to the Santa Fé Depot at Los Angeles. I waited until Cal had gone and then bought a second-class ticket and a tourist sleeper for home. I had only a few dollars left. My trip had not been profitable.

When I returned home, my sister Mary and the old dog were waiting at the gate. I was cheered a whole lot: They cared . . .

One night I went home; my sister was at the gate and the old dog raced down the road to meet me. He had a piece of yellow paper in his mouth. It was a telegram!

'Can offer you one-twenty-five per week as a star. One-year contract. You to direct your own pictures. Wire answer. Tom.'

It had come! We did not talk much that evening. We thought and thought much. The little white house on the hill was home. The old dog sat between us looking anxiously from one to the other. He knew something of great moment had happened. He knew it affected us and him. He suffered! He was afraid the little home would be closed up; that we would go away, and that he would again be put in a box and sent to the kennels, and he knew if he was sent to the kennels any more that he would die.

His master and mistress did go away . . . the little white house on the hill was closed up. Annie, who used to steal small pieces of cake for him and feed him in the kitchen, followed to the top of the hill, threw her apron up over her head, and cried. But old Mack was not in a box; he was not going to the kennels; he was leading on ahead, tugging at his chain, taking his master and mistress to their new home . . .

Six weeks from the time I had gone away, I commenced work again. We rented a cottage at Ocean Park.

*The Bargain* had been shown in some little beach theater and was such a hit that it had been immediately purchased by Famous Players. The contract contained a clause that after three years the picture returned to the first owner. This clause was in all such contracts merely to protect the ownership of the negative; the life of any picture was never three years. When the three years had expired, *The Bargain* came back to the New York Motion Picture Company and they made a great deal more money out of it. It is still being played. The success of *The Bargain* was responsible for my contract and my return to pictures . . .

In one of my first pictures I used a pinto horse named Fritz. He weighed only one thousand pounds, but his power and endurance were remarkable. We had a lot of desert riding to do. Our desert was the sand dunes, just below Playa del Rey. The action of our story called for Cliff Smith and myself to be attacked by Indians.

His horse was killed and he mounted behind me, and we were chased for a long distance before my horse was shot while going at a full gallop, and we went down and fought behind his body. The combined weight of Cliff and myself with our guns and a heavy stock saddle was close to four hundred and fifty pounds, yet that little horse carried us for hours until all our scenes were taken. But when I was lying across his neck shooting Injuns, he rolled eyes at me that plainly said:

'Say, Mister, I sure was glad when you give me that fall.'

He never called me Mister again. He is on my ranch to-day, monarch of all he surveys.

On Christmas Day, 1914, we did not work. I went to Hollywood to look at some furnished bungalows that my sister had selected as possibilities, our main need being an enclosed yard for old Mack, so he could neither attack nor be attacked by his canine brothers. I found one place that filled the bill perfectly. I asked the lady how far it was to the nearest restaurant. There were no restaurants in Hollywood! Not even a lunch-stand where one could buy a sandwich. Meals could be had at the Hollywood Hotel, but for guests only. I found quarters at 534 South Figueroa Street, and we moved to Los Angeles.

I worked very hard. I would get my breakfast at a little restaurant on Sixth Street, take the Edendale trolley, and at the junction of Lakeshore and Sunset catch the old Ford bus from the Sennett Studio, where our laboratory was. This bus took film to camp every morning and returned at night with the day's work. It meant fifty miles a day of travel, and getting up at five o'clock every morning to be at camp at eight o'clock. I never reached home, via the same route, before seven or seven-thirty in the evening.

After giving old Mack a walk, my sister and I would go to the Hoffman Café for dinner. Some evenings we would spend our two nickels at the Lyceum Theater, a few doors away, to see a picture show — but I usually fell asleep. When we reached home I would go over the story for the next day's work. For three years I worked sixteen hours a day and worried eight.

Several years previous I had attempted to write a poem. It was published in *The Morning Telegraph*. I grew so fond of Fritz that I asked Tom to allow me to make a picture out of it. He did allow me to do so, and it was released under its title, *Pinto Ben*. It has been shown under many different titles and is playing yet. The little horse stole the picture from me.

All the actors and actresses in camp liked to work in my pictures.

When working with other directors, they would often spend their spare time on our set.

The scenario department, of which C. Gardner Sullivan and J.G. Hawkes were the principal writers, could not keep all of the directors supplied with material. Many stories which had cost the company fifteen or twenty dollars, written in long-hand on a few sheets of paper, were handed to me to make a picture. That this was accomplished was not the result of brains, but of application, hard work, and a determination to succeed.

Early in the spring of 1915, after I had made over twenty two-reel pictures, the Triangle Film Corporation was formed. The new company absorbed the New York Motion Picture Company, the Reliance-Majestic Company, the Keystone Comedies. The owners of Triangle were Harry E. Aitken, Kessell and Bauman, and their associates. The director-generals were D.W. Griffith, Thomas H. Ince, and Mack Sennett. The Knickerbocker Theater, in New York City, was leased. Triangle pictures were to play at two-dollar prices. . . .

In front of a theater in the Bronx at New York City, the crowd tore the top clear off a seven-thousand-dollar limousine.

At the New York Theater, downtown, the reception was so great that I could not speak for many minutes, and Marcus Loew presented me with a huge silver cup, inscribed:

> To William S. Hart, Greatest Screen Actor.
> As an indication of the esteem in which he is
> held by millions

I was appearing in New York, Brooklyn, and surrounding cities for three days. Tom was there. He told me that Triangle was trying to force him out; that his lawyer and J. Parker Read, his personal representative, were trying to effect a settlement. I begged him to stick to Triangle. I told him of my love of the old camp, and how it would hurt me ever to think of leaving it. He said he would do his best to patch it up. . . .

Tom had quit Triangle and I had sent in my resignation. Tom was calling me from New York every day or night on the telephone begging me 'to stand by him.' The Triangle Company was sending Mr. Quinn, or other representatives, once every other week with bags of gold containing $9500, my weekly salary, which I declined to accept. One week — two weeks — passed; three weeks — four weeks — passed; still I was salaryless, and still I was turning down bags of gold and the biggest producers and distributors in America. Friendship was costing me dearly.

I would tell Tom over the telephone when he called me:
'Mr. (whoever it might be) is out here offering me $10,000 per week.'
He would still beg for time and say that he was negotiating with
Mr. Zukor.

My friends, Joe Weber and Arthur Hopkins, and many other
friends in New York made urgent appeals for me to do business
with them, but I stuck to Tom.


And then it came! Tom signed a contract to deliver me to Famous
Players within thirty days. He also signed a contract for himself
to make two pictures a year with a $50,000 guarantee for each pic-
ture; and a second contract involving three other stars with a
guarantee of $35,000 for each picture.

My contract was for sixteen pictures with a guarantee of $150,000
for each picture. Each of the other contracts contained a clause which
made them void, provided a contract was not made with me deliver-
ing me to Famous Players within thirty days. This fact I did not
learn until three years later.

I felt a bit hurt at Tom going for wholesale producing, but I knew
from my previous experience I could make the pictures myself, the
same as I had done. The worst thing I had to face was the 'I told
you so' of dozens and dozens of men who had predicted just what
happened. . . .

My first picture, *The Narrow Trail*, was made at the Lasky Studio
and my first big quarrel with Tom was about my horse. For some
unaccountable reason Tom, who always could see anything that
had a money value, could not see Fritz. He just did not like the
horse and I was never able to find out why. *The Narrow Trail* was
conceived and written in my love for Fritz, and when Tom wanted
me to use another horse, I began to doubt either his or my own
sanity. The horse made the picture a great success, and it is still
playing.

In the next fifteen pictures, although Tom tried in various ways
through Allen and Sullivan and others to get me to use Fritz, the
little pinto never earned another dollar that Tom shared in. That
is why the little fellow was idle for fifteen pictures.

Perhaps our row about the pony might have been patched up
had I not found that I was being charged a proportionate share of
the overhead expense of running Tom's own studio. I was
dumbfounded. I went to see Tom immediately, expecting him to
make some excuse and rectify the mistake at once. He did adjust
the matter, but instead of an excuse, he attempted to justify his
position.

This busted the breach wide open. Tom and I were never friends afterward. During the two years that passed in the making of the sixteen pictures, I never saw him but three or four times of probably five minutes each. All our quarreling — and there was a heap of it — was done through E.H. Allen, my studio manager. We leased the old Mabel Normand studio in East Hollywood from Mack Sennett. I remained in this studio for four years.

# [MOVING PICTURE WORLD]
# *The Bargain*

*This was William S. Hart's first feature film and his first big success. It convinced Tom Ince to hire him on a longterm basis. The* Moving Picture World *seems to have been of two minds about the picture. Their credits and synopsis were reprinted in Diane Kaiser Koszarski's book,* The Complete Films of William S. Hart, *(N.Y., Dover, 1980). Her introduction has many insights about Hart's acting and his sense of the western genre which we shall want to note in later volumes.*

Produced by the New York Motion Picture Company under the supervision of Thomas H. Ince; distributed by Paramount; in production June 11 — August 5, 1914; released December 3, 1914; © as a reissue by Tri-Stone Pictures, October 12, 1923; five reels.
    Directed by Reginald Barker; story and screenplay by William H. Clifford and Thomas H. Ince; photographed by Robert Newhard.
    Print sources: LC; Newhall; Em Gee.

CAST: Clara Williams (*Nell Brent*); J. Barney Sherry (*Phil Brent*); William S. Hart (*Jim Stokes*); J. Frank Burke (*Bud Walsh*); James Dowling (*Rev. Joshua Wilkes*).

SYNOPSIS: The country is alarmed by advice that Jim Stokes, the "Two-Gun Man," is in the neighborhood headed for the border, and warning is given to place a double guard around the stage on its trip through the canyon.
    The warning is timely, for Jim is planning to hold up the stage and obtain a package of gold on it consigned to the express company. The stage is seen traversing a winding roadway through the marvelous scenery of the Grand Canyon, and at an opportune bend

in the route Jim cleverly holds up and robs the stage, extra guard and all.

Jim has the lead in his attempt to escape, but his pursuers are close on his trail. He is wounded and his horse killed from under him. However, he manages to lose himself in the Bad Lands, and painfully makes his way to a spring, where he falls unconscious.

From this situation Jim is rescued by Nell Brent's father, who takes him to their home, where Nell nurses him back to health. He falls in love with his pretty nurse, and without revealing his identity is married to her. Conscience-stricken, he determines to return the stolen money to the express company, and riding to the nearest station for that purpose, is horrified to find a poster announcing a thousand dollars reward for his capture. He is seen and recognized almost immediately, and the sheriff organizes a party for that purpose even while Jim's horse is hitched at the railing of the store. He learns the intent, however, and again makes a daring escape with his pursuers crowding close behind. He rides his horse into a pool of water, to lose the trail, puts a note under the saddle for his waiting bride, and sends his horse home. Again he starts on foot, but is finally captured in a typical western hotel combining saloon, gambling rooms, and dance hall.

While waiting with his prisoner until train time, the sheriff is attracted by the revelry of the rooms below, and going downstairs, gets into the game and loses all of the stolen money he had just recovered from Jim. Returning then to his prisoner, whom he had left in handcuffs, the sheriff said, "I'm a bigger thief than you are, Jim Stokes. I've lost the money you stole from the express company."

Seeing the sheriff's predicament, and wishing himself to be free, Jim proposes the bargain that if the sheriff will let him go, he will recover the money. This is agreed upon, and Jim's handcuffs are removed. He then arms himself, and going out through the window, enters the gambling room and holds up the cashier. He gets the money, rushes out in the wildest excitement, mounts a horse, and is again pursued. The flight this time takes him to the edge of a great precipice with the posse at his heels. Without hesitation he chooses the plunge to capture and horse and rider are seen falling over and over down the steep cliffside. Jim again escapes, covers his trail, and reaches the hotel just in advance of the searching party. He enters the room in a semi-fainting condition, turns over the money to the waiting sheriff, is handcuffed, and hastily tumbles into bed just as the party comes to the door and gaining admittance, explains that the game has been held up and they thought in some way Jim might have escaped and "turned the trick."

The next day the sheriff starts with his prisoner, but safely away from the town, he looses the handcuffs, gives Jim two hours' start to get his bride, and wishes him good luck, thus fulfilling his part of the bargain. Jim returns to Nell, is forgiven, and they go across the border to another state. [*Moving Picture World*, December 19, 1914]

*The Bargain* is nothing more than an old-fashioned Western. I cannot truthfully say that it is one inch above the average of such pictures. Its scenic background is superbly beautiful, but not more so than that shown in many old single reels. Its plot follows the old familiar lines: the outlaw, finely enacted by William S. Hart, robs the stagecoach . . . the outlaw escapes happily and something like six felonies committed by two men go unpunished.

It is said that pictures of this sort are still popular in certain sections of the country and that nickelodeons in many big cities still yearn for them. This may be true, but it does not alter the fact that pictures of this sort have in the past been the most dangerous weapon in the hands of our enemies [the censors]. There can be no doubt whatever that a picture of this kind has a bad influence on youthful minds . . . [Stephan Bush, *Moving Picture World*, December 5, 1915].

## BRUCE FIRESTONE
# A Man Named Sioux

*Carrying the subtitle, "Nostalgia and the Career of William S. Hart," this article appeared in* Film and History *magazine, December 1977, pages 85-89. The author was at that time professor of English at Clemson University and editor of* South Carolina Review. *He is particularly concerned to call to our attention not only the impact of the wilderness on the frontier settlements, but also the individuals who lived that experience and carried it with them right into the movies. For Firestone, Hart's version of the west was a personal view of human nature as much as it was a call for dramatic realism.*

One of the most popular and productive approaches to American literature in this century has focused on the interplay between wilderness and civilization in the American experience. That confrontation between the old and the new, the known and unknown, is recorded in the earliest writings of American settlers, and it remains an important element even now in that vast conglomerate we call American culture. Frederick Jackson Turner spelled out the significance of the frontier in his famous address to the American Historical Association in 1893, and the thesis which he proposed — that our national imagination was formed by "the existence of an area of free land, its continuous recession, and the advance of American settlement Westward" — has become a landmark in American studies.

More recently, the Turner thesis has been adopted by film historians searching for a clue to the early and rapid surge in popularity of the American Western film. Most film historians agree that the closing of the frontier in the 1890's set the stage for the successful introduction of the Western film, and that the genre grew quickly in popularity because, along with the Western novel, it perpetuated an important cultural myth. Our need for a fictional frontier grew in proportion to the recession of the real one, and when that imaginary line finally went awash in the Pacific, dumping the last vestiges of Manifest Destiny somewhere on the beaches of Santa Catalina, we chose to relive the process — and thereby perpetuate it — in our fiction. The advent of the motion picture, which coincided roughly with the closing of the frontier, was fortuitous. It provided a popular medium even more accessible than the dime novel, one which seemed especially well suited to Western themes. Edwin S. Porter's advances in editing underscored the action; the pictures that moved seemed a good deal more realistic than words; and the large screen upon which these pictures were projected made the wide open spaces seem both wider and more open.

This is ground which has already been covered well by scholars of both film history and popular culture. George Fenin, William Everson, Richard Etulain, John Cawelti, Katherine Esselman and others have explored the literary, dramatic, political and social origins of the genre in great detail. What is often overlooked, however, is that this nostalgia was not simply a cultural phenomenon. It had a personal dimension as well. Some of those involved in making Western films during the silent era were dealing with a place and a time that they knew quite well. What they captured in their films was not simply a mythic landscape of the Old West. They were re-creating their own youth, and the way they saw that youth — nostalgically, sentimentally, whatever — helped shape the films they made. These men were certainly not the majority, and they rarely held positions of authority in the fledgling film companies.

But they did exist, and in one or two cases, especially that of William S. Hart, they did leave their mark.

We tend to forget how quickly Western films succeeded the era they portray, how rapidly they filled the void left by that vanishing frontier. The first Western films were actually quite topical. Like Edwin S. Porter's *The Great Train Robbery* and its many imitations, they were often re-creations of recent events. At the time city folk around the country were gaping in awe at that famous Wyoming train robbery, Butch Cassidy and the Sundance Kid were well and alive in South America — first Argentina, then Bolivia — doing what came naturally. Los Bandidos Yanquis kept doing it, too, until 1909 — a full six years after the film. Census statistics may indicate that the frontier had closed by 1890, but the Old West, like television's Bat Masterson, was really a legend in its own time. The last big cattle round-ups occurred as late as 1907; Wyatt Earp was somewhere in Nevada prospecting for silver and running a saloon when *The Great Train Robbery* was released; and both Buffalo Bill Cody and Bat Masterson survived the film (by 14 and 18 years respectively).

So it should come as no surprise that some of the earliest actors to work in Western films were men who had grown up in the 1880's in the West and Midwest. A 1908 sequel to *The Great Train Robbery* — this one called simply *The Bank Robbery* — was directed by the famous frontier marshall, William M. Tilghman, and featured well-known bank robber Al Jennings, who was just out of jail and figured to cash in on some of his well-earned notoriety. The Indians that appeared in Tom Ince's early films in the teens were actually still wards of the government, loaned out by the government and later returned (mostly intact) by Ince.

The figure whose life best dramatizes this personal dimension, however, is William S. Hart, because Hart was a good deal older than his co-workers by the time he entered motion pictures, and because Hart did rise to a position of influence. Although Ince and others often claimed credit for Hart's work, most scholars of the period agree that the films which Hart starred in bore his distinctive imprint.[1] They expressed a quite personal vision, a rare blend of austerity and sentimentality. One of the reasons Hart's career foundered in the twenties was that he refused to abandon that vision long after everyone else had. The more the times changed, the more Hart seemed to cling to his own individual style.

Hart was born in 1870 in Newburgh, New York — closer to Cooper's West than Wister's — but he spent most of his childhood on the prairie. His father was a miller who made his living by traveling the Midwest and setting up flour mills in new settlements. The family never stayed in one area very long, and by the time Hart had reached his teens he knew life on the prairie — especially the Dakotas — pretty well. According to his autobiography, *My Life East and West*,[2] the family lived for awhile beside an Indian reservation, and since most of Hart's playmates were Sioux children, he learned to speak Sioux language. In fact, if we can believe what Hart recounts in that book, it was his ability to converse in Sioux that extricated him and his father from several precarious situations in the early 1880's.

There is no way of knowing, of course, if these incidents are true, but there seems little question that Hart's nomadic upbringing gave him firsthand knowledge of prairie life, and that those experiences stayed with him all his life. When Hart stumbled into a Cleveland theatre in 1911 and saw his first Western film, he was appalled by its lack of authenticity. In the autobiography he describes the sheriff of this film as looking like a "cross between a Wisconsin woodchopper and a Gloucester fisherman." He goes on:

> "Here were re-productions of the Old West being seriously presented to the public — in almost a burlesque manner — and they were successful. It made me tremble to think of it. I was an actor and I knew the West. . . The opportunity that I had been waiting for years to come was knocking at my door.
> Hundreds of ideas seemed to rush in from every direction . . . the die was cast. Rise or fall, sink or swim, I had to bend every endeavor to get a chance to make Western motion pictures . . . I had been waiting for years for the right thing, and now the right thing had come! I was a part of the West — it was my boyhood home — it was in my blood." [pp. 198-99].

As this and numerous other passages in the autobiography illustrate, Hart liked to present himself as an authority on all things Western. But it was not this passion for realism which finally prevailed in Hart's films. Hart's objection to *The Virginian*, which he calls "a monument to the fact that a truly great writer can make the moon look like green cheese and get away with it," is a good illustration of the other passion which characterizes much of his work. What Hart finds most rancid about Wister's cheese is the character of the Virginian himself, who as foreman of the ranch leads a posse to capture and hang some cattle rustlers — one of whom has been his friend. Notice how little *realism* actually has to do with the objection:

> In the first place, the foreman would have refused flat-footed to trail his friend, and the ranchers would have respected him for so refusing. In the next place, if he had led the posse he would have led them the wrong direction and the ranchers would have expected him to do so, and again, respected him for it. And if he had led them to his friend and found his friend, he would have done it for a reason. He would have

stepped to his friend's side and said: "Well, gentlemen, I have done my duty and brought you here, but if you hang him, you've got to hang me, too! And we ain't neither of us strong for being hung while we've got our guns on" [pp. 175-76].

If the autobiography and the fiction which Hart published later in his career are any indication, the meaning of the West and the meaning of his own youth became nearly indistinguishable. Hart saw the West as the last bastion of all those virtues he had once believed in, and the older he got the more he became convinced that it was really like that: that cowboys — unlike the Virginian — were loyal (those that didn't drink, anyway); that Indians were pure and noble (before white men corrupted them); and that poetic justice ruled fairly but firmly (mounted no doubt on a pinto pony not unlike Hart's favorite Fritz). If there was an evil in this West it was the future — all those forces which threatened his world.

Hart tries very hard in his autobiography to avoid bitterness in describing his career, but it comes out anyway. As you read through it, it becomes evident that what draws him so strongly to his past is clearly its utter lack of resemblance to the present. After all, Hart had a tough time in the movies. Ince and everyone else exploited him, his fans turned on him, and he was the much-suffering victim of a well publicized and quite fraudulent paternity suit. To Hart, all this could not have happened in his youth, in the Old West. When friends would ask Hart what it was really like back then, he would tell them

> of a country where there are no spies or newsmongers — only kind-hearted, friendly things, those that would fight to the death in battle, but in peace would shrink from inflicting pain . . . of the land where none are strangled for free speech, where none are stoned for adultery of mind or body, because there is no adultery of mind or body [p. 161].

Most telling of all though, and most blatant in its contrast of past and present, is Hart's description of the days he would camp out in the hills with his production company. These were the best times, and it's evident that to Hart making films about the Old West was almost like being there.

> If this mimic world of toil where I was earning a living and reproducing days that were dear to me was to be the top of my mountain, I was content. I was surrounded by no greedy grafters, no gelatin-spined, flatulent, slimy creatures — just dogs, horses, sheep, goats, bulls, mules, burros, and white men and red men that were accustomed to live among such things. If we wanted a snake, we could go out in the hills and catch one — one that would warn us that he was a snake, with his rattles . . . I was happy [p.225].

For Hart, at least, making movies about the West became a way of reliving and recreating it, and while he often strove for a gritty kind of realism in his films, what Hart sought most was an antidote to the present — *his* present. The Old West was life measured out in ten gallon hats, not coffee spoons, and if Hart distorted it and sentimentalized it, that was because the West came to represent his own lost youth and innocence. An old Indian woman once told him: "I can only think and live in the past. The white people have taken away all of the Indian's future" (p. 15). It's no wonder that as he grew older, William Surrey Hart identified more and more with the plight of the Indian.

NOTES

1. See George N. Fenin and William K. Everson, *The Western: From Silents to the Seventies* (New York: Penguin, 1973), and John Tuska, *The Filming of the West* (New York: Doubleday, 1976).

2. New York: Benjamin Blom, 1929. All subsequent page references are in brackets in the text.

*C. Gardner Sullivan*

# JOE FRANKLIN
## *Hell's Hinges*

*Starting in 1948 on WABC radio in New York, and continuing on television in 1953, Joe Franklin was one of the earlier talk show hosts — a show business fan with a memory, an acquaintanceship, and a record collection all properly described as phenomenal. His useful and enthusiastic book,* Classics of the Silent Screen, *(N.Y., Citadel, 1959) profiles 50 films and 75 stars. It offers on pages 23-24 this review of a spectacular film made by William S. Hart in 1916.*

*Hell's Hinges* is classic of its kind. Together with the simpler *The Toll Gate* and the more actionful *The Narrow Trail*, it is one of the best of Hart's pictures. To dismiss it casually as a western would be a mistake, for it more closely resembles the Swedish *The Atonement of Gosta Berling* or Somerset Maugham's *Rain* than it does the traditional western, such as *Riders of the Purple Sage*.

*Hell's Hinges* has elements quite alien to the standard western — including the systematic seduction of a minister by the town trollop, and the minister's subsequent drunken madness and savagery, going so far as to burn down his own church. ("To Hell with the Church — let's burn it down!" reads his subtitle!)

Hart has been accused of being too sentimental a director, which at times he undoubtedly was. But there was always real power behind that sentiment. It is astounding that his tremendous talent as a director has gone unrecognized for so long. The camera placement in *Hell's Hinges*, the simple yet effective symbolism, and the flair for spectacle, as in the brilliantly handled mob scenes in which all of Inceville goes up in flames, the real "feel" of the old, dusty, unglamorized West, all should have earned Hart a reputation as one of the great directors. Certainly Hart, on the strength of his directorial performance here, is entitled to rate as one of the leaders among the rivals to Griffith, lower down on the artistic scale though they were.

For the most part, *Hell's Hinges* offers high-powered drama rather than straightforward western action. It is the story of a minister, weak-willed, and with no belief in his calling, who comes West to assume the spiritual leadership of a frontier community. His sister, knowing of his weakness, hopes it will make a man of him. Hart plays Blaze Tracey, an outlaw, feared yet respected, and having his own curious code of honor. He and Silk Miller (Alfred Hollingsworth) decide to run the minister out of town before religion can take root in Hell's Hinges. But Hart, although he sees through the minister's facade right away, is impressed by the sincerity of the man's sister. Because of her, he champions the minister's cause, stands up against the lawless elements, and helps in the building of a church.

But Silk Miller has no intention of giving up so easily. He has the town's trollop, Louise Glaum, seduce the minister the night before he is to open the new church. Disgraced before his flock, the minister launches into a wild orgy of drinking and, while Hart is out of town, leads the saloon element in an attack on the church. Despite fierce opposition by the God-fearing townspeople, the church is burned, and the decent citizens put to rout. The minister is shot and killed in the melee.

Returning to town, Hart finds the girl he now loves by the body of her dead brother — and in fury marches on the saloon-stronghold of Silk Miller's gang in this Sodom of the West. In a rugged climax, he kills Miller in a duel, and sets fire to the saloon. The whole town burns to the ground, and Bill and the heroine set out to find a new life together somewhere "over the mountains."

Apart from a single blow, there are no fisticuffs, and only one short riding sequence. Hart reserves his action for the final two reels of mob fighting and the blazing town, withdrawing all restraints to slam over one of the most powerful and spectacular action sequences that he ever created. Fine camerawork, utilizing long panoramic shots and beautiful lighting, excellent editing, and a sure control over the masses of extras, fuse these scenes into an episode of astonishing vigor. Hart, his assistant, Cliff Smith, his writer, C. Gardner Sullivan, and cameraman Joe August (who later did such fine work for John Ford) were one of the sturdiest (and least recognized) teams of craftsmen the cinema ever produced. Sullivan was one of the finest of early screen-writers, and one of his most interesting plot-lines was the one he developed here in *Hell's Hinges* — the contrasting of Hart's reformation ("a man wholly evil," as an early subtitle tells us) with the parallel degeneration of the minister. . . .

# THOMAS H. INCE

# The Challenge for the
# Motion Picture Producer

*Sudden illness and death in 1924 prevented Thomas Ince from writing a full account of his life and work. But a manuscript of ten short chapters had been completed. The typescript (together with a more polished version of chapters 3 to 9) is in the possession of the Museum of Modern Art. It was published after his death, with minor changes in style and diction, as "The Memoirs of Thomas H. Ince," in the* Exhibitors Herald *(later the* Motion Picture Herald*) in five installments from December 13, 1924 to January 10, 1925. The final section is reproduced here. The last five and a half paragraphs were omitted in the* Herald.

*A more remarkable statement of ideal goals by a producer-director would be hard to find in motion picture history. It establishes in plain language what Ince considers the best formal structure for dramatic stories and why this serves the audience as he sees it. It is also a manifesto in favor of realism on the screen — "the faithful portrayal of life" as against "forced dramatic situations." And it expresses a rare faith that a motion picture may have a therapeutic effect, for "seeing real characters with real problems to solve . . . will give us courage to meet our own problems."*

We are living in an age when the white light of criticism is turned upon accepted and established standards in all phases of life. The old order of things has passed, and all over the world worn-out traditions and methods are toppling. We are in the grip of another renaissance, a revolution of ideals. Like the phoenix of mythology, the new world order is rising out of the ashes of the old.

The picture of yesterday fulfilled its mission, giving way to the newer and higher standards demanded of the picture of today. And because some of the modern productions are now reaching such a high standard, the public has learned to expect even greater achievements. Picture-goers have shown their faith in us, and by that very faith they have thrown us a challenge to produce bigger and better pictures. Are we going to accept that challenge and make the picture of tomorrow take its rightful place in the onward march of progress? I, for one, pledge myself to this task.

The demand for better pictures is universal. On that point we all agree. But that demand brings up the question, 'What constitutes better pictures?' This question must be answered first by the producer and finally by the public itself, for in the final analysis it is the public who is the court of last appeal on the merits of a picture. It is in their hands to make it or break it.

But the producer with insight and a real desire to perfect his art, can and must feel the pulse of the vast American audience, and anticipate its desires and demands.

I hold it not only a duty but a privilege to study carefully the reactions of various types of pictures on the average audience, for only in that way can I reach my conclusions and give my interpretation of what constitutes better pictures.

The really successful photodrama of today, and I believe tomorrow, is one that catches the interest and holds the eager attention through sheer force of HUMANNESS AND FIDELITY TO DETAIL OF LIFE. The day has long since passed when our characters move like marionettes across the screen.

The public demands, and justly so, the faithful portrayal of life as it is lived by real flesh and blood people in all its various walks. They demand true characterizations, that they may see themselves reflected on the screen. The problems of human existence vary only in degree. Basically they are identical and fundamental. Therefore a picture with forced dramatic situations and emotions does not ring true. It is based upon a false premise and the audience leaves the theatre unsatisfied and unconvinced.

But a picture that is written and produced by those who are close students of human nature — and who portray faithfully the problems and desires of the human family — holds up the mirror of life to us and we see ourselves in circumstances and surroundings that are familiar to us. But that is not all. Seeing those everyday things of life worked out on the screen to successful or non-successful issues, as the case may be, we will get a new angle, perhaps, on how to handle our particular problems. Seeing real characters with real problems to solve, which parallel our own, we will get reactions that, in many instances, will give us courage to meet our own problems, our own successes and our own heartaches, and to handle them to our own satisfaction.

Nor do I mean by that, that the screen must preach. That is not its mission. It must entertain and give us the form of amusement that relaxes and at the same time stimulates. But it must do this through the portrayal of life as we know it, and it must give us something that will enhance the value of our own lives, which are too often drab and colorless.

It makes no difference whether the story is a comedy, a tragedy, or a straight dramatic exposition of life, so long as it rings true and gives us life as we know it, and something to take away with us that is finer and bigger than what we may have had before.

A striking instance of this comes to mind which had just that result. A play was put on the stage several years ago which was a brilliant comedy. I use that term in its finest sense. It was not a frothy farce. It was a story which dealt with one of the accepted tragedies of life, and would have been treated as such by nine playwrights out of ten. But this particular playwright chose to treat his theme as a comedy.

The principal character was played by a woman of perhaps forty who had been jilted by her lover on the eve of her wedding, twenty years before. Instead of accepting this condition as a tragedy and allowing it to cloud her life, she overcame it and developed into a woman of poise, charm, and power, handling her life with that light touch that laughs at grim tragedy, and handling all whom she contacted as she would handle pawns on a chessboard, bringing them all to her feet as willing victims of her charm and beauty of nature.

It is not the story that I wish to dwell upon in this instance, but the effect that it had upon the audience. At the end of the first act, the middle-aged people in the audience were sitting up with a new sense of their own power and importance. At the end of the second act there was a sparkle in the eyes of those who had felt that life was slipping into the background. When the curtain fell on the last act, which was the final triumph of the jilted lady, there was a tumultuous applause, and in the faces of the audience that left the theater, old and young, men and women, there was a look that bespoke a new lease on life and a courage to handle each individual problem that was uppermost in their own lives.

That play was a slice of life, faithfully portrayed. There was not one action that did not ring true, not one characterization that was false, and its effect crashed across the footlights and found a response in the hearts of all who saw it.

When pictures were in their infancy, which was but a few short years ago, the one idea seemed to be to make something happen on the screen. Action, and more action, with little thought of making that action portray the emotions and true experiences of life.

Action is absolutely essential to the successful photoplay. Without it there would be no screen drama. But it must be action which conveys the coordination of mind, heart, and body, rather than meaningless action alone. Because of this a distinct technique of creating screen material has developed and is in the process of larger and fuller development.

In the last few years there has been an enormous demand for rights to the published story and the successful play, but the field for that type of material is becoming exhausted. Furthermore, producers are realizing that the published story and play are not always adapted to the screen.

Stripped of the brilliant, intense, and humorous lines which have put a play over, or the literary style of a published story, there is, in many cases, very little left to carry five reels of plot and action on the screen. In other words there is not enough meat in the plot itself.

Therefore the producer is compelled to pad it, or to entirely rebuild the story, and when it is finished it has either lost its spontaneity or is so unlike the original that the public is disappointed. It is not a new story and it is not the one that they know and love. It is neither fish nor fowl nor good red herring.

This is not necessarily true of every published story or play, however. It is the exception that proves the rule, and in some instances a producer procures the rights to a Broadway hit or a best seller which is admirably adapted to the screen and then we have a double hit.

But for a sustained and consistent source of photoplay material the screen must develop its own writers, men and women who possess insight into the lives and emotions of their fellow beings, and who are able to depict the characterizations about them with sincerity and simplicity.

The theme or keynote of the story must be REAL. It must be based upon a fundamental principle of life, something which every man and woman knows in common with his neighbor — some underlying basis of human existence which touches the lives of the laborer or the capitalist, the show girl or the queen. The theme must be a universal language — love, greed, sacrifice, fear, or any emotion which is generally known to the human family.

Building on the theme, the plot should be no less one of sincerity and simplicity. It should have one clearly defined logical plot thread running unbroken through the story, with the counter plots converging to the main thread of the story and never distracting the attention from it.

Plots should be constructed UP, not DOWN. Situations and episodes should be gauged to lead to a climax that will accentuate all preceding scenes. The climax should be strong, virile, picturesque, colorful — redolent of life's passions.

Sequences should be arranged with strict attention to coherency and continuity of action. Each situation should be better and stronger than its predecessor, almost independent of its forerunner, so far as quality and story values are concerned.

Many writers have fallen short of their mark because they opened their plot with a crash, so to speak, and depending on this intensity at the start, allowed interest to lag, through failure to provide subsequent situations and climaxes of real dramatic merit. The successful photoplay is one that is well balanced throughout, always leading on and on, stimulating imagination and preparing for the ultimate finale which appeases and satisfies the expectant spectator.

It is a mistake to pile in many complications to force the action. This distracts the mind of the audience from the main story plot and is confusing. After such a picture has been viewed, it is almost impossible for the average person to relate the story in any logical sequence, and the result is that their brains are muddled and the reactions they get are a hodge-podge of complications and forced action.

The situations which carry the plot to its climax must be the everyday experiences that happen in the lives of the human family. Nor does that destroy the dramatic values of the story.

A dramatic scene portrayed on the screen will thrill an audience with its intensity even though that same scene lived in a Harlem flat or on a Texas ranch would impress those who were living the episode as commonplace or at least pleasant or unpleasant as the case may be. They would fail to realize the dramatic value of their own lives.

That is the art of the screen, as I see it, and the secret of better pictures: to hold up the mirror of life and show us to ourselves.

The stories that are going to lead to better pictures must be deeply human, expressed in such a way that every ounce of pathos, humor, characterization, and dramatic quality is felt by the audience, without forcing these elements to an illogical point or permitting imagination to make inroads upon truth.

# Chapter 3

# Griffith

*What happened within the next few years is probably*
*without parallel in the emergence of any art form.*
— Arthur Knight.

The strands of culture and personality are various and tangled. However much we try to make a pattern out of the puzzle of influences brought to bear on a creative person — and in turn passed on to others — there must still be mystery and guesswork.

D.W. Griffith's was the most influential career in the history of American motion picture directors. Among those who worked with him on his pictures were such future directors as John Ford, Raoul Walsh, W.S. Van Dyke, and Erich von Stroheim, while King Vidor, Cecil DeMille, and many others watched from afar. He trained and developed, from his first day's work at Biograph, a multitude of future stars of the screen.

He made a very large number of films — the total, by one count, 486. While only 28 of these were feature-length, they were all so early that they inevitably became models for other film makers. And of course in the judgment of his peers and his audiences, his were films of exceptional excellence.

This does not mean Griffith was brilliantly original, in the sense of being the first to use certain technical methods, despite his claims in the *Dramatic Mirror* advertisement, December 3, 1913:

"The large or close-up figures, distant views as represented first in Ramona, the switchback, sustained suspense, the fade-out, and restraint in expression." Certainly he and Billy Bitzer, his cameraman, tried out a great many things by accident and by design. But they were, as most film historians prefer to put it, innovative primarily in developing and using these methods over and over again, so that they became familiar, natural, accepted. And the creative contribution, above all, for Griffith, was to try to integrate his cinematic effects with the drama.

Louis Lumière and Georges Méliès will always have top billing in world film history as the first to provide us with, respectively, nonfictional and theatrical film styles. But Griffith took both strands of precedent and wove them repeatedly and vigorously into the kind of realistic settings and romantic stories which set the mode for the mainstream of American film.

His works were seen all over the world. *Intolerance* (1916) was a textbook for future Soviet directors. *Broken Blossoms* (1919) was well known by German writers and directors who later chose similar interior sets for expressionist effect. For contrast, he took his best outdoor social realist style to Germany in 1924 and made *Isn't Life Wonderful*. It was followed the next year by *The Joyless Street* and in 1931 by *Kameradschaft,* both directed by G.W. Pabst.

Less has been said, perhaps, about the influences Griffith absorbed from others. The forms of melodrama Griffith knew so well from his days on the road — ranging from Belasco to Sudermann, Sardou, and Ibsen — interacted with his discoveries of the powers of montage. Of course he was well aware of the contemporary competitive works of Thomas Ince and others.

In addition, the movies he saw from abroad taught him a thing or two and gave impetus to his epic impulse. He claimed he never went to the Italian spectacle *Quo Vadis* (1912) but Blanche Sweet told Kevin Brownlow she saw it with him. (*The Parade's Gone By*, p. 92.) He surely must have seen the Danish chase films which were so like his own and were available only two doors down the street. Could he have missed a 1908 Pathé chase film which featured cross-cutting and was so very much like his *Lonely Villa* (1909)? (Ron Mottram, "Influences Between National Cinemas," *Cinema Journal*, Winter 1974-75; Barry Salt, "The Physician of the Castle," *Sight and Sound*, Autumn 1985.)

The broader, underlying influences were from his early life.

His recollections of meadows and brooks in his childhood environment are clearly enough reflected in his films, and the obverse image of the treacherous city is there, as well.

Nostalgia can be very selective, but it is a powerful source of creative energy for many film makers: one thinks of Ford and Fellini, even Renoir. For Griffith it was not only a sustaining impetus for his work but undoubtedly a strong connecting link with his audiences, even in the twenties. He saw the pains that came with change, yet he also sometimes seemed aware of the dangers of faith in the old individualism in an era of increasing population, urban confusion, and complex community needs. In this he was the first of a special line of Hollywood directors — John Ford, King Vidor, Frank Capra — who were often willing to try to present within dramatic forms the relationship of the individual and society.

It should be of the greatest interest to working film makers (and instructive for critics as well) to look behind the screen and watch how this man worked — rehearsing with actors, learning to use the camera, achieving his purposes through editing. *The Adventures of Dollie*, made on location in Connecticut, was previewed on a quiet night (July 14, 1908) at Keith and Proctor's theater in Union Square, and earned the new director a contract of $45 a week with a royalty of a tenth of a cent per foot on every print sold in the future. Accepting a percentage was quite a gamble, but "the first year his royalty check went from practically nothing to four and five hundred dollars a month before the end of the year."

We have this on the authority of Linda Arvidson, the young actress who was Griffith's first wife and played the mother in the film. Her book, *When the Movies Were Young*, came out in 1925, fourteen years after they had been separated, but her account is characteristically generous, recalling (like any student film maker of today) the fun they had acting out that one-reel adventure.

Critical responses to Griffith's films, while they were predominantly supportive, ranged widely over the years, and a considerable anthology could be put together using simply the conflicting views of his pictures during the 1920s. As the following selections show, critics have found in Griffith's films "deliberation and repose" (Frank Woods), "magnificent pathos" (Sergei Eisenstein), "roaring climaxes" (Alan Casty), "infinite shadings of human emotion" (Blake Lucas), and "lyrical affirmation of life" (Eileen Bowser).

# D. W. GRIFFITH
# My First Real Battles With Life

*This is from a fragment of autobiography Griffith titled "The Hollywood Gold Rush." It began with some remembrances of childhood and broke off in 1916. It was dictated to Jim Hart, a Louisville newspaper reporter who was out of work, as Griffith was, in the late 1930s. In 1972 the notes became part of a biographical scrapbook called* The Man Who Invented Hollywood *(Louisville, Ky., Touchstone Publishing Co.).*

*Hart came to realize that the great director was doing little more than "rehearsing and directing scenes out of his past," and Richard Schickel, in his 1984 biography, warns us against it as "veracious only in the poetic sense." We may believe as much of the detail as we like (doubting perhaps that his shoes were ever tied on with rags). But what so vividly remained as memory must have affected what he would put on the screen.*

*Our brief extracts from pages 19 to 55 are intended to represent certain emotional backgrounds that stayed with him — his peculiar reverence for his father, his family's decline in status, his first embarrassment as an actor. Griffith's school of hard knocks in northern cities found reflection in* The Musketeers of Pig Alley *(1912), a sketch for future "gangster films," and* The Mother and the Law, *the modern story incorporated in* Intolerance. *His nostalgia for the fields and streams of the Kentucky countryside, here described so earnestly, found dramatic expression in* True Heart Susie *and* A Romance of Happy Valley *(both 1919).*

Down in old Kentucky, near Louisville, was the house of my father, Colonel Jacob Wark Griffith, a Confederate cavalry officer. The house was on a small hill and on all sides sloped meadows where sheep and cows and horses often grazed. Beyond a field in front of the house ran a dusty turnpike that had been laid by my father.

Once there had been quite a pretentious place — more or less like the popular conception of Kentucky mansions — with poplar and osage orange groves leading up to its portals. Guerrillas, disguised as union raiders, burned the house in the first year of the war. This second house that father built was quite small. And it was here that I was born. Here also was whelped the wolf pup of want and hunger that was to shadow me all my life.

A narrow lane led from our house to the turnpike. Sometimes by day along this old pike moved droves of cattle, white splashes of sheep, rattling carts and wagons, jogging buggies. By night these same buggies carried sweethearts and the flapping leather covers were often gilded by the new white spring moon . . .

As a small child, after having been sent to bed, I remember crawling cautiously back and hiding under the parlor table. I don't imagine it was so much to listen to father's literary readings as just to stay around with the grown-ups. A few neighbors would come in to gather round with the family and listen to father's dramatic readings from Shakespeare and other classics.

I got quite a little praise for my picture, *The Birth of a Nation.* Even Hollywood seemed to rather like it, but I think that that picture owes more to my father than it does to me.

The stories told of my father, particularly by veterans who had fought under his command, were burned right into my memory. I remember particularly one old soldier, Josh Long, of Crestwood, Kentucky. He said, "I believe if your father thought he had one drop of cowardly blood in his veins, he'd knife it out." Although he died many years after the war, it was the wounds and crude dressings that finally brought his death.

One could not find the sufferings of our family and our friends — the dreadful poverty and hardships during the war and for many years after — in the Yankee-written histories we read in school. From all this was born a burning determination to tell some day our side of the story to the world . . .

When I was making the picture *Way Down East* with Lillian Gish and Richard Barthelmess, it was necessary to introduce into the picture as much pastoral beauty as possible. Not only in this picture but in all others where similar scenes were required, I tried to find a scene that would match a vivid memory of our old farm down in Kentucky.

There was a small field close behind that farmhouse. I went out to it early one spring morning, when a boy, with a little pail to gather dewberries. The berry patch was on a gently sloping hillside. Behind it was a double log cabin where lived two Negro families that had been slaves of my parents. Beside the rambling cabin flowed a small stream and on one side of the patch there was a stake-and-rider rail fence. Several larks were soaring up and down from this rail fence, singing ecstatically in the clear spring morning. In memory, I always seem to see around this entire scene a luminous glow of joy. As I walked, it seemed that my bare feet hardly touched the ground. Of course, I did not realize then that never again would I know such pure joy, such singing, soaring ecstasy as that which my childish heart knew that spring morning long ago.

Often afterwards, I have thought what a grand invention it would be if someone could make a magic box in which we could store the precious moments of our lives and keep them with us . . . and later on, in dark hours, could open this box and receive for at least a few moments a breath of its stored memory . . .

At the time of my father's death, I was ten years old, the youngest in a family of seven with tremendously varying ages. My elder brothers and sisters were old enough to have been my parents.

After father's death came the deluge. Mother learned he had been paying ten percent compound interest on several mortgages and that we were now among the poorest of poor. The old wolf, whose mournful whine had been heard at the doors of so many unfortunates, now made a personal appearance in our back yard. Everything was on my poor mother's shoulders. Before the war she had never done work of any kind. Now, she was at it from dawn to dark — and then some. She even made the clothes I wore . . .

Conditions went from bad to worse on the old estate and we were soon forced to give it up. We moved to Shelby County, Kentucky — to what, I am sure, was the most useless farm in the entire world. It seems that my eldest brother was guilty of buying this farm because of a pretty face next door. Shortly afterward, he married the girl. Until I was twelve, we waged a losing fight against rocks, roots, bugs, and worn-out soil, in a desperate attempt to pay off an $1800 mortgage. We never made a dent in it.

From our new home we went to a school about two and a half miles away. In later years I have often thought that this was the cause of why I did not grow up overly bright. It seems that as time rolled on and the family kept moving that the schoolhouses kept getting farther and farther away from me. This particular one was near the village of Southville. We had to ford a winding stream seven times in making our way from home to schoolhouse. But we went to school, rain or shine, sleet or snow.

Those were the busy days: Up before daylight and milking the cows; general chores around the house and then a two-and-a-half mile tramp to school. In good weather, we enjoyed it, but in the event of rain or snow we always arrived at our destination thoroughly drenched and chilled to the bone. Then we would sit on our hard benches and depend upon the small stove or the mercy of the good Lord to dry us and prevent pneumonia. Here my first real battles with life began . . .

Thomas Coffin Cooke, the stage director, was going to put on a play in Louisville. The play was *The District School,* and he gave me the role of the dunce. All I had to do was sit on a high stool two hours and remark once during every performance, "The breeze from the lake blows chilly tonight."

Was I good in that part? (I rather suspect that I have been playing it ever since.) But this show soon folded, and then I got a substantial part with a real company, the Meffert Stock Company. These people took in hard cash and actually paid their actors' salaries. And their leading people were the idols of Louisville.

After the matinees, whole coveys of fluttering belles waited outside the stage door for a brief close-up of their favorites. I bore this in mind . . .

As the stock company gave two performances a day, we had little time for rehearsals. It seems, however, that I waded through them satisfactorily and invited everyone I knew and many I did not know to witness my initial performance. Of course, my mother and sisters would not come, but Jacob, with his lady friend and a small party, bought tickets for my Monday night premiere and prepared to give me a big send-off.

The great day came. At last I was on a real stage, acting. I knew my part and never dropped a word. In fact, in my enthusiasm, I added a few lines just to congeal the cheese. When my big dramatic scene came, I knew I had that matinee audience spellbound . . . or maybe earbound, anyway. Believe me, there was no one in that audience who did not *hear* me.

After the matinee I hesitated, bathed in perspiration, as I saw the manager advancing. He came up and presented me with one dollar and a half. (My weekly salary was "eight per.") I fancied that he had liked my acting so well that he intended paying me some in advance. I asked quickly "You liked it?" He responded quietly, "You are too grand for us." Then he said goodbye, and I knew then that I had been fired. It stunned me . . .

Ashamed to go home and ashamed to be seen on the streets, I bought a sandwich and a new drink called Coca-Cola and then found an obscure poolroom and sat in the back for hours . . .

I decided to storm the theatrical center of America — New York. Fevered by the virus of stage life, I sold my bicycle, drew out my savings, and with a sum total of $19 bought a round trip excursion ticket to Atlantic City. Selling the return ticket, I journeyed on roundabout to New York.

In all New York I did not know one person. For three days I lived in the shadow of the Brooklyn Bridge in a fifty-cent flophouse under the illusion that I was in New York City proper. It didn't take me long, however, to locate the theatrical agencies. And I haunted them for any kind of part. Soon, I was eking out a living by shoveling concrete. Finally, I was tossed a bone in the form of a part in one of the ten-twent-thirt melodramas of that day, but this show passed into the Great Beyond in Tonawanda, New York. So I became an ore shoveler and puddler in the Tonawanda Iron and Steel Company in order to ride the cushions back to Broadway.

Again I made the rounds and again I got a part in a melodrama. This time it was *London Life* — booked from coast to coast. It was a fairly good company and I went to bed each night dreaming of California, that state of golden dreams. We started out boldly enough, but then our success began to peter out. We did a complete fold in Minneapolis.

My salary had been $25 a week during the several months of fair success with this company and I had lived cheaply, sending home a chunky slice of it weekly. But now pride stopped me from wiring home for aid. Doubtless, the family exchequer was running low, anyhow.

In subzero weather I crept into the blinds of a Chicago-bound baggage car and covered quite a distance before being booted off. After getting well thawed out in a roundhouse in company with a half dozen other hoboes, I hopped freights — trying the rods for awhile — and finally landed in Chicago, a well-frozen ham.

The next lap was the home stretch to Louisville. I trudged from Cermak and State streets towards Englewood fifteen miles away. The 'boes had posted me that this latter spot would prove the best chance for making the blinds. First, I stopped at a small tavern at Twenty-second Street. The place was well known to actors. It was a half block from the American Theatre stock company and its free lunch counter was famous. There I spent my last nickel for a small beer and promptly committed assault and battery on the free lunch.

With a slightly mixed provender safely inside me I hiked briskly to Englewood and managed to hop a fast passenger train bound for Louisville.

Grabbing the blinds is a little known art. You must wait until the brakeman has pulled in the coach doors and the train is fast picking up speed. Then you make a desperate leap for the rail handles on either side of the front of the baggage car, which is directly behind the locomotive tender. A slight miscalculation may put you in an unmarked roadside grave. Once aboard, however, and you're safe until the next stop, there being no way for the brakeman to get at you.

Huddled in an exposed blind baggage car with the bitter wind driving icicles clear through you is no picnic. And I had eaten exactly ten cents worth of food in three days.

After about eighty-five miles I was discovered by the brakeman that night at a water stop and unceremoniously kicked off. After hitting the hard-packed earth and cinders there was no resistance left in me. I laid there for some time — so done up that I was just about ready to call the whole thing off and stay there when some hidden reserve hoisted me to my feet and shivered me into a nearby village. After stumbling around the main street (my shoes were tied to my feet with rags), I found a Dutch baker who was just opening his shop in the early morning light. He let me toast my toes in his bake oven. For a few minutes thereafter the baker paid me no attention, but when he looked at me again he gave an astonished shout, "Ach! Gott!" — for I had crawled completely into the warm oven like Service's immortal Sam McGee. The Dutch baker — peace to his ashes — gave me twenty stale doughnuts. Nineteen I ate on the spot, making Louisville on the twentieth.

Years later, I employed this incident in W.C. Fields' *Sally of the Sawdust.*

# ARTHUR KNIGHT
# The Father of Film Technique

*From one of the most widely used film history textbooks, here is a felicitous passage summarizing Griffith's growing confidence and understanding as he learned the possibilities of his new medium. It will be continued later as we observe his departure from Biograph. (Later scholar's note: Schickel believes it was J. Searle Dawley, Porter's assistant at the time, who actually hired Griffith for Edison as an actor.)*

*Knight was on the staff of the Museum of Modern Art film library before becoming motion picture critic for the* Saturday Review of Literature. *In 1962 he was appointed professor of cinema at the University of Southern California and subsequently became a reviewer for the daily* Hollywood Reporter. *Pages 23 to 26 are quoted from his world film history,* The Liveliest Art *(N.Y., Macmillan, 1957, 1978).*

"Lawrence" Griffith had spent a decade barnstorming through the United States, more often than not with shows that folded on the road. He had tried his hand at playwriting, at poetry and, when all else failed, had sold subscriptions to magazines, picked hops in the fields, worked on ships and construction jobs. Christened David

Wark, the fifth child of an impoverished Confederate colonel, Griffith chose to preserve his real name for the success he felt certain would one day come to him. It was as "Lawrence" that he approached Edwin S. Porter at the Edison Studio in the Bronx with his screen adaptation of the opera *Tosca*. Porter rejected the script, but offered Griffith the leading role in a film he was just about to start, *Rescued from an Eagle's Nest* (1907). This was an era in which actors from the legitimate stage viewed the movies with the utmost scorn, and felt that to perform in them was degrading. But Griffith, newly married, needed the money badly. He consented to play in it, at $5 a day. A few months later, armed with more scripts, he turned up at the Biograph Studio at 11 East 14th Street, New York City. He not only sold a few, but again was invited to act. Again, presumably, necessity forced his hand; but within a few months Griffith had become a fixture at Biograph and his wife, Linda Arvidson, had also joined the little company. Griffith, however, was still "Lawrence."

What happened within the next few years is probably without parallel in the emergence of any art form. Between 1908 and 1912 Griffith took the raw elements of movie making as they had evolved up to that time and, singlehanded, wrought from them a medium more intimate than theater, more vivid than literature, more affecting than poetry. He created the art of the film, its language, its syntax. It has often been said that Griffith "invented" the close-up, that he "invented" cutting, the camera angle, or even the last-minute rescue. This, of course, is nonsense. What he did was far more important. He refined these elements, already present in motion pictures, mastered them and made them serve his purpose. He discovered ways to use his camera functionally, developed editing from the crude assembly of unrelated shots into a conscious, artistic device. Apparently to Griffith each new film was a challenge, a chance to experiment, to try out new effects. Certainly, Biograph gave him every opportunity. In his first year there he turned out well over a hundred pictures — more than two a week!

One of his first moves was to break the standard distance maintained between audience and actor by changing the camera's position in midscene. There is no need, he argued, to photograph an entire sequence from a single setup when, by simply shifting to a new vantage point, we can always keep the most significant action in screen center. Pursuing the same line of reasoning, he continued to push the camera ever closer to his players to emphasize a gesture or a reaction. "The public will never buy only half an actor," his employers protested. But the public saw, and understood.

Grasping instinctively the fact that the movies are in reality a form quite apart from theater, Griffith went further still. Why go through all the tedious business of having an actor open a door, step into a room, close the door, then walk to the center of the stage before the significant action begins? He started his scenes instead directly, upon the action itself, and halted them as soon as the action was completed. Again the audiences understood. He became interested in the composition and lighting of his scenes. He discovered that by placing the camera at an angle to the action he could create a greater dynamism than was possible in the conventional head-on shot, that deep shadows and key high-lights — "Rembrandt lighting," he called it — would intensify the mood and heighten the visual impact of his scenes. He edited his own pictures and found that the length of time a shot remained on the screen could create very real psychological tensions in an audience: the shorter the shot, the greater the excitement. As early as 1909 he introduced this principle to build a climax of suspense in *The Lonely Villa*. A trio of thugs are forcing their way into the house. The father has learned by telephone that his wife and children are in danger, and drives frantically to the rescue. The burglars batter on the doors. The mother stands guard over her little brood. By cutting back and forth from one to the other, making each shot shorter than the last, Griffith heightened the excitement of the situation. It was a device he was to use again and again, a device in which time and space were shuffled freely at the will of the director.

Griffith felt his way gradually, ever more sure of himself, ever widening the gap between film technique and stage methods. He worked his actors to and from the camera, devising groupings and compositions which, while meaningless on the three-dimensional stage, proved highly effective on the two-dimensional screen. As he moved his camera closer to the players, he perceived that the theater's eloquent gestures and overemphatic facial expressions became awkward and artificial. He trained his performers in a quieter, more intimate acting style, and developed a host of young people, preferably without previous stage experience, to work in his films. The Griffith "stock company" at Biograph came to include such future luminaries as Mary Pickford, Lillian and Dorothy Gish, Mae Marsh, Mabel Normand, Robert Harron, Owen Moore, Blanche Sweet, Mack Sennett, Arthur Johnson, H.B. Walthall and Lionel Barrymore. Actors who could not follow his direction, actors who persisted in the melodramatic style of gaslit melodrama, either left Biograph or worked with other directors there.

# KARL BROWN
# The Great D. W.

*Sixteen years old when D. W. Griffith moved into the old Kinemacolor
studio in Hollywood, Karl Brown talked himself into a job as assistant
to cameraman Billy Bitzer. "All I require of an assistant is a strong back
and a weak mind," Bitzer told him. But Karl was an eager worker: he
invented a better kind of slate for recording the takes and a cheap way
of combining real waves with miniature ships. He stayed, with raises
in pay, till 1919.*

*Better still, he observed and remembered. When Kevin Brownlow
found out, in 1970, that Brown was still alive, he tracked him down and
got him to write a book.* Adventures With D. W. Griffith *(N.Y., Farrar
Straus Giroux, 1973), turned out to be, in Brownlow's estimation, "the
most vivid, and the most perceptive volume of reminiscence ever published on the cinema." Pages 27-29,14-17,20 show us Griffith's way of
working.*

To me, at my time of life and with my theatrical background,
Griffith was a puzzle to be solved, a challenge to the mind. This
was not because of any precocious gift for character analysis but
a simple, normal desire, shared by teenagers everywhere, to know
what makes the wheels go around. I had known stage directors,
dance directors, musical directors all my conscious life. These had
fallen, to my mind, into three easy categories. There were the
Teachers, who sat and expounded patiently all that was to be said,
done, or conveyed by indirection. According to my father, probably
the best of this class was W.S. Gilbert, who while rehearsing *Iolanthe,*
admonished the chorus girls with, "A little more virginity if you
please, ladies." Then there were the Showers, hams to the bone, who
insisted upon getting up and acting out every part of every player.
And finally, there were the Tyrants, the loud, sarcastic, domineer-
ing slave drivers who could never get through a rehearsal without
going into hysterics at least once. There were of course subcategories
and line-crossing individual directors, but all of them, almost without
exception as far as my observation went, were united in one fixed belief:
that their way was the only way and that no other way would do.

Griffith fell into none of these convenient pigeonholes. He did not
teach or preach, he did not act things out, and strangest of all, he
never knew what he wanted except in a broad general way. Obviously, if the scene called for a confrontation and a fight, there had to

be a confrontation and a fight. But just how the confrontation was to be played and the precise blow-by-blow fight was to be managed were always in question. His idea seemed to be that although he had a vivid mental picture of how that or any other scene should appear on the screen, he realized that there were always physical checks and balances to be overcome if he were merely to approximate the ideal of his imagination. Hence the rehearsals.

These rehearsals were managed in accordance with the tradition of the stage. A bare floor, plenty of kitchen chairs, the cast in street clothes ready for a first run-through. But in Griffith's case, everyone connected with the production was on hand with notebooks and sketch pads to determine the settings, the props, the costumes, and everything else that went into the playing of the picture from first to last, long shots and close-ups, reverse shots and cross-shots, the works.

Everything was played out fully with invisible props and invisible doors, windows, drapes, or whatever. This was easy for the cast. They could simulate anything. But it called for the closest possible attention by the stage crew, from his incredibly capable master carpenter, Frank ("Huck") Wortman, who could build anything Griffith could imagine, down through his equally capable prop man, Ralph DeLacey, to the lowliest of his second, third, fourth, or fifth assistants, who were really errand boys, forever on the run.* His first assistant was the big-bodied, brutal-faced, soft-spoken George Siegmann, whose ferocious appearance concealed a heart of purest mush.

Griffith's direction of these rehearsals was strictly ad lib, off-the-cuff improvisations to see what would work and what would not. He started with a central idea from which the story grew and took shape and came to life through his manipulation of these living characters. It was his way of writing, and a very fine way it was indeed. Instead of working with pen or pencil, or through the mind and artistry of a professional writer, however skilled, he sculptured his thoughts in living flesh, to see and feel and sense what could be achieved and what could not, and to know in advance which scenes would "play" and which would not. This called for a sort of cut-and-try, or trial-and-error procedure. A simple scene, apparently meaningless in itself, possibly a mere "bridge" to carry the story from one phase to another, would be tried two, three, five, or a dozen different ways to settle at last into the one pattern that would work for everyone concerned: camera, setting, lighting, the placing of props, everything. This persistent haggling over trifles brought to mind the famous remark attributed to Da Vinci: "Trifles make perfection, and perfection is no trifle."

These rehearsals were no mere walk-throughs to determine positions. They were fully acted out to the minutest details. Mae Marsh, rehearsing for a picture called *Apple Pie Mary*,** played much of the action in an old-fashioned country kitchen. Here she pared apples from a pan held in her lap. She cut her finger slightly and carried it instinctively to her mouth. Inspected the tiny cut carefully and dismissed it as nothing. Continued paring, becoming tensely eager as she managed to peel one whole apple with a single unbroken skin. She threw it over her shoulder, then inspected the curled-up coil of apple paring to see if it would spell the initial of the one she would someday marry. She mixed dough, rolled crust, fitted pans, held the pans to eye level for trimming with a knife. A pause for discussion. Should she crimp the edges with her thumbs, to make ripples, or with a fork, to make a fluted edge? Decision: thumbs. More like the pies mother used to make.

And so the pie was made ready for the oven. Opens oven door, tests heat with hand. Too cool. Lifts stove lid with an iron handle, looks at fire. Needs wood. Gets wood from wood box at side of stove, forces it into stove. Stick a little too long. Has to wedge it in. Replaces lid, opens grate damper, opens stove-pipe damper. And with all of this conjured up out of empty air, so vividly that you could all but see the stove, the lid, the wood box, the dampers.

She washes smudged hands at an old-fashioned indoor pump beside the sink. Fluffs her hair at a mirror, quite a small one because she has to stoop and bend to see the reflection. Picks up damp cloth to wipe the table where she has been working.

Interruption from DeLacey. "What do you want on that table, Mr. Griffith? Checkered tablecloth or oilcloth?"

"Oilcloth, of course. Didn't you just now see her wipe it?"

Silent retreat by Mr. DeLacey while he resolves to be more observant in future.

These rehearsals, in which everything was not only worked out but *thought* out to the finest detail, told everybody everything about everything. Huck came away knowing exactly what sets to build and how to build them. DeLacey had a clear picture in his mind of everything that would be needed. He could set about ordering the stuff to be sent out at any time. This would call for hunting and rummaging in secondhand shops, pawnshops, or even cellars and attics of old-timers who had such things cluttering their barns and outbuildings. Even Bitzer had ample foreknowledge of the sort of scenes he would have to light, and he could begin to plan how to go about it, what he might need in the way of extra equipment, and everything else.

Sometimes Bitzer would say, "Mr. Griffith, with Miss Marsh crowded into a corner like that we won't be able to see her face."

Griffith never resented intelligent questions. "Let's see, now," he'd answer musingly. "If we see her face, it will be Mae Marsh washing dishes. If we see only her back and arms, it will be every woman in the audience washing dishes. We'll play it with her back to the camera." . . .

The company arrives. The cast in costume, Griffith groomed and tailored to perfection, as always. Apparently vain of his appearance, a holdover from his acting days. He tells Bitzer the setup. Bitzer moves camera to proper position and begins to light the scene. A diffuser pulled back here, another run forward there. White flats angled to catch the sunlight and throw it in from one side of the set. During this, Griffith has taken off his coat and has begun to shadowbox, weaving and bobbing and ducking, dancing forward and back, throwing whole series of left jabs, darting his fist like a rapier as he charges forward at his invisible opponent, his face aglow with the joy of combat. He becomes savage, a killer, throwing whistling rights and deadly left hooks while ducking and blocking a barrage of blows from the Invisible Man . . .

All was ready. Griffith abandoned his athletics to take his seat beside the camera in an ordinary kitchen chair. A rehearsal was run through, more of positions than anything else, because the actors had already been rehearsed and they knew the mood and timing of every scene. Shooting was merely a matter of committing to film what had already been worked out in rehearsal . . .

Late as some of my night chores might be, whenever I had finished and had locked up the camera room for the night, the projection room was always going. We had two projectionists, Billy Fildew and George Teague, who divided the work between them. The projection room was open and ready from eight in the morning until twelve, one, or two, or even longer past midnight if Griffith so desired.

For the projection room was really Griffith's cutting room. Here he would sit, hour after hour, studying scenes he had run dozens of times before. They might be good. Very good indeed. But then again, there might be a way to make them even better, if only he could think of it. Over and over, endlessly over and over . . .

And then I would trudge on home past darkened houses where everyone was asleep, leaving behind the whirring projection room and the man within it, trying to drive his dreams into a corner where he could capture them and show them to the world.

NOTES

* Among these may be listed Joseph Henabery, Erich von Stroheim, Monte Blue, Edward Dillon, W.S. Van Dyke, Tod Browning, Elmer Clifton, and whoever else happened to be handy and not otherwise engaged. They couldn't have chosen a better school in which to learn their trade. (Author)
** The final film was entitled *Home, Sweet Home.* KEVIN BROWNLOW

# TOM GUNNING
# Weaving a Narrative

*From a special issue on Griffith published by the* Quarterly Review of Film Studies *(Winter 1981, pages 17 to 24), here is a fascinating analysis of distinctive varieties of parallel editing in some of the less well known short films made for Biograph. The author says that cross-cutting may be Griffith's chief narrative innovation and he wants to make it clear that creating suspense was only a small part of his usage of it.*

*Gunning has taught film history at Harvard and at the State University of New York at Purchase. With Ron Mottram, he organized a showing of a wide range of Biograph titles for the Museum of Modern Art centennial of Griffith's birth in 1975.*

*A first course in film editing or film production would benefit considerably from close observation of these early Griffith films.*

The history of parallel editing before 1908 still needs to be written. Although isolated examples of it appear before 1908 (particularly in European films), it is extremely rare in American films before Griffith. Further research may reveal that the role of Griffith in making it a common element in film narrative will be his strongest claim as one of the fathers of the narrative film style. In any case, by 1909 Griffith structures parallel editing in such a way that the pattern overrides the unfolding of action within individual shots. In 1908 Griffith had already cut between two threads of actions (from rescuers speeding to save victims from some imminent disaster, such as a lynching about to take place, or a mechanically rigged pistol about to go off) to build suspense. With *The Drive for Life* (1909), Griffith begins to place his edits so that they interrupt the action at a crucial point, in the middle of a gesture. In this film a woman scorned has sent her ex-lover's fiancee a box of poisoned chocolates. The lover finds out and rushes off in a car to warn his fiancee. Griffith cuts from the speeding automobile to the innocent girl at home about to eat the chocolates. At the end of each shot of the fiancee, she is in the middle of an action: holding the chocolate to her lips or opening her mouth. Of course when we cut back to her, she hasn't eaten the chocolate (she is interrupted by her sisters, or drops it, or merely kisses it). Griffith builds suspense, then, not only by cutting away from the dangerous situation, but also by placing his edit at a point where the action is incomplete. The pattern of the editing overrides the natural unfolding of the action. The action's continuity is noticeably interrupted, its unity sliced and its development suspended, by the structure of the shots. One senses, then, the intervention of the storyteller, the manipulator of narrative signs, who directly invokes the audience's participation by withholding — for a moment — the desired information.

Griffith used a structure similar to parallel editing in non-suspense sequences as well. The most famous example of this is in *A Corner in Wheat* (1909). In this film Griffith cuts from the financial gain of the Wheat King to the suffering he causes farmers and the poor. In this case the primary thrust of Griffith's editing is not simultaneity (though that is not ruled out) but contrast (Metz's "parallel syntagm"). This contrast pattern of editing, alternating rich with poor, is found in a number of Griffith's Biograph films. First sketched in *The Song of the Shirt* (1908), it also appears in *The Usurer* (1910), *Gold Is Not All* (1910), and *One Is Business, the Other Is Crime* (1912). The interweaving in these films of rich and poor, exploiters and exploited, is articulated by pairs of shots that sharply contrast. The death of a poverty-stricken woman is cut with bosses eating heartily at a restaurant *(The Song of the Shirt)*; The Wheat King's lavish entertainment is contrasted with poor people unable to buy bread *(A Corner in Wheat)*; a poor couple plays with their children while a rich woman's daughter dies *(Gold Is Not All)*. The intervention here of the storyteller allows the creation of a moral voice, who not only involves the audience in reading the narrative signs — recognizing the contrast — but also instructs them by causing them to draw a moral conclusion.

It is interesting to note that, in *The Usurer*, a 1910 near remake of *A Corner in Wheat*, Griffith combines this contrast pattern with the practice of suspending the outcome of an action by an edit. In one shot we see Henry Walthall as a poor man ruined by the Usurer's greed. He stands alone in his apartment, points a gun to his breast, and shuts his eyes. We cut to the usurer at a lavish party raising his glass. We return to Walthall staggering and falling dead on the floor. The pattern here is very interesting. On the one hand we have the structure, already established in the film, of contrasting the evil joys of the rich with the miseries of the poor. In addition, we have the intensification given by interrupting actions (both the pistol shot and the Usurer's raised glass; in the shot following Walthall's death we return to the usurer as he drinks). The editing pattern (and particularly the ellipses of the actual firing of the gun, which presumably occurs while we see the usurer raise his glass) certainly seems to indicate simultaneity. The edit involves a degree of suspense, but since no rescue is attempted this is not the main effect of the edit. The ironic juxtaposition with its indication of cause and effect becomes the principal meaning. Later in the film, Griffith cuts from the usurer, accidentally locked in his own safe and beginning to suffocate, to Walthall's dead body, underscoring the irony.

In Griffith's later Biograph films, some form of alternating pattern increasingly underlies the narrative form, even in cases that don't involve suspense or contrast. In 1912 and 1913, the first two shots frequently introduce two characters (or two groups of characters) before they have actually met. The characters' stories will be intercut in the opening sections of the film until a scene where they are finally narratively linked. Such interweaving seems to be Griffith's basic narrative schema. Griffith also further articulates its use for dramatic effects. In *A Woman Scorned* (1911), Griffith uses interruption of an action and contrast to accent an act of violence. A doctor (Wilfred Lucas) has been lured to an apartment by a gang of thieves who knock him unconscious. As he falls, we cut on this action to his wife and child at home sitting down to supper. In this shot, the father's empty place at the table is prominent in the left foreground. Although one might be dubious that this is intentional (similar structuring of space across edits in other Biograph films leads me to think that it is), it is worth pointing out that this empty place occupies the same area of the frame that Lucas collapsed into in the previous shot.

Later in the same film, Griffith enhances a contrast edit by presenting two radically opposed but visually similar actions. He cuts from the mother untying her daughter's shoes as she lies on her bed to the thieves tying a gag on Lucas, who is also lying in bed. By this kind of visual rhyming, Griffith develops a visual structure that overlays and articulates the narrative action taking place in the shots themselves. This elaboration of the formal elements of the shots beyond the necessary narrative information is one of the clearest examples of Griffith's tendency to make the storyteller evident to the audience. The act of arranging the narrative information becomes as important as simply conveying it.

During the Biograph period, Griffith's use of patterns of alternating shots takes on several meanings, usually distinguishable from each other, but at points shading into one another, as though not yet moulded into rigid formulas. The meanings of parallel editing patterns become particularly complex when they are used in relation to the psychological development of characters. Very early in his career appears a type of parallel editing based on the thoughts of his characters. Here we can see Griffith using parallel editing to provide one of the most basic *desiderata* of a bourgeois narrative — psychological motivation. By the intercutting of disparate locations and characters within certain narrative contexts, Griffith creates, as it were, a sort of psychological space. Significantly, its first use is in an adaptation of a respected literary source, his 1908 version of Tennyson's *Enoch Arden, After Many Years*.

The intercutting of the faithful wife at home with her distant shipwrecked husband provides one of Griffith's first cuts on action. As the husband on his desert island kisses his wife's locket, we cut back to her standing on her porch, arms outstretched, as if yearning for her absent husband; the splicing together of the gestures metaphorically unites the characters across vast space. Later in the Biograph period, Griffith's editing frequently joins characters separated in space. The vehicle of these connections is often a prayer *(The Fugitive, The Broken Locket, The Last Deal, A Pueblo Legend)*. Many shots of this sort include a token of the absent person, a locket or necklace, which the characters gaze at as they long for reunion *(Rose of Salem Town, The Broken Locket, After Many Years)*. This pattern is often combined not only with an interrupted action (like the kiss in *After Many Years*), but also with a contrast. In *The Fugitive*, for instance, we cut from a mother praying, to her son's death on the battlefield. The defining quality of the parallel editing in these instances is its participation in the characters' desires; the motive for the editing springs form their desire to cross space and join their loved ones. Through the editing their emotional union is stressed along with their physical separation.

There are films in which the expression of an emotional sympathy between separated characters takes on a nearly supernatural overtone. This is especially true in those cuts where the simultaneity of events is stressed. In both *As It Is in Life* (1910) and *In Life's Cycle* (1910), Griffith cuts from a pair of lovers embracing to a male relative of the girl far removed from the scene. The relatives (who in both films disapprove of the girl's lover) suddenly look very disturbed or shiver involuntarily. When we return in the following shot to the couple of *In Life's Cycle*, the girl too suddenly looks upset, as if aware of her brother's distant disapproval.

In *Sunshine Sue* (1910), Griffith expresses this type of emotional connection over distances through composition as well as editing. A beloved daughter (Marion Sunshine) is first introduced playing the piano for her parents. Later in the film she is stranded, penniless, in a big city. Getting a job at a music store, she is preyed upon by the store's manager. Upset, she leans against a piano in the left foreground of the shot and weeps. Griffith cuts to her father in the family parlor looking at a piano (which is associated with the daughter from the first shot) and patting it fondly. Not only do both shots contain pianos, both pianos occupy the left foreground of the frame. Through this edit and the similar arrangement of space in each shot, Griffith transfers the father's caress from the piano to his distant daughter who occupies the same area of the frame in the preceding shot.

Less dramatic than these shots of emotional union, but perhaps more revealing of the psychological meanings Griffith derived from parallel editing, is what I will call the "motive shot." An early example of this kind of editing appears in *A Salvation Army Lass* (1908). A tough (Harry Salter) has scorned his girlfriend's (Florence Lawrence) attempt to dissuade him from joining a burglary with his cronies, and has knocked her down. As he and his gang creep along the edge of a building, he suddenly stops and looks off screen. Griffith cuts to a brief shot of Lawrence still on the ground. In the next shot we return to Salter, who changes his mind about the burglary, hands his gun back to his companions, and leaves the frame. The editing pattern articulates and explains Salter's decision. It splits in two the moment when Salter changes his course of action, interrupting it with a shot of the factor that causes the change. The editing portrays a mental act and supplies a motive for the action ("He thinks of his true love. . . ").

However, it is the double nature of this shot which reveals the still fluid stage in the evolution of film syntax which characterizes Griffith's Biograph films. The shot of Lawrence is not univocally defined as a mental image, released from the objective space and time of the diegesis. The use of parallel editing remains an intervention of the storyteller who "points out" the character's motivation, rather than assigning the shot unambiguously to the subjectivity of the character. Salter's off-screen look could define the shot of Lawrence as an awkward sort of point-of-view shot. Or we could stress the simultaneity of the shot and see it as a strict parallel edit, conveying the information of what is happening to Lawrence as Salter sets off on the burglary. But since it neither offers new narrative information (at most it tells us that Lawrence is *still* lying there), nor develops a suspense situation, its articulation of Salter's decision remains its primary effect.

This three-shot pattern frequently recurs in Griffith's Biograph films to portray a decision by a character. Its appearance in *A Plain Song* (1910) is typical. A girl (Mary Pickford) is leaving her aged parents and running off with a carnival man. At the train station, she sees a group of old people being taken off to the poor house. Struck by the scene, Pickford stands motionless in the foreground. Griffith cuts to her parents at home. We then return to Pickford, still frozen in her previous position. The carnival man approaches with the train tickets, but she turns away from him and runs home. Again the interpolated shot of the parents articulates and motivates a decision. In this case there is no possibility of its being a point-of-view shot. Mary's frozen stance, as if she were in deep thought, also stresses the psychological nature of the shot. We can find the same pattern in *The Sands O'Dee* (1912). Mae Marsh has decided not to keep an arranged meeting with an artist on the beach. She stands motionless by her window. We cut to a shot of the artist wrapped in a shawl, waiting at the beach. We cut back to Mae, who apparently has changed her mind and climbs out her window to keep the assignation.

In both these instances, we must hesitate before we describe the interpolated shot purely as a mental image. Pickford's parents *are* waiting at home for her, and the artist *is* waiting on the beach for Mae. The shot of the artist includes details that Mae could not "imagine," such as his paisley shawl. The shots therefore are also parallel edits to events occurring at the same time. This dual role of expressions of the characters' thoughts and parallel edits to autonomous events shows the still pliable nature of Griffith's film syntax at this point.

Interestingly, in 1913, we find Griffith modifying this pattern, probably in order to present the interpolated shot more unequivocally as a mental image. In the opening of *Death's Marathon* (1913), a clerk (Walter Miller) looks up from his work with a dreamy expression. The next shot begins extremely underexposed and then brightens in a camera-made "fade-in." We see a girl (Blanche Sweet) seated on a bench in a garden facing the camera in a rather static posture (this is her first appearance in the film). The shot fades and we return to Miller, who rouses himself as if to shake off his reverie and return to work. The use of fades and the actionless shot of Sweet seem to signal the shot as Miller's mental image, rather than a parallel edit which indicates that Sweet is sitting in a garden at this precise moment. It is in this way that Griffith presents memories in *The Birth of a Nation,* by a thoughtful look of a character and an interpolated shot bracketed by fades. The fades signal an entrance into another dimension, that of unequivocal mental images. However, even this example is not an unambiguous image of a single character's subjectivity. The three shots from *Death's Marathon* just described are themselves bracketed by two shots of Walthall, who plays a coworker of Miller. Walthall too is in love with Sweet, and this rivalry forms the basic dynamic of the plot. At the end of the first shot of Walthall he pauses. When we return to him after the shots of Miller and Sweet, he too seems to be emerging from a daydream. The shot of Sweet, then, could be interpreted as a shared mental image. Again the pattern seems to be a gesture of the storyteller unwilling to relinquish the authority of the image to the subjectivity of any one character.

Griffith's use of parallel editing in the films at Biograph created not only a narrative form, but a form of narration, a storyteller to tell the story. Through parallel editing Griffith could create suspense by interrupting action and delaying information, make moral judgments, underscore characters' desires, and reveal motivation. All of these techniques fulfilled essential conditions for a new bourgeois narrative form, the rival of theater and the novel. However, the process of fulfilling these demands does not explain away all effects of the technique. The multiple meanings gained from this one technique in different situations show something of its enormous power and far-reaching implications. By breaking the continuity of actions, by composing similarly frames that are separated in space, by interpolating shots in the middle of decisions, Griffith both creates a fissure in the continuity of the narrative and forms a synthesis on a new level. Griffith's editing becomes a noticeable force which suspends, interrupts, and yet knits together actions within his narratives. What is sensed behind this narrative labor is the storyteller. This invisible but sensed hand will reach its apogee in Griffith's commercial disaster *Intolerance.* The "uniter of here and hereafter" will prove an obstacle to much of his audience, a frustration rather than a guide. Already towards the end of his tenure at Biograph the trade journals (which had praised some of his earlier films for their "high class" appeal) were finding his style too disjoined, too brutal, and were complaining about the large number of shots in Biograph films, the disorienting nature of their editing. This kind of dissatisfaction may have had a role in the tension between company executives and Griffith that led to his leaving Biograph in 1913.

Increasingly in the feature era, the storyteller would blend indistinguishably into the unfolding of the action of the narrative, and Griffith's style would be found old-fashioned or clumsy. Writing the history of this process and the many factors that contribute to it — the rise of the studio style as pioneered by Ince, the importance of film stars, and a new economic organization of the film industry — will require a great deal of new research. Griffith's place within that history is complex. But it is clear that Griffith's development of parallel editing during the Biograph years opens a tradition that not only moves toward the invisible editing of the classical Hollywood narrative, but also to (as he was the first to admit) the radical understanding of montage in the films of Sergei Eisenstein.

# FRANK WOODS
# Deliberation and Repose

*Under the heading of 'Spectator's Comments' in the* New York Dramatic Mirror, *Frank Woods offered frequent advice for the emerging movie industry. This column was dated June 4, 1910. Woods was something of a partisan of the Biograph films. He submitted scenarios of his own and before long was hired as head of Biograph's script department. This led him also into a good deal of publicity work, as Karl Brown explains later on.*

*The calmer, more thoughtful sort of acting was not at first Griffith's style. Florence Lawrence, in a January 1915 issue of* Photoplay *(reprinted in Gerald Mast,* The Movies in Our Midst*), complained of being asked in the early days to be "quick and snappy" because film buyers (who paid by the foot) wanted lots of action. As an actor Griffith himself had been criticized for overdoing his physical movements. Evidently the imported French* Films d'Art *encouraged him to have more confidence in naturalness.*

Probably the most marked change that has taken place in the style of picture acting in the last year or two has been in the matter of tempo. In the old days the pictures were literally "moving" pictures, and lively moving at that. Everything had to be on the jump. The more action that could be crowded into each foot of film the more perfect the picture was supposed to be. Some of this manner of picture acting still survives, usually when an old-timer does the acting or directing, but, generally speaking, it has given place to more deliberation. People in the pictures now move about somewhat after the style of human beings, instead of jumping jacks. For all of which let us give due thanks to the special divinity that rules over motion picture affairs.

One producing company, the *Biograph*, was a pioneer among American producers in this reform, and its films have long been distinguished by deliberation and repose, to such an extent that at one time it was a matter of much comment and criticism on the part of those who looked on the innovation as little short of sacrilege. Indeed, it may now be told as a matter worthy of record that the Biograph's first experiments along this line were undertaken with no little hesitation and fearsome doubt. Those having the responsibility for the change felt that they were treading on thin ice. So deeply rooted was the notion that speed was the thing that the experimenters were fearful that their attempts to introduce real acting into the films would be met with derisive laughter. Possibly to their astonishment the change at once met with the approval of the public. The people who paid their money to look at the pictures applauded the new idea (new in American pictures), and from that moment the habit commenced to grow, and has kept on growing ever since.

There is good reason why the public approves of slow acting without itself knowing or realizing why. The spectator who is reading the story by the action of the picture is better able to understand the things that are going on when the acting is properly timed. The slow, impressive, and deliberate speaker is always more effective as an orator than the rapid-fire talker. Even the successful actor or popular singer is obliged to make himself understood, and the actor employs both speech and acting. The same rule applies to picture acting, with this difference, that in the pictures the action alone must tell the story; there are no spoken words to aid in conveying the idea. The public is not rapid in comprehension, as a general rule. We have only to remember how slow many people often are to see the point of an obvious joke when it is told to them from the stage to understand the truth of this statement. It is not strange, therefore, that spectators generally prefer deliberation in picture acting.

How far can and should this matter of deliberation and repose be carried in motion picture work? Again we find the answer in the one rule: Be natural. Let there be as much deliberation as the character of the action will naturally permit. Any more deliberation is ridiculous; any less is tempting failure. It is the mark of the good director to know just how far he can go in this direction. Some of them — one in particular that this writer has in mind — very often go to the limit in seeking for effective deliberation, but the one referred to seldom if ever goes too far, although to some people there may be times when he appears to do so. But excessive deliberation is not a matter that can be safely handled by novices or by those who are not sure of their ability to master the situation. It requires rare skill and delicacy of feeling to avoid overstepping the limit and to get just the proper degree of deliberation for the most impressive effect. Unless perfectly sure of himself, the average actor and director would do well to steer his craft by the signal light already pointed out: Be natural. Small boats should sail close to shore . . . .

# LEWIS JACOBS
# Griffith Leaves Biograph

*From Jacobs' landmark history,* The Rise of the American Film *(N.Y., Harcourt Brace, 1939), here is a lively section (pages 109-118) of one of the chapters on Griffith. He is making a special effort to get inside the directing experience. First he suggests that Griffith found it exhilarating to use California architecture and topography as aesthetic building blocks for his narrative. Jacobs, ever the montage enthusiast, says he was learnng that "guiding the camera, even more than directing the actor" is the basis of cinema, that "the unit of the film art is the shot." Then he traces Griffith's efforts to expand the importance and length of his productions, which brought him into conflict with his Biograph bosses and finally led him to quit.*

About this time California had become the mecca of the independent movie makers. Griffith, seeing the pictures made there, was impressed with the landscapes and pictorial possibilities the state offered. Upon investigation he learned that not only mountains and beaches but historic missions, tropical vegetation, and deserts were easily accessible. His love for the picturesque, his eye for the sweep of scenery and his enthusiasm for "artistic" backgrounds, urged him to leave New York and go West. Weather conditions, moreover, always a serious problem in the East, seemed better in California: they would help him to meet his expanded production schedule.

In the winter of 1910 Griffith took his company of Biograph players to California, and on the outskirts of Los Angeles he improvised a studio. Wanting for his initial production a theme that would impress the Biograph office back in New York, he wrote a religious story about the old San Gabriel Mission. This film, *The Thread of Destiny*, proved notable for three reasons. It featured Mary Pickford; it employed a new lighting effect that was both "dim" and "religious"; and, most important, its editing demonstrated conclusively that the shot is the basis of scene construction.

Griffith desired to imbue the film with as much of the Mission atmosphere as possible. He photographed the Mission in great detail, with its weatherbeaten walls, decorative interiors, stairways, choir loft, and cemetery-shots which were not called for in the plot but which, when carefully edited, created an atmosphere and background that greatly reinforced the narrative and action of the story. No one, not even Griffith himself, had as yet taken shots of the various details of a setting to build a scene. Any shot which did not present a major phase of the scene's action had always been regarded as impeding, even intruding upon, the flow of the story; it was "a waste of footage" in the usual one-reel film. Griffith's realization that the details of a background could not only enhance a scene's mood and strengthen its action, but could also be basic in a scene's construction, was a daring step forward in the refinement of movie technique.

It was now clear to Griffith that the director must use the camera not only to take the total content of a scene, but to select details within the scene that bear relations to the content of the film as a whole. This meant that a shot need not be regulated and restricted by an imaginary proscenium: freed from this spatial bondage, the camera could be stationed at any point, according to the director's desire to select details and angles of the content that would lend strength to a scene's structure and intensify its interest. This liberty to direct attention to a vital element of a scene, to vary time and space relationships for the sake of emphasis or contrast, gave the director a powerful means of stimulating the spectator's responses. Griffith suddenly understood how the art of the movie director differs from that of the stage director: in movie making, guiding the camera, even more than directing the actor, is the trick.

Acceptance of this new principle meant that hereafter the screen story would have to be conceived from a new point of view. Griffith had hit upon a truth with implications that all motion picture directors since then have been trying to command. It is that the primary tools of the screen medium are the camera and the film rather than the actor; that the subject matter must be conceived in terms of the camera's eye and film cutting; that the unit of the film art is the shot; that manipulation of the shots builds the scene; that the continuity of scenes builds the sequences; and that the progression of sequences composes the totality of the production. Upon the composition of this interplay of shots, scenes, and sequences depends the clarity and vigor of the story. Here, Griffith saw, is the epitome of motion picture method.

Working under commercial pressure, producing pictures at a steady pace in California throughout the winter of 1910, Griffith strove to apply what he had divined about camera composition, lighting, shot details, scene construction, transitions, and other phases of film technique. He constantly tried, moreover, to weld these elements into a personal style. The pictures he turned out during this period were *The Converts, The Way of the World,* and *The Two Brothers,* utilizing the missions and topography of California; semi-historical pieces such as *In Old California, Love Among the Roses, The Romance of the Western Hills;* and *Ramona,* romanticizing Dons, Senoritas, and Indians.

*Ramona* provoked the most public excitement. For the privilege of adapting it Griffith had paid $100, an extraordinary sum for a story in those days. Biograph issued a specially illustrated folder which declared proudly that *Ramona* was the most expensive picture ever made. In this film appeared what Griffith subsequently was to call "the extreme long shots." These were shots of vast, distant panoramas and were intended to emphasize the spaciousness of the scene as a dramatic foil to the close shots.

*Ramona* was followed by a series of film sermons told in the idiom of the day: *Gold Is Not All, Over Silent Paths, The Gold Seekers, Unexpected Help, A Rich Revenge, As It Is in Life,* and *The Unchanging Sea.* The last is remembered as the "first masterpiece" of Griffith's West Coast series.

Returning to New York in the spring, Griffith set himself to work so industriously that Biograph's president, Arthur Marvin sighed, "He'll die working." Besides editing his Western-made pictures, Griffith kept up with a production schedule more ambitious than ever. *In the Season of Buds, A Child of the Ghetto, What the Daisy Said, The House with the Closed Shutters, The Sorrows of the Unfaithful, The Call to Arms,* and *The Usurer* led a colorful array of dramas too numerous to list. The hard-working director's activity was constantly spurred by the increased attention of the trade papers to his pictures. The growing demand of exhibitors for Biograph products, and the new phenomenon of fan letters singling out Griffith's pictures for praise indicated his increasing ability to outshine his contemporaries.

In the summer of this year Griffith signed his third contract with Biograph. This contract stipulated the relatively high salary of $75 per week and one-eighth of a cent per foot royalty on all films sold. What made this agreement significant for Griffith was not so much the raise, however, as the fact that in it he abandoned his pseudonym "Lawrence" and for the first time used his real name, David. At last he was wholeheartedly accepting his career. From now on he was to work under his own colors. Happy over his decision, he set his face toward future accomplishments.

In 1911, again in California, Griffith produced *The Last Drop of Water*, *Crossing the American Prairies in the Early Fifties*, *The Lonedale Operator*, *The White Rose of the Wilds*, and *The Battle of Elderbush Gulch*, the last being released under the shortened title *The Battle*. All these films were distinguished from the general run of contemporary pictures by their content, careful attention to detail, and freshness of treatment. But in these pictures Griffith was seeking to master something new: movement of the action. Without knowing it, all he had discovered thus far had been an approach to it. Now he set about deliberately to create it by all the means he knew, and in *The Lonedale Operator* he was most successful. This was the usual last-minute rescue type of story, stemming from *The Lonely Villa*. A girl held captive in a train depot telegraphs her father and sweetheart, railroad men, for help, and they commandeer a train and speed to her rescue. In filming the scenes Griffith seized every opportunity for emphasizing movement. Not only was there action with the shot, but the camera itself moved — not as in a pan shot, but by being placed on the moving train. The cutting back and forth from the speeding train to the captive gave momentum to the whole. The fluency of action which Griffith achieved by these devices brought a new kinetic quality to the screen.

Now Griffith began to chafe under the arbitrary limitation of a picture to one reel. One reel was hardly adequate to unfold a complete story; the limitation hindered development, curtailed incidents, and proved a general barrier to the choice of deeper themes. If the movie was ever to become a vital medium, reasoned Griffith, its length would have to be increased. But just as Porter in 1903 had

had to convince his doubting employers that the public would sit through a picture a full reel in length, Griffith now had to struggle with Biograph's reluctance to lengthening films to two reels. Finally disregarding protests, he made a two-reel picture, another version of the story which had already proved successful in one reel, *Enoch Arden*. Biograph refused to release the film as a whole; it was sold in two parts. But the movie audiences, unsatisfied after viewing only one reel, forced exhibitors to obtain both reels and show them one after the other. Biograph in turn had to comply with the requests of the exhibitors, and so the two-reel film was introduced.

The American two-reeler appeared none too soon, for almost immediately afterward two-reelers from European studios appeared. Their reception by audiences was anxiously watched by American producers. So enthusiastic was it that by 1912 two- and even three-reelers were acknowledged by the trade as inevitable.

Now allowed to expand his stories whenever he felt that they demanded more length, early in 1912 Griffith made two films which, for size and content, were his most ambitious efforts up to that time. Unlike any of his previous pictures, the first of these, *Man's Genesis*, was produced by a definite esthetic urge, not a commercial one. The seriousness of its theme, "a psychological study founded upon the Darwinian Theory of the Evolution of Man," indicated Griffith's lack of concern for so-called entertainment values and his desire to do something "worth-while." Needless to say, his employers were strongly opposed to the undertaking.

The philosophical and scientific aspects of the theme were dramatized in the conflict between the intelligence of "Weak-hands" and the body of "Brute-force." In the struggle brain finally conquers brawn. Though the film seems naive to us today, it was then considered very advanced. The picture turned out to be one of the most discussed films of the year, provoking Vachel Lindsay to declare in his book *The Art of the Moving Picture:*

> It is a Griffith masterpiece, and every actor does sound work. The audience, mechanical Americans, fond of crawling on their stomachs to tinker their automobiles, are eager over the evolution of the first weapon from a stick to a hammer. They are as full of curiosity as they could well be over the history of Langley or the Wright Brothers.

Griffith's intuitive choice of such a serious subject was proved sound, for it inspired deeper respect for the screen among those who had been wont to scoff.

Encouraged by this response, Griffith next ventured an ambitious historical re-creation of Custer's last stand, called *The Massacre*. Like *Man's Genesis*, this film was to be more than another program picture. Griffith went far beyond his budget in the production, paying no attention to the pained protests from Biograph's Eastern offices: he was determined to turn out a film greater than any he had yet done. With its casts, costumes, and sets on an unprecedentedly lavish scale, with its "hundreds of cavalrymen and twice as many Indians," the production forced Griffith to reach a new high in his series of technical triumphs. The film abounded in mass scenes, detailed shots of close fighting, vast panoramic pan shots, all skillfully blended and given a rapid continuity in a manner that presaged his later style in *The Birth of a Nation*. *The Massacre* was, in a sense, America's first spectacle film; for Griffith it was the beginning of a new and profounder turn of his talents.

But before the picture was released the American film world was disconcerted by a sudden and unexpected influx of European pictures of such dimensions that everything which had preceded them faded into insignificance. These foreign pictures, three, four, and even five reels in length, elaborately produced, with classics for subject matter, and starring such world-famed figures as Sarah Bernhardt, Helen Gardner, Asta Nielsen, Mme. Réjane, stirred America deeply. *Queen Elizabeth, Camille, Cleopatra, Gypsy Blood, Mme. Sans Gene*, in their length and power of conception, dwarfed contemporary American productions. The American companies, particularly those in the motion picture patents-trust group, regarded the invasion with mixed feelings of contempt and jealousy. Trade papers uneasily exhorted American producers to oust the foreigners. The aloof legitimate theatre itself turned a fearful eye upon these new threats of celluloid. But the climax came with the startling announcement that a young arcade and nickelodeon upstart, Adolph Zukor, had signed a contract to feature "Famous Players in Famous Plays," all to run the foolhardy length of four reels. The industry was aghast.

In the midst of this excitement Griffith's *The Massacre* was released. Much to Griffith's chagrin, it was overlooked. Other events of momentous meaning had caught the attention of the movie world; in some quarters the anxiety over the rising popularity of long features, the foreign productions, and Zukor's Famous Players verged on hysteria. Everyone was wondering and fearing what would happen next. Griffith himself wanted to return to New York to view the foreign "miracles," but Biograph's winter production schedule kept him in California.

Smarting with the realization that foreign producers had thrust him into the background, Griffith set to work angrily on the production of what he called his masterpiece, *Mother Love*. His impatient disregard of time and money threw Biograph into a panic, but he insisted on his way: this new film was to be his answer to the European invaders. His entire personnel sensed his anxiety; they worked like demons, hoping to make the production come up to Griffith's expectations. But their industry was in vain. Like *The Massacre, Mother Love* was scarcely acknowledged in the sweeping course of events. Even before the picture was completed, word reached Griffith of a new sensation, the Italian picture *Quo Vadis*, by far the most elaborate and best picture made to date. The news was a shock to Griffith: twice now, with staggering suddenness and finality, he had been outclassed.

His ambition reinforced by intense envy, Griffith now resolutely planned a reprisal that would force the world to acknowledge his supremacy. His new production would be of such dimensions as the world had never seen. To prevent rumors of his vast undertaking from spreading to the rest of the industry, he took his company to the town of Chatsworth, miles from the Los Angeles picture center. Not unnaturally, everyone working with Griffith was highly curious. What was he up to? Never before had he taken so many shots or been so exacting; never before had there been so much activity and so little known of its nature. He was rehearsing scenes over and over again, photographing and rephotographing unceasingly. How many pictures was he making, anyhow? What had inspired his new meticulous firmness? What was he driving at? Why was he so secretive? But to all questions Griffith maintained an unbroken reserve. Bitterness and envy rankled deep in him. His only concern was to achieve a triumph so outstanding that every movie ever seen before would, in comparison, seem like trash.

Finally in 1913 the secret production was completed: the first American four-reel picture, *Judith of Bethulia*. And once again the coincidence of events interfered with Griffith's hopes for an overwhelming success. *Judith of Bethulia* was not released until almost a year after its completion, when, ironically enough, Griffith had already forgotten it in an undertaking of far greater consequence.

As it turned out, *Judith of Bethulia* became Griffith's Biograph swan song. When it did appear in 1914, it proved to be an extravagant treatment of the Bible story rewritten by Thomas Bailey

Aldrich, and without question the ablest example of movie construction to date. Though it appeared too late to overshadow *Quo Vadis*, it was a far better film. Even if Griffith had done nothing further than *Judith of Bethulia*, he would still be considered a sensitive and outstanding craftsman. A comparison of the usual puny American film of 1913 with the opulent and vigorous *Judith of Bethulia* proves Griffith's stature conclusively.

The unusual form of *Judith of Bethulia*, modeled on the fourpart pattern of Griffith's earlier *Pippa Passes*, presaged the form of Griffith's future masterpiece, *Intolerance*. The four movements were in counterpoint not unlike a musical composition; they reacted to each other simultaneously, and the combination produced a cumulative, powerful effect. The individual episodes had a tight internal structure. The imagery was not only lavish in detail but fresh in camera treatment and enhanced by expert cutting.

The picture was produced in a deliberate effort to surpass the splendors of the Italian spectacle *Quo Vadis*, which, in fact, Griffith himself had not seen. *Judith of Bethulia* was crammed with colorful mass scenes and tremendous sets in a style that was later to be embraced by other American directors, notably Cecil B. DeMille. Such episodes as the storming of the walls of Bethulia, the chariot charges, and the destruction of the Assyrian's camp by fire "out-spectacled" any movie yet produced in America.

Satisfied with his completed achievement, Griffith returned to New York to learn that Biograph, now in a new and modern studio in the Bronx, had contracted with the theatrical firm of Klaw and Erlanger to film their successful stage plays after the policy introduced by Zukor. During Griffith's absence a new tempo had been felt in the industry; the air was full of exciting predictions that the stage and the screen were henceforth to work together. European features had made America conscious of her own movie and stage talent and had started a craze for stage names and plays. All the Eastern companies were negotiating for stage alliances.

Griffith was now notified by Biograph that, because of his reckless extravagance with *Judith of Bethulia*, he would in the future supervise production instead of direct. Angered at his employers, bitter at being misunderstood, envious of the acclaim given the foreign pictures, Griffith decided to leave Biograph. He saw in a new company, Majestic-Reliance (Mutual), the opportunity to carry out a fresh and a more elaborate artistic offensive.

After getting his bearings and studying the foreign pictures for a time, he dramatically announced his break with Biograph. The announcement, listing all his technical discoveries, appeared as a full-

A rare photograph of Thomas H. Ince, evidently giving make-up instructions to a cowboy actor in his costume department.

Fritz and friend, William S. Hart. [Photos from Academy of Motion Picture Arts and Sciences.]

Portrait of Ince in studio advertising. [Motion Picture News Studio Directory 1918.]

"Victims of the black mobs" after the war, according to *The Birth of a Nation*. [Frame enlargement.]

The Ku Klux Klan rides to battle. [Marc Wanamaker Bison Archives.]

The great gate of Babylon in *Intolerance*. (AMPAS photo.)

**D.W. Griffith directing *The Birth of a Nation*.** [Bison Archives.]

**The Babylon palace in *Intolerance*.** [Eastman House photo.]

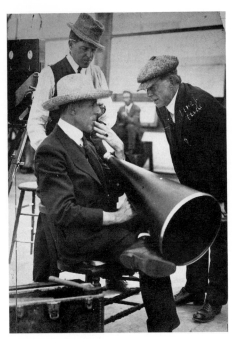

Billy Bitzer, photographer, and Frank Woods, scenario editor, with D.W. Griffith. [Wisconsin Center for Film and Theater Research.]

Stars of the Triangle Film Corporation: First row, Douglas Fairbanks, Bessie Love, Constance Talmadge, Constance Collier, Lillian Gish, Fay Tincher, DeWolfe Hopper. Second row, Robert Harron, Harry Aitken, Sir Herbert Tree, Oliver Moore, Wilfred Lucas. Third row, Dorothy Gish, Seena Owen, Norma Talmadge. [Marc Wanamaker Bison Archives.]

Richard Barthelmess and Lillian Gish in *Broken Blossoms*. [From Academy of Motion Picture Arts and Sciences.]

A recently discovered photo: Griffith appears to be directing Bitzer and Josephine Crowell while Erich von Stroheim checks a soldier's cap. [Bison Archives.]

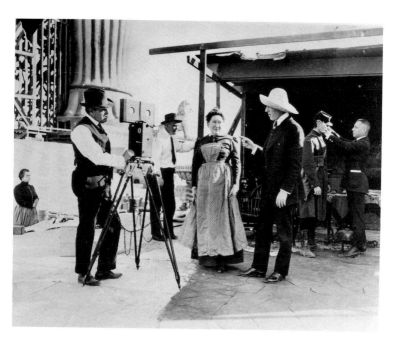

Griffith's own studio at Mamaroneck, N.Y., former estate of a Standard Oil executive.

Scenes of the French revolution for *Orphans of the Storm* were produced at his studio.

Griffith directed W.C. Fields and Carol Dempster in *Sally of
the Sawdust*. [Marc Wanamaker Bison Archives.]

Lillian Gish as *True Heart Susie*
determines to give up her cow.

Erich von Stroheim at the camera. . . .
and in uniform as Count Karamzin in
*Foolish Wives*. [Bison Archives.] **Zasu
Pitts** sleeping on her precious gold
pieces in *Greed*. [AMPAS photo.]

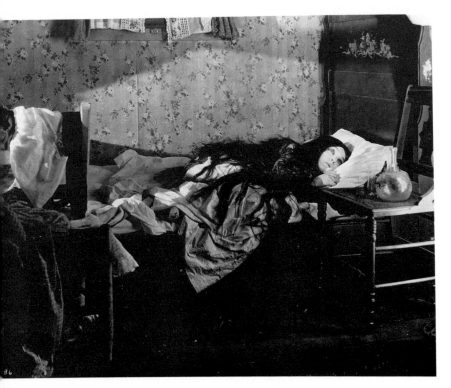

page advertisement in *The New York Dramatic Mirror* for December 31, 1913. On October 29 the trade papers had already broken the news that Griffith was henceforth to be with Mutual Movies, and they had heralded a new era for the "Belasco of the Screen." The advertisement in *The New York Dramatic Mirror* confirmed what in October had been thought to be a mere rumor.

## LILLIAN GISH
# Planning *The Birth of a Nation*

*More on Griffith's way of working, this time from the point of view of his finest actress. Griffith often tried to get more out of people by putting them in competition with one another. Yet it's hard to imagine Lillian Gish, so generous, studious, and self-contained, ever fighting for a role. The way she writes about being chosen is singularly objective, and in general her autobiography reflects respect for others and for the medium of film. The Movies, Mr. Griffith, and Me (Englewood Cliffs, N.J., Prentice-Hall, 1969) was written with Ann Pinchot. These pages, 131-133, should make readers want to savor more of it.*

One afternoon during the spring of 1914, while we were still working in California, Mr. Griffith took me aside on the set and said in an undertone, "After the others leave tonight, would you please stay."

Later, as some of the company drifted out, I realized that a similar message had been given to a few others. This procedure was typical of Mr. Griffith when he was planning a new film. He observed us with a smile, amused perhaps by our curiosity over the mystery that he had created.

I suspected what the meeting was about. A few days before, we had been having lunch at The White Kitchen, and I had noticed that his pockets were crammed with papers and pamphlets. My curiosity was aroused, but it would have been presumptuous of me to ask about them. With Mr. Griffith one did not ask; one only answered. Besides, I had learned that if I waited long enough he would tell me.

"I've bought a book by Thomas Dixon, called *The Clansman*. I'm going to use it to tell the truth about the War between the States. It hasn't been told accurately in history books. Only the winning side in a war ever gets to tell its story." He paused, watching the cluster of actors: Henry Walthall, Spottiswoode Aiken, Bobby

Harron, Mae Marsh, Miriam Cooper, Elmer Clifton, George Siegmann, Walter Long, and me.

"The story concerns two families — the Stonemans from the North and the Camerons from the South." He added significantly, "I know I can trust you."

He swore us to secrecy, and to us his caution was understandable. Should his competitors learn of his new project, they would have films on the same subject completed before his work was released. He discussed his story plots freely only over lunch or dinner, often testing them out on me because I was close-mouthed and never repeated what anyone told me.

I heard later that "Daddy" Woods had called Mr. Griffith's attention to *The Clansman*. It had done well as a book and even better as a play, touring the country for five years. Mr. Griffith also drew on *The Leopard's Spots* for additional material for the new movie. Thomas Dixon, the author of both works, was a southerner who had been a college classmate of Woodrow Wilson. Mr. Griffith paid a $2,500 option for *The Clansman*, and it was agreed that Dixon was to receive $10,000 in all for the story, but when it came time to pay him no more money was available. In the end, he reluctantly agreed to accept instead of cash a 25 per cent interest in the picture, which resulted in the largest sum any author received for a motion-picture story. Dixon earned several million dollars as his share.

Mr. Griffith didn't need the Dixon book. His intention was to tell his version of the War between the States. But he evidently lacked the confidence to start production on a twelve-reel film without an established book as a basis for his story. After the film was completed and he had shown it to the so-called author, Dixon said: "This isn't my book at all." But Mr. Griffith was glad to use Dixon's name on the film as author, for, he told me, "The public hates you if it thinks you wrote, directed, and produced the entire film yourself. It's the quickest way to make enemies."

After the first rehearsal, the pace increased. Mr. Griffith worked, as usual, without a script. But this time his pockets bulged with books, maps, and pamphlets, which he read during meals and the rare breaks in his hectic schedule. I rehearsed whatever part Mr. Griffith wanted to see at the moment. My sister and I had been the last to join the company, and we naturally supposed that the major assignments would go to the older members of the group. For a while, it looked as if I would be no more than an extra. But during one rehearsal Blanche Sweet, who we suspected would play the romantic part of Elsie Stoneman, was missing. Mr. Griffith pointed to me.

"Come on, Miss Damnyankee, let's see what you can do with Elsie."

My thin figure was quite a contrast to Blanche's ripe, full form. Mr. Griffith had us rehearse the near-rape scene between Elsie and Silas Lynch, the power-drunk mulatto in the film. George Siegmann was playing Lynch in blackface. In this scene Lynch proposes to Elsie and, when she rebuffs him, forces his attentions on her. During the hysterical chase around the room, the hairpins flew out of my hair, which tumbled below my waist as Lynch held my fainting body in his arms. I was very blonde and fragile-looking. The contrast with the dark man evidently pleased Mr. Griffith, for he said in front of everyone, "Maybe she would be more effective than the more mature figure I had in mind."

He didn't tell us then, but I think the role was mine from that moment.

At first I didn't pay much attention to Mr. Griffith's concept of the film. His claim that history books falsified actual happenings struck me as most peculiar. At that time I was too naive to think that history books would attempt to falsify anything. I've lived long enough now to know that the whole truth is never told in history texts. Only the people who lived through an era, who are the real participants in the drama as it occurs, know the truth. The people of each generation, it seems to me, are the most accurate historians of their time.

Soon sets were going up; costumes arrived; and mysterious crates, evidently filled with military equipment, were delivered. As we gradually became aware of the magnitude of the new project, we grew even more anxious than usual about being assigned roles in the film. All the young players wanted to prove their worth before it was too late. This distress from young girls in their teens may seem strange today, but the photography of that time aged one so drastically that we believed that by the time we reached eighteen we would be playing character roles.

# ARTHUR KNIGHT
## *The Birth of a Nation*

*Continuing his analysis of Griffith's development of the screen's visual aspects, Knight gives us a compact index of some of the memorable scenes in his epic story of the Civil War. (Pages 27-31,* The Liveliest Art.*)*

Leaving Biograph, Griffith — now at last David Wark Griffith — joined the Mutual Company and supervised for them a number of five-reel features, potboilers that, for the most part, reveal all too clearly Griffith's essential lack of interest. For during this period Griffith was gathering together his resources to tackle a subject so great, so ambitious and daring as to astonish the imagination. He had read Thomas Dixon's novel *The Clansman*, a story of the Civil War and the Reconstruction period that followed, a story of the rise of the Ku Klux Klan. Being a Southerner, the son of a Confederate officer, Griffith was drawn instinctively to its theme. But his film sense responded even more strongly to the sweep and melodramatic power of the novel — a little family ruined by the war, then fighting to preserve its integrity amidst carpetbaggers and renegade Negroes. He flung himself into the production, poured into it all his own finances and those of his friends. Working without a scenario, he devised new, unheard-of effects — battle scenes photographed in extreme long-shot and reminiscent of the Brady Civil War photographs, action shots taken in extreme close-up, the climactic ride of the Clans photographed with the camera mounted low on the back of a moving truck. He drew on all the known resources of the camera and invented still more — the iris, the mask, the vignette, split-screen and triple split-screen shots. He worked out every action, every gesture for the principals in his huge cast. He mustered all his knowledge of editing to impart fluency and mounting tension to the scenes that poured from Bitzer's camera. The result was a film of extraordinary eloquence and power, *The Birth of a Nation*.

Released early in 1915, *The Birth of a Nation* took its audiences by storm. Twelve reels long (almost three hours), with a special score performed by a full symphony orchestra, it swept along with a cumulative force that a present-day viewing of the film can only par-

tially suggest. There simply had never been a picture like this before; "like writing history in lightning," Woodrow Wilson described it. The passions it aroused, the tensions it created lasted beyond the theater. They overflowed into the streets, and race riots and mob action followed in the wake of its presentation in many cities. But whether loved or hated, *The Birth of a Nation* established once and for all that the film was an art in its own right — and Griffith was its master.

Even today, after more than forty years, the strengths of this remarkable film are still apparent — the characterization through vivid symbol, the epic swelling of its first act from scenes of warm intimacy to the broad panorama of battle, then closing quietly on the Little Colonel's return to his ravaged home; the fevered melodrama of its second half dominated by the sweeping ride of the Clans. Individual scenes reveal still more clearly Griffith's sure instinct for the perfect film image. Incomparable is his portrayal of Sherman's vengeful march to the sea. Beginning with a tight iris shot of weeping women and children huddled together high on a hill, as the iris opens out to fill the screen the camera pans to the right, to an extreme long-shot of Sherman's army far below spreading destruction through the countryside. Individual shots depict the pillage, the burning, the slaughter. The sequence ends with a closing iris glimpse of the tearful women on the hill. The ruthless devastation of war is made poignant by relating it to the innocents who suffer. Again, in a scene that still seems breathtakingly daring, Griffith intercuts shots of the old people at home on their knees in prayer with cold, pitiless glimpses of trenches piled high with corpses frozen in the agony of death. The realism of the scene in the Union hospital, the painstaking authenticity of the reconstruction of Lincoln's assassination, the heart-warming moment of the homecoming, the virtuoso cutting from the wild ride of the Clansmen to the besieged family in a squalid cabin — these are passages of pure film that rank among the greatest in all motion-picture history.

What makes *The Birth of a Nation* difficult to view today is precisely what touched off the controversy that raged about the film in 1915 — its use of Negro stereotypes and its sympathetic account of the rise of the Klan. Griffith seems to have been genuinely shocked at the charges of anti-Negro bias leveled against him on all sides when the film appeared, and not without reason. One has only to read *The Clansman*, on which it was based, to become aware of the pains that Griffith had taken to eliminate from his version the rabid hatred that seethes through Thomas Dixon's book. But Griffith was a Southerner, brought up in an embittered, impoverished household.

His father had been a colonel in the Confederacy, and Griffith grew up hearing tales of the good old days before the war. He balanced his renegade Negroes and vengeful mulattoes with happy, faithful "darkies," and thought he was being fair. He could never comprehend that to many one stereotype was as repugnant as the other. Set against this, such minor blemishes as Griffith's eternally twittering young girls and a painfully poetic epilogue depicting the arrival of universal brotherhood pale into insignificance. But perhaps the true measure of this film is to be found in the very depth of the passions it aroused. Certainly, not for another ten years was there to be a movie capable of affecting its audiences so profoundly.

# KARL BROWN
# The Proof of the Pudding

> *We're back with Brown again, now a veteran Bitzer assistant but still a teenager, approaching with misgivings the Los Angeles premiere of* The Clansman (Adventures With D. W. Griffith *pages 86-89, 91-96.) He finds it is not "just another movie." His eyewitness account, though written many years later, is unique, graphic, and revealing. The stamping, yelling crowd showed not only the power of the film but the power of its racist message.*

Frank Woods knew absolutely everybody worth knowing and a good many that were not. A printer and newspaperman himself, and keenly aware of the power of the press, he entertained mostly newspapermen and columnists, writers and editors, some of whom were his oldest cronies, like Bob Davis and Ben De Casseres, with whom he cut up old touches about the care and feeding of authors like O. Henry, the most popular and the most difficult writer of the day. And of course little words, little stories, little human-interest anecdotes, delivered in Frank Woods's inimitable manner, somehow found their way into the conversation, with the result that Griffith was ceasing to be a man and was rapidly becoming a legend.

Not that he lied or misrepresented even by inference. Frank Woods was incapable of deceit or misrepresentation. He told the absolute truth at all times, but he told it with such art and such gusto that the truth became entertainment at its best, which is an art that almost surpasses art. For, as everyone knows, nothing is so unreasonable as the truth, and it's a rare personage who can make the truth believable.

It was probably Frank Woods's doing that had the picture world waiting and counting the days for the first glimpse of Griffith's most ambitious effort to date, the showing of *The Clansman* at Clune's Auditorium.

It was a packed house, with swarms of people standing around outside, hoping for cancellations so they could get in anywhere at all, even in the top gallery. I never saw or felt such eager anticipation in any crowd as there was at that opening night. We three, my father, my mother, and I, had been given choice seats saved for us by Frank Woods. My parents, old-stagers at the business of opening nights, were all keyed up to a state of high tension, while I — well, I was feeling a little sick because *I* knew what the picture really was, just another Biograph, only four times as long. I simply couldn't help feeling that it had been a tragic mistake to build up such a fever pitch of eager anticipation, only to let them down by showing them what was bound to be just another movie. Only longer, much longer, three hours longer. What audience, however friendly, could possibly sit through that much of nothing but one long, one very long movie of the kind they had seen a hundred times before?

My first inkling that this was not to be just another movie came when I heard, over the babble of the crowd, the familiar sound of a great orchestra tuning up. First the oboe sounding A, then the others joining to produce an ever-changing medley of unrelated sounds, with each instrument testing its own strength and capability through this warming-up preliminary. Then the orchestra came creeping in through that little doorway under the proscenium apron and I tried to count them. Impossible. Too many. But there were at least seventy, for that's where I lost count, so most if not all of the Los Angeles Symphony orchestra had been hired to "play" the picture.

Not that I hadn't known about a special score having been prepared for the production. Joseph Carl Breil had been around the studio a lot, talking with Griffith, so I knew what was up. But Carl Breil was no Beethoven. Thus far he had produced only one song, "The Song of the Soul," which had become a great favorite among those who like that kind of music, but he was no great shakes as a composer in the grand manner. Oh, he was capable enough in his own limited way. He *was* a musician, there was no denying that. He could arrange, he was good at instrumentation, and he could conduct. He could do just about anything known to music except think up tunes. Well, maybe Griffith had supplied that lack. We'd soon find out, because the orchestra pit was crammed to overflowing with the finest performers in Los Angeles and more, many more instruments of different kinds than I had seen anywhere before except at full-dress, all-out symphony concerts. He had the big doghouses, as we called the double basses, and a lot of little doghouses, as the cellos were called, with as many fiddles as there was room for and enough brass to make up a full brass band all by itself. And as for the kitchen, or hardware shop, as the drum section was called, there was everything known to percussion, while at the console of the massive pipe organ sat a little man lost in a maze of stops and manuals, ready to turn on the full roar of that monster at the tip of a baton. Yes, it was a complete orchestra, all right. I even glimpsed two or three banjos in that crowded orchestra pit, but what they could be doing there was more than I could imagine.

The house lights dimmed. The audience became tensely silent. I felt once again, as always before, that strange all-over chill that comes with the magic moment of hushed anticipation when the curtain is about to rise.

The title came on, apparently by mistake, because the curtain had not yet risen and all I could see was the faint flicker of the lettering against the dark fabric of the main curtain. But it was not a mistake at all, because the big curtain rose slowly to disclose the title, full and clear upon the picture screen, while at the same moment Breil's baton rose, held for an instant, and then swept down, releasing the full impact of the orchestra in a mighty fanfare that was all but outroared by the massive blast of the organ in an overwhelming burst of earth-shaking sound that shocked the audience first into a stunned silence and then roused them to a pitch of enthusiasm such as I had never seen or heard before.

Then, of course, came those damned explanatory titles that I had shot time and time again as Griffith and Woods kept changing and rechanging them, all with the object of having them make as much sense as possible in the fewest possible words. Somehow, the audience didn't seem to mind. Perhaps they were hardened to it. They should have been, by now, because whenever anybody made any kind of historical picture, it always had to be preceded by a lot of titles telling all about it, not to mention a long and flowery dedication thanking everyone from the Holy Trinity to the night watchman for their invaluable cooperation, without which this picture would not have been possible.

The orchestra sort of murmured to itself during the titles, as though to reassure the audience that they couldn't last forever. And then . . . the picture, gliding along through its opening sequences on a flow of music that seemed to speak for the screen and to interpret every mood. The audience was held entranced, but I was not. I was worried in the same way that young fathers, waiting to learn whether it's a boy or a girl, are worried. I was worried, badly worried, about the battle scenes, and I wished they'd get through fiddle-faddling with that dance and all that mushy love stuff and get down to cases. For it was a simple, open-and-shut matter of make or break as far as I could see; and I could *not* see how that mixed-up jumble of unrelated bits and pieces of action could ever be made into anything but a mixed-up jumble of bits and pieces.

Well, I was wrong. What unfolded on that screen was magic itself. I knew there were cuts from this and that, but try as I would, I could not *see* them. A shot of the extreme far end of the Confederate line flowed into another but nearer shot of the same line, to be followed by another and another, until I could have sworn that the camera had been carried back by some sort of impossible carrier that made it seem to be all one unbroken scene. Perhaps the smoke helped blind out the jumps, I don't know. All I knew was that between the ebb and flow of a broad canvas of a great battle, now far and now near, and the roaring of that gorgeous orchestra banging and blaring battle songs to stir the coldest blood, I was hot and cold and feeling waves of tingling electric shocks racing all over me.

The Confederate charge was simply magnificent. Once again, there was nothing choppy about it, no sense of scenes being cut one into another. That whole line of men simply flowed across the field, stumbling and dropping as they ran somehow into solid sheets of rifle fire from the Union entrenchments, while bombs, real bombs and not Fireworks Wilson's silly little powder puffs, burst with deafening roars among these charging heroes. Oh yes; I knew. I knew perfectly well that the backstage crew was working furiously to create these explosion effects just behind the screen, but I was too caught up in the magnificence of the spectacle to care *how* it was achieved.

And that scene with Walthall snatching up the flag and racing forward with it: holding it high and waving it defiantly as he ran with it in one hand and his drawn sword in the other straight at the cannon, to mount the parapet, and then — in a single, magnificent, overwhelming glimpse of one man, alone against a sky full of bursting bombs, thrusting that standard down the cannon's throat and shouting his defiant yell, while the trumpets in the orchestra split the air. Nor were those trumpets alone. I think every man in that packed audience was on his feet cheering, not the picture, not the

orchestra, not Griffith but voicing his exultation at this man's courage
— defiant in defeat, and all alone with only the heavens for his
witness.

Suddenly I remembered; and with the memory came shame, deep
and bitter, for this was the very scene I had convinced myself was
so very bad, so utterly silly. And yet it was the greatest of them
all, inconceivable except in the mind of an inspired genius. Of *course*
he was right. For every man stands alone, in the ultimate moment
of truth. How could I have been so stupid as to have missed anything
so starkly obvious, so universally true?

The same humiliation came repeatedly to drown me in shame
through the length of the showing. I was forced to admit to myself
over again how pitifully little I knew about anything at all. . .

Somewhere during my self-castigation a title came on reading
INTERMISSION. So soon? I asked my father the time. He pulled
out his watch, snapped open the case, and said it was nine thirty.
Preposterous. Somehow during the past fifteen minutes, or not more
than twenty, an hour and a half had sneaked away.

We went out with the rest of the crowd to stretch our legs and,
in true backstage fashion, to eavesdrop on the comments of the
others. There was enthusiasm, yes; lots of it. It had been exactly
as grandpa had described it was the consensus, only more real. There
were also a few professionals who were wisely sure that Griffith was
riding for a fall. "You can't shoot all your marbles in the first half
and have anything left for your finish" was the loudly expressed opinion of a very portly, richly dressed gentleman. "That battle was a
lulu, best I've ever seen, and that assassination bit was a knockout,
I ain't kidding you. But what's he going to do for a topper, that's
what I want to know. I'll *tell* you what's going to happen. This thing
is going to fizzle out like a wet firecracker, that's what it's going to
do. Don't tell me, I know! I've seen it happen too many times. They
shoot the works right off the bat and they got nothing left for their
finish. You wait and see. You just wait and see."

Chimes sounded from inside, to signal the end of the intermission. Loudmouth threw his cigar away and shouldered his way back
inside. I crept to my place with a sense of cold foreboding. I knew
what was coming: no more action, no more battles, nothing until
way down at the very end, which was a virtual repeat of *Elderbush
Gulch,* only with renegades instead of Indians, and with clansmen
instead of the good old tried-and-true United States Cavalry, complete with flags and pennons, bugles and flashing sabers, and if need
be, a full-screen shot of the flag itself with the National Anthem

blared out by a regimental band for a surefire finish that would bring 'em up cheering.

Yes, this would work. Of that there could be no possible doubt, no possible doubt whatever. But it was so old, so very old as to be threadbare.

And yet it wasn't the finish that worried me so much as the long, dull, do-nothing stuff that I knew was slated for the bulk of the second half. Stuff like the hospital scenes,* where Lillian Gish comes to visit Henry Walthall, she in demurest of dove gray, he in bed with a bandage neatly and evenly wrapped around his head. Now what in the world can anyone possibly do to make a hospital visit seem other than routine? He'll be grateful, naturally, and she'll be sweetly sympathetic, but what else? How can you or Griffith or the Man in the Moon possibly get anything out of such a scene? Answer: you can't. But *he* did, by reaching outside the cut-and-dried formula and coming up with something so unexpected, and yet so utterly natural, that it lifted the entire thing right out of the rut and made it ring absolutely true.

Since this was an army hospital, there had to be a sentry on guard. So Griffith looked around, saw a sloppy, futile sort of character loitering about, and ran him in to play the sentry, a fellow named Freeman, not an actor, just another extra. Well, Lillian passed before him and he looked after her and sighed. In the theater and on the screen, that sigh became a monumental, standout scene, because it was so deep, so heartfelt, and so loaded with longing for the unattainable that it simply delighted the audience. . .

If so, then what of Griffith's long-established principle of making the audience love a character and of then putting that same character in the direst possible danger, only to stage a rescue at the last instant? Because he had made the audience love Little Sister, he was going to put her in the gravest possible danger, but he was *not* going to rescue her. She was going on over that peak to her death. I knew, because I had thrown her over myself. How could he dare to do such a thing? Audiences would never stand for it. They'd hate him. And they'd hate his picture for letting such a thing happen to this heroic little girl.

But before that came the interminable walk of Walthall to the doorway of his ruined mansion, the walk that had nearly cost me my job. I waited with squirming anxiety for that scene to come on, and when it did appear, I was caught up, along with the rest of the audience, with what seemed to me to be the most restrained yet most powerful scene I had ever seen. Of course, Carl Breil helped enormously. As Henry's eyes drifted over the smoke-blackened pillars and the broken gates and windows of his formerly immaculate home, little hints of happy memory came fleeting past from the orchestra. And when he reached the door and the arms came out to greet him, the muted strings brought a lump to every male throat and a flow of tears from the eyes of the gentler sex. I looked at my mother. She was frankly weeping; and I didn't feel so absolutely indifferent myself.

I endured the "drama" — all that stuff with Ralph Lewis being shown up as a fake when he wouldn't let his daughter marry George Siegmann because he was a mulatto — all because I was itching to get to the part where Walter Long chased Mae Marsh all over Big Bear Valley, running low and dripping with peroxide.

What came on the screen wasn't Walter Long at all. It was some sort of inhuman monster, an ungainly, misshapen creature out of a nightmare, not running as a human being would run but shambling like a gorilla. And Mae Marsh was not fluttering, either. She was a poor little lost girl frightened out of her wits, not knowing which way to turn, but searching, searching for safety, and too bewildered to know what she was doing. So she ran to the peak of that rock, and when the monster came lumbering straight at her, she . . . well, all I can say is that it was *right*, absolutely, perfectly, incontestably right.

And did the audience hate Griffith for letting them down? Not a bit of it. When the clansmen began to ride, the cheers began to rise from all over that packed house. This was not a ride to save Little Sister but to avenge her death, and every soul in that audience was in the saddle with the clansmen and pounding hell-for-leather on an errand of stern justice, lighted on their way by the holy flames of a burning cross.

Ah, but those rides. Sure, there were people in trouble, bad trouble, fighting in trapped positions for their lives, but the concern of the audience didn't seem to be at all with the plight of the besieged. On the contrary, their hearts and souls seemed to be riding with the clansmen, who kept pounding through, over hills and through streams and along lanes, all of them in a long-continued, never-slackening charge.

A thing that hit me like a paralyzing electric shock was to hear Griffith's voice — not his real voice, of course — but the brasses imitating his voice as he sang that "Ha-Haaaah — Yah!" over and over again. Griffith had undoubtedly sung it for Breil, who wrote it down and then orchestrated it for trumpets, trombones, and horns, backed by the thunder of hoofs created by the sound-effects men behind the screen.

The effect was tremendous. There was one shot in particular that made the audience duck and scream. The horses swerved from their path in a huddled bunch and ran straight for the audience, to *jump over* the screen as though to land right square in row M of the orchestra seats.

I watched this shot with the greatest of interest because I had never seen it. True, I had shot it. That was the one where the horse kicked the magazine off the camera as he passed over me. But I had never seen it, because although I was turning the camera as a sort of reflex action, I personally was huddled down in as tight a knot as I could manage, with both my eyes screwed tightly shut. Not that I was frightened. No, never that. But I was a cameraman and cameramen have to protect their eyes. So I was only doing my duty by looking — no, not looking, but *guarding* the company's best interests.

So everyone was rescued and everyone was happy and everyone was noble in victory and the audience didn't just sit there and applaud, but they stood up and cheered and yelled and stamped feet until Griffith made an appearance.

*If* you could call it an appearance. Now I, personally, in such a situation would have bounded out to the center of the stage with both hands aloft in a gesture of triumph, and I would probably have shaken my hands over my head, as Tom Wilson had told me was the proper thing for any world's champion to do at the end of a hard-fought but victorious fight.

Griffith did nothing of the sort. He stepped out a few feet from stage left, a small, almost frail figure lost in the enormousness of that great proscenium arch. He did not bow or raise his hands or do anything but just stand there and let wave after wave of cheers and applause wash over him like great waves breaking over a rock.

Then he left. The show was over. There was an exit march from the orchestra, but nobody could hear it. People were far too busy telling one another how wonderful, how great, how tremendous it had all been.

The street cars were all crowded. My father and mother managed to get a rear seat together on the fourth or fifth car, and I took the little wooden bench that ran sideways just back of them. The conversation was all about the picture and what a miraculous experience seeing it had been. I lost all this babble in a seething sea of my own thoughts. . .

Somewhere in this welter of confused images came a new concept of Griffith. I was not wrong in thinking that some of his scenes had been pretty bad, definitely overdone and in some cases actually hammy. But how was I to know that these *had* to be so because he was intending to use only the shortest of flashes, measured in frames and not feet, and that he had to punch everything possible into these shots or the effect could never be felt? So I began to feel less bad about myself, even though ignorance is no excuse, and better about Griffith, not so much as a great man but as a great craftsman. And the heart of his craft was in what we fumblingly called cutting, or editing, or some other such inadequate term.

What he really was — it seemed odd to think so — was a great composer of visual images instead of notes. What I had seen was not so much a motion picture but the equivalent of Beethoven's *Eroica* or his Fifth. That picture had been perfectly orchestrated and the instrumentation flawless.

NOTE

* In the prints we now see, the hospital scenes Brown refers to occur before the intermission. GEORGE PRATT

# FRANCIS HACKETT
# Brotherly Love

*Once* The Birth of a Nation *began to be seen around the country, it racked up huge grosses but also met riots, cuts, and bans. Griffith claimed the right of free speech, but the film's worst flaw was its attack, not on people's opinions, but on something no man could change, blackness. This profoundly angry review appeared in* The New Republic, *a liberal weekly, on March 20, 1915, page 185. Hackett (1883-1962), the magazine's associate editor from 1914 to 1922, was an Irish immigrant who became a well known author and book reviewer.*

*The Birth of a Nation, a motion picture drama in two acts, founded on Thomas Dixon's story,* The Clansman. *Presented at the Liberty Theatre, New York.*

If history bore no relation to life, this motion picture drama could well be reviewed and applauded as a spectacle. As a spectacle it is stupendous. It lasts three hours, represents a staggering investment of time and money, reproduces entire battle scenes and complex historic events, amazes even when it wearies by its attempt to encompass the Civil War. But since history does bear on social behavior, "The Birth of a Nation" cannot be reviewed simply as a spectacle. It is more than a spectacle. It is an interpretation, the Rev. Thomas Dixon's interpretation, of the relations of the North and South and their bearing on the negro.

Were the Rev. Thomas Dixon a representative white Southerner, no one could criticize him for giving his own version of the Civil War and the Reconstruction period that followed. If he possessed the typical Southern attitude, the paternalistic, it would be futile to read a lecture on it. Seen from afar, such an attitude might be deemed reactionary, but at any rate it is usually genial and humane and protective, and because it has experience back of it, it has to be met with some respect. But the attitude which Mr. Dixon possesses and the one for which he forges corroboration in history is a perversion due largely to his personal temperament. So far as I can judge from this film, as well as from my recollection of Mr. Dixon's books, his is the sort of disposition that foments a great deal of the trouble in civilization. Sometimes in the clinical laboratory the doctors are reputed to perform an operation on a dog so that he loses the power to restrain certain motor activities. If he is started running in a cage, the legend goes, he keeps on running incessantly, and nothing can stop him but to hit him on the head with a club. There is a quality about everything Mr. Dixon has done that reminds me of this abnormal dog. At a remote period of his existence it is possible that he possessed a rudimentary faculty of self-analysis. But before that faculty developed he crystallized in his prejudices, and forever it was stunted. Since that time, whenever he has been stimulated by any of the ordinary emotions, by religion or by patriotism or by sex, he has responded with a frantic intensity. Energetic by nature, the forces that impel him are doubly violent because of this lack of inhibition. Aware as a clergyman that such violence is excessive, he has learned in all his melodramas to give them a highly moral twang. If one of his heroes is about to do something peculiarly loathsome, Mr. Dixon thrusts a crucifix in his hand and has him roll his eyes to heaven. In this way the very basest impulses are given the sanction of godliness, and Mr. Dixon preserves his own respect and the respect of such people as go by the label and not by the rot-gut they consume.

In "The Birth of a Nation" Mr. Dixon protests sanctimoniously that his drama "is not meant to reflect in any way on any race or people of to-day." And then he proceeds to give to the negro a kind of malignity that is really a revelation of his own malignity.

Passing over the initial gibe at the negro's smell, we early come to a negrophile senator whose mistress is a mulatto. As conceived by Mr. Dixon and as acted in the film, this mulatto is not only a minister to the senator's lust but a woman of inordinate passion, pride and savagery. Gloating as she does over the promise of "negro equality," she is soon partnered by a male mulatto of similar brute characteristics. Having established this triple alliance between the "uncrowned king," his diabolic colored mistress and his diabolic colored ally, Mr. Dixon shows the revolting processes by which the white South is crushed "under the heel of the black South." "Sowing the wind," he calls it. On the one hand we have "the poor bruised heart" of the white South, on the other "the new citizens inflamed by the growing sense of power." We see negroes shoving white men off the sidewalk, negroes quitting work to dance, negroes beating a crippled old white patriarch, negroes slinging up "faithful colored servants" and flogging them till they drop, negro courtesans guzzling champagne with the would-be head of the Black Empire, negroes "drunk with wine and power," negroes mocking their white master in chains, negroes "crazy with joy" and terrorizing all the whites in South Carolina. We see the blacks flaunting placards demanding "equal marriage." We see the black leader demanding a "forced marriage" with an imprisoned and gagged white girl. And we see continually in the background the white Southerner in "agony of soul over the degradation and ruin of his people."

Encouraged by the black leader, we see Gus the renegade hover about another young white girl's home. To hoochy-coochy music we see the long pursuit of the innocent white girl by this lust-maddened negro, and we see her fling herself to death from a precipice, carrying her honor through "the opal gates of death."

Having painted this insanely apprehensive picture of an unbridled, bestial, horrible race, relieved only by a few touches of low comedy, "the grim reaping begins." We see the operations of the Ku Klux Klan, "the organization that saved the South from the anarchy of black rule." We see Federals and Confederates uniting in a Holy War "in defense of their Aryan birthright," whatever that is. We see the negroes driven back, beaten, killed. The drama winds up with a suggestion of "Lincoln's solution" — back to Liberia — and then, if you please, with a film representing Jesus Christ in "the halls of brotherly love."

My objection to this drama is based partly on the tendency of the pictures but mainly on the animus of the printed lines I have quoted. The effect of these lines, reinforced by adroit quotations from Woodrow Wilson and repeated assurances of impartiality and goodwill, is to arouse in the audience a strong sense of the evil possibilities of the negro and the extreme propriety and godliness of the Ku Klux Klan. So strong is this impression that the audience invariably applauds the refusal of the white hero to shake hands with a negro, and under the circumstances it cannot be blamed. Mr. Dixon has identified the negro with cruelty, superstition, insolence and lust.

We know what a yellow journalist is. He is not yellow because he reports crimes of violence. He is yellow because he distorts them. In the region of history the Rev. Thomas Dixon corresponds to the yellow journalist. He is a clergyman, but he is a yellow clergyman. He is yellow because he recklessly distorts negro crimes, gives them a disproportionate place in life, and colors them dishonestly to inflame the ignorant and the credulous. And he is especially yellow, and quite disgustingly and contemptibly yellow, because his perversions are cunningly calculated to flatter the white man and provoke hatred and contempt for the negro.

Whatever happened during Reconstruction, this film is aggressively vicious and defamatory. It is spiritual assassination. It degrades the censors that passed it and the white race that endures it.

ROLFE COBLEIGH
# A Propaganda Film

*What is truth in a motion picture? Cobleigh's friends told him that*
The Birth of a Nation *"glorified lynching and falsified history." Thomas*
*Dixon's easy answer was that there was at least some true history in the*
*film. He admitted openly he wanted to teach the white people of the*
*United States to have a "feeling of abhorrence" against black men. And*
*he wanted to ship them all back to Africa.*

*This is a deposition included in a packet of materials prepared by the*
*National Association for the Advancement of Colored People in 1915*
*in Boston, called* Fighting a Vicious Film: Protest Against The Birth of
a Nation. *It was reprinted in Harry M. Geduld (ed.)* Focus on D. W.
Griffith *(Englewood Cliffs, N.J., Prentice-Hall, 1971) pages 97-100.*

I, Rolfe Cobleigh, of Newton, in the County of Middlesex and
Commonwealth of Massachusetts, being duly sworn depose and say,
that:

I am associate editor of *The Congregationalist* and *Christian*
*World*, published at 14 Beacon St., Boston, where our offices are
located.

My attention was attracted to the moving picture play entitled,
*The Birth of a Nation*, by editorials which appeared in the *New York*
*World*, the *New York Evening Post*, the *New York Globe* and other
newspapers condemning the production when it was first shown in
New York. Several of my friends, who saw the show in New York,
soon reported to me their disapproval on the grounds that it incited
race prejudice against the Negro race, that it glorified lynching and
falsified history. Influenced by this evidence I wrote a letter to Mr.
D.W. Griffith, who was advertised as the producer of the film, and
protested against the exhibition of such a series of moving pictures
as these were represented to be. I received in reply a letter from Mr.
Thomas Dixon, whose interest in *The Birth of a Nation* was indicated
by the paper upon which he wrote, the letter-head being printed with
the words: "Thomas Dixon's Theatrical Enterprises," under which
was *The Birth of a Nation*, with D.W. Griffith, following the titles
of five other plays written by Mr. Dixon. He said in the letter referring to "our picture": "The only objection to it so far is a Negro Society
which advises its members to arm themselves to fight the whites."
He also wrote that Rev. Charles H. Parkhurst, D.D., was "making
a report on this work," and that if I would "await Dr. Parkhurst's

report" he would send it to me. This letter was dated March 27.

Under date of April 3, I wrote in reply: "I shall await Dr. Parkhurst's report, which you say you will send me, with interest." I asked for the name of "a Negro society which advises its members to arm themselves to fight the whites."

Mr. Dixon wrote again under date of April 5, enclosing Dr. Parkhurst's report of which he said: "As this letter has been forwarded to Mayor Curley by Dr. Parkhurst I will appreciate it if you will publish it in *The Congregationalist*, with any comment you may make. Also Dr. Gregory's letter except one clause." Both the Parkhurst and Gregory letters were in approval of *The Birth of a Nation*. Mr. Dixon referred to his opponents as a "Negro Intermarriage Society," a term used in Mr. Gregory's letter to Mayor Curley and he gave the name of the organization as the National Association for the Advancement of Colored People, and suggested that it might produce a play to answer him, and that, "The silly legal opposition they are giving will make me a millionaire if they keep it up." I did not reply to this letter.

On the morning of April 9, 1915, Thomas Dixon called at my office and I had a long talk with him about *The Birth of a Nation*. He tried to convince me that it deserved my approval. He referred especially to the favorable reports of Dr. Parkhurst and Mr. Gregory. Mr. Dixon asked what I thought of Dr. Parkhurst's approval of the play. I replied that the evidence which had come to me was so strongly against the play that I was not influenced by Dr. Parkhurst, but that I would try to judge the play impartially when I saw it. He talked at length with reference to the artistic and dramatic merits of the play and of its value for the teaching of history, and ridiculed those who disapproved it. In reply to my questions with reference to the treatment of the Negro race in the play, he said that the subject was a debate, that he presented one side and that those who disagreed were at liberty to present the other side.

Mr. Dixon admitted that some of the scenes as originally presented in New York were too strongly suggestive of immorality and that he told Mr. Griffith they went too far.

I asked Mr. Dixon what his real purpose was in having *The Birth of a Nation* produced, what he hoped to accomplish by it. He began to read from the copy of Thomas B. Gregory's letter to Mayor Curley six things that Mr. Gregory said the play did in its effect on an audience. I interrupted to say, "Yes, but what is your chief purpose, what do you really want to accomplish through the influence of this play?" He replied in substance that he wanted to teach the people of the United States, especially the children, that the true history of the Reconstruction period was as it was represented in *The Birth of a Nation*. He said that in the play he presented the historical fact that Thaddeus Stevens became dictator of the United States government immediately after the death of President Lincoln, and that he appeared in the play under the name of Stoneman. Mr. Dixon said that one purpose in the play was to suggest Stevens' immorality in his relationship to his colored mistress for many years. He said the alleged sensual character of this woman, who in the play is called "Lydia Brown, Stoneman's mulatto housekeeper," was emphasized. Mr. Dixon described bad conditions in the South during the Reconstruction period, alleging that the Negroes gained control politically incited chiefly by Thaddeus Stevens, that the white Southerners were insulted, assaulted, robbed and disfranchised and that white girls and women were in constant danger of assault by colored men. He emphasized the alleged dominant passion of colored men to have sexual relations with white women and said that one purpose in his play was to create a feeling of abhorrence in white people, especially white women against colored men. Mr. Dixon said that his desire was to prevent the mixing of white and Negro blood by intermarriage. I asked him what he had to say about the mixing of the blood outside marriage and if it was not true that white men had forced their sexual relations upon colored girls and women all through the period of slavery, thus begetting children of mixed blood outside marriage, and if it was not true, as I am creditably informed, that such conditions prevail to a wide extent even among white men who occupy high social and political positions in the South today.

Mr. Dixon hesitated and finally answered that there was less of such conditions than there had been. Mr. Dixon said that the Ku Klux Klan was formed to protect the white women from Negro men, to restore order and to reclaim political control for the white people of the South. He said that the Ku Klux Klan was not only engaged in restoring law and order, but was of a religious nature, as represented in the play, having religious ceremonies and using the symbol of the cross. He said that the best white men of the South were in it, that Mr. Dixon's father was a Baptist minister in North Carolina and left his church to join the Ku Klux Klan, and that he remained with the organization until it was disbanded.

I asked Mr. Dixon what solution of the race problem he presented in *The Birth of a Nation* and he replied that his solution was Lincoln's plan. He said this was the colonization of the Negroes in Africa or

South America, which he said President Lincoln favored during the last of the Civil War. Mr. Dixon said that he wished to have that plan carried out, that he wished to have all Negroes removed from the United States and that he hoped to help in the accomplishment of that purpose by *The Birth of a Nation.*

I suggested the difficulty of getting ten million people out of the country, and asked if he seriously advocated such a scheme. He replied with great earnestness that he did, that it was possible to create public sentiment such that a beginning could be made in the near future, that a large faction of the Negroes themselves would cooperate in the enterprise and that within a century we could get rid of all Negroes.

Mr. Dixon informed me that the first presentation of *The Birth of a Nation* in Boston would be given that evening for censorship before the mayor and other city officials and newspaper critics and gave me two tickets for that exhibition. He said that in anticipation of a hostile demonstration he and his associates would have thirteen Pinkertons scattered through the audience at the first performance and that as many or more Pinkertons would be employed in the Tremont Theatre at the exhibitions that would follow in Boston, with orders to rush anyone into the street instantly who started any disturbance. He said that he had feared there would be trouble in New York and that many Pinkertons were employed when the show was presented in New York, but that up to the time I saw Mr. Dixon there had been no disturbance in the Liberty Theatre, where the play was presented in New York. Mr. Dixon said that he owned a one-fourth interest in *The Birth of a Nation* Company.

I asked Mr. Dixon to what cities the show would be taken next and he replied that all plans had been held up until they knew the result of the protests in Boston. He said he regarded Boston as the critical point for their enterprise, that it was more likely to object to such a play than any other city and that he and his associates believe that if they could get by in Boston they would be able to go anywhere else in the country with the show without trouble.

As he went away he asked me to let him know what I thought of the play after I had seen it and expressed the hope that I would approve it.

I saw *The Birth of a Nation* that evening, April 9, and saw it again three weeks later, after omissions had been made to comply with the decision of Judge Dowd. I have expressed my disapproval of *The Birth of a Nation*, following each view of it on the grounds of falsifying history, in a riot of emotions glorifying crime, especially lynching, immorality, inviting prejudice against the Negro race, falsely representing the character of colored Americans and teaching the undemocratic, unchristian and unlawful doctrine that all colored people should be removed from the United States. I especially disapprove the play because Mr. Dixon frankly explained to me that his purpose in the play was to promote a propaganda with the desire to accomplish the results that I have stated.

ROLFE COBLEIGH

Personally appeared Rolfe Cobleigh and made oath to the truth of the foregoing affidavit by him subscribed before me in Boston, Massachusetts, this 26th day of May, A.D. 1915.

GEORGE R. BRACKETT, NOTARY PUBLIC

| 5th and Olive Streets | *Clune's* PROGRAM | Theatre Beautiful |

**LLOYD BROWN, Manager**

MR. W. H. CLUNE presents
## 22nd and Positively Last Week
# The Clansman
### Photo-Drama in Twelve Reels

Amplified from the famous novel of Thomas Dixon, Jr., produced by D. W. Griffith, the world's foremost motion picture director. The greatest mot.on picture ever staged.

#### Cost $500,000

Required seven months to stage it.
Includes most spectacular battle scenes ever enacted

Presented by the following all-star cast:

Benjamin Cameron ...........................Henry Walthall
His sister Florence...................................Mae Marsh
His sister Margaret ...................... .........Miriam Cooper
Mrs. Cameron ............................Josephine Crowell
Dr. Cameron ............................Spottiswood Aitken
Austin Stoneman ...............................Ralph Lewis
His daughter Elsie ...................... ............Lillian Gish
His son Phil ......................................Elmer Clifton
His second son ..................... .............Robert Harron
Silas Lynch .............................George Siegmann
Gus .....................................Walter Long
Lydia Brown ......................................Mary Alden
Abraham Lincoln .........................Joseph Hennaberry
Charles Sumner .............................Sam de Grasse
Gen. Lee ...................................Howard Gayo
Gen. Grant ......................................Donald Crisp
Jake ...............................................Wm. de Vaull
Cyndy .............................................Jennie Lee
   Scenic effects in prologue built by J. D. Martin Scenic Co. Los Angeles, Cal.

# THOMAS CRIPPS
# The Year of *The Birth of a Nation*

*In* Slow Fade to Black: The Negro in American Film 1900-1942 *(N.Y., Oxford University Press, 1977), Cripps has given us on pages 59-60 a concise yet colorful summary of what happened in Boston. A professor of film history at Morgan State College in Baltimore, the author was one of the earliest film scholars to call attention to the varying treatment of blacks over the years in Hollywood and in Hollywood films.*

Boston — "Freedom's birthplace," the home of William Monroe Trotter's militant *Guardian,* and the liberal Boston *Post* — opened the attack on *The Birth of a Nation* from both pulpit and press even before the picture arrived. Mayor James Curley understood grassroots politics and granted a hearing in the opening blare of Tremont Theatre advertising.

Curley allowed both sides full expression, perhaps hoping they would burn themselves out so that he would not need to act. Griffith footnoted his work with historians and offered $10,000 for proof of distortions. Early in the game the NAACP judged Curley to be "a democratic and very kindly Irishman," even though they suspected him of lack of sympathy with their demand for censorship. The Epoch group won the opening rounds largely because they trapped Moorfield Storey of the NAACP into admitting he had not seen the film and because other NAACP delegates seemed "shaky" and buried in their notes, and prone to interrupt the proceeding. At last Curley touched off the rage below the surface of the meeting when he straddled, promising to cut the picture while admitting his powerlessness. "Bosh," carped one of the NAACP group who thought Curley to be shamelessly "playing to the colored galleries" and no more. The blacks tried everything during the short-fused session: they hissed a mention of Wilson, urged the banning of the film under the laws governing boxing movies, cited shots of race hatred and "sexual excesses," invoked the Women's Christian Temperance Union, and read letters from Rabbi Wise, Jane Addams, Ovington, and other liberal whites. At one point Curley, piqued at the growing mountain of redundant testimony, asked if Macbeth tended to incite feeling against whites. Storey bristled and charged the Mayor with representing "the other side." The meeting broke up amid Curley's denials, Griffith's insistence on filming "history" as he saw fit, and an offer to cut a few shots.

Curley made good his offer, and the movie opened on April 10 with the chase scene, several leering Negroes, the marriage sequence, Stoneman alone with his mistress, and the South Carolina legislature excised, as concessions rather than acts of conscience or requirements of law. During the second week the *Post* began to take the Negroes' side despite Epoch's considerable advertising space. Its writers reported the murderous moods of New York audiences, discovered that Curley's predecessor had banned *The Clansman* in 1906, and chided the producers for using clergymen as "authorities" in the ad copy.

Then toward the end of the week the small black community of Boston made its strongest stand, taking to the streets for a direct confrontation. Two hundred police turned out when a group of blacks attempted to buy tickets at the segregated theatre. Active in the melee was Trotter, who had cut short a lecture tour. In the lobby he railed against the discrimination, then as the heat rose a cop hit him, and other policemen poured in and arrested ten blacks. A few blacks managed to get inside and at the death leap smashed an egg against the screen and tossed a stink bomb into the crowd. Outside, brawls sputtered in the street.

The next day a wild, hooting crowd gathered at Faneuil Hall, where a crowd of blacks heard Trotter castigate Curley for his betrayal of Negro voters. Michael Jordan of the United Irish League chipped in with an attack on Wilson, and the old Abolitionist Frank Sanborn added a few words. On Monday the blacks marched up Beacon Street to the gold-domed State House, singing "Nearer My God to Thee." Trotter and sixty others pressed inside, while perhaps two thousand waited grimly on the steps. Hurriedly, Governor David Ignatius Walsh and Attorney General Attwill thrashed out the limits of their authority to deal with the film, as moderates led by Booker T. Washington's friend and high ranking black officeholder, W. H. Lewis, reached them ahead of Trotter, revealing the continuing stress within black ranks. Reluctantly, they allowed Trotter to speak from the steps, while the Governor disarmed his impact by promising to ask the legislature for a law prohibiting inflammatory material. Then he ordered the police to stop the show because the gathering was *prima facie* evidence of the movie's power to breach the peace.

Satisfied for the moment, the Negroes called off the demonstration at the Tremont Theatre. But again, marginal success produced friction within black ranks. Trotter used the occasion to squeeze in a bitter denunciation of "colored traitors," meaning Lewis, and by extension, Booker T. Washington and his moderate National Negro Business League, which, Trotter claimed, had issued a conciliatory statement that the movie was "historical and would have good effect." For their part the moderates thought the demonstrations had "suffered from too much Trotter."

Yet, unlike the tag end of the New York fight, the blacks of Boston, even the extremes of Lewis and Trotter and their white allies, had been brought together by the exhilaration of direct action. Also, despite the failure to break the run of the film, they had forced whites to deal with a black united front, had created a model for the future, and had shown how the New York office could nurture local leadership. To stand together across the street from the Robert Gould Shaw monument, with its dedication to the brave black troops of the Civil War, and to catch a glimpse of the Crispus Attucks monument through the trees on the Common, to sing "The Battle Hymn of the Republic," to raise two hundred dollars, was to act in a new drama in the theater of the streets. "The colored troops fought nobly," a witness reported.

# JOSEPH HENABERY
## *Intolerance*

*A few handy hints on problems to be faced in preparing a spectacular film. Henabery was an office file manager for a railroad firm and directing amateur theatricals on the side when the movie industry began to come to California. He saw it as a new opportunity, gave up his secure job, and went to work as an extra player. His lanky looks and his make-up research won him the role of Lincoln in* The Birth of a Nation. *Soon he was the whole research department for Griffith, a staggering task at that moment, since Babylon and three other historical periods were to be used in a single movie. Henabery (1888-1976) was one of the few associates at this time who dared to offer Griffith criticism, and one of the first to be offered a directing job.*

*This remarkable interview (from which we reprint only pages 57-63) must surely encourage any reader to want more of Kevin Brownlow's* The Parade's Gone By *(N.Y., Knopf, 1968), one of the most valuable of all cinema history books. On page 101 Brownlow reports that Allan Dwan told him he personally proposed to Griffith the "elevator" idea.*

We had one of the grand shots of all time in *Intolerance*. We built a tower facing the Babylonian set, with an elevator in it, a studio-constructed elevator. The camera platform was mounted on top of this device. As it descended vertically, the tower moved forward on wheeled trucks which rode on railroad tracks. These trucks had cast-iron wheels, eighteen inches across; they were the kind of platform trucks used by railroad maintenance men.

Four people rode on the camera platform: Griffith; Bitzer; Karl Brown, his assistant; and myself. The scene opened on a full, high setup of the palace with thousands of people in the scene. Without any cut or break, it gradually descended to a medium shot which included just the principals. The shot was repeated a number of times. During the rehearsal, Griffith would call attention to background action he wanted corrected. At the end of the rehearsal move, I would run back into the set and tell the group captains about the changes. Griffith made corrections to the foreground action himself. Then we would return to the camera platform and ride up to the top. We rehearsed for about one and a half hours. Now we had to begin shooting to catch the light at the proper angle. The scene itself was made three or four times. As I recall it, each shot appeared to be okay. However, as retakes would have cost a fortune, the shot was repeated for protection with some minor changes in exposure.

I never put a tape measure to the camera platform, but one figure is firmly fixed in my mind, a figure which can be used to scale most of the sets. The walls of Babylon were ninety feet high. The walls were about the same height as the columns on which the elephants were erected; it is safe to estimate the overall height at one hundred and forty feet. The camera platform was between a hundred and a hundred and fifteen feet; as I recall it, we were in a line horizontally with the elephant platforms, and the camera was slightly below them. At its widest point, the tower structure was forty feet.

Altogether we spent little more than a couple of hours on the scene. We had to shoot with the light. If we wanted the full effect of the settings, we had to take the scene when the lighting was appropriate. We couldn't take it in backlight, for instance. We'd have to take it in maybe a nice crosslight, or half-backlight. So we were limited to a period between ten a.m. and eleven a.m.

I found the locations for the battle scenes which were supposed to be along the rivers Euphrates and Tigris. They were shot a little below what we call the Baldwin Hills. Historically, it was about the same type of land. Acres and acres of swampy plain. I got permission from the heirs to the Dominguez Estate and arranged with the Pacific Electric Railroad to take special electric cars, hauling our extras, to within a short distance of where we wanted to work.

Assisting Griffith meant that I also had to cope with the mobs of people. Let's say we were going to have two thousand people; how do you get two thousand people costumed and ready, early in the morning, unless you break it down some way? I figured that I would give each man a card. This would indicate which booth he would get his costume from — and he would be one of, say, one hundred and fifty people who would get their costume from that booth. I had the backs of the Babylon sets divided into booths, and labeled, and had the costumes placed as I wanted them, so they'd be orderly. And I had two thousand ready by eight a.m.

Technically speaking, George Siegmann was the principal assistant director. He was a grand fellow, but he didn't care too much about either organization or research, and lots of times he'd come to me when they were making a scene and say, "Which way should they go? Left or right?" But he did more for me than any human being would ever do for someone working in a similar capacity. He was a wonderful guy.

Lunches were ordered the night before. I had to take a gamble on the weather. Many a time I've boiled in oil when the fog didn't break until way late, and we had a couple of thousand extras standing by.

A cafeteria in the city would work all night to prepare these lunches, and I was very strict about leftovers. I'd tell them to make up just the right number, and I insisted that the food be fresh because the lunches were a great psychological help. Extras got their carfare, their lunch, and a dollar and a quarter a day. They only got a dollar and ten cents a day when they worked on *Birth of a Nation;* this wasn't much of a raise, but it was more than other companies paid their mobs.

I could get two thousand boxed lunches on two trucks. And they were nice lunches. These cost thirty-five cents apiece, which in those days meant a darn good deal. I would arrange for them to be distributed from the same places that I had for the costumes, and I could feed the whole mob in no time at all. When the trucks came on, they'd make a run for it, yelling "Hey! L-u-n-c-h! L-u-n-c-h!" and you couldn't control them. They'd grab their lunches and their milk, and oh boy, they were very happy with that.

I had noticed one old guy who always seemed to get away from the rest, after he'd got his box lunch. He'd go over to where we had kind of a canvas fence surrounding the property, the barrier that kept the public out, and he'd sit on the ground. I couldn't figure what was going on over there — until one day I strolled over to a point where I could see both sides of the fence. And there, on the other side, was his poor old wife. He was passing part of his lunch to her, under the fence. . .

The time came when the picture was to be taken over to Pomona for its first showing. I had never seen any rushes, let alone any completed cuts of the picture. That was always Griffith's privilege. I'd stand outside the projection room and wait for him. I could recall that near the end of *The Birth of a Nation* he said to me: "Well, how do you like yourself?"

"What do you mean?"

"As Lincoln."

"How do you suppose I'd ever get to see Lincoln?"

He laughed.

I rode to Pomona in Griffith's Fiat with Bobby Harron, Mae Marsh, Lillian Gish, Mr. Griffith, and his chauffeur. In those days is was a terrible thirty-mile ride to Pomona; there were no paved highways then. We plowed through to Pomona because it was an out-of-the-way place where we could be sure of an unprejudiced reaction.

We had the showing — and I was utterly confused by the picture. I was so discouraged and disappointed. On the way home, everyone was raving, raving, raving — "Oh, it's wonderful."

Sure, it had wonderful scenes in it, wonderful settings and many wonderful ideas. But to me it was a very disconnected story. I knew that Griffith had had a problem trying to utilize all this material in a sensible way. But he had ended up with cuts a foot long. He had switched from period to period and he had it all chopped up. He just had too much material.

A modern audience might be able to grasp it, because they follow such techniques more often. But in those days people expected continuity.

The thing that disturbed me more than anything else was the subtitles. I was the last one to be dropped off, and as the chauffeur drove me home I gave the picture a lot of thought.

At ten next morning, I met Griffith in the little open area between his office and the scenario department. He stopped and said, "Well, what did you think about last night?"

I was very hesitant to say anything. Finally, I came out with: "Well, I was disappointed. The worst feature, as I see it, is that you have many titles in there that mean absolutely nothing to the audience. You and I, and a few people around here, have been close to the subject. We know the relationship between certain characters and certain events. But you're asking an audience, some of whom are almost illiterate, to absorb points beyond their grasp. It's impossible. It's —"

Griffith suddenly got very angry, something he very seldom did.

"You don't know what you're talking about," he snapped. He left me and walked up to the scenario department.

I didn't feel bad about what I had said. I had it off my chest; at least that was one thing. I would have felt very remiss if I hadn't expressed my opinion.

Several hours later, I was standing on the stage, not too far from where he was working, waiting till he came out. He might want to order something for the next day; I could never tell. Eventually, he emerged from the scenario department and began to walk to his office across the stage when he noticed me.

"Hey, Hanabery!" he said, and came over to meet me. "What was this you were saying this morning about titles?"

I started to recite some of the points once more. Then Frank Woods came from the scenario department, and Griffith called him over.

"Frank," he said, "Hanabery's right. How *do* they know that Cyrus the Great was related to so-and-so? How *could* they know?" He turned to me. "Come into the office after lunch."

I sat in there for about three hours. I hit the titles I particularly objected to. I made suggestions and they worked my ideas over and revamped the titles.

# RUSSELL MERRITT
## *Intolerance*

*In this critical study, published in the* International Dictionary of Films and Filmmakers *(Volume I, Films, P. 212-213), Russell Merritt stresses the cultural and aesthetic determinants of Griffith's epic film. He also links the "modern story" ("The Mother and the Law") with contemporary economic strife, specifically the war between John D. Rockefeller Jr. and strikers in Colorado.*

*It might be added that the influence of* Intolerance *on Soviet film makers carries special weight when "The Mother and the Law" is compared to Sergei Eisenstein's first film,* Strike.

*Merritt is professor of communication arts at the University of Wisconsin, Madison. His work on D.W. Griffith is extensive and in due course will culminate in a documented study of his life and works, a study which began with his 1970 Harvard dissertation.*

Critical judgment remains sharply divided on *Intolerance*, Griffith's most expensive and flamboyant spectacle. Those critics who pronounce the film a failure generally point to the four stories which, they claim, are thematically too diverse to be effectively collated. Taking their cue from Eisenstein's famous indictment, they argue that the film suffers from purposeless fragmentation and thematic incoherence. Others, notably Vachel Lindsay, George Sadoul, Edward Wagenknecht, and more recently Pauline Kael, list *Intolerance* among the masterworks, stressing its formal complexity, experimental daring, and thematic richness. René Clair, taking a middle position, writes, "it combines extraordinary lyric passages, realism, and psychological detail, with nonsense, vulgarity, and painful sentimentality."

Historians agree, however, that *Intolerance* remains Griffith's most influential film, and that among its most precocious students were the Soviet directors of the 1920s. As Vance Kepley states, "When *Intolerance* was shown in the Soviet Union in 1919 it popularized a montage style already evolving in the hands of Soviet artists. It was reputedly studied in the Moscow Film Institute for the possibilities of montage and agitational cinema (agit-film) and leading Soviet directors, including Eisenstein, Pudovkin, and Kuleshov, acknowledged a debt to Griffith in their writings."

True to his customary practice of starting one film while finishing another, Griffith began work on *Intolerance* while editing *The Birth of a Nation* in the fall of 1914. *Intolerance* began with the modern story, originally entitled "The Mother and the Law." It was intended as a companion piece to *The Escape* (released by Mutual earlier that year), a study of white slavery and the corruption of city slums.

"The Mother and the Law" was virtually completed before *The Birth of a Nation* was released. Not until May, 1915, after *Birth's* controversies were at their peak, did he resume work on it. Determined to surpass the Civil War movie, he decided to expand his modern story to epic proportions. He built lavish sets (notably, the Mary Jenkins ballroom and the Chicago courtroom) and — most important — expanded the story to include the famous strike sequence.

This was, in part, an effort to capitalize on the headlines surrounding John D. Rockefeller, Jr., who had been called up before the Commission on Industrial Relations to explain his role in the 1914 Ludlow massacre. *Intolerance's* strike is loosely based on this incident, in which 23 striking employees of Rockefeller's Colorado Fuel and Iron Company were shot down by the national guard. In these new sequences, Griffith also attacked the Rockefeller Foundation, which, like its founder, came under severe public criticism as the creation of a hypocritical plutocrat, a philanthropy paid for by the exploitation of workers to enhance the reputation of their taskmaster.

Griffith continued shooting his modern story through the summer of 1915. Meanwhile, he began work on a French story, directly patterned after Meyerbeer's *Les Huguenots* which had enjoyed great popularity at the Metropolitan Opera with Caruso and Toscanini. Originally this was to be the lustrous counterpoint to the drab modern story. In original prints, the interiors of the Louvre palace were hand tinted, while considerable attention was paid to royal costumes and lavish Paris sets.

Not until the end of the year did he begin his most elaborate and expensive story. The Hall for Belshazzar's Feast has become perhaps the best-known set created for a silent film. Griffith had his set festooned with Egyptian bas-reliefs, Hindu elephant gods, and Assyrian bearded bulls. Practically every Near Eastern style was represented somewhere on the walls or in the costumes — except the styles of Babylon. Until Douglas Fairbanks' castle set for *Robin Hood*, it remained the largest backdrop ever created for a movie scene.

The result, when combined with the Passion sequence, was a conglomerate of stories and styles in search of a unifying principle. Part morality play and part three-ring circus, the movie was part of the new eclectic aesthetic that had all but buried the older ideal of organic synthesis. Along with Scott Joplin's "Treemonisha" and Charles Ives' Third Symphony, it remains one of the period's great hybrids.

As such, it won uniformly enthusiastic critical notices, but proved disappointing at the box office. Produced at a cost of $386,000 (almost four times the expense of *The Birth of a Nation*) and endowed with an extraordinary cast, it left audiences cold. Although the film cost considerably less and earned more than historians have generally reported, Griffith himself was convinced he had failed. Two years after its release, he released the modern and Babylonian episodes as two separate films. Traditionally, these productions have been dismissed as footnotes to *Intolerance*, simple attempts to relieve the producer of *Intolerance's* burden of debt. Several recent critics, however, have argued that the modern story — released as *The Mother and the Law* — is improved when separated from the other stories and should be evaluated as a self-contained feature.

Griffith was the most eclectic of American directors, an artist whose work consistently absorbed and reflected American popular culture. Of all his films, *Intolerance* remains the one most firmly rooted in its own time, a work representing the cultural phenomena of its day. Probably no film before *Citizen Kane* touched on as many aspects of American popular taste.

Griffith's instincts cannot be called infallible. In his sweeping dragnet of the fine arts, he intuitively missed every important art movement of his time; the raw materials he gathered were an unsorted miscellany of official art treasures (like the Cluny unicorn tapestries and the Assyrian winged bulls) and parochial 19th century *kitsch*. As a muckraker, he had trouble distinguishing important social evils (like America's bloody labor wars and horrible prison conditions) from ephemeral parochial problems. The demons he fought most bitterly, like the Anti-Saloon League, the Rockefeller Foundation, and settlement workers, represented issues far more complex than he ever perceived. He had infinite charity for prodigals, but none for Pharisees, and he depicts "uplifters" as onesidedly in *Intolerance* as he depicted blacks in *The Birth of a Nation*.

Today, *Intolerance* is usually discussed according to memorable isolated sequences, notably Belshazzar's feast, beginning with its famous crane shot; the strike sequence; the courtship of Mae Marsh and Bobby Harron; the courtroom scene with the famous close-ups of Mae Marsh's hands; and the Babylonian battles. Although considerable attention has recently been paid to Griffith's treatment of mise-en-scene, the most durable aesthetic debate continues to center on his intercutting techniques, especially the rhythmic climax built on four intertwined catastrophes, one averted, the others not.

# SERGEI EISENSTEIN

# Dickens, Griffith, and the Film Today

*The idea of montage may not have developed in Russia solely as the result of looking at Griffith films. American scholars like David Bord-well and Vance Kepley Jr. have pointed out the independent contribu-tions of avant garde artists and such early film makers as Lev Kuleshov and Dziga Vertov. But according to Eisenstein, the most brilliant theorist and film maker of them all, Griffith's works represented "a revelation" for young film makers in Soviet Russia. The film which gets the chief credit for this influence is the one with the grandest editing scheme of any film in history.* Intolerance, *imported in 1916, but not shown until 1918, was studied at the Moscow Film Institute. It persuaded Vsevelod Pudovkin to give up science for film.*

*In this elaborate critical study written years later, in 1944, Eisenstein wanted to show that popular fiction was a natural forerunner of film, both in content and form. Charles Dickens, the English novelist, he declares, was not only a favorite source for Griffith in terms of characters and melodramatic plots. He also provided a pattern for cinematic parallel editing. Hence these two types of conflict — melodrama and montage — are related.*

*The essay is 60 pages long. We have tried to include the heart of his argument about Dickens and Griffith. (*Film Form, *Harcourt Brace, 1949, pages 198-201, 205-207, 213, 216-217, 233-235, 241-245.) We had to omit the explications of Dickens texts pointing out the use of objects similar to close-ups, a long conclusion explaining Russian styles of montage, descriptions of several old U.S. melodramas, and a witty introduction about city and country contrasts in America. (Eisenstein visited the U.S. during a futile job negotiation with Paramount in 1930.)*

*In his surprisingly sharp critique of* Intolerance, *Eisenstein deplores Griffith's lack of abstract ideological thinking but in turn he fails to show how such a generalizing impulse might have been expressed.*

In order to understand Griffith, one must visualize an America made up of more than visions of speeding automobiles, streamlined trains, racing ticker tape, inexorable conveyor-belts. One is obliged to comprehend this second side of America as well — America, the traditional, the patriarchal, the provincial. And then you will be con-siderably less astonished by this link between Griffith and Dickens.

The threads of both these Americas are interwoven in the style and personality of Griffith — as in the most fantastic of his own parallel montage sequences.

What is most curious is that Dickens appears to have guided *both* lines of Griffith's style, reflecting both faces of America: Small-Town America, and Super-Dynamic America.

This can be detected at once in the "intimate" Griffith of contemporary or past American life, where Griffith is profound, in those films about which Griffith told me, that "they were made for myself and were invariably rejected by the exhibitors."

But we are a little astonished when we see that the construction of the "official," sumptuous Griffith, the Griffith of tempestuous tempi, of dizzying action, of breathtaking chases — has also been guided by the same Dickens! But we shall see how true this is.

First the "intimate" Griffith, and the "intimate" Dickens . . .

I can't recall who speaks with whom in one of the street scenes of the modern story of *Intolerance*. But I shall never forget the mask of the passer-by with nose pointed forward between spectacles and straggly beard, walking with hands behind his back as if he were manacled. As he passes he interrupts the most pathetic moment in the conversation of the suffering boy and girl. I can remember next to nothing of the couple, but this passer-by, who is visible in the shot only for a flashing glimpse, stands alive before me now — and I haven't seen the film for twenty years . . .

Instead of going into detail about this, let us rather return to that more obvious fact — the growth of that second side of Griffith's creative craftsmanship — as a magician of tempo and montage; a side for which it is rather surprising to find the same Victorian source.

When Griffith proposed to his employers the novelty of a parallel "cut-back" for his first version of *Enoch Arden (After Many Years, 1908)*, this is the discussion that took place, as recorded by Linda Arvidson Griffith in her reminiscences of Biograph days:

> When Mr. Griffith suggested a scene showing Annie Lee waiting for her husband's return to be followed by a scene of Enoch cast away on a desert island, it was altogether too distracting. "How can you tell a story jumping about like that? The people won't know what it's about."
> "Well," said Mr. Griffith, "doesn't Dickens write that way?"
> "Yes, but that's Dickens; that's novel writing; that's different."
> "Oh, not so much, these are picture stories; not so different."

But, to speak quite frankly, all astonishment on this subject and the apparent unexpectedness of such statements can be ascribed only to our — ignorance of Dickens.

All of us read him in childhood, gulped him down greedily, without realizing that much of his irresistibility lay not only in his capture of detail in the childhoods of his heroes, but also in that spontaneous, childlike skill for story-telling, equally typical for Dickens and for the American cinema, which so surely and delicately plays upon the infantile traits in its audience. We were even less concerned with the technique of Dickens's composition: for us this was non-existent — but captivated by the effects of this technique, we feverishly followed his characters from page to page, watching his character now being rubbed from view at the most critical moment, then seeing them return afresh between the separate links of the parallel secondary plot.

As children, we paid no attention to the mechanics of this. As adults, we rarely re-read his novels. And becoming filmworkers, we never found time to glance beneath the covers of these novels in order to figure out what exactly had captivated us in these novels and with what means these incredibly many-paged volumes had chained our attention so irresistibly.

Apparently Griffith was more perceptive.

But before disclosing what the steady gaze of the American film-maker may have caught sight of on Dickens's pages, I wish to recall what David Wark Griffith himself represented to us, the young Soviet film-makers of the 'twenties.

To say it simply and without equivocation: a revelation. . .

The brilliant new methods of the American cinema were united in him with a profound emotion of story, with human acting, with laughter and tears, and all this was done with an astonishing ability to preserve all that gleam of a filmically dynamic holiday, which had been captured in *The Gray Shadow* and *The Mark of Zorro* and *The House of Hate.* That the cinema could be incomparably greater, and that this was to be the basic task of the budding Soviet cinema — these were sketched for us in Griffith's creative work, and found ever new confirmation in his films. . .

Griffith arrived at montage through the method of parallel action, and he was led to the idea of parallel action by — Dickens!

To this fact Griffith himself has testified, according to A. B. Walkley, in *The Times* of London, for April 26, 1922, on the occasion of a visit by the director to London. Writes Mr. Walkley:

He [Griffith] is a pioneer, by his own admission, rather than an inventor. That is to say, he has opened up new paths in Film Land, under the guidance of ideas supplied to him from outside. His best ideas, it appears, have come to him from Dickens, who has always been his favorite author . . . Dickens inspired Mr. Griffith with an idea, and his employers (mere "business" men) were horrified at it; but, says Mr. Griffith, "I went home, re-read one of Dickens's novels, and came back next day to tell them they could either make use of my idea or dismiss me."

Mr. Griffith found the idea to which he clung thus heroically in Dickens. That was as luck would have it, for he might have found the same idea almost anywhere. Newton deduced the law of gravitation from the fall of an apple; but a pear or a plum would have done just as well. The idea is merely that of a "break" in the narrative, a shifting of the story from one group of characters to another group. People who write the long and crowded novels that Dickens did, especially when they are published in parts, find that practice a convenience. You will meet with it in Thackeray, George Eliot, Trollope, Meredith, Hardy, and, I suppose, every other Victorian novelist . . . Mr. Griffith might have found the same practice not only in Dumas *père*, who cared precious little about form, but also in great artists like Tolstoy, Turgeniev, and Balzac. But, as a matter of fact, it was not in any of these others, but in Dickens that he found it; and it is significant of the predominant influence of Dickens that he should be quoted as an authority for a device which is really common to fiction at large.

Even a superficial acquaintance with the work of the great English novelist is enough to persuade one that Dickens may have given and did give to cinematography far more guidance than that which led to the montage of parallel action alone.

Dickens's nearness to the characteristics of cinema in method, style, and especially in viewpoint and exposition, is indeed amazing. And it may be that in the nature of exactly these characteristics, in their community both for Dickens and for cinema, there lies a portion of the secret of that mass success which they both, apart from themes and plots, brought and still bring to the particular quality of such exposition and such writing.

What were the novels of Dickens for his contemporaries, for his readers? There is one answer: they bore the same relationship to them that the film bears to the same strata in our time. They compelled the reader to live with the same passions. They appealed to the same good and sentimental elements as does the film (at least on the surface); they alike shudder before vice, they alike mill the extraordinary, the unusual, the fantastic, from boring, prosaic and everyday existence. And they clothe this common and prosaic existence in their special version.

Illumined by this light, refracted from the land of fiction back to life, this commonness took on a romantic air, and bored people were grateful to the author for giving them the countenances of potentially romantic figures.

This partially accounts for the close attachment to the novels of Dickens and, similarly, to films. It was from this that the universal success of his novels derived. In an essay on Dickens, Stefan Zweig opens with this description of his popularity:

> The love of Dickens's contemporaries lavished upon the creator of Pickwick is not to be assessed by accounts given in books and biographies. Love lives and breathes only in the spoken word. To get an adequate idea of the intensity of this love, one must catch (as I once caught) an

Englishman old enough to have youthful memories of the days when Dickens was still alive. Preferably it should be someone who finds it hard even now to speak of him as Charles Dickens, choosing, rather, to use the affectionate nickname of "Boz." The emotion, tinged with melancholy, which these old reminiscences call up, gives us of a younger generation some inkling of the enthusiasm that inspired the hearts of thousands when the monthly installments in their blue covers (great rarities, now) arrived at English homes. At such times, my old Dickensian told me, people would walk a long way to meet the postman when a fresh number was due, so impatient were they to read what Boz had to tell . . . How could they be expected to wait patiently until the letter-carrier, lumbering along on an old nag, would arrive with the solution of these burning problems? When the appointed hour came round, old and young would sally forth, walking two miles and more to the post office merely to have the issue sooner. On the way home they would start reading . . .

I don't know how my readers feel about this, but for me personally it is always pleasing to recognize again and again the fact that our cinema is not altogether without parents and without pedigree, without a past, without the traditions and rich cultural heritage of the past epochs. It is only very thoughtless and presumptuous people who can erect laws and an esthetic for cinema, proceeding from premises of some incredible virgin-birth of this art!

Let Dickens and the whole ancestral array, going back as far as the Greeks and Shakespeare, be superfluous reminders that both Griffith and our cinema prove our origins to be not solely as of Edison and his fellow inventors, but as based on an enormous cultured past; each part of this past in its own moment of world history has moved forward the great art of cinematography. Let this past be a reproach to those thoughtless people who have displayed arrogance in reference to literature, which has contributed so much to this apparently unprecedented art and is, in the first and most important place: the art of viewing — not only the *eye*, but *viewing* — both meanings being embraced in this term.

This esthetic growth from the *cinematographic eye* to the *image of an embodied viewpoint on phenomena* was one of the most serious processes of development of our Soviet cinema in particular; our cinema also played a tremendous role in the history of the development of world cinema as a whole, and it was no small role that was played by a basic understanding of the principles of film-montage, which became so characteristic for the Soviet school of film-making.

None the less enormous was the role of Griffith also in the evolution of the system of Soviet montage: a role as enormous as the role of Dickens in forming the methods of Griffith. Dickens in this respect played an enormous role in heightening the tradition and cultural heritage of preceding epochs; just as on an even higher level we can see the enormous role of those social premises, which inevitably in those pivotal moments of history ever anew push elements of the montage method into the center of attention for creative work.

The role of Griffith is enormous, but our cinema is neither a poor relative nor an insolvent debtor of his. It was natural that the spirit and content of our country itself, in theme and subjects, would stride far ahead of Griffith's ideals as well as their reflection in artistic images.

In social attitudes Griffith was always a liberal, never departing far from the slightly sentimental humanism of the good old gentlemen and sweet old ladies of Victorian England, just as Dickens loved to picture them. His tender-hearted film morals go no higher than a level of Christian accusation of human injustice and nowhere in his films is there sounded a protest against social injustice.

In his best films he is a preacher of pacifism and compromise with fate *(Isn't Life Wonderful?)* or of love of mankind "in general" *(Broken Blossoms)*. Here in his reproaches and condemnations Griffith is sometimes able to ascend to magnificent pathos (in, for example, *Way Down East*).

In the more thematically dubious of his works — this takes the form of an apology for the Dry Law (in *The Struggle*) or for the metaphysical philosophy of the eternal origins of Good and Evil (in *Intolerance*). Metaphysics permeates the film which he based on Marie Corelli's *Sorrows of Satan*. Finally, among the most repellant elements in his films (and there are such) we see Griffith as an open apologist for racism, erecting a celluloid monument to the Ku Klux Klan, and joining their attack on Negroes in *The Birth of a Nation*.

Nevertheless, nothing can take from Griffith the wreath of one of the genuine masters of the American cinema.

But montage thinking is inseparable from the general content of thinking as a whole. The structure that is reflected in the concept of Griffith montage is the structure of bourgeois society. And he actually resembles Dickens's "side of streaky, well-cured bacon"; in actuality (and this is no joke), he is woven of irreconcilably alternating layers of "white" and "red" — rich and poor. (This is the eternal theme of Dickens's novels, nor does he move beyond these divisions. His mature work, *Little Dorrit*, is so divided into two books: "Poverty" and "Riches.") And this society, perceived *only as a contrast between the haves and the have-nots*, is reflected in the consciousness of Griffith no deeper than the image of an intricate race between two parallel lines . . .

And, naturally, the montage concept of Griffith, as a primarily parallel montage, appears to be a copy of his dualistic picture of the world, running in two parallel lines of poor and rich towards some hypothetical "reconciliation" where the parallel lines would cross, that is, in that infinity, just as inaccessible as that "reconciliation." . . .

. . . if *Intolerance* — in its modern story — stands unsurpassed by Griffith himself, a brilliant model of his method of montage, then at the same time, along the line of a desire to get away from the *limits of story* towards *the region of generalization* and metaphorical allegory, the picture is overcome completely by failure . . .

The reason for this failure was . . . particularly in Griffith's misunderstanding that the region of metaphorical and imagist writing appears in the sphere of *montage juxtaposition*, not of *representational montage pieces*. . . .

Griffith announced his film as "a drama of comparisons." And that is what *Intolerance* remains — a drama of comparisons, rather than *a unified, powerful, generalized image*.

Here is the same defect again: an inability to abstract a phenomenon, without which it cannot expand beyond the *narrowly representational*. . .

However, the failure of *Intolerance* to achieve a true "mingling" lies also in another circumstance: the four episodes chosen by Griffith are actually un-collatable. The *formal failure* of their mingling in *a single image* of *Intolerance* is only *a reflection of a thematic and ideological error*. . .

The question of montage imagery is based on a definite structure and system of thinking; it derives and has been derived only through collective consciousness, appearing as a reflection of a new (socialist) stage of human society and as a thinking result of ideal and philosophic education, inseparably connected with the social structure of that society.

We, our epoch — *sharply ideal* and *intellectual* — could not read the content of a shot without, before all else, having read its ideological nature, and therefore find in *the juxtaposition of shots an arrangement of a new qualitative element*, a new *image*, a new *understanding*. . .

ALAN CASTY
# Griffith and
# the Expressiveness of Editing

*At one point in the midst of a suspended paragraph, the original
Eisenstein essay included a provocative remark about melodrama: "its
methods must have been stored away in Griffith's reserve fund." He
developed this thought only in general terms, since he did not have access to Griffith's own records, his experience on the road as an actor.
Alan Casty, a film teacher at Santa Monica College, has tried to put the
point in a somewhat wider American perspective.* (Development of the
Film, *N.Y., Harcourt Brace Jovanovich, 1973, pages 20-22, 25-27.*)

*Casty is with Eisenstein and Jacobs in valuing Griffith primarily for
his montage achievements. But he is far more critical of Griffith than
Eisenstein (who admires American directors like Griffith and Ford). Casty
is not even willing to put Griffith on the same level as Dickens, calling
him more superficial and addicted to inadequate "mannerisms" of acting,
dependent on remembered patterns of stage melodrama and its spectacular
"realism." These passages summarize part of the argument of Nicholas
Vardac in a book about the carryover, in the early 1900s, of realistic
techniques* From Stage to Screen *(1949).*

*Casty goes on to propose that there was a three-way interaction among
dramatic modes, political attitudes, and cinematic styles which came to
a climax in Griffith's work. Similar kinds of clear-cut polar oppositions
occur, he says, in melodramas, in Progressive theories, and in parallel
editing. This is not a neutral kind of structuralist analysis. Casty instead
is blaming Griffith for drawing from the Progressive era a too-simple
preoccupation with good and evil. This, he suggests, together with his
favorite style, the "split world" of parallel editing, led to the "roaring
climaxes" of Griffith's films. (See also Myron Lounsbury on the Progressive era and film in his 1973 book* The Origins of American Film
Criticism 1909-1939.*)*

*Casty then gives us a rather careful attempt to convey the complex
structure and action of* Intolerance. *He agrees with Henabery that it is
confusing, but it is also "awesome."*

Eisenstein was the first to examine the significant relationship between Griffith and Charles Dickens, although Griffith's references
to Dickens to support his own use of parallel editing had appeared
earlier. In "Dickens, Griffith, and the Film Today" (still one of the
most intricately wrought and persuasively argued pieces ever written on the film art), Eisenstein particularly focuses on the similarity
of Griffith's technique — the use of physical detail and close-ups and

especially the use of abrupt shifts of scene to build tempo and emotion. Although he remarks in passing on similarities of content, attitude, and world view, he does not penetrate far enough. For what we have in Griffith is the surface of Dickens — that which made him so popular because it touched only the nerve ends of the public — but not the wit or penetration, the insight into complexity, and the emotional depths that underlay the surface simplicities, the types, the sentimentalities of situation and emotion. What is left is the energetic rendering of the shell: Griffith's cinematic embodiment of sentimental emotionalism; naive, simplistic conflict and tension; and character stereotypes.

These sentimental simplifications and episodic rendering of many scenes had long been a popular staple of the stage. It was this late nineteenth- and early twentieth-century stage melodrama that established the patterns of expectations shared by Griffith and his audiences. The theater of Henry Irving, Scott MacKaye, and David Belasco, among other producers and directors, had imparted to the young film industry the impetus of its own movement toward more and more surface realism — conceived as the presence on the stage of real objects and settings. It had moved toward the rendering of impossible spectacle — locomotives, fires, sawmills, ice floes — and had developed rapid scene-shifting and a flourishing of physical action in fights, chases, and last-minute rescues.

But it had done more. It had provided the film-makers and the audiences who would smoothly make the transition from stage melodrama to film with a pervasive, habitual conception of dramatic oversimplification of character, emotion, conflict, and theme.

Griffith, along with others, was to move beyond this melodrama in terms of the inventiveness, the verve and vitality of tempo with which he rendered the melodrama. He would apply it more seriously and sincerely to grave problems of the world. But even here his themes were more simplistic *theses,* naively applied, without the depth of conception or powers of self-analysis to see the contradiction in following the sensationalized bigotry and prejudice of *Birth* with an equally sensationalized attack on bigotry and prejudice in *Intolerance.* In 1944, in a late and rare statement of his aims, Griffith replied to a question about what makes a good film:

> One that makes the public forget its troubles. Also, a good picture tends to make folks think a little, without letting them suspect that they are being inspired to think. In one respect, nearly all pictures are good in that they show the triumph of good over evil.

This approach to human problems — in terms of clear-cut absolute distinctions between the forces of light and darkness — was the legacy of melodrama. But it also was a typical popularization of the ideals and attitudes of the Progressive Era in the first decade and a half of the century in America. More than a political movement, Progressivism seemed to capture a national tone: an innocent, optimistic faith in progress and human potential, in the efficacy of change; a moralistic seriousness, a no-nonsense soberness; a mixture of sentimental idealism and gruff, athletic confidence. Theodore Roosevelt was the type writ large. The movies, it was felt, were to be, in Vachel Lindsay's phrase, the prophet-wizard of the new millennium. Lindsay was one among many who stressed the role of the movies in uplifting society. An especially instructive voice of the times was that of Louis Reeves Harrison, an influential spokesman within the industry and the critic for the *Moving Picture World*. With insistent regularity, Harrison repeated his belief that we — especially in America — "seem to be at the dawn of enlightenment" and that it was the film that would hasten the dawn, with "its cultivation of the social muscle," its ability "to affect the manners and habits of the people, to cultivate their taste for the beautiful, to soften harsh temperament by awakening tender sympathy, to correct primitve egotism and avarice, to glimpse history and travel, to nourish and support the best there is in us."

The expressive style of Griffith, and of the period, reflected these attitudes — the innocent enthusiasm of discovery and Progressive meliorism, extreme polarizations and finger-pointing emphasis of melodrama and moral absolutism. Like the histrionics and mannerisms of the acting that has become one of its most bothersome aspects, Griffith's approach was a bold and bald iconography of broad gestures. His parallel editing most fully exemplifies his personal version of this collective style and its relationship to the conglomeration of attitudes — emotionalist, melodramatic, Progressive, reactionary, absolutist — that he brought to his films. Emotionally, it produced the extremes of tension and emotion that he sought, the roaring climaxes of his favorite narrative structures. Technically, it freed the film from the limitations of time and space. But even more important, it intensified the facile, absolute oppositions of his plot conflicts; it became the visual structure for his feelings about a world of totally distinct but directly opposed forces, of irreconcilable poles of good and evil. It is a split world, but clearly, neatly split. For all the rapidity and variety of his parallel editing, it is clearly oriented, sharply demarking, ordering editing. Unlike the rapid editing of today — and its context of relativity and ambiguity — it does not seek to blur, or overlap, or dislocate. . . .

*Intolerance* . . . is a film of paradoxes — beyond those ironies intended by Griffith. Its grandiose conception weighs it down. Its thesis is too broad and vague. Its four plots don't clearly develop the thesis in a consistent manner: In the modern plot, the most extended of the four, the term "intolerance" might apply to the actions of the lady do-gooders but not to the bosses who mistreat workers, the police who shoot the workers down, the criminal who misuses the girl and boy, the boy who, through bad luck and sheer stupidity, twice gets caught holding a gun, the court that stupidly sentences him to death for murder, or the ludicrous coincidences of the murder itself. Its sheer flood of detail gets in the way of even maintaining a response to the plots as plot, especially when so many of the plot details are bathetic, banal, oversimplified. Yet this very grandiosity gives the technique its challenge, gives Griffith the opportunity to carry it out with a plastic vitality, a flow of movement, an audacious inventiveness that, especially in the last third of the movie, is, for all of its artificiality, awesome.

The key is again parallel editing — on a monumental scale. The basic structure embodies Griffith's intuition of the space-and-time fluidity of film technique. Throughout, he juggles all four plots simultaneously, intercutting from one to the other. Through roughly two-thirds of the film, the segments devoted to each plot are several minutes long, although there are some exceptions, and there is some parallel intercutting during a segment between actions that occur within that plot. As the climaxes of the four plots approach, he begins to cut more rapidly from one plot to another. But in three of the four he also begins to use more intercutting *within* the plot, creating his characteristic three-way, chase-and-rescue pattern. (From the fourth plot — Christ moving to his crucifixion — relatively few shots appear.) Thus, in the last third of the movie, the three-way structures *within* each of the three plots are in turn part of what is basically a three-way structure *among* the three plots. The result is an intricate interleafing, as an element in one plot is juxtaposed against a similar element in another: Evil ones in Plot A gather, evil ones in Plot B gather; good guys in Plot B wait, good guys in Plot C wait.

In the contemporary episode there is actually a double chase as well, or a chase in two movements. In the first movement, the boy is being readied for execution by hanging, while the girl speeds in a racing car to catch the governor, who is seen on a speeding train. Griffith cuts back and forth among these three elements, and then he cuts to a parallel three-cornered situation in the French Huguenot plot. Here the girl and her family are inside their house, the besieging army in the streets, her lover racing across the city to save her. Again, Griffith cuts back and forth among the three elements and then cuts to a parallel three-cornered situation in the Babylonian plot. Here, the Babylonians are celebrating a previous victory, while the evil hordes move on the city and a young servant girl races in a chariot to warn the Babylonians. Again, the three-way cutting, and then back to the three elements of the contemporary plot.

At the successful climax of the first movement of the contemporary rescue — the stopping of the train — Griffith achieves his most striking juxtaposition of shots. Without the intervening title that he often uses in his transitions between the plots, he cuts from a shot of the girl's happy success to a shot of the Huguenot girl being stabbed by her tormentor. From this point on, the continuing suspense of the race back to save the boy (and intercutting between the two points) is interleaved with the tragic final stages of the two other plots. With reversed contrast, the last shots of the defeated Babylonians are followed by the successful last-minute rescue of the boy. By this point the acceleration produces a flurry of images, with shots of shorter and shorter duration within each sequence and a resultant acceleration of alternation between sequences. By fragmenting space and action into component details, this acceleration produces a corollary sense of impeding time as well.

The virtuosity and excitement of this sustained crescendo of editing burst the bindings of ideological and esthetic conception; still, the basic stylistic structure underlies them. For all the visual fireworks, the images still build the conventional rhythm of emotion and linear progression of the dualistic narrative. In *Intolerance*, however, Griffith does use contrast editing with a sharper, ironic sense of counterpoint. The ironic reversals reinforce the clear-cut oppositions, rather than undercutting with any skeptical ambiguity: for example, between plots, the trial of the boy and the trial of Christ; within a plot, the workers visited by the "Vestal Virgins of Reform" to save their souls and (in the next scene) the workers denied work and shot down by the militia. Immediate visual juxtapositions reinforce the situational irony: the lavish home of the boss and the plain room of "The Dear One"; "Babylon's greatest noble" served wine with great pomp at the feast and "The Mountain Girl" milking a goat in a poor section of Babylon to get a drink for herself.

The selection of close-ups is one last indication of the mixed nature of the film's multitude of effects. A sudden cut to the eyes of one actress, another to the lower part of an actress' face, a shot in the shadows of the face of Mae Marsh ("The Little Dear One") as she returns to her child and darkened room after the trial, the brief shot of her stoic face at the verdict — these are in sharp contrast to the many facial close-ups of banal, exaggerated expressions. The shot of Mae Marsh in the courtroom is immediately followed by the famous close-up of her hands, twisting together, gripping tightly in anguish — the two shots together expressing her character, her state of mind and heart. But it should not be forgotten that the selective nuance of these two close-ups had been preceded by dozens of other shots of her face and hands, intercut with shots of the boy, as she encourages him during the trial, twisting her handkerchief, biting the end of it, blinking her eyes, essaying a flickering smile again and again and again. In Griffith's world of Armageddon, even the quiet nuance is shaped into the hyperbole of the booming voice.

# BLAKE LUCAS
# Infinite Shadings of Human Emotion

*Now we have a critical estimate of Griffith's work from still another quarter. Lucas is a Los Angeles writer who will have nothing to do with the notion that Griffith is "dated" or "primitive" or that he "declined" after 1917. He wants us to look at both the early short films and the features made in 1919 as revealing Griffith's continuing grasp and greatness, his skill in presenting the depth of human experience. These are conveyed, Lucas suggests, not so much through the wondrous mechanics of montage, but through luminous acting and* mise en scène *(which we might define as "action placed within a background").*

*This is part (pages 51-55) of a longer essay, 'A Directorial History of Silent Films' (*Magill's Survey of Cinema: Silent Films, Volume I, *Englewood Cliffs, N.J., Salem Press, 1982). It is similar to revisionist analyses offered in 1974 by such writers as John Dorr (*Film Comment*) and William Cadbury (*Film Quarterly*). Dorr proposed that Griffith entered a new phase about 1919 and de-emphasized editing, while Cadbury insisted that this may have been true but there was nothing new about it — he was still doing all the same things he had always done so well. Lucas explores the implications of a Griffith who was versatile, forward-looking as well as nostalgic, aware of ambiguity, more expressive as a dramatist than as an editor.*

The American director who made the most sustained contributions to the language of film throughout the silent period was David Wark Griffith. The prodigious creativity of Griffith was opportune, for while it is an exaggeration to state that he invented much of the vocabulary of cinema, as is sometimes claimed, he did deepen and refine much of that vocabulary. More importantly, his films in these crucial early years demonstrated conclusively that a film director could find a personal style which would make his work as artistically resonant as that of the masters of other art forms. Between 1908, when he made his first one-reel film, *The Adventures of Dollie*, and 1915, when the cinematic range he had achieved permitted the ambition of a lengthy feature, *The Birth of a Nation*, Griffith made approximately five hundred short films for Biograph. Many of these films survive, but only a relative few such as *The Battle of Elderbush Gulch* (1913), a seminal Western, and *Musketeers of Pig Alley* (1912), a precocious gangster film, have been widely seen. It is well known that Griffith experimented with lighting, composition, close-ups, cross-cutting, narrative structure, and poetic suggestiveness in these films. A viewing of many of these films reveals that they are not valuable simply for the fundamental cinematic techniques which resulted; almost invariably, Griffith was successful in making his ideas dramatically expressive. A great variety of subject and approach, unified by Griffith's sensibility, made these individually modest films one of the central achievements of the cinema.

At their simplest, the films tell action-oriented, melodramatic stories. *The Lonedale Operator* (1911), for example, relates the story of a girl who works for the railroad foiling the nefarious plans of the villains and finding love in the process. It does not sound like an especially compelling film, but the sureness with which the elaborate action sequences are cut and the director's ability to establish immediately sympathetic identification with his charming heroine make the film a very fresh and remarkably pleasing cinematic experience. More adventurously, Griffith tackled subjects without simple, clear-cut stories. *A Corner in Wheat* (1909), adapted from a story by Frank Norris, does not concentrate on a central protagonist. Instead, it presents a fairly complex social situation, relating in its brief running time the relationship between the corrupt and greedy tycoons of the wheat business and the poor farmers who stick to their task with little change of fortune. Throughout the film, Griffith returns to recurring images, such as the sowing of the wheat as two figures walk back and forth over a field in a long shot. The film is not a documentary and does present its narrative in a dramatic style, but the drama is overshadowed by images which make it expand into a more powerful statement.

In addition to social issues, Griffith explores psychological ones. *The Female of the Species* (1912), one of the earliest films to feature Mary Pickford, contrasts the behavior of various women in a melodramatic situation which has the appearance of a fragment of a more detailed narrative. Griffith's interest here is in exploring character rather than resolving all of the intricacies implied by the story.

Often, Griffith seemed disdainful of nineteenth century conventions. His films become especially interesting, both aesthetically and dramatically, when his creative energy is concentrated on visually expressing the emotional states of his characters. *The Mothering Heart* (1913) is a modern story of adultery which boasts no surprises. The husband is unfaithful with a café dancer, and the loving wife discovers their affair. The husband is repentant, but his wife is consumed by rage and grief. Finally, she forgives her errant husband. It is very difficult to think of a contemporary film on the subject which treats it more persuasively. The wife is played by Lillian Gish (who was only seventeen at the time), and the range of emotions which the actress expresses in the final scenes is truly remarkable. In this context, the camera's distance from the action, especially with regard to the selective employment of close-ups and the staging of related shots occurring in exteriors and interiors, has a precise effect on the emotional mood of a situation, which is timeless. *The Mothering Heart* is one of many films which shows its director to be completely uninhibited by the apparent limitations of the medium at that time. It is the nuances of the stories which bring out his cinematic astuteness, not the stories themselves.

The height of Griffith's artistry is reached when fragmentary moments, representative of the consciousness of a character, are displayed visually to underline the relationship of the character to the world of the film. Griffith never tired of this technique, which looks forward to modern directors as diverse as Alain Resnais, Luis Bunuel, and Hideo Gosha. Memory, subjectivity, and the crystallization of unexpressed thoughts are the facets of this remarkable predilection, brought to perfection in such films as *Broken Blossoms* (1919) and often evident in the Biograph shorts. Griffith's ability to break up a narrative with these free-flowing reminiscences and projections of feeling are more daring in intent and execution than a great deal of the narrative manipulation of the 1960's and 1970's. Although other directors have demonstrated greater surface complexity in reordering dramatic experience to a special design, none has done it with less constraint and less self-consciousness than Griffith. His sensibility seems to have a natural tendency to break down the most old-fashioned material into a glowingly modern, formal structure. The result in the Biograph period was poetic distillation in films such as *The Sands of Dee* (1912). This masterpiece, one of the many Griffith shorts which deserves far more exposure, centers on a young woman who spends most of the film waiting on a beach in a reverie over an unresolved romance. Its images of loneliness and inward existence are uncommonly moving. It evokes the exterior moods of its landscape and the interior moods of its heroine's fluctuating emotions without recourse to transparently exciting drama, but it is as engrossing as the most elaborate chase film, arguably more so. In the face of such films as *The Sands of Dee*, conventional descriptions of this period of cinema as "primitive" break down completely.

The subtler aspects of Griffith's style deserve emphasis for several reasons. One reason is that Griffith has drawn a great deal of attention to crosscutting between related spheres of physical action. The suppleness with which the director could clearly delineate diverging and converging sequences within a single elaborate drama led to the sureness with which the many spectacular sequences of his two greatest films, *The Birth of a Nation* and *Intolerance* (1916), are composed and edited. Unfortunately, he is usually measured solely by those remarkable accomplishments, although his more intimate and subtle works are often superior and, at the same time, more representative of what is traditionally celebrated as artistic. Additionally, Griffith is sometimes spoken of as a dated and faded figure whose films owe too much to Victorian melodrama. As the Biograph films and the best of his later films demonstrate (and as is also evident in numerous graceful and discreet moments woven into the tapestries of *The Birth of a Nation* and *Intolerance*), Griffith used the narrative conventions of the nineteenth century as a basis from which to explore freely modern situations, often imparting an ambiguous moral tone which implicitly and intriguingly questions the values of his own background. From this perspective, the apparent naiveté of outworn melodramatic structures is extremely effective, providing counterpoint to the sophistication with which Griffith's style describes the most profound aspects of human experience in a visually poetic manner.

Griffith's films are filled with beautiful close-ups of captivating heroines, poignant iris shots, theatrical flourishes adapted to cinema, and astute editing which sometimes creates rhythms that are virtually musical. More significantly, however, he remains one of the most modern directors. His films treat adult situations with delicacy, sensitivity, and perception. The boldness with which he developed and refined the language of cinema is actually of less interest than the care of his *mise-en-scène*. The actors and actresses (among them Lillian Gish, Mae Marsh, Miriam Cooper, Blanche Sweet, Robert Harron, Henry B. Walthall, Clarine Seymour, Richard Barthelmess,

Carol Dempster, and many others) to whom he remained loyal and who constituted an evolving repertory company, lent themselves with great trust and skill to a recognizable style, a style which sought to describe the infinite shadings of human emotion and interaction. The best moments in his films are almost always very simple from a technical point of view. These moments are affecting because of the genuineness of the actors, the thoughtfulness of the compositions and a consummate attention to detail.

Griffith's features made use of the stylistic attributes of the Biograph shorts. As the features did not need to compress material within the disciplines of one or two reels, these longer films tend, at least superficially, to have more conventional formal structures. Actually, Griffith used the opportunities afforded by his features to treat his material in a similar way but with more depth. The precise touches required to give the one- and two-reel films density become diffused throughout the film. Individual moments might be less startling, but the cumulative effect is often richer. *Intolerance* aspires to tell four stories, widely separated in historical time, simultaneously, each with a distinctive tone of its own although all treat the same theme. Initially, the audience is permitted to spend considerable time acquainting itself with each story, but as the film progresses toward a climax, the four stories alternate with increasing rapidity and, in an aesthetic sense, become one, which adds to the power of the single happy ending in the modern story and the almost abstract epilogue in which a free-flowing series of images underlines the director's theme with great force.

In *True Heart Susie* (1919), the most revered of his pastoral romances, Griffith unerringly accords value to certain key images, such as the shot early in the film when William (Robert Harron) and Susie (Lillian Gish) almost kiss. Later, after William has mistakenly married another woman (Clarine Seymour), these early images are recalled. The costume Gish wears as the younger Susie is very distinctive so that it can be recognized even in long shot in the final image. The couple has reconciled after the death of William's wife, although each is older and considerably less innocent. Griffith wrote a beautiful title to precede this final shot, suggesting that viewers may now think of Susie and William as they once were. This is precisely what the final image permits the audience to do, for it is clearly a shot of the young William and Susie in the untroubled love they might have enjoyed. The events of the story have stolen away this untroubled love. The memory image, which on its face seems to underline the happy ending, reveals on another level that a gentle tragedy has been insinuated into the film with exquisite grace. No one can ever be as they once were: one can only think of them that way. Griffith instills this painfully affecting thought in a fleeting moment because he has been careful throughout the film not to overstate or solemnize his dramatic material. In *True Heart Susie*, a deceptive simplicity serves the visual and emotional texturing of remarkable emotional power.

Also made in 1919, *Broken Blossoms* confirms Griffith's mastery in delineating subtle exchanges of feeling between his characters. The story involves a tender young Chinese man (Richard Barthelmess) and a battered adolescent girl (Lillian Gish) in London's Limehouse district. In the film, the director evokes the separate lives of each before they meet by fragmenting their respective existences into a series of sad and bitter moments. These moments are transformed into drifting reflections of their bruised hearts by the images which establish them and introduce these reveries. The girl is a pitiful figure sitting on the docks and staring down at the water; the young man stands against the wall on the streets and gazes absently and passively at the milieu which has destroyed all of his ideals. In this manner, Griffith not only provides a formally interesting exposition but also evokes the subsequent harmony between the two characters which will briefly illuminate their lives before tragedy descends. It is a measure of Griffith's enduring artistry that such images still seem to suggest the essence of cinema.

ARTHUR LENNIG

# An Unconventional Masterpiece

Broken Blossoms, *Griffith said, was a "labor of love." Condensed from an article in* Film Journal, *Fall-Winter 1972, this profile of the preparation, story, and script of the 1919 film shares with us some useful research, revealing some of Griffith's attitudes toward adaptation. Lennig is professor of film history and film making at the State University of New York at Albany. He is the author of* Classics of the Film *(1965) and* The Silent Voice: A Text *(1969).*

Broken Blossoms, *according to Eileen Bowser, not only won praise from the critics; it gained a profit, by 1934, of more than $700,000 for United Artists.*

*I would rather be able to produce something like* BROKEN BLOSSOMS *than to own the most gorgeous country estate imaginable . . . If one can't be happy in doing the thing worthwhile, what else matters?*[1]

D. W. Griffith's fame rests mainly on his two epic films, *The Birth of a Nation* (1915) and *Intolerance* (1916). In them he proved himself a great innovator, the master of editing, a director able to control his viewers' passions and evoke their awe; he proved that films could be important. Much less stress has been placed on his smaller, more intimate works, such as *True Heart Susie* (1919), *The Romance of Happy Valley* (1919), *Broken Blossoms* (1919), *The White Rose* (1923), and *Isn't Life Wonderful* (1924). But in them Griffith revealed another, equally important facet of his nature — the gentle, poetic side. Perhaps the most famous of his smaller films is *Broken Blossoms*, and deservedly so; a simple tale, simply told, it had delicacy and exoticism, without any loss of his powerful dramatic sense.

As with most things in Griffith's life, there are several versions of how he decided to film *Broken Blossoms*. Lillian Gish has said that during the fall of 1918, while Griffith was planning to become a partner in United Artists, Mary Pickford and Douglas Fairbanks called his attention to Thomas Burke's story "The Chink and the Child."[2] Griffith, however, told a quite different story to an interviewer in 1919. He explained that one night while he was in London in 1917 he had had trouble sleeping, so he picked up Burke's recently published book, *Limehouse Nights*, and read "The Chink and the

Child." This tale of a sensitive boy, a cruel father, and a pathetic waif didn't just appeal to him — it fascinated him. "It made an impression on me that I could not overcome and my dramatic sense was so touched that I kept repeating over to myself that here was a story demanding production."[3] This reaction isn't surprising, as the plot contained several elements that Griffith had succeeded with before: a suicide (Mae Marsh in *Birth*), miscegenation (again, *Birth*), and the evils of the urban setting (*Escape* and *The Mother and the Law*).

Although Griffith was enthusiastic about the story, he worried whether it would be good box-office. After all, his grandiose scheme for *Intolerance* — although it satisfied the poet in himself and impressed critics — proved hardly tolerable to his creditors. "The Chink and the Child" ran counter to almost every American precept by dealing with poverty and ugliness, and offering an unhappy ending. The murder of the heroine and the suicide of the hero were bad enough, but to compound the audacity, the heroine wore rags and the hero was a slant-eyed, impassive foreigner. Griffith knew that audiences went to the movies to be entertained and did not want unhappy endings, yet the deaths at the end of the story were built right into its fabric. They couldn't be changed; he would make either a film with an unhappy ending or no film at all. He mentioned the new project to others, but they were skeptical. "It would never succeed," he was told, yet the desire to make this poetic film remained. After much hesitation he finally decided that if costs could be kept down he would go ahead with it. As he said later, "If ever I indulged in a labor of love it was in *Broken Blossoms.*"[4]

To Griffith the message was as important as the medium. In *The Birth of a Nation* he had told the story of the Civil War and Reconstruction, and in *Intolerance* he graphically pointed out the evils of injustice and conflict. *Broken Blossoms* would also have its message. He wanted, as he later said,

> to help riddle the fallacious notion that Americans are superior to those they call "foreigners." Too many Americans labor under the delusion that they are the greatest people in the world, and that all others are "foreigners." Now I believe that so long as we Americans speak out with shallow contempt of Italians as "wops," of Frenchmen as "frogeaters" and of Chinese as "Chinks," so long as we imagine that we alone represent all the heroism and beauty and ideals of the world first, so long will the efforts of such idealistic leaders as President Wilson *fail.*[5]

If the tragedy of *Broken Blossoms* appealed to his poetic self, and its message to his didacticism, there was yet another desire, a timeless one. Writers penned sonnets to their loved ones, painters sketched the fascinating fleshiness of their mistresses, and now Griffith, working in a new medium, would try to bring to the screen what Lillian Gish meant to him, not only personally but also artistically. She would become the idealized image of womanhood, the personification of his dreams. But how to render such a vision? How to capture the soft haze of beauty without wrinkles, dew-laps, and all the imperfections the flesh is heir to? No one, he later said, was ever really beautiful,[6] but he would make Lillian just that: more exquisite than reality, a youthful face metamorphosed through the magic of the camera into the ethereal. He would capture the delicate, wistful overtones in her personality; he would render on the screen the misty phantom of a man's dream.

The whole film was a challenge to Griffith, as he later explained in a letter to Thomas Burke:

> When I first contemplated making a cinema drama of your story, it met with fierce objection among all the distributors connected with our industry. Of course, as I don't need to tell you, the presentation of tragedy, either in moving pictures or on the stage, is a very daring thing as I cannot recall any that have been successful with the people.
>
> It was my intention to attempt a real tragedy with the motion pictures and so used your story for this purpose. . . .
>
> We tried very hard to keep the spirit of the story, making only such changes as we deemed necessary for our audiences, and of course, as you know, you cannot picturize words.[7]

Although Burke was able to plunge right into the middle of his tale, Griffith could not rely just on titles to provide exposition; instead, and wisely so, he *showed* the past of his characters. For example, Griffith begins his story in China with a sensitive boy (Richard Barthelmess) who believes in his peaceful oriental philosophy. When some American sailors start fighting among themselves, he tries to settle the argument: "Do not give blows for blows. The Buddha says, 'What thou dost not want others to do to thee, do thou not to others.'" But the sailors are loutishly indifferent to his efforts and in the ensuing melée he is thrown to the ground. "Just a sociable free fight for the Jackies — but the sensitive Yellow Man shrinks in horror," says a title. Convinced "more than ever . . . that the great nations across the sea need the lessons of the gentle Buddha," the young man, after receiving advice and wisdom from an elderly man in the Temple, decides to go to the warring nations of the West.

The next part of the film opens in the Limehouse district of London "some years later" where the sordid life, the poverty, the cruelty, and the indifference have had their effect — his youthful dreams have vanished. Although he is now a shopkeeper and is shown visiting an opium den, this young Chinese man remains at heart a good person. One does not have to be ingenious to see the obvious parallels with Griffith's own life: read Kentucky for China, New York and Hollywood for London, and artistic integrity for the young Chinaman's idealism.

In direct contrast to the sensitive Chinaman is Battling Burrows (Donald Crisp), a symbol of intolerance, hatred, and moral indifference. A prize fighter, he does not find his profession adequate release for his sadism and consequently torments his little girl, Lucy, a product of one of his casual liaisons. This girl (Lillian Gish) is beaten on the slightest provocation. To Griffith she represents the innocent waif sacrificed in the moral and emotional slaughterhouse of the world. Despite her poverty, her rags, and the fog-filled streets, she is beautiful in both appearance and soul. To dramatize her situation Griffith has her visit a married woman who, surrounded by her starving and lice-ridden children, warns the girl against marriage. The girl also talks to some prostitutes who caution her against the evils of their profession. What can such a blossom do in this universe but be broken? Griffith has her open a little box of mementos left by her mother to show that she is not the only one, that her mother too probably went through the same syndrome before she died. The girl, longing for beauty, takes her saved-up roll of tin foil to the flower vendor, but she does not even have enough to buy a flower.

When the father finds out that he must go into training for his next fight, and thus must forswear drinking and women, he lets out his resentment on the girl. Beaten for no reason, she is left alone in the little shack. Finally, she staggers out and wanders through the streets, only to collapse at the Chinaman's door and fall into his store. This action is an improvement over the story in which a prostitute picks her up and takes her to a den where the child's virginity is going to be sold for a good price. . . .

Burrows finds out where Lucy has gone, breaks into the boy's place, smashes everything, and drags the girl back. Frightened, she crawls into a closet, and writhes in an agony of dread, surely one of Lillian Gish's greatest moments. Burrows breaks in, raises his whip, and finally beats her to death. The boy, meantime, returns to his apartment, sees the havoc, and runs off to Lucy's home. There he finds her dead body. Burrows enters the room and is about to kill him with a hatchet when the boy shoots the murderer, picks up the girl in his arms, carries her back to his own place, and commits suicide before his little shrine.

Griffith's changes in the story are almost always improvements. Certain aspects which Burke only mentions in a summary sentence or two, such as Burrows' discovery of the girl in the apartment and the smashing of the room, and later his beating of the girl, Griffith illustrates more fully. He also modifies the ending by having the boy kill Burrows in self-defense, whereas in the story he leaves a poisonous snake to achieve his justice. . . .

Basically, the film is the triangle of a good man, a bad man, and an innocent waif — the elemental substance of so much of Griffith's work. But Griffith also offers a new twist on the merits of East-West morality. At a time when most orientals appeared as murderers or insidious monsters, Griffith opposed American prejudices by showing that the Chinaman is the "white person" and Burrows the monster.

Despite the exoticism of the story and some of the oriental flavor, the film is also realistic. As a depictor of low life, Griffith has few rivals among American directors in the silent period and is challenged only by Erich von Stroheim. Both of these men knew the seedy aspects of life and were able to draw upon them in their films. But whereas Erich von Stroheim for the most part observed cruelly and sardonically, Griffith always provided some character or scene to show that beauty and love still exist in the world along with horror and ugliness. . . .

NOTES

1. "Griffith's Ideas," *Ohio State Journal* May 25, 1919.
2. Lillian Gish, *The Movies, Mr. Griffith, and Me* (Prentice-Hall, 1969), p. 217.
3. New York *Sun*, October 26, 1919.
4. *Ibid.*
5. *National Magazine*, August 19, 1919.
6. D.W. Griffith, "What Is Beauty?" *Liberty Magazine*, October 19, 1929.
7. Griffith, "Letter to Thomas Burke," October 1, 1918, Griffith Collection.

# RICHARD SCHICKEL
# *Way Down East:*
# Finances and Responses

*It's a pretty seamless fabric, but we have torn some threads from* D.W.
Griffith: An American Life *(N.Y., Simon & Schuster, 1984, pages 426,
428-430, 433, 436-438, 442-443) which we hope will reveal the special
quality of Schickel's 647-page biography. The book is an extraordinary
feat of research and sympathetic imagination which does not shirk the
task of evaluating every major feature film.*

*Included here, besides a synopsis of the story, is an effort to place
Griffith the producer-writer against the background of writings of the
time, and thus to suggest that he was more in touch with contemporary
popular culture than some of his critics claimed. Then there is a dizzy
trip through some of Griffith's financial dealings — a page which can
only begin to tell us what burdens he must have undertaken, year after
year, to keep himself in business. Finally there are a couple of notes on
contemporary evaluations of this film, which was Griffth's greatest success at the boxoffice since* The Birth of a Nation.

. . . The most cursory glance at the commercially successful films
of the decade — many of them critically well received, as well —
reveals among them almost all the popular classics of the late-
nineteenth-century stage and literature, highly romantic and highly
melodramatic, receiving either their first production, or their first
feature-length production: *Daddy Long Legs, Pollyanna, Dr. Jekyll
and Mr. Hyde, Treasure Island, Little Lord Fauntleroy, The Prisoner
of Zenda, The Trail of the Lonesome Pine, The Hunchback of Notre
Dame, Romola, The Three Musketeers, The Phantom of the Opera,
Peg O' My Heart* and so on and on. There was no reason for Griffith
not to contemplate doing material of this kind, and no reason to
suppose that the commercial failure that would attend him in this
decade could be blamed on his being "out of touch" with public taste.
Far from it; many men, many film companies, made fortunes by
being precisely as "out of touch" as he was. And whether you were
P.C. Wren or Rafael Sabatini, it was obviously possible to go on
creating hugely successful new works that employed variations on
the old formulas at great profit to yourself and to the great pleasure
of your public.

It would have been convenient for his admirers if Griffith had not aligned himself, now that he had some power, with gentility and cultural conservatism. It would have been better for his reputation, then and later, if he was going to go broke, that he do so heroically, following an esthetically radical course, leaving behind him some masterpieces in which the eager student could find the first traces of the modernist spirit, rather than masterpieces (which, indeed, he once or twice managed to make in this era) that depend for their appeal on their crystallization, in images, of the past.

When a cultural sharpster might have been reading *Jurgen,* Griffith was in touch with the General Lew Wallace estate about the screen rights for *Ben-Hur* (the asking price, alas, was a million dollars!) and engaging in mutually flattering correspondence with H. Rider Haggard about acquiring one of his novels. When he might have been snapping up *Winesburg, Ohio,* or even *Main Street,* he was buying the rights to Joseph Hergesheimer's much different view of small-town life, *Tol'able David,* not to mention his exotic romance *Java Head.* And he would leave it to someone else (Thomas Ince) to be the first to bring O'Neill to the screen (*Anna Christie* in 1923, starring Griffith's discovery, Blanche Sweet). Of course, he had little choice in the matter. For better or worse his taste and his talent were fully formed, and so was his character.

The perils and potentials of being able to exercise his taste to its fullest were illustrated by his first major purchases for production at Mamaroneck. Both were plays of long-standing popularity, both were hugely expensive to acquire and to mount. One, long since forgotten, was *Romance.* The other, the source of what is, arguably, Griffith's most nearly perfect expression of his spirit and sensibility, was *Way Down East. . . .*

*Way Down East* was first performed, in a version considerably different from its final form, at Newport, Rhode Island on September 3, 1897, the work of an inexperienced writer named Lottie Blair Parker, who brought her script to William A. Brady, the producer-writer. . . . It became a staple for road and resident companies throughout the United States, and Brady estimated that he earned some $200,000 in royalties from it, Mrs. Parker contenting herself with whatever money Brady had paid her to buy out her interest, plus the rights she retained to foreign-language productions.

Brady understood the commercial as well as the sentimental power of the piece and was not about to surrender it cheaply to the movies, even to a friend like Griffith. The price they finally arrived at was $175,000, breaking the record-setting price Griffith had just paid for *Romance.* Nor was that the end of his story costs. Mrs. Parker had to be paid $7,000 for her rights to the non-English speaking territories, and Griffith engaged a playwright, Anthony Paul Kelly, to prepare a scenario of which Griffith in the end used very little. That cost him another $10,000. These preproduction charges set the pattern for the picture; *Way Down East*, which contains no spectacular settings, no mobs of extras, no overpaid stars, nothing of the sort that usually runs the cost of a movie up, turned out to be the most expensive film Griffith had made to date.

Mostly what he paid for was the passage of time, time for the seasons to turn, time for the elements to produce some of their more wondrous effects. He would have to hold his company on call and tie up his studio for better than six months — far longer than his usual production schedule — with interest charges mounting up on the extensive borrowings the production required. But it was worth it. One of the distinguishing qualities of the film, perhaps the most significant factor in permitting it to transcend the limits of its primitive genre, derives from his careful rooting of his characters in their environment, from the manner, as well, in which nature's moods seem to reflect their emotional weather. These were qualities no amount of stage machinery could produce, and it may be that *Way Down East* represents the culmination of the process, stretching back almost to the beginning of the movies, by which film, possessing a superior technology, finally rendered its rival obsolete: the triumph of optics over mechanics.

Griffith did not tamper with the basic story he had spent so much to acquire. In the film as in the play Anna Moore (Lillian Gish) is a "down east" country lass — the phrase refers to that portion of Maine which lies geographically east of Boston — who comes to the Hub to seek financial aid from rich relatives. They treat her condescendingly, but she meets and falls in love with Lennox Sanderson (Lowell Sherman, who made a career out of playing overhandsome cads and weaklings). He arranges a mock marriage to trick the girl into sleeping with him. He also insists that their "wedding" be kept a secret, so as not to anger his father and cost him his financial support. When she becomes pregnant, she, of course, insists that their marriage be revealed, whereupon Sanderson then tells her the truth — and deserts her. She returns home, but her mother dies, and she takes refuge in a rooming house, where she bears her child — very realistically by the standards of the time, too much so according to some moralistic critics, and some censorship boards. The child sickens and dies and it may be that the emotional high point of the film is Anna's vigil with him — in which she baptizes him (no minister is called) before death comes.

Thereafter, Anna wanders the roads until she comes upon the Edenic farm of Squire Bartlett and his family. There, after convincing the stern but essentially benevolent owner of her worth, she finds both work and warmth, winning the love of the son, David (Barthelmess). Unfortunately, the Bartlett farm is quite close to the Sanderson estate and the dastardly Lennox, now enamored of a Bartlett cousin, Kate Brewster, who the squire hopes will marry David, finds Anna's presence an uncomfortable reminder of his past and he keeps asking her to leave. She refuses, but when her former landlady, visiting a nearby small town, sees Anna, she tells her story to Martha Perkins, the village gossip, who retells it to the Squire, who orders Anna from his home, in the theater's classic casting-out scene, inspiration since of a thousand cartoons and parodies. Lennox happens to be present, taking dinner with the Bartletts, and before Anna exits into the ferocious blizzard that has blown up, she denounces him as her seducer. David believes her story and rushes out to find her.

There ensues one of the most remarkable sequences in film history, in which the hysterical Anna, blinded by her emotions as much as she is by the storm, wanders through the gale and then on to a frozen river, where at last she collapses. In the morning the river ice begins to break up and, still unconscious on her ice floe, she is carried perilously close to the edge of a falls, from which, at the last possible moment, she is rescued by David.

. . . During one of the numberless takes required for the river sequences, as the current gathers speed, Barthelmess, hampered by a raccoon coat and heavy spiked boots, must leap from floe to floe trying to reach her before she is carried over the falls. There was nothing like a Niagara (an insert shot of which was placed — rather ineptly — into the sequence to build menace) near White River Junction. Still, Gish was being carried at ever increasing, and quite unexpected, speed toward dangerous rapids as the actor made his way to her. Directing from a bridge over the torrent, Griffith shouted to him to pick up his pace, but the command was lost in the roaring of the water. Barthelmess himself, however, soon saw Gish's danger, and racing toward her, leaped onto a piece of ice too small to bear his weight. The look of panic on his face as he starts to sink, then heaves himself onto a sturdier bit of ice is utterly real. And there are similar fearful moments — clearly not acting — as he carries Gish to safety across the highly untrustworthy ice. The effect of these shots in the final film is to break through fictional conventions and send a clear signal to the audience of the dangerous trouble taken

on this film. They may therefore represent a poor choice esthetically. But they are also undeniably thrilling as documentary footage,
and Griffith was justified in surrendering to their undeniable impact.

. . . He never brought a higher measure of energy or concentration to any film. And he never risked more, financially. Consider:
to buy the rights to *Way Down East* he had borrowed $175,000 from
the Central Union Trust Company, putting up as collateral 80 percent of his personal interest in the film. Then on April 23 he borrowed another $150,000 from another bank, the Guarantee Trust
Company, putting up as collateral his personal interest in five of
the six Artcraft pictures, plus *Hearts of the World*. A month
thereafter, he had to put up the negative for *The Love Flower* in
order to receive a $315,000 loan at 6 percent in order to buy the
rights to the film from First National so he could then turn it over
to United Artists for distribution — his contribution to peace among
the partners and to the company's continuing need for product. But
that was still not the end. In June, just as plans for incorporation
and the public offering of shares in the D.W. Griffith Corporation
were coming to fruition, he borrowed another $200,000 from the
Central Union, this time putting up his rights in the four latest
Dorothy Gish comedies, his remaining 20 percent interest in *Way
Down East*, plus a $150,000 life insurance policy he held. His ex-
posure at this point thus amounted to $525,000, most of it at-
tributable to production costs on *Way Down East*. Adding in loans
that were still outstanding on *The Love Flower* and *Romance*, it is
clear he had managed to run up close to a million dollars in debt
during the first six months of 1920, retirement of which was entirely predicated on the performance of his pictures at the box office.

And then, in June, just about everything else he had was placed
in the hands of the Chicago firm of Counselman & Company, which
was handling his corporation underwriting. This included: all the
physical assets of his studio, 300 shares of United Artists common
and preferred stock, contracts with artists (valued, very generously, at $250,000), all his extant distribution contracts, his mortgaged
rights in *Hearts*, the Artcrafts, the Dorothy Gish pictures, the First
National releases, and all other films then in production, plus "good
will," which was also generously evaluated. Thus virtually everything
Griffith had was, in effect, twice encumbered — first to pay for current production, then to establish the corporation. Just to service
production debt all his pictures had to turn at least a modest profit.
If they did not, creditors obviously had recourse to the films
themselves, which meant, in turn, they would be attaching the cor-

poration's only real assets, It also meant that Griffith himself could, in the worst imaginable case, be rendered penniless.

To be sure, he had received, in return for the assets he had placed with Counselman, all the Class B stock of the corporation — 375,000 shares of it plus a note for $150,000 giving him a claim against his own corporation for money he had advanced it during the period he was awaiting flotation of the public stock issue. But that issue, which was to consist of 125,000 shares of Class A stock, to be sold at $15 a share, had a prior claim on the company's assets — up to $25 per share in the event of voluntary liquidation, up to $20 in the event of bankruptcy. At either figure, the pay down on the Class A stock would require far more than the company had in realizable assets, particularly since the only truly valuable property among them, the films themselves, were already pledged to the banks as loan security. Worse, Griffith was obligated to pay a dividend of $1.50 per share per year on the Class A stock, a feat he never fully accomplished. Indeed, to keep the company afloat in the years ahead, Griffith deferred much of the $200,000 annual salary to which he was contractually entitled, leading him, in the end, to sue his own concern for back pay. To put the matter simply, and mildly, if *Way Down East* were not a hit, his company would be out of business almost before it started.

He was thus under tremendous pressure, as he ended his shooting and began editing, titling and scoring, not only to finish as quickly as possible, but to make the picture as good as possible. As was his wont, he pursued his postproduction working long into almost every night, right up to the day of the premiere. Others might fall asleep as he screened dailies, but never Griffith, and his colleagues, according to Carr, were always hearing his voice drifting across "a chasm of sleep." "Do you like the second shot or the fifth best?" The questions were particularly insistent on *Way Down East*, with Carr claiming there was 80,000 feet of film, the result of multiple camera coverage, to select from for the 12,000 feet used in the final negative.

. . . taking an old but well-liked work, allowing the new medium to freshen it without distorting it or losing its basic value as a simply unbeatable entertainment, Griffith had made a film that was irresistible on almost any level on which it was approached. A simple comparison merely with his own work shows that. Though it traffics in many of the same values as the Gish pastorals of the previous year, its scale transforms it into a major work, while unlike that other minor candidate for designation as a masterpiece, *Broken Blossoms*, it avoids poetical and "prettifying" excess (the word is Gilbert Seldes's). Yet among the long films, it avoids the moral blindness

of *Birth*, the structural imbalances of *Intolerance* and the simple
failures to understand observable reality that marred *Hearts*. And,
of course, it was unmarked by the cynicism, or perhaps more properly the attempts at cynicism (a manner Griffith was quite bad at),
to be found in some of his other work of the time.

To some critics *Way Down East* might be old hat, but it wasn't
to Griffith and he brought authentic feeling, authentic emotion to
it, as he did to all his best work. He liked and believed in these people, liked and believed in the conventions through which they were
seen. In short, this may well have been the film he had been aspir-
ing toward since Biograph days, the perfect matching of man and
material on a project that lay at the dead center of his range. There
is an ease to the film, a comfortable stride to its pace, even a certain
control in its titling that make it a delight for a modern audience
to watch. By dropping back in time Griffith here frees us from the
discomfort we often feel in the presence of an old-fashioned sensibility
working in an inherently modernist medium. For once, we can relax
and have a good time with him, enjoy him enjoying his confidence
in himself and his material.

And so the picture went forth. And it did travel "far and long."
Two statements, perhaps, indicate as well as anything the breadth
of its appeal. One was a letter from John Barrymore, then at the
height of his powers, to Griffith. Having seen *Way Down East* twice
he wrote that "any personal praise of yourself or your genius . . .
I would naturally consider redundant and a little like carrying coals
to Newcastle," but not "having the honor of knowing Miss Gish personally," and fearing direct address might be considered "imperti-
nent," he asked Griffith to tell her that "her performance seems to
me to be the most superlatively exquisite and poignantly enchant-
ing thing that I have ever seen in my life." He had seen Duse and
Bernhardt on the stage and thought Gish matched them "for sheer
technical brilliancy and great emotional projection, done with almost
uncanny simplicity and sincerity." It was, he said, "great fun and
a great stimulant to see an American artist equal, if not surpass, the
finest traditions of the theater." What music for the movie people!
Greater respect than that from one's peers cannot be hoped for and
Griffith quoted from the letter in his advertising campaign.

But more useful than that was the outpouring of praise from people who did not ordinarily have much to say about the movies, except perhaps to condemn their pernicious influence on public morals.
Typical of this support from quarters previously unheard from was
a lead editorial in the *Omaha World-Herald*, when *Way Down East*
reached that hinterland. It began by saying the motion picture had,

at birth, come "into the hands of those who were striving not for the best art but for the most dollars." Yet despite this "debasement" here was *Way Down East,* and here was the man who made it. "David Wark Griffith is not merely a keen businessman exploiting 'the movies.' He is a man of culture and refinement and ideals — a true and a great artist. He is a man of vision and convictions — a great preacher. And he has shown us, in this 'simple story of plain people,' how the screen can be used. With true art of a high order of excellence, not alone to entertain the people but to serve them. He has made the combination of beauty with truth. He has put art to its loftiest practical use as the handmaiden of simple goodness. He has given us a foretaste of what 'the silver screen,' in its free and unimpeded development, under the hand and inspiration of genius, can and will become even within the lifetime of men and women now in their youth."

---

# 44th St. Theatre 44th Street, near Broadway New York City

### D. W. GRIFFITH'S

# HEARTS OF THE WORLD

Opening Thursday Evening, April 4, 1918
The Story of a Village
An Old-Fashioned Play with a New-Fashioned Theme
In Two Parts
Scenario by M. Gaston de Tolignac
Translated into English by Capt. Victor Marier
Under Personal Direction of D. W. Griffith

**The Characters.**
(In the order in which they first appear.)

| | |
|---|---|
| The Grandfather | Adolphe Lestina |
| The Mother | Josephine Crowell |
| The Girl, Marie Stephenson | Lillian Gish |
| The Boy, Douglas Gordon Hamilton | Robert Harron |
| The Father of the Boy | Jack Cosgrave |
| The Mother of the Boy | Kate Bruce |
| The Littlest Brother | Ben Alexander |
| The Boy's Other Brothers | M. Emmons / F. Marion |
| The Little Disturber | Dorothy Gish |
| Monsieur Cuckoo | Robert Anderson |
| The Village Carpenter | George Fawcett |
| Von Strohm, agent of German autocracy | George A. Siegmann |
| The Innkeeper | Fay Holderness |
| A Deaf and Blind Musician | L. Lowy |
| A Poilu | Eugene Pouyet |
| A French Peasant Girl | Anna Mae Walthall |
| A Refugee | Mlle. Yvette Duvoisin |
| (Courtesy Max Duruy, Comedie Francaise, Paris) | |
| A French Major | Herbert Sutch |
| A Poilu | Alfonse Dufort |
| A Poilu | Jean Dumercier |
| Stretcher Bearers | Jules Lemontier / Gaston Riviere |
| A Poilu | Georges Loyer |
| A German Sergeant | George Nichols |
| Refugee Mother | Mrs. Gish |
| Woman with Daughter | Mrs. Harron |
| Wounded Girl | Mary Harron |
| Refugee | Jessie Harron |
| Boy with Barrel | Johnny Harron |

ACT. I.
(1) The first part is given up to the village in time of peace.
(2) The latter part is the struggle with the Germans for its possession.

ACT II.
(1) The village under German occupation.
(2) The Allied Forces attempt to drive out the invader.

## JAMES R. QUIRK

# An Open Letter to D. W. Griffith

*The publisher of* Photoplay *considered himself something of a sage, a father figure for the whole movie industry. His magazine earned a position of considerable respect and a wide readership. But sometimes he got a little high handed, as he did in this unfortunate editorial (December 1924). It is rather weirdly contradictory. How could Griffith be austere and brutal, on the one hand, and sentimental on the other? If he is to get more in touch with the real world, why would it help to become more like Cecil DeMille? What Quirk meant was that DeMille seemed to be "in touch," at the moment, with audience tastes.*

*The notions so carelessly offered in this "letter" were to follow Griffith to his grave. They were copied by critics and historians for many years afterward, claiming that the Victorian Griffith was behind the times in the twenties. The 1920s reflected changes in moral codes caused by World War I, the widespread refusal to obey Prohibition, the rise of racketeering, and new "freedoms" for women. But for Griffith simply to try to conform to these changes in audience expectations would hardly represent any kind of directorial leadership.*

*Griffith was actually just on the point of submitting himself to studio budgets and schedules at Paramount. His independence was ending and he was giving up his Long Island studio. He made a "jazz age" picture,* That Royle Girl, *and one that had been bought for DeMille,* The Sorrows of Satan *(both 1926). He could do these things, but not very well. He was far closer to "facing the world" when he was allowed to make the semi-documentary stories suited to his temperament and skills:* America, Isn't Life Wonderful, *(both 1924) and* Abraham Lincoln *(1930).*

The time has come when, for the good of motion pictures, you should take an accounting of yourself.

You have contributed more to the progress of the photoplay than any human force. You come nearer to being the one positive genius of the screen than any other worker in filmdom. Von Stroheim and Chaplin have revealed their flashes of genius but you have come to be considered the dean of our directors, the guiding spirit of the silent drama.

But, Mr. Griffith, you have reached a point where you are before an *impasse.* Your abilities are at a dead stop. You must do something to yourself — and for the good of the pictures.

Permit me to delve into your real self in pointing out a remedy. Your very habits of life have made you austere. You literally have withdrawn from contact with things about you. You have created a wall between yourself and the outside world. You have made yourself an anchorite at Mamaroneck. Such a withdrawal soon means a Puritanical repression, an unyielding eye upon humanity. You see men and things in sharp blacks and whites, as being very good or very bad.

Your pictures shape themselves towards a certain brutality because of this austerity. Much the same thing overtook the Puritans with their ducking stools and stocks and the high bred Spaniards with their racks and thumb screws. Austerity is a dangerous thing.

Your refusal to face the world is making you more and more a sentimentalist. You see passion in terms of cooing doves or the falling of a rose petal. You refuse to face the world because it would wreck your ideals of things as you think they should be and you create a false world of things as you would like to have them. But, remember, the screen — in order to advance — must portray life as it is.

Your lack of contact with the world makes you deficient in humor. You must know people to see the laughter of life.

In other words, your splendid unsophistication is a menace to you — and to pictures. You must not look upon yourself as the evangelist of the screen. You have too great genius to let it waste. You have demonstrated that in dozens of unforgettable screen episodes. The photoplay has reached its highest points in these episodes.

One of the penalties of isolation is the fact that it draws bad advisers. You must stop seeing life at second hand. . . .

I am not recommending that you acquire puttees, a swimming pool and a squad of Jap valets. Nor am I suggesting that you pal around with Elinor Glyn. Yet, if I had my way, I would imprison Cecil De Mille at Mamaroneck for a while and I would loan you his Hollywood trappings, each and every one of them.

You, Mr. Griffith, could select your players anywhere, at your own figure. You are a tradition. You have the supreme advantage over every other director. Players, authors and technical workers would flock to you, once you dropped your austerity.

You must sacrifice yourself for the good of pictures. Let someone else take charge of your soul for a year or so. Faust tried it — and had a good time. Otherwise he would have been forgotten by poetry and history.

I fear you exaggerate your capacities as a business man. The sale of stock in your company to the public earned you nothing but trouble. Why not do as Allan Dwan and Marshall Neilan have done

— let some proven business organization handle the other end of it? You have a wonderful brain, but only one.

You made the screen of the past, Mr. Griffith. Now make it in the future.

# BLAKE LUCAS
## *Lady of the Pavements*

*From a 1980s perspective, Lucas wants to convince us that Griffith (who, as we have seen, could not easily change himself into a DeMille) was capable of entertaining us as subtly as Lubitsch and with a similar kind of warm observation. Such versatility has seldom been ascribed to Griffith, and leaves us wishing for a double bill of this rare 1929 film with, say, The Marriage Circle (1924). Of course the Lubitsch couples were all upper middle class, whereas Lady of the Pavements at least included some ironic contrasts between the cruelties of the upper class and the sincerity of a poor cabaret performer. This naturally would have appealed to Griffith. Contemporary reviews, according to Schickel, were at best "indifferent" and the New York opening of the film was humiliating in paying more attention to Lupe Velez than to the director. Lucas' revaluation appeared in Magill's Survey of Cinema: Silent Films, Vol. II, 1982.*

The alleged decline of D. W. Griffith is one of the most unfortunate and unwarranted myths in conventional histories of the cinema. In recent years, renewed attention to some of his later films has revealed that in the final phase of his career, Griffith remained a creative and evolving artist who was not content to offer pale copies of his earlier triumphs. Griffith's last film, *The Struggle* (1931), has more recently been considered a landmark early talkie. Film historians now recognize its lasting artistry based on the film's "considerable dramatic and emotional power." *Lady of the Pavements* has been neglected even more than *The Struggle*, perhaps because it is an extremely rare film of which no more than a few prints survive. The relative unavailability of this film is very unfortunate because it is one of Griffith's most beautiful and perfect films, ranking with the more famous *True Heart Susie* and *Broken Blossoms* (both 1919). Lacking the scale and ambition of Griffith's most celebrated films, *The Birth of a Nation* (1915) and *Intolerance* (1916), these films are more intimate and subtle, possessing an extraordinary delicacy of emotional texture. *Lady of the Pavements* is especially notable in this respect because, on the surface, it is nothing more than an unoriginal romantic comedy in the manner of Ernst Lubitsch's films.

The story concerns a deception and the resulting romantic complications. Count Karl von Arnim (William Boyd), a member of the Prussian Embassy in Paris, discovers that his fiancée, Countess Diane des Granges (Jetta Goudal), has been unfaithful. Angered by her cavalier treatment, he tells her that he would prefer to marry "a woman of the streets" and breaks off with her. The scorned Countess conspires with Baron Finot (Albert Conti) to obtain an elaborate form of revenge. They find a soubrette named Nanon del Rayon (Lupe Velez) singing at the Smoking Dog cabaret and groom her to pass as a lady. As planned, Count von Arnim falls in love with her. Nanon and the Count become engaged, then Countess des Granges reveals the deception. Nanon feels hurt and guilty and flees, but Count von Arnim's reaction is unexpected. Although he has been tricked into falling in love with Nanon, he recognizes that, essentially, she is innocent and that his callous former lover has manipulated them both. Indifferent to his rank and social position, he finds Nanon at the Smoking Dog and the two are reconciled.

Stories like this were very popular at the time *Lady of the Pavements* was made and remained so into the 1930's when sound demonstrated their adaptability to the musical genre. Allegiance to any real time and place was incidental, and the romantic intrigues of the upper classes could be treated with a light hand, resulting in elegant escapism of wide popular appeal. Lubitsch was the master of this type of film. He possessed wit and sophistication and undercut the superficial lightness of his films with his genuine affection for the characters and his insightful treatment of the relationships. It was not easy to imitate Lubitsch's sensibility without seeming graceless and awkward. *Lady of the Pavements* compares favorably with Lubitsch's films because Griffith projects his own personality into it. It was not a project he initiated or developed. He simply stepped in and directed it when the assignment was offered. The material might have seemed out of his range, but the warm mood with which he imbues the film shows that his response was profound. Unlike Griffith's earlier virginal heroines, Nanon del Rayon is an experienced "woman of the streets," but he treats her with the same respect. He appreciates her beauty, her sweetness, and her sincerity. He demonstrates that his lovers do not need to be innocent to be appealingly guileless.

The assumption that Griffith was ill-suited to anything other than Victorian melodrama and pastoral romance had always been a false one. In his Biograph shorts, he had treated a wide variety of stories, many of which were notably modern and free of sentiment. He is best appreciated as an artist bridging two worlds, the Victorian world into which he had been born and the twentieth century which questioned the values of that earlier world. His characters reflect this. Anna Moore (Lillian Gish) in *Way Down East* (1920) suffers from the same puritanism as those who persecute her, but both she and the film ultimately reject that puritanism. The one character in that film who is consistently admirable is the hero (Richard Barthlemess) whose values are far more flexible than those of his family and the community in which he lives.

There is a trace of irony to the moral codes evoked in many Griffith films. The punishments the characters suffer for transgressing, particularly in the case of the women, always seem ludicrously extreme. In this context, the lighter tone required in *Lady of the Pavements* permits Griffith to express a mature attitude to the realities of love. The heroine's virtue is never a cause of concern to the hero. Once the deception has been exposed, he does not hesitate for a moment to reconcile with her. The amusing irony of the film is that the Countess des Granges, who seeks to deceive and hurt the hero, is the one who gives him what he really wants by bringing the heroine into his life.

*Lady of the Pavements* was made partly to show off young Mexican actress Lupe Velez. As a result of Griffith's careful direction, the somewhat limited Velez displays a charm and sensitivity worthy of better actresses, such as Lillian Gish, Mae Marsh, and Miriam Cooper, with whom Griffith had been associated earlier. She is beautifully photographed and costumed throughout the film and makes a credible transformation from soubrette to refined lady. Jetta Goudal and William Boyd also give skilled performances, the latter in a role far removed from the Hopalong Cassidy characterization with which he came to be identified in later years. The distinctive tone of romantic comedy in this period is enhanced by the presence of Franklin Pangborn as a prissy etiquette professor whose fights with Velez are hilarious. Pangborn made a career out of playing this type in many famous films of the sound era.

The romantic aura which surrounds Velez is imparted to the entire production. It is one of the loveliest films of its type, with sets by the prodigious William Cameron Menzies, who later made immense contributions to the overall design of *Gone with the Wind* (1939) and *Kings Row* (1942), among many other films. Griffith does not stress cinematic virtuosity in any obvious sense. The camera moves with great fluidity at times, as in the subjective shot when the Count runs to the window and looks down at the street after Nanon has run away, but on the whole, the direction is distinguished by superb pacing, a fairy-tale visual atmosphere, and nuances which make the tender feelings of the characters vivid and affecting. The film demonstrates Griffith's versatility and undiminished mastery, but it is most memorable for the pure pleasure it affords.

In 1929, many silent films were to an extent made over as sound films, and this is marginally true of *Lady of the Pavements*. Irving Berlin wrote a haunting song, "Where Is the Song of Songs for Me?" which Velez sings to Boyd during a romantic sequence. A trade review indicates that this song and a synchronized music score constituted the extent of the film's use of sound, but another, very favorable, review which appeared when the film opened at the California Theater indicated there was also some spoken dialogue by Velez as well as additional songs. The film survives in a strictly silent version and is completely satisfying in that form. Fortunately, a recording of Velez singing "Where Is the Song of Songs for Me?" also exists. At a rare showing of the film during a Griffith retrospective in 1969, the recording was played just prior to the actual screening of the film. The melody was utilized by the organist in his subsequent accompaniment and the song was able, once again, to become an integral part of the film. This unusual presentation is worth recalling because of the magical effect the song had before a single image had been projected and the way this effect informed the experience of watching *Lady of the Pavements*. Although the image of Velez actually singing the song in the film can no longer be experienced as it was in 1929, it may be evoked as an uncommonly touching souvenir of cinema.

# EILEEN BOWSER
## *Isn't Life Wonderful*

*Curator for the Department of Film at the Museum of Modern Art in New York City, Eileen Bowser is internationally known as a discriminating film critic and historian. She was editor and chief contributor to a volume called* Film Notes, *published in 1969 by the Museum as a guide to their American fiction films available for circulation. This review appeared in the book at pages 55-56.*

D. W. Griffith's last film as an independent (until his final work, *The Struggle*) was *Isn't Life Wonderful*. A fiction-document of depression conditions in postwar Germany, it was a surprising film for Griffith to have made at a time when he needed to make money more than ever before. However, he knew that he would have no more opportunities for a while to make movies to please himself: he had already secretly signed up with Paramount. The unusual subject of the film was probably suggested to him by his lifelong financial advisor, J.C. Epping, a German citizen who had visited his relatives there during the terrible year of 1922.

It was also Griffith's last great film, the last to blaze new trails. Forswearing spectacle, thrills, and large-scale action, he produced an intimate, sharply realistic study of poverty, hunger, and the debasement of people by the evils of war. He showed himself sympathetic to the same country he had condemned six years earlier in the propaganda film *Hearts of the World*. The story was based on contemporary events, and the film was made on the German locations, using local people as extras: during July and August of 1924, he shot the street scenes in Old Berlin, the forests in Crampnitz and Sacrow, the shipyard at Köpenick, the potato patch at Grünau. Hunger and malnutrition, breadlines and riots are portrayed with penetrating presence in the somber grays of newsreel photography. The scene in which the family of Polish refugees sit dully at their dinner of turnips, for example, is a masterpiece of observation.

The film stops short of slice-of-life naturalism, however, imbued as it is with the lyrical affirmation of life expressed by the reiteration of the title, as well as the addition of Griffith's naive and sentimental touches and comedy scenes to Major Moss's original story.

The actors play their parts with unusual restraint and understatement: Carol Dempster, her hair pulled back and in shabby clothes, attains a stature she never achieved in any of her other films and justifies Griffith's long preoccupation with her. Even the villains are not Griffith's typical leering caricatures, but ordinary workingmen driven to crime by hunger. When Inga calls them beasts, they reply, "Yes, beasts we are, beasts they have made of us."

The climactic chase sequence is a stirring one unlike any other Griffith chase: there are no contrived effects, and the suspense is not pushed beyond belief. In a beautifully staged and photographed series of shots, Inga and Paul with their precious store of potatoes hurry home through the tall trees as darkness approaches, pursued by the desperate workers who at last overtake and rob them. To judge by the reviews, at the time of the opening the picture ended here, with the two lovers trying to console each other. But within a few days Griffith had tacked on a happier ending, which weakens the simple and poetic finish. The addition consists of the scenes with the titles, "A year later — the aftermath," "The family escort them to their new home," "And this time enough potatoes for all!" This presents a perplexing problem for the historian and archivist: does one show the film as Griffith originally intended it, or as he (unfortunately) decided to improve it, no doubt after being told it was too depressing to attract a wide audience? Historical truth seems to demand the latter.

Made the year before Pabst's *The Joyless Street, Isn't Life Wonderful* had a wide influence on European and American film-making. Fritz Lang noted in an interview in 1925: "Griffith has again revolutionized the film world . . . he has given a veracious picturization of conditions in Europe after the war, conditions little understood in America . . . which gave rise to most poignant dramas." These films were perhaps too isolated to have composed a movement, though they present an interesting parallel to the growth of neorealism in Italy after World War II.

# Chapter 4

# Stroheim

*This was, obviously, the straight dope on European decadence.  — Richard Griffith and Arthur Mayer[1]*

*Stroheim's apparent obsession with sex, sadism, and seduction is indeed noticeable in all his films.*
                                        *— Peter Noble[2]*

If D.W. Griffith, American-born, had a dream of success which was to a great extent fulfilled in his life and reflected in the energetic optimism of his films, Austrian-born Erich von Stroheim seems to have been afflicted with paralyzing nightmares.

In his adopted country, after many struggles and rejections similar to Griffith's, Stroheim eventually benefited from the same opportunities and advantages Griffith had, and in fact worked as his production assistant. Yet these encouraging events did not shake the gloomy philosophy underlying all his films.

Louis Hartz, a Harvard political philosopher, has claimed that America's dominant pragmatic liberalism, during and after the 1776 revolution, reflected the fact that Americans — that is to say, white Americans — never experienced an intrenched feudal system, as Europeans did.[3] When Stroheim came to the U.S. in 1909, he brought with him an obsession with middle European feudal traditions which haunted him all his life. Seven of the nine

1.  *The Movies*, (1957, 1984) p. 213.
2.  *Hollywood Scapegoat*, (1950) p. 62.
3.  *The Liberal Tradition in America*, (1955).

stories he brought to the screen were about middle European "nobility," and they were depicted for the most part as venal, vapid, and cruel.

Whether his treatment of barons and countesses drew upon direct personal experience is none too clear. Peter Noble confidently asserts (on the basis of conversations with Stroheim) that "he had lived in a world of intrigue and lasciviousness. At court he had seen drunken officers at midnight dragging protesting maidservants into their quarters."[4] Yet it is now well known that Stroheim was not related to powerful personages at court, as he claimed. It is highly unlikely that he was in a position to see scenes of this sort. He may have simply read the newspapers, listened to gossip, and used his imagination.

Stroheim claimed for years that he had been an officer in the imperial guard, that his father grew up as a member of the Austrian court and his mother was a lady-in-waiting. Actually he was the son of a hatmaker who joined the army — and was compelled to leave it — as a private. When he came to the United States at 24, he decided to impress Americans by adding the aristocratic 'von' to his name. But for a long time the new immigrant had to work at odd jobs, including extra work in the movies, before he made himself noticed and valuable during World War I as an expert on German uniforms and a performer in villainous Prussian roles.

"I have always told them the truth as I saw it," he wrote in his Foreword to Peter Noble's biography. What more could anyone ask of a film director — especially a director who invented his entire personal history? But are we compelled to take Stroheim seriously when he equates truth with ugliness and life with determinism, saying he gives us "life as real as it actually is for people: harsh, unexpected, hopeless, fatalistic"?[5]

Stroheim was echoing the dark vision of the philosopher Thomas Hobbes, to whom man's original "state of nature," dominated by selfishness, was "solitary, poor, nasty, brutish, and

---

4. *Op.cit.*, p. 83.
5. Georges Sadoul, *Dictionary of Film Makers*, (1965, 1972) p.244. The Stroheim manifesto in the front of the Noble biography is a close paraphrase of the end of the next to last paragraph in one of Norris' many essays in criticism, "The True Reward of the Novelist," *World's Work*, October 1901: "I never truckled, I never took off the hat to Fashion and held it out for pennies. By God, I told them the truth."

short."[6] Yet Hobbes at least proposed, as an improvement on that state, that human reason was bound to reach out for self-preservation (thereby inflicting on society an absolute ruler).

Stroheim seems to have had no coherent view of society at all, except as a habitat for fools, villains, and inept lovers. He certainly had no prescriptions for the improvement of humanity. However much he proclaimed his debt to D.W. Griffith, he shared very little of Griffith's faith in messages. In a Griffith film a character might learn from experience. Stroheim only exposed them to cruel ironies. William Everson makes the comparison:[7]

> Griffith liked to find beauty amid squalor and despair *(Broken Blossoms, Isn't Life Wonderful)*. Stroheim preferred to find ugliness and depravity amid luxury and elegance *(Foolish Wives, The Merry Widow)*.

This suggests that he could be consciously discrediting wealth and aristocracy in order to promote a more disciplined or idealistic way of life. But in a Stroheim film it is extremely hard to find any lurking positive alternative. In fact there is a certain ambivalence which becomes more pronounced in the later films, an underlying fascination with the old regime, a regret that the dreadful old traditions have passed away.[8]

He certainly did not see America itself as an alternative, for when he dealt with Americans, it was not to turn attention to the values of freedom, the frontier, or a new civilization. In his films Americans were either naive stuffed shirts, unable to cope with sophisticated Europeans, as in *Foolish Wives*, or ignorant and stolid lower-class clods, as in *Greed*.

Stroheim's first three films were about attempted seduction. This prudent state of incompletion served to satisfy the Puritan preferences of the American audience, although there was plen-

6. Thomas Hobbes, *Leviathan*, (1651). See also George H. Sabine, *A History of Political Theory*, (N.Y., Holt, 1937).

7. "Erich von Stroheim 1885-1957," *Films in Review*, August-September 1957. Another comparison Stroheim himself made: "Lubitsch shows you first the king on his throne, then as he is in his bedroom. I show you the king first in his bedroom so you'll know just what he is when you see him on the throne."

8. Richard Koszarski offers a thoughtful comment on this: "No matter what his true origins, von Stroheim completely identified himself with the *ancien regime*, and its fall was traumatic. He dwells on the injustice of prewar society, but in the end finds it preferable to what replaced it." *The Man You Loved to Hate*, (1983) p. 99.

ty of hanky panky clearly going on in the background and before the movie started. Furthermore, the death of the character played by Stroheim himself in *Blind Husbands* (1919) and *Foolish Wives* (1922) seemed to add tension and seriousness to the atmosphere of petty eroticism.

In later films, there was an increasing intrusion of the notion of romantic love denied. A prince with some pretensions toward charm, but with no intentions of giving up his harem-like contacts at the bordello, may be attracted to a pretty commoner, but with no hope of happiness. In four films, people of noble birth are forced to marry ugly and unloved characters in order to benefit from their wealth. In three of them the spouse is aged, crippled, or both. In *Merry Go Round* (1923) and *The Wedding March* (1928) it is the male protagonist who is required to go through an undesired marriage. Old Baron Sadoja in *The Merry Widow* (1925) appears as a decrepit suitor for the female lead. A similar character, also played by Tully Marshall, turns up in the last half of *Queen Kelly* (1928).

The list of minor characters who are unfortunate in their ugliness or unrepentant in their depravity would be a long one. Stroheim's pessimistic view of human nature was displayed in the range of despicable, money-grubbing, decadent, and stupid characters he wrote into his scripts. Devotees of the Stroheim world in fact have found his various hags and wastrels rather endearing — a distinct change from the sweetness and light so predominant in Griffith's screen characters. For those who liked to hiss the proper hero and cheer the wily villain, there were entertaining rewards in Stroheim pictures.

Although Stroheim seemed depressed about the corrupt lives he displayed on the screen — and usually gave the cruel ones a fairly savage kind of punishment — he clearly felt that what they represented was more "real" than goodness. It is a keyhole kind of realism he offers us, a process which seems to be "revealing" but can also be seen as a simple philosophy of pessimism. André Bazin thus characterized his "one simple rule for direction":[9]

> Take a close look at the world, keep doing so, and in the end it will lay bare for you all its cruelty and its ugliness.

For Stroheim, romantic expectations by mortal man are naive and almost always bound to be frustrated. There are implied

9. *What is Cinema?* (1967) p. 27.

happy endings in *Merry Go Round* (completed by Rupert Julian under Irving Thalberg's supervision) and *The Merry Widow*, but it is obviously questionable whether these belong to Stroheim, and the second half of *The Wedding March* is ambiguous, since war separates the married lovers at the end. All of these heroines, as well as "Queen" Kelly, go through so many vicissitudes before snaring their true loves that we find the whole charade far from romantic and the endings more than likely a concession to the boxoffice. Stroheim himself could frequently be heard deploring the "tyranny" of the happy ending.

The reason for the failure of all romantic hopes, of course, is that fate intervenes. Something goes wrong because of character flaws or power struggles or accidents or outside forces. No one is permitted to have what he or she wants, or even deserves. This may be called naturalism, but it is so consistent that it seems more forced than natural. In this respect, Jonathan Rosenbaum links Stroheim with "his first literary models, Zola and Norris":[10]

> The fictional worlds of all three are so charged with metaphysical forces and intimations of fatality that the "realism" they project is not one in which free will predominates; characters are usually doomed to be what they are by class and social position, heredity, mysterious turns of fate, or some malign combination of all three.

*Greed*, which Stroheim made from the Frank Norris novel, *McTeague*, is his chief claim to fame and his only serious attempt to portray American life. Here he was dealing with the lower classes, but he applied much the same treatment to them as he had to the upper classes in Europe: he made them look ugly, ignorant, avaricious, and tiresome. It was essentially an outsider's view, as he managed to admit in a curiously self-contradictory statement to Edwin Schallert:[11]

10. "Second Thoughts on Stroheim," *Film Comment*, May 1974. Thomas Dean, a Ph.D. candidate in English at the University of Iowa, in an unpublished paper on Frank Norris and Stroheim explores the differences among Stroheim, Zola, and Norris, suggesting that Norris was more American than either of the others in his faith in possible personality improvement through environmental influences (although in the case of McTeague this is reversed), whereas Stroheim accepts the "Judeo-Christian" view of man as naturally depraved and necessarily punished. "The Flight of McTeague's Soul-Bird," 1987.

11. "Stark Realism — At Last!" *Picture Play*, October 1923, quoted in Koszarski, *op.cit.* p. 117. Schallert later became movie reporter and critic for the Los Angeles *Times*.

They have said I could not make an American story, and I want to prove that I can. Of course, it is foolish to say that *McTeague* is American any more than that *Nana* is French. They are international. You can, in fact, trace the inspiration of *McTeague* to *L'Assommoir* of Zola, and it appealed to me more than any other story written by an American, because it is so universal, and because, perhaps, basically the viewpoint and style are those of the European continental.

This "European continental" view of Americans was of course what Stroheim expected to bring to *McTeague.* And whether or not his sensibility was up to that of Zola, he accepted fully not only the determinism and pessimism of the naturalist tradition, but also its style of overwhelming concentration on details. Stroheim did not flinch from the challenge, as he saw it, to create the first completely naturalistic motion picture. In the grandest possible gesture of fidelity to "life," he attempted to make his film the length of the novel — that is, to reproduce it scene by scene and with the same number of characters.

Such a notion was doomed from the start, since theater owners were not prepared to run a movie that started in the afternoon and ended late at night. The footage submitted to the Metro-Goldwyn studio in 1924 was cut and cut and cut again.

Nor was this enough to make it attractive to audiences. The crude German peasant types with which he populated the screen offered not a single character an average middle class American wished to identify with. Richard Griffith and Arthur Mayer summed up the reaction: "Audiences were not indifferent to it or bored by it — they actively hated it."[12]

*Greed* therefore has the same popular standing among the works of Stroheim as *Intolerance* has among Griffith's films. On the other hand, there has been over the years a consensus among critics that *Greed*, like *Intolerance*, though for somewhat different reasons, is an absolutely unique achievement. In the history of

12. *The Movies, op.cit.* Koszarski quotes (*op.cit.*, p. 146) from the trade paper, *Harrison's Reports*, December 13, 1924: 'In my seven-year career as a reviewer and in my five-year one as an exhibitor, I do not remember ever having seen a picture in which an attempt was made to pass as entertainment dead rats, sewers, filth, rotten meat, persons with frightful looking teeth, characters picking their noses, people holding bones in their hands and eating like street dogs or gorging on other food like pigs, a hero murdering his wife and then shown with hands dripping with blood; I have never in all my life seen a picture in which all the principal characters were people of the gutter and remained such to the end."

American films, there are not many stories of working class people that show relentlessly those aspects of their lives that are dreary, clumsy, and commonplace. Linked with this milieu, on the one hand, was an insistent theme of worship of money, and on the other, a strictly tragic structure, in which not one of the protagonists is left alive.

Tragedy is uncommon in the movies, and it is believed by many critics to be the highest form of drama. *Greed* aspired to that distinction, yet it was not the traditional tragedy of kings or of attractive star-crossed lovers. Griffith's *Broken Blossoms*, with its "low-life" lovers, had been praised in 1919 as "the first genuine tragedy of the movies." But *Greed* was grim beyond imagining, and its combination of milieu, theme, and structure carried an aura of innovation. It still does today, and it was one of the gross miscalculations of the Mayer-Thalberg regime at M-G-M that the director's complete version was not preserved, whatever judgment might be made about the length that had to be used in theaters.

*The Merry Widow* (1925) was less innovative, and its tunelessness was a handicap, but the story of the Franz Lehar operetta was enough to make it Stroheim's most popular and profitable production. The *New York Times*, among others, included the film in a "best ten" list. The irony of a small principality being dependent on the wealth of a single outsider perhaps was appealing to Stroheim, and it seems that Thalberg also gave him leave to make changes. He is supposed to have refused at first to undertake such a well known trivial love triangle, and later turned his back on a scene between Mae Murray and John Gilbert, saying, "Tell me when it's over." His antiromantic inclinations were no doubt satisfied by the grisly bridal-night scene he invented, in which Baron Sadoja, expiring, fails to make Sally his wife but does make her a rich widow.

*The Wedding March* offered a similar situation of a nobleman attracted by a beautiful commoner. But in this case Stroheim, age 43, short of stature and plain of face, famous from World War I as "the man you love to hate," attempted to play the romantic role. He is even polite to the sad-eyed limping millionaire he has married (played by ZaSu Pitts) while longing for the "apple blossoms" associated with petite Fay Wray, whose oafish suitor later threatens to destroy everybody. It is hard to imagine this flaccid melodrama as a popular success and in fact it was a disaster except in a few cities. This was also the scenario in which the princess-mother greets the morning smoking a cigar, and the prince, his father, works out the terms of a marriage of convenience for the son in a drunken stupor on the floor of a brothel.

After that, it only remained for Stroheim to try to sell Gloria Swanson on playing the inheritor of a whole chain of African brothels. She supposedly never agreed to this plot point, being convinced that her American fans would find it loathsome. One version of the story has it that she wasn't told about this until ten reels of *Queen Kelly* were already shot (in 1928). Griffith and Mayer report that shortly after being given this bit of news Swanson simply said to Stroheim at the end of a scene, "I have to make a phone call," (to Joseph Kennedy, her very close friend and financing partner) and never came back. Stroheim, for his part, claimed there was no bad feeling between them, and that the reason for stopping the picture was simply the cumulative realization that the sound film had arrived. "The cumulative effect of von Stroheim's directorial extravagance" is a better explanation, Richard Koszarski says, referring not so much to the budget as to the outrageous decadence of the whole story as it was emerging in the rushes.[13]

There was one more script, based on a play, which attempted to deal with two young American couples. Again ZaSu Pitts is the rejected woman, and her suicide keeps the story in the tragic mode. Most of the footage Stroheim shot at the Fox studio was rejected and reshot. Stroheim indicated that there was a quarrel between two supervising producers and he was caught between them. *Walking Down Broadway* became *Hello Sister* (1933) and Stroheim became, for the rest of his life, an actor and occasional screenwriter.

He had already accepted acting jobs in Hollywood, as a sadistic film director in *The Lost Squadron* (a caricature of himself), and as a sadistic novelist in *As You Desire Me*, for which Greta Garbo had specifically requested him. After several discouraging jobs in poverty row studios, he was glad to accept an offer in France, where he discovered there was still an enormous reservoir of appreciation for his films. He worked steadily for three years, in a wide variety of roles. The peak of his performing career was the prisoner-of-war camp commandant, Von Rauffenstein, in Jean Renoir's *Grand Illusion* (1937).

13. *The Man You Loved to Hate*, pp. 218-222.

During and after World War II he worked again in the United States, notably for Billy Wilder as Field Marshal Rommel in *Five Graves to Cairo* (1943) and as Gloria Swanson's butler (and former director) in *Sunset Boulevard* (1950). He did not like this — his last Hollywood role — very much. It was the mad film director again, this time rejected by the industry.[14] But the part was more sympathetic than most, and of course his reunion with Swanson after twenty years was symbolic of the film's purpose as a sad salute to the silent era.

Stroheim as a human being was as full of contradictions as some of the more entertaining characters in his films. According to the accusations of his first wife (in divorce proceedings, reported by Richard Koszarski), he was physically abusive and yelled at her inside and outside the house.[15] In his earliest days as an actor in short films, Everson says, Stroheim the egotist simply could not hold still: he had to be noticed, had to try to steal attention from the leading players.[16] Lillian Gish "saw him break into tears when the part for which he had rehearsed was given to another actor" in a Griffith film.[17]

When he became well known, he made a point of dressing smartly and arriving at his studio office in a chauffeured limousine. His treatment of stars was based on breaking their spirit and bending them to his will. He was not quiet on the set. He berated extras of high and low degree to demonstrate who was in charge. Yet the loyalty of his "stock company" was part of his legend: he always found places in his cast and crew for those who had worked with him before. And when L.B. Mayer suspended him at a time of crisis on *The Merry Widow*, the extras rebelled openly and Mayer backed down.[18]

His private life seems to have become far quieter as he became more successful and, presumably, more sure of himself. In fact his third wife, who frequently came to work with him, brought

14. Thomas Quinn Curtiss, *Von Stroheim*, (1971), p. 321. From 1941-1943, Stroheim played Jonathan Brewster in a touring company for the stage production, *Arsenic and Old Lace*.

15. *Op.cit.*, p. 12

16. *Films in Review, op.cit.*

17. *The Movies, Mr. Griffith, and Me*, (1969) p. 174.

18. Curtiss, *op.cit.* pp. 126-127, 210-211.

a noticeably moderating influence right onto the set. Peter Noble
provides us with personal data (as of 1950) and a comment:

> . . . His first wife was Margaret Knox of Oakland, California, who died
> in 1915. His second wife, May Jones, a designer for D.W. Griffith, was
> the mother of his eldest son, Erich, now an assistant director at Twen-
> tieth Century-Fox Studios in Hollywood. Stroheim's third wife, follow-
> ing his divorce in 1918, was actress Valerie Germonprez, whose brother
> Louis was Von's devoted assistant director for ten years. She was the
> mother of Stroheim's second son, Joseph Erich.
>
> Whether Stroheim's deep interest — some have termed it an obsession
> — with sexual themes in his films was an expression of his own sublimated
> desires is doubtful, but it is certainly curious that the man who did most
> to bring a sophisticated approach to sex into the silent cinema was himself
> a loving and faithful husband for more than thirty years.[19]

The story of Erich von Stroheim is usually told in terms of the
puzzling excesses he insisted on during production and the agon-
ized reactions of studio bosses when the bills came in. His pictures were almost always too long for commercial release, and
the costs of production were said to be inflated by such foolishness
as precisely toned bells which could not be heard by the audience
and expensive woven monograms on military underwear (never
to be seen on the screen but supposedly contributing "realistically" to the wearer's dignity).

Stroheim very often acted as his own costume designer and
worked in close collaboration with Richard Day, who was usually
his art director. In his grasp of all the aspects of production and
his concern for every single detail, on or off the screen, he was
certainly Griffith's disciple. But his eagle-eye perfectionism,
focused on the most trivial properties on the set, seemed to many
people to verge on the irrational.

After he built a replica of much of Monte Carlo on the Universal
lot for *Foolish Wives*, it was no wonder that publicists were in-
structed to try to get some money back at the boxoffice by making him into an exotic character, spelling his name with a dollar
sign, calling $troheim the costliest film maker in the world, and
his movie "the most fascinating spectacle ever conceived by man."[20]

19. *Hollywood Scapegoat*, pp. 82-83. Possibly 20 years. During his time in France,
    1937-1939, Denise Vernac — actress, journalist, and Stroheim fan — became his
    companion, and this relationship lasted until the end of his life in 1957.

20. Herman Weinberg, *Stroheim: A Pictorial Record of His Nine Films*, (1975). Adver-
    tisement reproduced on p. 37.

*Foolish Wives* made him truly famous, and it gave Universal a touch of class. It did not, however, reach the screen as he planned it. There had already been a conflict over late-night shooting with Irving Thalberg, the new chief of production at the studio. As soon as Stroheim made it clear that he wanted to run the picture in two three-hour parts in two separate theaters, Thalberg locked him out of the editing rooms. The premiere in New York, as a concession to him, was three hours long, but there were complaints about the length and even more protests about the morality of the story. The prints for general release were cut to the usual ten reels.

Almost all of Stroheim's pictures were taken over by others — changed, shortened, re-shot. This was not really unusual in Hollywood, then or later, since negatives are owned by the people who pay for them, not by their directors. But Stroheim managed to carve out for himself a place as perhaps the most unhappy victim of studio revision in Hollywood history. This was the more irksome in view of his early successes as a director.

His sudden arrival on the scene as a writer-director-star for *Blind Husbands* was the gift of Universal's president, Carl Laemmle. His impassioned selling of himself and his script won the support of the man who had founded one of the first great independent companies. Stroheim says they were friendly throughout that first picture, the next *(The Devil's Passkey)*, and the start of *Foolish Wives*. But then Laemmle went to Europe, leaving his now-famous Viennese director in Thalberg's charge.

Not yet well known as Hollywood's executive "boy wonder," Thalberg was nevertheless ready to assert the primacy of the studio hierarchy over the creative hired hands. It was the beginning of the end of the director's domination, a precedent established by Griffith. In the case of Stroheim's fourth film, *Merry Go Round*, it was possible for Thalberg to cut back on what he saw as endless rehearsals and retakes by actually removing Stroheim during production and replacing him with another director. He could do this because he had already seen to it that Stroheim did not perform as an actor in the picture and therefore was not indispensable.

Thalberg was the perpetrator of most of the unkind cuts, not only at Universal but again at Metro-Goldwyn. Stroheim, after the shocking dismissal at Universal, was riding high with a new contract. He was working hard on *Greed* at Goldwyn when the company was unexpectedly sold to Loew's Inc. L.B. Mayer was brought in as studio head, and Thalberg was his new production chief. Soon *Greed* underwent a painful shrinkage. Still, after all those repeated hot confrontations, Thalberg decided to give Stroheim the go-ahead to make *The Merry Widow*.

Such paradoxes make the story of Stroheim both interesting and emotional. Claims of "brutal" changes made by "hacks" have given us a continuing legend of nine ruined masterpieces. It is a great shame, certainly, that we are now unable to see the footage Stroheim wanted us to see. But it is at least debatable whether a picture twice as long about the same people would be a greater artistic achievement than the version of *Greed* we have. As William Everson suggests, this version must have been cut, not by hacks, but by experts, since it is the one which critics all over the world have placed among the greatest films.

As for his reputation for profligate spending, Lewis Jacobs has a few well-placed doubts as to whether that was the main reason for Stroheim's separation from Hollywood. He had "no more failures than less worthy directors" and at M-G-M far more money was spent, wasted, and lost on *Ben Hur* than on *Greed*.

It was what he was trying to say that isolated Stroheim from American film makers. Was he trying to tell the world some profound, obscure, and valuable truth? "Hollywood," Jacobs says, "steered clear of von Stroheim because it was steering clear of reality and endorsing claptrap."[21] But was it reality that Stroheim gave us, or was it claptrap just like the rest — with a negative twist?

Controversies over what might have been — and recriminations on both sides about the self-indulgent artist versus the philistine studio — tell us much about the beginnings of the Hollywood studio system. But these things cannot be as significant for us today as the films themselves and a continuing examination of the philosophy expressed in them.

We may view them as simply "unAmerican," products of a sensibility oblivious to our familiar ideals of get-ahead gumption, equal opportunity, free individualism, and the democratic spirit. On the other hand, we may look at Stroheim's film stories as cautionary tales, giving us graphic examples of the perpetual cussedness of human nature, warning us that corruption and

21. *The Rise of the American Film*, (1939), p. 344.

hidden power might some day become as familiar a part of our experience as in an older Europe.

Whatever we may eventually say of Stroheim as prophet, his consistent pessimism set the tone for a long line of European visitors, from the lightheartedness of Ernst Lubitsch through the dark warnings of Fritz Lang to the dogged cynicism of Billy Wilder. Certainly in his films there is none of the familiar American trait of confidence in the future. If such a notion raises its head (in *Greed* or *Walking Down Broadway*) it is quickly discredited. His films celebrate no beckoning frontiers. They aren't about an individual taking thought and getting ahead. They are about being frustrated and slipping back. They are grotesque contradictions of the American dream of success, studies in corruption and evil with no hints at all on the ways to a better life.

Whereas Griffith looked upon evil as an external temptation which can be successfully resisted, Stroheim saw evil as an endless pressure on us, from within or without, which can never be overcome. This struck the postwar generation — which had suffered specific losses of life and hope and some of the old familiar standards of behavior — as a bitter "truth." He offered them an echo of a darker world, plus an entertaining, sardonic treatment of it. This paralleled the more pedestrian sophistication already being promoted by Cecil B. DeMille, for whom evil was mainly a useful ingredient in showmanship.

Those who were not rich enough or nervous enough to expatriate themselves to Paris after the war looked at Stroheim's films and said, "Life in Europe was cruel — but fascinating." Others said, "If that's the way it was, we don't want it here." In either case, they felt he had brought them new, more mature experiences and they were impressed.

Despite his many disappointments, it was not an especially unlucky time for Stroheim to be making films in America. He wrote his own scripts, directed as he wished, saw his films reduced in length but in most cases the internal style of his scenes retained and his philosophy kept largely intact. He was replaced on two films and "excesses" were censored in others. But his public impact in his own time was enormous and his influence on other film makers, then and now, has been considerable. When his films went abroad, they found wide recognition. During his latter years in France, his personal fame and circle of friends gave him satisfaction.

The characters and themes in his films contrasted sharply with the characters and themes in the films of Griffith and Ince. His world view was different from theirs and different from that of most Americans. But he got our attention all the same. He brought to movie theaters a sensibility reminiscent of Goya and Hogarth. He had a talent for despair and a flair for publicity, and he made the most of them.

# ERICH VON STROHEIM
# The Seamy Side of Directing

*This brief statement about the extravagance of the movie industry (as opposed to his own) appeared under Stroheim's name in* Theatre Magazine, *November 1927. It was discovered and reprinted by Richard Koszarski in his book,* Hollywood Directors, 1914-1940, (N.Y., Oxford University Press, 1976) *pages 172-175. The telling blow is the last sentence: 'What we want is better pictures, but restraint will never produce them.'*

There has been much talk, today, of the waste of money in motion pictures. Most of the accusation is thrust upon the director's shoulders. That, at least, has been my experience. But the extravagance is committed long before the director enters the scene.

This is one of the follies of the industry. Take, for instance, *An American Tragedy*. Two or three companies buy it. When I say "it," I mean, most often, the title. Let us say $97,000 is paid for it. That is but the initial expense. It is like buying a car without spare parts. Then there is the expense of adaptation, script, continuity, and so forth, which aggregates approximately an additional $75,000. That is before the picture is begun. Then the director with vision, who wants authentic details, surroundings and general atmosphere, is watched with a hawk-eye. He is lucky if he can enforce his own interpretation, incidentally the reason he has been engaged.

My greatest handicap has been the fact that when I started directing one of the publicity men thought that since motion pictures impress people with the huge sums entailed in the making, it would be a capital stunt to advertise the amount of money I was spending. And so, this publicist chose Forty-second Street and Times Square New York, as the target for all hungry eyes, and each day, with the help of his widely imaginative mind, posted the latest figure, increasing the numbers in leaps and bounds. The result was most harmful to me in the industry, for while the producers were pleased to boast of their extravagance, they privately resented it.

A human characteristic this and not unlike incidents that arise in one's own family. I recall when a very young man, a student in the Austrian army, boots were the most fastidious part of my uniform. I used to order six pairs at a time, instead of one, so that I would not be compelled to wear the same pair until they grew shabby, at the same time keeping them all in good condition. While my father, well able to afford the expenditure, proudly beamed at my well-groomed appearance, he ranted and fumed at my extravagance, just the same.

How can a director be expected to turn out an artistic work if he is ever conscious of money — of an amount he is supposed to spend. The holes in the motion picture industry are not in the prodigality entailed by the director, but in the salaries paid to stars for months and months while they are not working, merely because their contracts call for salary. A director has many "white elephants" on his hands, too; often the producer's relatives. Sometimes he is given one of these prize purchases that is no more suited to the motion picture than a violin. If the director should change the story very obviously, as he often has to because of the difference in vehicles between spoken and silent drama, he is severely criticized.

I must record a word of sympathy here for the smaller director. He is usually watched so closely on the financial budget that he daren't begin to express himself. He is rarely given the wherewithal to make a picture that would turn out to be "big." He is limited to time, expense and also usually given poor actors with whom to work. In that way he is forced into a snag. His work is grouped with the less important, and eventually he is classified as "just an ordinary director," with the result that when a producer has a big story on which he can spend freely and which calls for an excellent cast, to whom does he naturally turn? To the man who has already made a "big" picture. That forces the "smaller" director into a rut, from which he can rarely extricate himself.

A director should no more be limited to the time and money spent on a picture than an author or a playwright. Neither of the latter can be told that he must write something within forty days, and see to it that the properties involved should not exceed $10,000. In the same way it is utterly impossible for a director to be told that he must complete a picture in a given time and see that it does not cost more than $ . . . . . A capable director is not necessarily content with a scene after it has been shot five or six times, or after he has spent the scheduled four days on it. Perhaps one more shot, or another day would give him the desired result; does that not justify his delay? After all, no director enjoys retakes any more than the producer does the additional expense, but if he feels that he has not achieved the desired result, that in itself is assurance something better is possible, and that he can give it. What we want is better pictures, but restraint will never produce them. . . .

# HERMAN WEINBERG
## Stroheim's Pictorial Art

> *Here speaks a longtime passionate admirer of the films of Stroheim, Sternberg, and Lubitsch. Weinberg edited three books of stills from Stroheim films, including* The Complete 'Greed.' *The passages which follow are from the introduction to* Stroheim: A Pictorial Record of His Nine Films *(N.Y., Dover Publications, 1975) pages xi, xiii, xvi, and xvii.*
>
> *It is noteworthy that such European masters of cinema as Jean Renoir and Luis Bunuel have declared they were greatly influenced at an early stage of their careers by the first director of European origin to find success in America.*

*Foolish Wives* — that acid dissection of social follies which left Renoir *bouleversé* and decided him on a film career, the film which William Wyler called one of the ten greatest of all time, of which the *New York Times* said in its review, "It teems with scenes that mean something, that throw light on character and action, that strike the spectator fairly between the eyes and make him sit up and read pictures. This is the chief value of the film. The picture is thus vitalized through Mr. von Stroheim's cinematographic skill." But in such a complex work one can find what one has the capacity to find. For the French critic Lo Duca, "Stroheim's terrible laughter and brutal skepticism shook the habitual American thinking of the time as it had never been shaken before"; Claude Mauriac discovered in it "a cruel eroticism, and black humor"; to Pierre Leprohon, it revealed "the disgust of man for man." There were other reactions, too, such as the one in the *New York Morning Telegraph* (cited by Marcel Lapierre in his *Les Cent Visages du Cinéma*, Grasset), which fulminated, "It should be prohibited. It's a case of high treason to America and an insult to women in general. I'd kill anyone who took my children to see this film."

But cinema as an art was jolted out of its puberty by *Foolish Wives*. Furtively in *Blind Husbands*, then more boldly in *The Devil's Passkey*, Stroheim had tested the reaction of the cinematic Pollyannism of the time to what he was trying to do, and then, when he was confident that his audience was ready for it, he unleashed his demon with this *danse macabre* in the form of a masque.

"A genius, the greatest after Chaplin," said André Bazin, foremost of French film critics, of Stroheim. An instinctive genius, one would have to add, considering that his first film, *Blind Husbands* (called that over his protests in defense of his own title, *The Pinnacle*), was one of the first of any consequence to appear on that eternal morning that saw the parturition and early development of the motion picture. "It is superior to most of the year's productions," said the *New York Times* of a year which included Griffith's *Broken Blossoms* and George Loane Tucker's *The Miracle Man*, "and, more importantly, its outstanding pictorial quality indicates that Mr. Stroheim, unlike many directors, grasps the fact that the screen is the place for moving pictures and that whatever is to be done on it with artistic finish, must be done pictorially. So many directors use moving pictures chiefly to ornament and enliven their stories. They do not depend upon them in crises. Whenever dramatic moments come, or when the plot is to be unfolded or carried forward, they turn to familiar but ineffectual words. But Mr. Stroheim . . . has evidently relied principally on pictures and in a number of his dominating scenes there are no words at all, only eloquent pictures, more eloquent than words could ever be." That was said in 1919. . . .

One thing Stroheim did was to kick out the artificial sets of Hollywood with their insipid "prettiness," demanding sets for his films that looked like the real thing. No one had ever demanded this before. This often led him to such far reaches as constructing what appears to have been a good portion of the Principality of Monaco for *Foolish Wives*, half the Prater for *Merry Go Round*, St. Stephen's Cathedral with the Stephansplatz and Graben before it in the Vienna of *The Wedding March*, etc. He could also go to the other extreme and build no sets at all, as in *Greed*, for which he utilized actual buildings of types called for by the Norris novel *McTeague*. And though basically a studio craftsman, like Griffith, Rex Ingram and other leading directors of the time, he could also go to such extreme places as Death Valley because Norris called for it in his novel, just as Griffith went to the actual postwar inflation-ridden Germany for *Isn't Life Wonderful* and Ingram to the Sahara for *The Garden of Allah* because Robert Hitchens' novel called for it. Stroheim was told, "A desert is a desert, shoot it in Oxnard or the Mojave," just as they told that to Ingram. But *McTeague* wasn't about Oxnard or the Mojave, just as *The Garden of Allah* wasn't. And so each man went where he had to go. Only sometimes did they go where it was expedient when faced with the studios' immovable dictum (first propounded by the now legendary Hollywood producer who reputedly told his director, who was looking for an "authentic location" involving a sylvan glade, "A rock is a rock, a tree is a tree. Shoot it in Griffith Park" [a well-known public park in Los Angeles]). Even the usually implacable Stroheim had to give in to that, and the duel in the early morning mist in *The Merry Widow* and the confrontation of the squadron of mounted cuirassiers and convent girls in the dazzling sunlight of high noon in *Queen Kelly* were both shot in Griffith Park — but how they were transfigured into the Balkans and the Baltic respectively is what ultimately mattered.

*Greed* . . . which stirred the cupidity that slumbers in everyone, but close to the surface of consciousness. In the film it is aroused to an uncontrollable frenzy on the part of all the principals concerned, each living in the private world of his own panic that the winning of a lottery unleashes. Everyone hopes to win the lottery. One has to go to Céline to find a counterpart for the fury and pessimism of this film in literature, though the saving grace of *Greed* is that it is without the nihilism of the savagely misanthropic author of *Journey to the End of Night*. . . .

Buñuel, who has directed his own *Diary of a Chambermaid*, also confesses to Stroheim as the first of his inspirers to "go and do likewise." When Carlos Fuentes asked him who were his strongest influences in the beginning, he replied, "The comedians, certainly, and von Stroheim." He particularly liked the scene in *The Merry Widow* where three men in a box at the theater have their binoculars trained on the lithe young dancer Sally performing on the stage — Prince Danilo looking at her face, Crown Prince Mirko looking at her middle and the degenerate old Baron Sadoja looking at her feet. . . .

"He wanted to show that the whole world was kin, that there was good and evil everywhere, and not always where we would expect to find them, and sometimes in the most surprising places," I once wrote about Stroheim. "Human nature was compounded of contradictory attributes, which Dostoievski realized so trenchantly, and no Stroheim character ever ceased for an instant to be a credible human being, whether cast in the role of hero or villain. A complete human being himself, with the wide latitude that this permits, he observed human frailty as he would observe it in himself, with irony or compassion, depending on the circumstances, but never losing his sense of humor, which was prodigious and, more often than not, withering.

"Round and round went the eternal game of lust that fascinated him as a scientist is fascinated by the developments in research he is undertaking . . . lust for the things men lust for, the lust for money, for love, for youth, before which borderlines of nationality and caste crumble. Like Asmodeus, he soared over the rooftops of the world and peered into the windows, and what he saw there is partially discernible in the pitifully few fragments that were permitted to remain of his work by those whom he angered or made afraid. But he loved life, and it was this that the buffoons who tried to 'put him in his place' did not understand, for how could they know that a man can have wings and rejoice only in the flight of his creative spirit?"

# S.J. PERELMAN
# Cloudland Revisited: Vintage Swine

*For Weinberg,* Foolish Wives *was an "acid dissection of social follies."*
*This essay by one of America's premier humorists is an acid dissection*
*of Stroheim's film, reprinted from pages 82-88 of* The Road to Miltown,
or Under the Spreading Atrophy *(N.Y., Simon and Schuster, 1957).*
*Perelman (1904-1979) worked in Hollywood from time to time. He*
*wrote the basic screenplays for the early Marx brothers' films* Monkey
Business *(1931) and* Horsefeathers *(1932) and also for* Around the World
in 80 Days *(1956).*

Some Hollywood flack, in a burst of inspiration, dubbed him the
Man You Love to Hate. He was a short man, almost squat, with
a vulpine smirk that told you, the moment his image flashed upon
the screen, that no wife or bank roll must be left unguarded. The
clean-shaven bullethead, the glittering monocle, and the ramrod back
(kept rigid by a corset, it was whispered) were as familiar and as
dear to the moviegoing public as the Pickford curls or Eugene
O'Brien's pompadour. No matter what the background of the picture was — an English drawing room, a compartment on the Orient
Express, the legation quarter of Peiping — he always wore tight-
fitting military tunics, flaunted an ivory cigarette holder, and kissed
ladies' hands profusely, betraying them in the next breath with utter
impartiality. For sheer menace, he made even topnotch vipers like
Lew Cody, Ivan Lebedeff, and Rockliffe Fellowes seem rank
stumblebums by comparison. He was the ace of cads, a man without
a single redeeming feature, the embodiment of Prussian Junkerism,
and the greatest heavy of the silent film, and his name, of course,
was Erich von Stroheim.

I first saw him in a tempestuous drama, presented by Carl Laemmle
in 1919, called *Blind Husbands,* which von Stroheim, with cyclonic
energy, had adapted into a photoplay, and directed, from *The Pinnacle,* a novel he had also written. Actually, I must have seen him
three years earlier as the Second Pharisee in the Judean movement
of *Intolerance,* wearing a fright wig and a gaudy toga and heckling
the Nazarene, but there was so much Biblical flapdoodle flying
around that I was too confused to peg him.

The picture that definitely canonized von Stroheim for me, though,
was *Foolish Wives,* a gripping exposé of the swindlers who were

popularly supposed to prey on rich Americans in Monte Carlo. In this 1922 chef-d'oeuvre, he impersonated a spurious Russian noble named Ladislaw Sergius von Karamzin, as ornery a skunk as ever flicked a riding crop against a boot. Everything about him seemed to me touched with enchantment: his stiff-necked swagger, his cynical contempt for the women he misused, and, above all, his dandyism — the monogrammed cigarettes, the dressing gowns with silk lapels, the musk he sprayed himself with to heighten his allure. For six months afterward, I exhibited a maddening tendency to click my heels and murmur "*Bitte?*" along with a twitch as though a monocle were screwed into my eye. The mannerisms finally abated, but not until the Dean of Brown University had taken me aside and confided that if I wanted to transfer to Heidelberg, the faculty would not stand in my way.

Not long ago, the Museum of Modern Art graciously permitted me to run its copy of *Foolish Wives*, on condition that if I became overstimulated or mushy, I would not pick the veneer off the chairs or kiss the projectionist. Such fears, it presently turned out, were baseless. The showing roused me to neither vandalism nor affection; in fact, it begot such lassitude that I had to be given artificial respiration and sent home in a wheelbarrow. Ordinarily, I would incline to put the blame on my faulty metabolism, but this time I knew what the trouble was. A certain satanic *Schweinhund* hadn't blitzed me as he used to thirty years ago.

*Foolish Wives* upsets precedent by first investigating the seamy side of Monte Carlo instead of its glamour. We fade in on a milieu brimful of plot — the tenebrous hovel of an aged counterfeiter named Ventucci. A visit from his principal client, Count Karamzin, establishes that the latter is using Ventucci's green goods to support an opulent villa as a front for his stratagems. During their colloquy, the Count's jaded appetite is whetted by his host's nineteen-year-old daughter, a poor daft creature fondling a rag doll. The old man stiffens. "She is my only treasure," he snaps at von Stroheim, unsheathing a stiletto. "If anyone should harm her . . . " Leaving this promissory note to be honored at whatever point von Stroheim has run his gamut, the action shifts to an exclusive hotel near the casino. Here we meet an overripe young matron with a face like a matzoth pancake, all bee-stung lips and mascara, the wife of an American millionaire called (*sic*) Howard Hughes, and played by a sluggish Mittel-europan identified in the cast of characters only as Miss Dupont. Von Stroheim ogles the lady, who seems complaisant, gets himself presented to her, and, baiting his hook with a sermon about the pitfalls of Monte Carlo, offers to introduce her to his cousins the Princesses Olga and Vera Petchnikoff. He further-more assures her, brazenly squinting down her bodice, that they — and, of course, he — would be enraptured to act as her social spon-sors. Mrs. Hughes, understandably, is *bouleversée*, and, consent-ing to accompany him to a water carnival several nights thence, lumbers away to loosen her stays and recover her wits. Whether she has any of either is debatable; both her figure and her deportment are so flabby that one cannot work up much moral indignation against von Stroheim. The man is earning a very hard dollar.

Disclosed next is the Villa Amorosa, the seaside lair of the Count and his confederates, Princess Olga (Maude George) and Princess Vera (Mae Busch). For my money, Mae Busch never possessed the spidery, ghoulish fascination of that consummate she-devil Jetta Goudal, but she ranked high as a delineator of adventuresses and Eurasian spies. At any rate, the two lady tricksters, far from being von Stroheim's cousins, live in what appears to be a languid state of concubinage, switching about in negligees and exchanging feline gibes. Over breakfast, the three agree on the *modus operandi* stan-dard among movie blackmailers, whereby the Princesses are to divert Mr. Hughes while von Stroheim compromises his wife. Ventucci, meanwhile, bustles into focus in the crisp, matter-of-fact fashion of a milkman, trailed by his daugher and bringing a satchel of fresh queer just off the press. He gives off ominous rumblings when the Count behaves familiarly with the girl, but nothing more consequen-tial than glowering results. The same is true of the water carnival that evening. Mr. Hughes, a silverhaired, phlegmatic wowser, whose civilian name escaped me in the credits, betrays mild pique at the sight of his wife paddling around the studio tank and pelting von Stroheim with artificial roses but, after a few heavy sarcasms, relapses into coma. Had the tempo not quickened in the ensuing scene, the picture might have ended right there for me. What with the whir of the projector and the weight of my eyelids, it took every bit of buckram I had, plus frequent pulls at a Benzedrine inhaler, to keep from sliding into the abyss.

Whittled down to essentials, the purport of the scene is that the Count takes Mrs. Hughes on an afternoon excursion, pretends to get lost in a thunderstorm, and steers her to a sinister house of assignation run by a crone called Mother Gervaise. The sole func-tion of this unsavory character, as far as I could tell, was to per-suade the young matron to doff her wet shimmy, so that von Stroheim, who has made a great show of turning his back, can stealthily appraise her in a pocket mirror — as neat a sample of voyeurism, I may add, as any ever reported by Wilhelm Stekel. After endless chin music calculated to allay her trepidation, von Stroheim has just maneuvered his sweetmeat into the horizontal when a wild-eyed anchorite reels in, ululating for shelter. Who this holy man is the picture never explains, but his scowls put a quietus on the high jinks, and Mrs. Hughes regains her hotel next morning shopworn but chaste. Inexplicably enough, the Count does not use the incident to shake down her husband — indeed, he has Princess Vera affirm that Mrs. Hughes spent the night with her — and the whole affair mystifyingly trails off with nobody the wiser, least of all the audience.

Up to now, the element of gambling has been so ruthlessly slighted in the story that the locale might as well have been a Scottish tabernacle or the annual dance festival at Jacob's Pillow. Suddenly, however, Lady Luck rears her head beside that of Sex. In addition to his other *chinoiserie*, von Stroheim has been shacking up with a bedraggled maiden named Malishka, a servant at the villa, whom he has glibly promised to wed as soon as the Bolsheviki are deposed. To still her importunities, the Count cooks up a pitiable tale of insolvency and borrows her life savings, which he loses at roulette. Mrs. Hughes, who is also having a flutter at the wheel, observes his despair and lends him her pile of counters — a gesture that abruptly changes his luck. Strong though the temptation is to pocket his winnings, he craftily relinquishes them to his benefactress, and then, a few hours later, lures her to the Villa Amorosa with a plea that his life and honor are at stake. The rendezvous takes place in a tower room. Outside the door, Malishka crouches in a fever of jealousy, and this time generates sparks in a quite literal sense. Infuriated by her lover's endearments to Mrs. Hughes prior to easing her of ninety thousand francs, the maid locks the pair in and sets fire to the stairs. They take refuge on an exterior balcony, from which they shout appeals for help, but the other guests at the villa are absorbed in being fleeced at baccarat by the Princesses and fail to respond. Hughes, meanwhile, has become increasingly worried about his wife's absence, pantomiming his solicitude by sitting on the edge of his bed and thoughtfully scratching his chin. Eventually, the Monte Carlo Fire Department, which has been snoozing under the bulldog edition of *Le Petit Monégasque*, bestirs itself, and, dashing to the scene, spreads a net under the balcony. Von Stroheim gallantly knees his companion aside and jumps first. Mrs. Hughes follows, almost hurtling through the roof of the limousine in which her husband has just driven up. Apart from the indignity of the *pompiers'* catching a glimpse of her bloomers, though, she sustains no perceptible damage, and the episode peters out, like all those preceding it, with Morpheus, the patron saint of the scenario, drowsily sharpening his quill for the next sequence.

Low as were the price of film and the salaries of actors in 1922, Mr. Laemmle and his aides must nevertheless have decided at this point in *Foolish Wives* that the consumer's patience was finite, and ordered the curtain down. The last reel, therefore, begins with Hughes' discovery, in his wife's corsage (while hunting for his pipe or a pair of shoe trees, I got the impression), of the note by which the Count had enticed her to his villa. He seeks out von Stroheim, knocks him down, and exposes his activities to the police. The Princesses are apprehended on the verge of flight, and unmasked as a couple of actresses named Maude George and Mae Busch, and now all that early scaffolding about Ventucci and his fey daughter comes in handy. Von Stroheim, in a stormy Dostoevskian finish, sneaks back to the coiner's hovel, ravishes the girl, is disemboweled by her father, and winds up being stuffed into a cistern. The concluding shot shows the Hugheses reunited — if two pieces of strudel can be said to be en rapport — lying in bed and reading, from a volume entitled *Foolish Wives*, the passage "And thus it happened that disillusionment came finally to a foolish wife who found in her husband that nobility she had sought for in — a counterfeit."

# A.R. FULTON

# Naturalism: From *McTeague* to *Greed*

*A professor of English at Purdue University, Fulton brought out one of the earliest American critical-historical film textbooks.* Motion Pictures *was published in 1960 by the University of Oklahoma Press, with the subtitle, 'The Development of an Art from Silent Films to the Age of Television.' The author undertook to illustrate special aspects of technical and artistic innovation through analysis of certain key films. His careful study of* Greed *is of special interest in view of Stroheim's announced determination to film the Frank Norris novel from beginning to end, page by page. Professor Fulton finds that the film maker in this case not only had to leave out a few things (even in his own long version, never released) but he also expanded on and added to some of the specific actions mentioned in the novel. Our excerpts are from the revised version of his book (Norman, University of Oklahoma Press, 1980) pages 104-108, 110-111.*

Von Stroheim's attempt to put *McTeague* completely on the screen resulted in a film of 42 reels, which would have meant a running time of about ten hours. The studio insisting that it be shortened, von Stroheim reduced it to 24 reels, and then permitted a further reduction to 18 reels, to be shown in two parts. Finally Metro-Goldwyn-Mayer, which the Goldwyn Company had become, turned the print over to a studio worker who cut it to 10 reels by eliminating not only the subplots but parts of the main plot as well, and by bridging gaps with subtitles. In the process McTeague's fight with Marcus in Frena's saloon was transposed so that in the released print it occurs after, instead of before, the wedding. The studio burned all the parts that had been cut, but the extant reels together with von Stroheim's script for the original film illustrate what von Stroheim meant by "putting a novel *completely* on the screen just as it was originally written." That *Greed* is not *McTeague* so reproduced can be seen from von Stroheim's own alterations, and that it could not have been is patent because the media of novel and film are different.

In the first place, von Stroheim changes the historical period of *McTeague*. His story commences in 1908, whereas Norris began writing *McTeague* in 1892 or 1893 and had completed it by 1898. Von Stroheim's purpose was apparently to bring the outcome of the story down more nearly to the time *Greed* was filmed — 1923. Inasmuch as *Greed* includes actual shots of San Francisco streets and environs, von Stroheim may have decided on this change for the sake of verisimilitude, but in making the change he sacrificed absolute verisimilitude to the novel and thus compromised his theory. Whereas Norris begins the novel by presenting the hero as an already established dentist, *Greed* opens with McTeague as a young man working in the gold mine. In the novel the gold mine episode is introduced indirectly and only briefly. Sitting in his dental chair in that scene at the beginning of the novel, McTeague is reminded by the tunes he is playing on his concertina of his life ten years earlier. In the film these recollections are presented directly — not in flashbacks, as they would have been if von Stroheim had put the novel on the screen just as it was originally written. This change to an earlier point of attack is significant, for it is characteristic of films to begin their stories at the beginning. *Greed* begins with an iris-in on the title "The Big Dipper Gold Mine, 1908, Placer County, California." For about ten minutes (an hour in the original print) and in contrast to the hardly more than two hundred words that Norris devoted to this part, the film presents McTeague's early life before it brings McTeague up to the point in the story at which the novel begins. Like many other films, *Greed* therefore requires no exposition.

*Greed* deviates from *McTeague* in the presentation of events near the climax. Chapter 21, which narrates McTeague's flight across Death Valley, ends as follows:

> He tramped forward a little farther, then paused at length in a hollow between two breaks, resolving to make camp there.
> Sudenly there was a shout.
> "Hands up. By damn, I got the drop on you!"
> McTeague looked up.
> It was Marcus.

The first part of chapter 22, the concluding chapter of the novel, tells of Marcus joining the posse to track down McTeague, of the rest of the posse giving up, and of Marcus going on alone. A third of the way through the chapter the action is brought up as follows to the point at which the preceding chapter ends: "'If he ain't got water with um,' he said to himself as he pushed on, 'if he ain't got water with um, by damn! I'll be in a bad way. I will for a fact.' . . . At Marcus's shout McTeague looked up . . ." This is the novelistic method of presenting simultaneous action. But, Griffith having shown how motion pictures can manipulate time and space to an extent beyond that possible in a novel, von Stroheim rearranges the order of these incidents so that action in separate places is more nearly simultaneous. The flight-and-pursuit sequence opens with a continuity title: "McTeague had been missing from San Francisco for weeks when — " There follows an insert of a poster announcing a reward of a hundred dollars for the capture of "John 'Doc' McTeague." Then after a medium-long shot of a crowd in western gear looking at the poster, there is a close-up of an individual in the crowd: it is Marcus. After a few more shots to emphasize Marcus's connection with the crowd and its interest in the poster, there is another continuity title — "The fugitive." The next shots are of a valley and of McTeague leading his mule. The film now cuts back to Marcus and his associates. It is night. A brief sequence shows Marcus joining the posse to track down McTeague. Again there is a continuity title — "that night desolation lay around Mac." A series of shots pictures the fugitive, unnerved, firing at imaginary pursuers, and then throwing his rifle away. Again the film cuts back to Marcus, who is starting out with the posse. This cut is made without a continuity title, for now the relationship between the two lines of action has been established. The sequence continues in this manner for fifteen minutes, crosscutting seventeen times between the pursuer and the pursued, before the lines of action are united by Marcus catching up with McTeague.

Such deviations from the novel are inherent in the difference between the epic and cinematic methods of narration. There are also arbitrary deviations, illustrating not only this difference but von Stroheim's failure to put *McTeague completely* on the screen. Mortimer Adler points out that "if a novel be adapted to the screen, it must be contracted in the direction of dramatic magnitude." (By "dramatic magnitude" Adler means the limited number of characters and incidents in a play as contrasted to the larger number in a novel.) Even in its original 42 reels *Greed* illustrated Adler's dictum. For example, in narrating the events of the picnic, Norris writes;

> In the afternoon Mr. Sieppe disappeared. They heard the reports of his rifle on the range. The others swarmed over the park, now around the swings, now in the Casino, now in the museum, now invading the merry-go-round.

Of the locales Norris mentions in this passage, von Stroheim included only the merry-go-round in his film, intercutting it with a scene in a shooting gallery as though to represent what "they heard." The merry-go-round would offer more interesting possibilities for filming than the other locales, and von Stroheim may have selected it for this reason. The point, however, is not that he selected the merry-go-round but that he selected. In the novel McTeague celebrates his engagement to Trina by taking the Sieppes to a variety show. Norris describes not only most of the acts in considerable detail but also their effect on the unsophisticated theatre party. Von Stroheim filmed only one of the acts — a pair of knock-a-bouts — deleted in the abridgement. As in the picnic sequence, he selects, and by selecting he not only fails to put the novel completely on the screen but again demonstrates the impracticality, if not the impossibility, of succeeding. In the truncated print, the contraction in the direction of dramatic magnitude is of course only greater. The deletion of the subplots is part of this kind of contraction. . . .

On the other hand, here and there von Stroheim expands even the scope of the novel. Whereas, for example, Norris has Marcus tell McTeague about Trina's falling out of a swing and breaking a tooth, von Stroheim includes two scenes that were deleted when the film was cut — one of Marcus telling McTeague about the accident and another depicting the accident itself. Similarly he filmed not only the scene in which McTeague tells Trina about losing his job at the surgical instrument factory but, to precede it, a scene — not retained in the extant print — in which he is dismissed and paid off. In the novel the last appearance of the Sieppes is at the wedding. As they are saying their good-byes, Mr. Sieppe keeps calling, "Gome, gome, we miss der drain." Taking "der drain" as a cue, von Stroheim planned a sequence — not retained in the cut version — that began with an iris-in of the Sieppes at the Santa Fe Railroad Station loaded with boxes, satchels, and valises, pushing their way through the crowd into the main entrance. Then a series of shots shows them going through the station, out to the platform, and onto the train. Von Stroheim planned the sequence with his usual detail: Mr. Sieppe neglects to present tickets to the ticket taker at the gate and has to come back and put down four boxes to find the tickets, other travelers say good-bye to friends and relatives, Mr. and Mrs. Sieppe get on the train and enter the day coach but have to go back to help the children up, the car gives a lurch and Mrs. Sieppe drops her hatbox, which falls under the wheels, Mr. Sieppe retrieves the box. The sequence ends with an iris-out on a long shot of the departing train.

Scenes such as these seem to originate in von Stroheim's compulsion to tell everything, as though he, had he written *McTeague*, would have included them. . . .

The deletions in *Greed* that reduce the magnitude of *McTeague* illustrate the kind of contraction to which Adler refers. But Adler also observes about the adaptation of a novel to the screen that "it must be expanded with respect to dramatic detail." (By "dramatic detail" Adler means the amount of detail in the development of single incidents.) Although the presentational nature of motion pictures makes this kind of expansion inevitable, the extent of the expansion depends on the director. That von Stroheim expanded Norris's two hundred words on McTeague's early life into an hour-long prologue is illustrative. Even the curtailed prologue illustrates this kind of expansion. McTeague recalls the episode that led to his becoming a dentist, Norris narrating it in two sentences:

> Two or three years later a travelling dentist visited the mine and put up his tent near the bunk-house. He was more or less of a charlatan, but he fired Mrs. McTeague's ambition, and young McTeague went away with him to learn his profession.

In the extant version of *Greed* the two sentences are represented in twenty-six shots. . . .

Von Stroheim filmed *Greed* before sound became an adjunct to the screen. In describing the wedding of Trina and McTeague, Norris writes:

> Then Trina and the dentist were married. The guests stood in constrained attitudes, looking furtively out of the corners of their eyes. Mr. Sieppe never moved a muscle; Mrs. Sieppe cried into her handkerchief all the time. At the melodeon Selina played "Call Me Thine Own," very softly, the tremolo stop pulled out. She looked over her shoulder from time to time. Between the pauses of the music one could hear the low tones of the minister, the responses of the participants, and the suppressed sounds of Mrs. Sieppe's weeping. Outside the noises of the street rose to the windows in muffled undertones, a cable car rumbled past, a newsboy went by chanting the evening papers; from somewhere in the building itself came a persistent noise of sawing.

The predominant image in that passage is sound: the sounds in the room itself, the sounds from the street, and, finally, a sound from somewhere in the building — "a persistent noise of sawing." Without specifically naming it, Norris implies that, in spite of the immediate concern of the characters with a momentous event, the everyday world is going on just the same, and in "a persistent noise of sawing" he implies a premonition of discord in this marriage.

How would von Stroheim express in pictures the idea that Norris expresses in the noise of sawing? A similar problem arose when *What Price Glory?* was filmed three years later. The problem in *What Price Glory?* is solved by a title which reads: "Deafening roar of guns . . . shrieks of shells." Von Stroheim's solution is different. Recognizing that the street noises and the sawing are symbolic, von Stroheim changes the audio symbols into a visual one. During the wedding scene he points his camera over the shoulders of the bridal couple and past the face of the minister to the window. Through the window is seen, passing in the street below, a funeral procession. Lest there be any doubt as to his intention, he interpolates three more shots of the procession, one of them at close range and at street level. And in his zeal to put *McTeague* completely on the screen he represented the noise of sawing itself by a medium-close shot of "a hand holding a piece of hardwood while the other hand works a saw." Among the deletions when the film was cut are six interpolations of this shot during the wedding.

Although this and other shots of the sources of sound — a train whistle, a bird singing, seals barking, the keyboard of the melodeon as Selina, playing, pulls out the stop labeled "Tremolo," a clock striking nine — were also cut out, comparable shots remain — a piano player (its open front showing the levers moving), the bellows of the concertina moving as McTeague plays, the bell in McTeague's office ringing, and so forth. . . .

The naturalists said that they were trying to write the truth. A prefatory title to *Greed* is a quotation from Frank Norris:

> I never truckled. I never took off the hat to fashion and held it out for pennies. By God, I told them the truth. They liked it, or they didn't like it. What had that to do with me? I knew it for the truth then, and I know it for the truth now.

In its naturalistic motivation, von Stroheim's film is true to Norris's novel. Man, according to the naturalists, is the product of his heredity and his environment. In keeping with this sociological approach, *McTeague* is a story of disintegration of character. McTeague's downfall is partly caused by fate — that, for example, he meets and marries Trina, whose character is also weak. A continuity title in *Greed* reads: "First, chance had brought them together. Now mysterious instincts as ungovernable as the winds of heaven were uniting them." Since Norris implies that the hero's heredity is also responsible, von Stroheim, paraphrasing a passage in the novel, inserts this subtitle: "But below the fine fabric bred of his mother ran the foul stream of hereditary evil, a taint given him by his father." The prologue of the original film details the degeneracy of McTeague's father and his death from alcoholic poisoning. Fate is against the characters. There is always the chance that they may escape, but there is also the chance that they may not.

The film is also faithful to the naturalism of the novel in its detailed picture of working-class life in California at the turn of the century. The neighborhood in which McTeague lives on Polk Street in San

Francisco is photographed with documentary like realism. Von Stroheim is no less realistic in his picture of the dental parlors and McTeague at work in them than Norris, who is said to have studied *A Textbook of Operative Dentistry* to get McTeague's dental procedures just right. The wedding feast is filmed in scrupulous accord with Norris's description. Nor is von Stroheim any less realistic in making up scenes of his own, for example, the scene in the shooting gallery, for which his script specifies "all kinds of Dutchmen, in funny hats, with moustaches, with and without glasses, beer-bellies and mush faces; plenty of tin and brass medals decorate their manly chests." Vividly recording the mores of a people at a particular time and place, *Greed* is no less a sociological document than *McTeague*.

The tendency of the naturalists to emphasize drabness of environment characterizes *Greed* as much as it does *McTeague*. The film by no means glamorizes. Von Stroheim even outdoes Norris in drabness. In the courtship scene in the novel, Trina and McTeague sit on the roadbed of the railroad along the muddy shore of San Francisco Bay. Von Stroheim, in still another deviation from Norris, has them perch on a concrete block over the sewer outlet, Trina having suggested, "Let's go over and sit on the sewer." The scene of the marriage proposal, the little railway station to which they return in the rain, could not have been represented on the screen less glamourously. . . .

# JOEL W. FINLER
# Reassessment: Stroheim as Stylist and Myth Maker

*Published in England by Movie Magazine Limited and in the U.S. by University of California Press (1968), Finler's heavily illustrated book spent 59 of its 144 pages on a close analysis of the surviving footage of* Greed *in relation to Norris' novel and the original shooting script. One of his main points is that the film as finally cut omits not only subordinate characters and details of the emotional build-up (Trina's suspicions, Marcus' fight with Mac) but also specific psychopathic elements which were expressed in terms of symbolism, surrealism, and dreams, and took the film beyond mere realism.*

*The chapter we are using here (pages 127-130, 132) is useful in calling attention to Stroheim's cinematic technique, which was about as minimal as Chaplin's. Editing dexterity is so rare that critics usually can find only one rather elementary example — the theater scene in* The Merry Widow *in which the three suitors are seen to be watching, respectively, Sally's face, body, and feet. Andrew Sarris, in* The American Cinema, *remarks on Stroheim's "technical chastity" in* The Wedding March, *which contains not a single camera movement. Finler calls this a conscious reaction against montage, a choice proposed thirty years later by the French critic André Bazin as more in keeping with the historic development of cinema. Finler's quotations from Lewis Jacobs also show how alert that historian was in 1939 to a difference made famous by Bazin in 1958.*

*Je distinguerai dans le cinéma de 1920 à 1940 deux grandes tendances opposées: les metteurs en scène qui croient à l'image et ceux qui croient à la réalité.*

Thus wrote André Bazin in his essay 'L'Evolution du Langage Cinématographique' in 1958. Both of these opposing lines of development can be seen to stem from the work of D.W. Griffith in the 'teens: he was the spiritual father both of believers in the image and of believers in reality.

Eisenstein, whose films and writing had an unparalleled influence for many years beginning in the 'twenties, openly acknowledged his debt to Griffith. He might be regarded as the leader of the image group for whom composition, lighting and angle of each individual shot was subordinate to the primary function of editing the shots together. The theory of montage depended on the great potential for the use of editing to achieve a meaning on the screen which could not be found within the individual shots. Apart from Eisenstein, such directors as Gance and Dovzhenko might be included in this group.

In the other line of development came those directors who emphasized the creation of a complete reality in front of the camera and included important details within a scene which was shot as a whole. In 'The Rise of the American Film', Lewis Jacobs had referred to the technique of such a director thus:

> His films are not based on the editing principle but on the piling up of detail within the scenes. In the scenes themselves he did everything that another director would do by cutting; his continuity and story were within the scene itself, and did not depend for meaning upon a particular combination or organization of shots. Details, action, and comment were selected and brought into the camera's scope without any changing of the shot.

Writing in the 'thirties, Jacobs could not help but be influenced by the widely accepted view of montage as the basis of the Art of Film. This conditioned his concluding remarks:

> Despite its weaknesses, *Greed* was an important contribution to movies in general. Stroheim's very incompetence in editing forced him to enrich the scene. This achievement was appreciated by other movie-makers, etc.

From Jacobs' viewpoint, these remarks might appear to describe Stroheim's technique, which was diametrically opposed to that of Eisenstein in the 'twenties. Stroheim is the connecting link between Griffith and Renoir in the 'thirties. Today the pendulum has swung the other way and this 'reality' line of development is the more highly regarded. One can now recognize that Stroheim's approach had a fundamental validity and was not merely an attempt to surmount his 'incompetence as an editor'. He was able to place his characters in an environment and to convey the atmosphere of the time and place. On the other hand, the montage film tended to be better suited for treating large-scale subjects in which people appeared more as types than as individuals.

Unfortunately, Stroheim was able to use his technique to the full only in *Greed*. Alone among Stroheim's films of the 'twenties, *Greed* attempted to be uncompromising in subject as well as in treatment. The resulting film was so mutilated and misunderstood that Stroheim never again repeated the experiment.

Stroheim won an international reputation for his artistic integrity and his refusal to compromise, which made him something of an exception in Hollywood. But this assessment was not entirely accurate. Like any other writer or director, Stroheim was strongly influenced by the need to gain the interest of a producer. He generally opted for subjects with considerable commercial appeal. His technique and approach were often uncompromising, but only within the limits set by the chosen subject.

His films invariably went beyond the confines of the usual Hollywood product, in depth as well as length. His style showed his antagonism to the star system in the interrelation of major and minor characters which counterpointed the main plot. He was unusual in his attention to every detail of decor and characterization, and in his wish to make his films in two parts with an interval.

The most important turning point in Stroheim's career came in 1925. After his great disappointment with the release version of *Greed*, he was able to make a complete change of direction in the same year. For the same studio he undertook the most 'commercial' assignment of his career: direction of *The Merry Widow*, starring John Gilbert and Mae Murray. Here he proved that his technique could produce an interesting and artistically successful result within the most stringent limitations of subject. And if the result was not the best of his films, it is work that is by no means unworthy of Stroheim.

Stroheim took great liberties with the story of the operetta, introducing into the plot two sadistic and debauched villains. His fondness for extremes of incongruity found its fullest expression in a project which was to Stroheim his least congenial.

The villains, who had been added to the original by Stroheim, brought with them commercially valuable elements of eroticism and violence. Prince Mirko is involved in numerous brawls and duels and throws a party which turns into an orgy. Baron Sadoja is a fetishist and lecher who has a heart attack on the night of his wedding to the innocent young heroine, Mae Murray. Stroheim undoubtedly saw a certain justice in the humiliations undergone by the star who had been imposed upon him, like Gloria Swanson, the star he was forced to use in *Queen Kelly*. Both are married to ugly old degenerates, played by Tully Marshall, in the most grotesque of matches. (According to Bosley Crowther, Stroheim had to explain Tully Marshall's foot fetish to the baffled producer, Irving Thalberg, who retorted, 'And you have a fetish for footage').

The juxtaposition of extremes of good and evil found in *The Merry Widow* is typical of Stroheim's later films. He was fond of contrasting the young and beautiful with the old and repugnant, violence with tenderness, vulgar eroticism with romantic love.

Yet the nineteenth century melodrama is integrated into his films by virtue of Stroheim's feeling for details and the subtleties of characterization and background. These are not just the puppet figures in the tawdry spectacle created by the many directors who attempted to imitate him. Stroheim's attention to detail gave rise to the many exaggerated stories of his extravagance, in spite of the commercial appeal of his lavish decor and spectacle. It is irrelevant today whether such stories were true or not, though most of them evidently were not. What matters is that they were believed at the time and contributed to an elaborate myth around Stroheim which helped to destroy his career as a director.

The success of Stroheim and his early films was probably partly due to his being known internationally as the Man You Love to Hate — and as the descendant of an aristocratic, military family from Vienna. The publicity stories began to reach new extremes while *Foolish Wives* was in production; he was publicized as $troheim, director of 'The First Million Dollar Film'. Although *Foolish Wives* lost money, it helped to establish Universal as a major Hollywood studio. And M.G.M. may have lost money on *Greed*, but it made back every penny, and more, from the success of *The Merry Widow* the following year. No, the black-balling of Stroheim was not based on simple economics. Many films and many directors had lost at least as much money. Stroheim was the victim of his own myth, created by all those publicity stunts and exaggerated stories, to which, over the years, he had even contributed himself. The myth, and a certain amount of bad luck, buried his creative aspirations.

The extravagant and romantic aspects of Stroheim's creative personality emerge from his own screen portrayal of the aristocratic officer: he values proficiency with gun and sword or in the saddle, he is chivalrous to ladies and always immaculately dressed. Even while he is satirizing the values of the nineteenth century, Stroheim seems to show some sympathy for them. Stroheim is a realist whose films are most often set around the time of the First World War. They portray the downfall of the way of life they depict when it is confronted with the harsh realities of the twentieth century.

Yet Stroheim is also a romantic, like Griffith, to whom he is greatly indebted. The heroines of his later films, with their pale faces framed by long hair and romantically photographed in soft focus and close-up, recall the innocent girls in Griffith's films. A Griffith villain, like the sadistic Battling Burrows in *Broken Blossoms*, is an antecedent for such Stroheim characters as Kallafati or Schani.

The difference between the directors is more one of attitude than of subject. Griffith's films are warm and sentimental while the coldly sophisticated Stroheim tempers his romanticism with cynicism.

Griffith's films often end happily with a last-minute rescue, like the Modern Story of *Intolerance*. The lack of happy endings in Stroheim shows that his heroes and heroines rarely emerge from their experiences unscathed. A Griffith heroine like the Dear One in *Intolerance* lives in a single bare room decorated with one flower in a pot, a statuette of the Madonna and a single crucifix or a religious painting on the wall. Contrasting with it is the fancy apartment of the Musketeer of the Slums, which is filled with erotic statues and pictures of naked women. This great contrast in decor related to character is used in a very similar way by Stroheim in every film from *Merry-Go-Round* to *Queen Kelly* with the exception of *Greed*. It is of course possible that Stroheim helped to design the decor for *Intolerance*. Just as the Boy in *Intolerance* attempts to break away from the evil Musketeer when he falls in love with the Dear One, so Stroheim's aristocratic heroes rebel against their luxurious backgrounds because of their new-found love.

The nineteenth-century custom of labeling a character by his name is not wholly discarded by Stroheim. Although he never called his heroine the Dear One, it is unnecessary to know German to appreciate such names as Nicki 'Wildliebe' or wild 'Wolfram'. The doctors are named Armstrong or Stahl (steel). Similarities in a name always suggest similarities in a character: Jan Vooyheid to Yan Vrenen, Sally O'Hara to the equally Irish Patricia Kelly, and obviously the Mitzis of *Merry-Go-Round* and *The Wedding March*, and the sadistic Sadoja, Schani, Schweisser, von Steuben, Zoltan and Strong.

Following in the tradition of Griffith and Stroheim, Renoir is a third great romantic of the cinema. His films also reflect a certain nostalgia for the last century, but whereas Griffith appears sentimental and Stroheim cynical, Renoir is tolerant. Stroheim and Renoir meet on common ground in *La Grande Illusion* with its First World War setting. The solitary flower which von Rauffenstein cuts to place on the body of the friend whom duty has forced him to shoot is a geranium, like the 'hopeful geranium' of the Dear One in *Intolerance*.

The work of all three directors can be related to the literature of the nineteenth century. Renoir has mentioned the influence of *Foolish Wives*, in particular, on his own approach to the filming of Zola's 'Nana', his first important work. His other sources for screen adaptations included Maupassant ('Une Partie de Campagne'), Flaubert ('Mme Bovary'), and again Zola with the strongly Naturalist novel 'La Bête Humaine', whose leading character is a forerunner of Norris's 'McTeague', as filmed by Stroheim.

And at least two of Griffith's adaptations from Norris had anticipated Stroheim by a number of years. *Two Men in the Desert*

(1913) foreshadows the concluding climax of *Greed* and is said to have been filmed in Death Valley. In *A Corner in Wheat* (1909), Griffith realized the value of remaining faithful to the original. He cross-cuts between a luxurious banquet of the rich, and bread lines, just as Norris had done in his book.

Stroheim's very first projects were Norris's 'McTeague' and his own story, 'The Pinnacle', which became his first film. In his last creative work, 'Les Feux de la Saint-Jean', Stroheim has returned to the subject and locale of 'The Pinnacle' over thirty years earlier. All Stroheim's novels, and particularly 'Paprika', are marked by his affinity with the Naturalist novelists of the nineteenth century.

In his novels as in his films, Stroheim was fond of depicting life at its most basic and comparing animal and human behaviour. The crudely primitive life of his gypsies would certainly have appealed to Zola or Norris. The dominant hereditary or 'external' forces which often control the lives of his characters shows Stroheim retaining the determinist philosophy of the Naturalist.

# ARTHUR LENNIG
## *The Wedding March*

*In the films after Greed, there is some softening of the grisly images of middle European "nobility." Marjorie Rosen, referring especially to* Blind Husbands *and* Foolish Wives *(in* Popcorn Venus: Women, Movies, and the American Dream, *p. 69) insists that "just as [Theda] Bara was the ultimate exaggeration of aggressive female libido, von Stroheim's uniformed gigolo was the extreme masculine distortion. . . . All women were his prey." Professor Lennig counters this with his view that there is a tendency in* The Wedding March *to idealize, at least for a moment in the experience of his characters, romantic love. This may be attributed to Stroheim's more relaxed experience of success in Hollywood, his distance in time from his native Austria, and his desire to appease producers and audiences. It did not go very far however. (See the plot summaries in Appendix C.)*

*Professor Lennig, who teaches film at the State University of New York at Albany, finds his admiration for Stroheim increased over the years since he was a student at Wisconsin and later published his own film reviews in a book called* The Silent Voice. *He has lately revised and extended his analysis of* The Wedding March, *from which we have extracted the evaluative passages. He is also convinced that those observers (Jacobs, Bazin, Finler, Sarris, et al.) who have downgraded Stroheim's use of cinematic techniques, especially editing, should look more carefully at the evidence: "There is more cutting in* Greed *within scenes than in* Broken Blossoms."*

In essence, *The Wedding March* tells the story of Prince Nicki, a rather charming rake who falls in love with and seduces (not necessarily in that order) Mitzi, a girl of the lower classes, and then leaves her so he can marry Cecelia, a crippled heiress.

The film is "Dedicated to the true lovers of the world." This opening statement involves the viewer in the first difficulty of interpretation. To the modern audience — an audience which, in Herman G. Weinberg's view, is a "savage" one because it will not admit to sentiment — this dedication might appear ironic. But it is not meant to be viewed ironically. Stroheim is honestly offering his work to the true lovers of the world; however, this does not mean that his characters are motivated only by pure love. In fact, his point may be that there is no such thing as pure love, for it is not in the nature of man. He realizes that the aim of every lover is to go to bed with his beloved; the gentleness, compassion, and understanding that lie beyond this basic fact are what separates the cad from the true admirer.

The presence of sexuality prevents *The Wedding March* from being merely a sentimental tale. The implications of the film are that man is a creature full of animal drives, perversions, greed, and hypocrisies, and that somehow, by some strange miracle, man does transcend his baseness. Havelock Ellis, in his *Studies in the Psychology of Sex* [III, 39], explains the problem:

> To look upon love as in any special sense a delusion is merely to fall into the trap of a shallow cynicism. Love is only a delusion in so far as the whole of life is a delusion, and if we accept the fact of life it is unphilosophical to refuse to accept the fact of love.

This delicate balance is important. Without an awareness of it, viewers tend to see the love story as a parody, a satirical thrust at romantic love, or, on the other hand, to see it as a pure romantic story, with the man and woman as star-crossed lovers. In actuality, the film is a mixture of both.

There is no doubt that Mitzi is a true lover. But what about Prince Nicki (played by Stroheim)? His name, Nicholas Ehrart Hans Karl Maria Wildeliebe-Rauffenburg, is obviously symbolic. "Wildeliebe" (wild-loving) Nicki is a non-working playboy who spends most of his time and all of his money in the pursuit of pleasure. And pleasure to Nicki is "Wein, Liebe, und Lieder." Although he is attracted to Mitzi and eventually falls in love with her, he has hardly become an innocent child in the process. He retains his worldly view, his cynicism, perhaps even a slight touch of sexual perversion (notice how he slips his overcoat over her, as if Mitzi dressed as an officer — or as himself — is more desirable).

Men of sophistication can fall in love, but they are not fools nor have they forgotten the ways of the world. It is possible for Nicki to spend the early part of an evening in a brothel and then to visit his beloved. Love, even an overwhelming kind, does not necessarily answer all of one's needs. Nicki may be a lover, but he is an aware one, aware always of the complexities of his own emotions. He is charmed by Mitzi's naivete and overwhelmed with her loveliness and dedication, but how long will these qualities last? How can they compete with the money he would get from marrying an heiress? These are not fanciful alternatives. Stroheim has not forgotten his realistic predilections. . . .

*The Wedding March* is in many ways Stroheim's greatest work; it doesn't have the reputation of *Greed*, but it is a more personal film in almost every way. It was written by Stroheim and played by him, and it touches upon many of his strongest obsessions. Its women, Mitzi and Cecelia, are most sensitively and sympathetically portrayed. When Cecelia limps down the aisle and speaks about apple blossoms, and when Mitzi is seen waiting in the rain with the reprehensible Schani, Stroheim reaches emotional heights he never quite achieved in his other films. He has also given dimension to his own role. He is no longer the complete heel of *Blind Husbands* or the over-sexed and calculating count of *Foolish Wives*. But if he has humanized his role, he has not sentimentalized it. He portrays a sophisticated man who has been touched by love, and although he will not act on it (that is, marry for love), he can feel.

Stroheim has captured in this film what he has not achieved in others: genuine emotion and empathy. Audiences feel for the characters, particularly Mitzi, and few can be unaffected at the end of the film when she looks after the departing carriage, with the rain pouring down on her saddened face.

The film's opening title, "Vienna — Anno Domini 1914," is not without its ironies and implications. This is indeed Vienna, the over-ripe capital city of an empire which is shortly to crumble, but it is also the year of God, and God is absent or certainly silent in this pitiful tale of greed and lust and love.

Many critics betray a kind of unconscious chauvinism when they praise Stroheim for showing the corruption of the old world as if somehow the new didn't have any. These critics seriously misinterpret Stroheim's *Weltanschaung*. He chooses the decadence of Vienna for its exotic qualities, its style, and its splendor; but it is not that Vienna is so extraordinarily decadent (what big city isn't?), but rather that the city is an example of man's institutionalized, organized folly. To a moralist like Stroheim, every city is Vanity Fair, and he could easily have done the same for New York, although America's class structure is not so strikingly defined. After all, isn't *Greed* as strong an indictment of American life as any of Stroheim's other films are of Europe's?

Are not the low-class friends of McTeague similar to Schani's family and isn't Schani really Marcus Schuler with an Austrian accent? Stroheim is no debunker of the upper class only, as some leftist critics have tried to make him. To the contrary, he is beyond such simplicity; each segment of society receives its due.

Like all moralists, Stroheim is fascinated by man's evil and corruption. Sodom and Gomorrah are well-known cities because of their sins, far better known than more virtuous places of the Holy Land. Stroheim feels genuinely the sins and corruptions of the world; but unlike most moralists, he is honest enough to acknowledge his own predilections for sin. For this reason, he is never selfrighteous — and this is perhaps his main strength as a commentator upon mankind.

Ruthlessly, he examines the sensual and the financial and the social lusts of man. His depiction, however, does not reek entirely of tragedy. To him, life is a macabre comedy; it is this quality which preserves his work from being soft and sentimental. Unfortunately, film critics betray that they are working with a young art and reveal all too often a partisanship that does injustice not only to themselves but to the works they wish to defend. Faults are granted even to Shakespeare, but somehow to criticize a movie master is to invoke a fanatic's ire. *The Wedding March* is not a perfect work. At certain times Stroheim over-stresses characterization to the point of caricature. For example, Schani spits too much; Stroheim does not have to continue to telegraph to his audience that Schani is not a delicate person. The apple blossom shots are perhaps excessive, and certainly the frequent cutting to a nightingale brings the scene almost to the point of parody. Such a grotesque and macabre shot as the hands which change to bones is effective once, but on repetition loses much of its power. These are matters of discretion and, although Stroheim is curiously heavy-handed at times, unwilling to make a point without also underlining it, they are minor flaws. His work may not be perfect, but it is superb.

# GAVIN LAMBERT
# Stroheim: He Didn't Really Belong to America

*For a last word on Stroheim we turn to a British critic, editor during the early 1950s of the film quarterly published by the British Film Institute,* Sight and Sound. *His title, 'Stroheim Revisited: The Missing Third in the American Cinema,' expressed his belief that Griffith, Stroheim, and Chaplin were the three most vital directorial figures of the silent era. The article (which appeared in the April 1953 issue) described the story and style of several of the major films and expressed regret that none of them were available in British archives.*

*The last section, appearing on page 204, is reprinted here, with a preliminary paragraph from page 166 categorizing the Stroheim films. In* Greed *he finds expressed such qualities as futility, drabness, folly, and human debasement and sees the film's theme not so much as lust for money but as thwarted sexual desire.*

*His attempt to place Stroheim in relation to Griffith and Chaplin is a striking example of analytical criticism ("all have studied, painstakingly, the face of poverty"). But his separation of "Stroheim the Austrian" from the others is perhaps more valuable. As a foreigner, "his past was not the American past." He not only rejected, Lambert says, the American dream of self-help but any "affirmation of human dignity" either in Europe or America — a philosophic pessimism to be reflected in films by other European directors who later came to work in the United States.*

Of the nine films that Stroheim was to direct between 1918 and 1932, four (*Blind Husbands, The Devil's Passkey, Foolish Wives, Walking Down Broadway*) were extremely bitter contemporary comedies of sexual manners, combining satire, melodrama and the pathological; four were set in the pre-World War I Austrian court (*Merry-Go-Round, The Merry Widow, The Wedding March, Queen Kelly*), and against a rich background analysis of its intrigue and corruption told the story of a prince who fell in love with a commoner; and one, *Greed*, stands apart, an onslaught on the social realities of America at the turn of the century. As a body of work, this is as substantial and idiosyncratic as anything in the cinema. . . .

To assess what Stroheim (and the American cinema) learned from Griffith, one needs to go back several years beyond *The Birth of a Nation*, to a marvellous two-reeler that he made in 1908 called *A Corner in Wheat*. With this film, probably, the "modern" American cinema was born. The subject might have been something from Frank

Norris' sketchbook: a simple story about unscrupulous Californian businessmen and the hardships their methods caused to poor people. The luxurious life of a man who has a corner in wheat, and the queues of starving poor people lining up for bread, which suddenly increases in price, are contrasted with a sharp bitterness. The capitalist dealer comes to an appropriate end, falling into a huge vat of flour at his own factory while showing a party of friends round, and vanishing as if in quicksands. In this historic vignette Griffith stated some basic social issues, depicted poor people in their own surroundings with directness and sympathy, satirised and condemned big business. Four years later, in *The Musketeers of Pig Alley*, a film of similar dimensions, he did another astonishing thing; this melodrama set in a city slum portrayed crime as the inevitable outcome of poverty, and described, against an authentic background of street corners, tenements and alleys, the growth of the hold-up gang.

It is all too easy to call Griffith a Victorian on the evidence of certain undeniably Victorian elements in his work, and dismiss his social ideas as outdated or confused. The fact remains that the ideas of *A Corner in Wheat* and *The Musketeers of Pig Alley* were taken up by, and are still embodied in, most "advanced" social documents produced by the American cinema. *The Birth of a Nation*, certainly, is disfigured by its attitude towards the negro race, and Griffith as philosopher in *Intolerance* is hardly to be taken seriously; and yet, as an observer of existing reality, he could be brave and acute. There is a case, I believe, to be made that his large-scale films are more historically important — in their development of many of the cinema's most vital narrative resources — than artistically satisfactory, and that his best works, as works of art, are the smaller, more intimate ones — these two early sketches, *Broken Blossoms*, *Isn't Life Wonderful*, *One Exciting Night*. At any rate, one can trace the influence of *A Corner in Wheat* through the uncompromising actuality of *Greed* to the poetic style of *The Grapes of Wrath*, just as *The Musketeers of Pig Alley* is the ancestor of the 30's gangster films, and remains even as contemporary as, say, *The Asphalt Jungle*.

From Griffith, in fact, the two main lines of American cinema start and diverge; and at the head of the first opposing lines of descent are Chaplin and Stroheim. Differently placed as they are, one is also struck by what they have in common — similarities, incidentally, that have caused all of them to be labelled Victorian. All are, undisguisedly, moralists; Chaplin as well as Griffith and Stroheim is an exile; all work on a solid 19th century scale, carpentering their plots, contriving their episodes, not much concerned with the plausibilities of coincidence but intent on depicting human beings in conflict with social injustice; all are fond of young, innocent, tender and ill-treated heroines from poor families; and all have studied, painstakingly, the face of poverty. Where they diverge is in their declaration of sympathies, for while Griffith and Chaplin appeal to common humanity, Stroheim does not. He approaches it in the love scenes of *The Wedding March* and *Queen Kelly*, but the final tone even of these films remains misanthropic. There are similarities between Chaplin's London and the London of *Broken Blossoms*, but none between the beautiful poverty of Charlie and the squalor of the McTeagues. Nothing in Stroheim is ever transfigured. The only parallel is Chaplin's most bitter film; one can imagine Stroheim having made a *Monsieur Verdoux*.

After Griffith's first disclosures, then, the two main lines of approach to the American scene become clear. The direct one runs through Chaplin, to the early Vidor, to Ford; between *Broken Blossoms, The Gold Rush, Hallelujah! The Grapes of Wrath*, there are evident affinities — a lyrical approach to simple and ordinary people, an affirmation of human dignity and love. The line from Stroheim contains no such reassurances. The violent satire of *Foolish Wives* leads through to Lubitsch's elegant and cynical comedies, finds a more recent echo in the ruthless upper class intrigues of Sturges' *The Lady Eve* and *The Palm Beach Story*, in the bizarre passions of Wilder's *Sunset Boulevard*. The cruel declining aristocracies of *The Wedding March* are transferred to America at the turn of the century in Welles' *The Magnificent Ambersons*, in Wyler's *The Little Foxes* and *Carrie*; and the unaffectionate surface texture of American life in *Greed* in the numerous crime and gangster films of the last twenty years, in Lang's *Fury*, in Huston's *Treasure of the Sierra Madre*, in *Citizen Kane*. All these, like Stroheim's, are films of "exposure," with an eloquent mistrust of society and of human motives.

In creating this antithesis in the American cinema, Stroheim also rejected some powerful elements: the American "dream," folklore, much that was ingrained and indigenous, homely and comfortable. Only a foreigner could have achieved it. From this point of view Stroheim's work epitomises that cross-fertilisation with other cultures which so much American art in this century has undergone. As in the 1900's the literary tradition had been divided between those who went to Europe and those who stayed at home, so twenty years later a parallel occurred in the cinema — only, this time, Europe came to America, and, like the novelists who had emigrated, Stroheim in Hollywood evoked the magnificence and treachery of European civilisation, the raw materialism of the new world.

So it happens that the triumvirate of the American cinema comprises only one American, and beside Griffith the Southerner are Chaplin the Englishman and Stroheim the Austrian. One cannot imagine an immigrant artist being allowed to create a comparable upheaval in Hollywood today; it seems, even, inevitable that after a few years Stroheim should have been rejected, that he should have returned to Europe and planned a last episode to his *comedie humaine*, in which once again the customs, the great and solid structures, the temperatures and preoccupations of an obsolescent society would emerge like a city rising from the sea. For he didn't really belong to America, any more than other artists who had left it; his past was not the American past, and he was altogether too stern with the present. Yet for a time he annexed it, and the occupation marks have remained. So it usually is with those who make revolutions. They seize power and are as suddenly deprived of it, but when they have gone, many things are different, and a part of them still remains.

# Appendices

## Appendix A
## RICHARD CORLISS
# Writing in Silence

*Film lovers are greatly indebted to Richard Corliss for his special con-
tributions to the history of screenwriting. Currently a cinema reviewer
for* Time *magazine and editor since 1970 of* Film Comment, *Corliss chose
to devote one of his first issues (Winter 1970-71) to "The Hollywood
Screenwriter," containing 66 filmographies and 12 special articles. This
became a book (N.Y.,* Discus/Avon, *1972) along with his* Talking Pictures, *(Woodstock, N.Y.,* Overlook Press, *1974/N.Y.,* Penguin Books,
*1975) a series of reviews focused on writers.*

*Finding out what writers did in the silent era is a really daunting task.
If screenplays were used at all they were seldom saved and few are
available for us to study them today. Lillian Gish gives us the impression that most of Griffith's films were done in his head. This may have
been true for many of the short films but it could rarely apply to films
after* Intolerance, *as the Griffith filmography shows. Thomas Ince required exact scripts, as we know, and Gardner Sullivan has been our
example of professional writing for that studio.*

*Here is a valiant attempt by Corliss to outline the situation by at least
naming some names. It is from an article in* Film Comment *for July-August
1985, pages 70-71. It will be noticed that he refers back to the single article in the 1970-71 issue by Gary Carey on Anita Loos, screenwriter for
Douglas Fairbanks.*

It was in 1898 that Roy L. McCardell, a columnist for the New
York *World*, went to work as a story editor for American Mutoscope
& Biograph Pictures. Epes Sargent, a critic for *The Moving Picture
World*, wrote a brief history of screenwriters, called "The Literary
Side of Pictures" (1914), in which he identified McCardell as "the
first man on either side of the water to be hired for no other purpose than to write pictures. . . . They were not moving pictures in
the sense now employed, though they were indeed moving." Sargent
means that the films were made, not for movie theaters, but the

penny arcades. He goes on: "McCardell used to write about ten captions telling a more or less complete story. Then he and the boss would hire a lot of models — mostly girls — and go out and make pictures for the captions." Sargent makes it sound as if Roy McCardell was not only our first screenwriter, he was the first American auteur.

McCardell went on to create a famous syndicated feature called "The Jarr Family," but he continued to work for the movies, specializing in farces. In 1915 he wrote a 30-part, 60-reel serial called *The Diamond from the Sky*, which prompted Terry Ramsaye, some years later, to remark that "McCardell is thereby the author of both the shortest and the longest pictures in the world." (This was before *Heimat*.) McCardell's script for *The Diamond from the Sky* was something of a ringer. He had written his script for a scenario contest held by the Chicago *Tribune*. The prize was $10,000; no fewer than 19,003 scenarios were submitted.

It was now 1915, when *The Birth of a Nation* was released. Movies were sweeping the country, and if John and Jane Doe couldn't be movie stars, they'd get into pictures by writing scripts. All they had to do was buy a book on How to Write a Scenario. This was a huge market. *The Film Index* lists more than a hundred instructional books and booklets on scenario writing. There were dozens of correspondence schools, like the E.Z. Scenario Company. The Palmer Institute of Authorship promised to teach the budding scenarist "how success can be won through mastery of the fundamentals of photoplay writing, as taught by a group of America's highest authorities in this subject." In 1915, one such manual was written by the eminent screenwriter Louella Parsons, who, according to Epes Sargent, "has written little, but many promising writers owe much to her helpful advice" — which she would later dispense in a gossip column. Indeed, Sargent referred to Frank Woods, who helped construct the scenarios for *The Birth of a Nation* and *Intolerance*, as "the one commentator on photoplay who never wrote a book on how to do it."

Even back in the Teens, a version of the auteur theory was raging. While Griffith and his actors were insisting that *The Birth of a Nation* sprang directly from the Master's head to celluloid, a critic for *The New Republic* was devoting 1500 words to a review of the film — and never once mentioned Griffith's name. Meanwhile, Sargent, in his *Moving Picture World* column, would inveigh against any craftsman who might tamper with the screenplay: "The successful, the continuously successful, photoplay maker is the man who will insist that every member of his staff devote his endeavor to preserving the originality of the writer, and whose editor merely edits for technical fault, whose director directs the script given him, and whose players do not know more than the author, editor, and director combined. Such things may come to pass some day. May that day be soon." For good or ill, that day never came to pass.

The names on Sargent's honor roll of early screenwriters read like the lines in a Christina Rossetti poem, or a Gilbert and Sullivan operetta. Rollin S. Sturgeon was the story editor at Vitagraph Pictures; Romaine Fielding and Shannon Fife both worked for Lubin in Philadelphia; Captain Leslie T. Peacock was the top writer at Universal; H. Tipton Steck toiled at Essanay; C.B. "Pop" Hoadley was story editor at Imp and Powers; Emmett Campbell Hall wrote the first original screenplay for a two-part (meaning two-reel) movie, *His Trust* and *His Trust Fulfilled*, directed by D.W. Griffith (1910). The name Epes Winthrop Sargent has its own lilt to it. Aside from writing a weekly column, he scripted several hundred movies for Lubin Pictures.

Louella Parsons was not the only writer to achieve greater fame, or at least notoriety. Bernie Schulberg wrote for Famous Players; as B.P. Schulberg he headed production at Paramount from 1928 to 1932. Herbert Brenon, a staff writer for Imp, later produced and directed the 1924 *Peter Pan* and other lovely spectacles; Lois Weber, arguably the greatest American director who happens to be a woman, started as a screenwriter.

Almost from the beginning, women were involved in screenwriting, and not just as a ladies' auxiliary. We may smile at the names of these pioneers (Hetty Gray Baker, Lillian Sweetser, Maibelle Heikes Justice) but we shouldn't underestimate their contribution to silent pictures. A second generation — comprising those women who came to the movies as it expanded to feature-film length — was even more influential. In a 1970 *Film Comment* article, Gary Carey wrote: "The industry's leading scenarists were, by large majority, women. Perhaps there is a good sociological reason for this: perhaps it was because women were more attuned to turning out the kitsch melodramas and hot-house romances that dominated the run-of-the-mill Hollywood product of the period. Whatever the reason, it was a phenomenon that remained constant until the mid-1920's."

Carey has his own list of mellifluously-named women screenwriters: "Clara Beranger, Christine Johnson, Frances Marion (who wrote the best of Mary Pickford's films and later was a specialist for Marie Dressler), Olga Printzlau, Josephine Lovett, June Mathis (remembered mainly and unfairly as the woman who cut *Greed* to shreds), Ouida Bergère, Grace Unsell, Jane Murfin, Beulah Marie

Dix, Jeanie MacPherson (C.B. De Mille's favorite scenarist), Bess Meredyth, Lenore J. Coffee." The monikers are poetic — or at least onomatopoetic — and so is the name of the writer we credit with bringing movies out of the rural and ruritanian hot-houses and into the snazzy, urban 20th century: Anita Loos.

While still in her teens, Loos had her first script produced: *The New York Hat*, made in 1912 by D.W. Griffith, and starring Mary Pickford and Lionel Barrymore. It was an impressive beginning, but not really a portentous one; temperamentally, Loos and Griffith were worlds apart, or at least a generation. His soul was attuned to the rhythms and sentiments of Victorian romance and confederate blood-and-thunder — in a word, melodrama. She marched to the beat of a different drummer: Noble Sissle, or some other ragtime strutter. So though Loos followed Griffith from company to company, he only occasionally brought her scripts to the screen. She was one of the first to learn the occupational hazard, or the fatal curse, of screenwriting: a script is only a movie if someone decides to produce it.

Loos got her chance when a director at Triangle, John Emerson, encouraged her to write a script for the company's young actor, Douglas Fairbanks. The result, *His Picture in the Papers* (1916), was an immense success, and the beginning of a beautiful professional friendship. (More than that in fact: Loos and Emerson were married in 1919.) The movies Loos wrote for Fairbanks were, for the adolescent art, revolutionary. Here was a brash young man with boundless energy and a will to succeed. In contrast to the heroes the movies had produced until that time — Broncho Billy Anderson, Francis X. Bushman, the courtly swains of the Griffith films, even Charlie Chaplin with his Victorian-valentine soul — Fairbanks was the movies' first 20th-century hero. He would serve as the model for other go-getting all-American types, from Harold Lloyd to Clark Gable and Errol Flynn to Burt Reynolds and even Eddie Murphy. To keep pace, and keep up to date, with this high-spirited hero, Loos developed the style of wisecracking dialogue that has been the American cinema's most bracing contribution to the English language. To be sure, the jokes weren't spoken, they were printed on intertitles; but the effect was still revolutionary. The Fairbanks films were not only excuses for the star's athletic feats, they were spoofs of contemporary fads, so the titles *had* to be just as contemporary.

Loos and Emerson made eight films with Fairbanks in 1916 and 1917. After they broke up, Fairbanks went on to become the swashbuckler for which he is remembered — a 20th century hero in 17th century drag. As for Loos and Emerson, they turned their writing talents to Constance Talmadge, and made her one of the first 20th-century heroines, fighting to retain her purity and her pluck in the Jazz Age. Later still, Loos wrote some of Jean Harlow's sprightlier comedies. . . .

# Appendix B
# Extant Films of Thomas H. Ince

*The following notable feat of filmographic sleuthing was part of Martin Sopocy's contribution to the article in* Cinema Journal *which translated* Jean Mitry's *study of Ince. (See page 82).*

Most of the films produced by Ince have already gone the way of all cinema on nitrate stock. Nothing remains of *The Battle of Gettysburg* but some stills, while other Ince classics survive only as fragments or in abridged or reconstructed versions. This list, a tentative round-up of the Ince holdings in the four chief American archives — The Library of Congress (abbreviated below as LoC). The University of California film archive at Los Angeles (UCLA below), George Eastman House (GEH) and The Museum of Modern Art (MoMA) — probably represents the bulk of what remains of his vast output in the United States. What may survive in the European archives is another matter. (The Cinemathèque Française reputedly has large holdings of French-release Ince films which await cataloguing and — a job even *more* hellish, as the translators of the foregoing text are prepared to testify — identifying them with the titles of their American release.) Archives are continually enlarging their holdings, but the listings for GEH and MoMA are complete as of May 1982; they are, however, only approximate for LoC and UCLA, whose extensive collections are catalogued in a manner which, while logical, makes it difficult to identify films according to producer. This, plus a time limitation, made it impossible to obtain exhaustive lists for either archive despite generous help from their staffs.

But while many omissions are thus accidental, those of *Almost a Friar, At Old Fort Dearborn, Carmen of the Klondike, Flying Colors, For the Freedom of Cuba, The Leopard Woman, Massacre of the Fourth Cavalry* and *Wenona's Broken Promise*, all of which have sometime been attributed to Ince, are not. They are omitted on advice from George Pratt, who finds they are the work of other producers. Similarly, the inclusion in the list of *Human Wreckage* is tentative, for while certain circumstances of its production connect it with the Ince organization, Mr. Pratt, whose rigorous scholarship has brought new standards of hard-headedness to a subject which badly needs it, points out that the published evidence leaves the nature and extent of that connection unclear. (The film, which followed hard upon Wallace Reid's tragic death and which starred his widow, was advertised as a sensational story of drug addiction by its producers who, for reasons of their own, remained anonymous when the film was released. This is certainly at odds with Ince's well-known flair for self-promotion, and its relation to the Ince canon remains one of the ambiguities of Ince studies.)

Thanks largely to research done by Diane Kaiser Koszarski for her book *The Complete Films of William S. Hart* (Dover Publications, 1980), the listing of extant Hart films is reliable for LoC, MoMA and GEH (her book does not list UCLA holdings), needing only George Pratt's correction that no prints of *In the Sage Brush Country* are known to survive, and Eileen Bowser's correction that MoMA does not hold prints of *The Narrow Trail* or *The Poppy Girl's Husband*. However, none of the four archives at present holds a print of Hart's *Tools of Providence*, or of the fragment of *The Dessert Man*, which Mrs. Koszarski lists as being available from commercial print suppliers.

Since the list is in no sense a filmography, titles are given in alphabetical order for easy reference. Each entry begins with the film's title (which in all cases is that of its original release), followed, in order, by the year of its release, its director, its principal player, its approximate length (whether "F" for *feature* or "S" for *short*, where the latter is understood to be any film of 4 reels or less, the exception being those cases, duly noted, where the film survives only as a fragment), and finally, the archive(s) in which it is to be found. Viewing prints are available for all films except where an asterisk precedes the initials of the holding archive; this signifies that the film survives either in nitrate which is in most cases too fragile to project, or in a gauge, such as 28mm, for which viewing equipment is presently unavailable. Scholars may find reassurance in knowing that, in these days of shrinking operating funds, these films are in the keeping of concerned experts whose care maximizes their chance of survival until money can be found to restore them to permanent and viewable form. But even for nitrate stored in optimum conditions, transfer to acetate is a race against time.

Finally, for their patient and disinterested help in compiling this list — under circumstances, in many cases, of understaffing and overwork — I wish to thank Eileen Bowser and Charles Silver of the

Film Department of MoMA; Paul C. Spehr, Emily Sieger and Patrick J. Sheehan of the Motion Picture, Broadcasting and Recorded Sound Division of LoC; Robert Rosen and Robert Gitt of the Theatre Arts Department of UCLA, and, especially, that tireless champion of Ince's work, George C. Pratt of GEH. — *M.S.*

*Alarm Clock Andy* (1920), Jerome Storm. Charles Ray. F. LoC, UCLA.
*Anna Christie* (1923), John Griffith Wray. Blanche Sweet. F. GEH, MoMA.
*The Army Surgeon* (1912), Francis Ford. Francis Ford. S. LoC.
*Artful Kate* (1911), Thos. H. Ince. Mary Pickford. S. LoC, *GEH.
*The Aryan* (1916), Wm. S. Hart. Wm. S. Hart. F. LoC.
*At the Duke's Command* (1911), Thos. H. Ince. Mary Pickford. S. MoMA.
*Back of the Man* (1917), Reginald Barker. Chas. Ray. F. GEH.
*Bad Buck of Santa Ynez* (1915), Wm. S. Hart. Wm. S. Hart. S. GEH, LoC.
*Beau Revel* (1921), John Griffith Wray. Lewis Stone. F. LoC, UCLA.
*Bell Boy 13* (1923), Wm. Seiter. Douglas MacLean. F. LoC.
*The Bargain* (1914), Reginald Barker. Wm. S. Hart. F. LoC, UCLA.
*Battle of the Red Men* (1912), Thos. H. Ince. J. Barney Sherry. S. GEH.
*The Beggar of Cawnpore* (1916), Charles Swickard. H.B. Warner. S. GEH.
*Below the Surface* (1920), Irvin Willat. Hobart Bosworth. F. LoC.
*Between Men* (1915), Wm. S. Hart. Wm. S. Hart. F. GEH, LoC, MoMA.
*Black Is White* (1920), Charles Giblyn. Dorothy Dalton. F. LoC, UCLA.
*Blazing the Trail* (1912), Thos. H. Ince. Francis Ford. S. GEH, MoMA.
*Blue Blazes Rawden* (1918), Wm. S. Hart. Wm. S. Hart. F. UCLA, GEH (print slightly abridged, with French titles).
*Branding Broadway* (1918), Wm. S. Hart. Wm. S. Hart. F. MoMA.
*Breed of Men* (1919), Wm. S. Hart. Wm. S. Hart. F. MoMA.
*The Bronze Bell* (1921), James W. Horne. Courtenay Foote. F. LoC.
*The Busher* (1919), Jerome Storm. Chas. Ray. F. GEH.
*The Captive God* (1916), Chas. Swickard. Wm. S. Hart. F. LoC, *GEH
*A Child of War* (1913), . . . . . . . S. MoMA.
*Civilization* (1916), Raymond B. West, Reginald Barker, et al. Howard Hickman. F. MoMA.

*The Clodhopper* (1917), Victor Schertzinger. Chas. Ray. F. GEH, LoC, MoMA.

*The Conversion of Frosty Blake* (1915), Wm. S. Hart. Wm. S. Hart. S. LoC.

*The Coward* (1915), Reginald Barker. Chas. Ray. F. MoMA, UCLA, *GEH.

*The Crab* (1917), Walter Edwards. Frank Keenan. F. GEH (has print with flash titles only).

*The Crisis* (1912), Thos. H. Ince. Francis Ford. S. GEH.

*A Crook's Sweetheart* (1914), . . . . . . UCLA (fragment).

*The Cup of Life* (1915), Raymond B. West. Bessie Barriscale. F. LoC.

*Custer's Last Fight* (1912), Thos. H. Ince. Francis Ford. S. LoC, GEH (has 1933 reissue print).

*Dangerous Hours* (1920), Fred Niblo. Lloyd Hughes. F. LoC, MoMA, UCLA.

*The Dark Mirror* (1920), Chas. Giblyn. Dorothy Dalton. F. LoC.

*The Darkening Trail* (1915), Wm. S. Hart. Wm. S. Hart. S. LoC, UCLA.

*D'Artagnan* (1916), Chas. Swickard. Orrin Johnson. F. LoC, *GEH.

*Days of '49* (1913), Jay Hunt. Thos. Chatterton. S. LoC, *GEH.

*The Death Mask* (1914), Jay Hunt. Tsuru Aoki. S. LoC.

*The Deserter* (1912), Francis Ford. Francis Ford. S. LoC.

*The Deserter* (1916), Scott Sidney, Chas. Ray. S. LoC, MoMA.

*The Devil* (1915), . . . Bessie Barriscale. F. LoC.

*The Disciple* (1915), Wm. S. Hart. Wm. S. Hart. F. GEH, LoC.

*The Drummer of the Eighth* (1913), Jay Hunt. Cyril Gottlieb. S. GEH, LoC, UCLA.

*The False Faces* (1919), Irvin Willat. Henry B. Walthall. F. GEH.

*The False Road* (1920), Fred Niblo. Enid Bennett. F. LoC.

*The Family Skeleton* (1918), Victor Schertzinger. Chas. Ray. F. LoC.

*The Favorite Son* (1913), Francis Ford. Chas. Ray. S. GEH.

*The Female of the Species* (1916), Raymond B. West. Dorothy Dalton. GEH (has one reel of original five).

*Flame of the Yukon* (1917), Chas. Miller. Dorothy Dalton. F. LoC.

*For the Honor of the Seventh* (1912), Thos. H. Ince. Mae Marsh. S. GEH.

*A Gamble in Souls* (1916), Walter Edwards. William Desmond. F. LoC, *GEH.

*Flare-up Sal* (1918), Roy William Neill. Dorothy Dalton. F. LoC, UCLA.

*The Gangsters and the Girl* (1914), Scott Sidney. Chas. Ray. S. GEH.

*The Girl Glory* (1917), R. William Neill. Enid Bennett. *GEH (has nitrate print of three of original five reels).

*The Green Swamp* (1916), Scott Sidney. Bessie Barriscale. UCLA (fragment).

*Hail the Woman* (1921), John Griffith Wray. Florence Vidor. F. MoMA, *LoC.

*Hell's Hinges* (1916), Wm. S. Hart. Wm. S. Hart. F. GEH, LoC, MoMA.

*Her Husband's Friend* (1920), Fred Niblo. Enid Bennett. F. LoC.

*His Mother's Boy* (1917), Victor Schertzinger. Chas. Ray. F. LoC.

*His New Lid* (1910), Frank Powell. Thos. H. Ince. S. LoC.

*The Home Stretch* (1921), Jack Nelson. Douglas MacLean. F. LoC, UCLA.

*Homer Comes Home* (1920), Jerome Storm. Chas. Ray. F. LoC, UCLA.

*Human Wreckage* (1923), John G. Wray. Dorothy Davenport. F. *LoC.

*In the Tennesee Hills* (1915), . . . Chas. Ray. S. GEH.

*The Indian Massacre* (1912), Thos. H. Ince. Francis Ford. S. GEH.

*The Invaders* (1912), Thos. H. Ince. Francis Ford. S. GEH, LoC, UCLA.

*The Italian* (1915), Reginald Barker. George Beban F. LoC, UCLA, *GEH.

*The Jailbird* (1920), Lloyd Ingraham. Dorothy MacLean. F. LoC.

*Jimmy* (1914), Scott Sidney. Cyril Gottlieb. S. LoC.

*John Petticoats* (1919), Lambert Hillyer. Wm. S. Hart. F. LoC, MoMA.

*Keno Bates, Liar* (1915), Wm. S. Hart. Wm. S. Hart. S. MoMA, *GEH.

*Keys of the Righteous* (1918), Jerome Storm. Enid Bennett. F. LoC.

*A Knight of the Trails* (1915), Wm. S. Hart. Wm. S. Hart. S. GEH, LoC.

*The Last of the Ingrams* (1917), Walter Edwards. William Desmond. F. LoC, *GEH.

*Last of the Line* (1914), Jay Hunt. Sessue Hayakawa. S. MoMA, UCLA.

*The Lieutenant's Last Fight* (1912), Thos. H. Ince. Ray Myers. S. LoC.

*Love Letters* (1917), R. William Neill. Dorothy Dalton. F. LoC.

*Love Me* (1918), R. William Neill. Dorothy Dalton. F. LoC.

*Love or Justice* (1917), Walter Edwards. Louise Glaum. F. LoC, *GEH.

*Lying Lips* (1921), John Griffith Wray. House Peters. F. LoC.

*Madcap Madge* (1917), Raymond B. West. Olive Thomas F. LoC, *GEH.

*Maid or Man* (1911), Thos. H. Ince. Mary Pickford. S. MoMA.

*The Man from Nowhere* (1915), Wm. S. Hart. Wm. S. Hart. S. GEH.

*Mary's Ankle* (1920), Lloyd Ingraham. Douglas MacLean. F. LoC, UCLA.

*The Millionaire Vagrant* (1917), Victor Schertzinger. Chas. Ray. S. LoC, *GEH.

*Mr. Silent Haskins* (1914), Wm. S. Hart. Wm. S. Hart. S. GEH.

*The Moral Fabric* (1916), Charles Miller. Frank Mills. F. LoC.

*Mother O'Mine* (1921), Fred Niblo. Lloyd Hughes. F. LoC.

*The Narrow Trail* (1917), Wm. S. Hart and Lambert Hillyer. Wm. S. Hart. F. GEH, LoC, UCLA.

*O Mimi San* (1914), Reginald Barker. Sessue Hayakawa. S. LoC, *GEH.

*An Old-Fashioned Boy* (1920), Jerome Storm. Chas. Ray. F. LoC, UCLA.

*On the Night Stage* (1915), Reginald Barker. Wm. S. Hart. F. GEH, LoC.

*One a Minute* (1921), Jack Nelson. Douglas MacLean. F. LoC.

*The Other Girl* (1912), Francis Ford (?). Harold Lockwood. S. GEH.

*Paris Green* (1920), Jerome Storm. Chas. Ray. F. LoC, *GEH.

*Partners Three* (1919), Fred Niblo. Enid Bennett. F. LoC.

*The Paymaster's Son* (1913), Thos. H. Ince. Richard Stanton. S. *LoC.

*Plain Jane* (1916), Charles Miller. Bessie Barriscale. F. GEH.

*The Pinch Hitter* (1917), Victor Schertzinger. Chas. Ray. F. LoC, *GEH.

*Pinto Ben* (1915), Wm. S. Hart. Wm. S. Hart. S. GHE, LoC.

*The Price Mark* (1917), R.W. Neill. Dorothy Dalton. F. LoC.

*The Quakeress* (1913), Raymond B. West. Louise Glaum. S. LoC.

*Red Hot Dollars* (1919), Jerome Storm. Chas. Ray. F. LoC, *GEH.

*The Renegade* (1915), Chas. Swickard(?) Chas. Ray. S. LoC (as *The Renegade Ranger*), *GEH.

*The Return of Draw Egan* (1916), Wm. S. Hart. Wm. S. Hart. F. GEH (has print with French and Spanish titles only).

*The Rookie's Return* (1921), Jack Nelson. Douglas MacLean. F. LoC.

*The Roughneck* (1915), Wm. S. Hart. Wm. S. Hart. S. GEH, LoC.

*Rumplestiltskin* (1915), Reginald Barker. Elizabeth Burbridge. F. LoC, MoMA, UCLA.

*The Ruse* (1915), Wm. S. Hart. Wm. S. Hart. S. GEH, LoC, MoMA.

*Satan McAllister's Heir* (1915), Walter Edwards. Walter Edwards. S. GEH.

*The Scourge of the Desert* (1915), Wm. S. Hart. Wm. S. Hart. MoMA (incomplete).

*Selfish Yates* (1918), Wm. S. Hart. Wm. S. Hart. F. MoMA.

*The Sergeant's Secret* (1913), Thos. H. Ince. Chas. Ray. S. LoC.

*Shark Monroe* (1918), Wm. S. Hart. Wm. S. Hart. F. MoMA.
*Shorty's Ranch* (1915), . . . Shorty Hamilton. GEH (has two-reel
abridgement of three-reel original).
*Silent Heroes* (1913), Jay Hunt. Thomas Chatterton. S. GEH.
*The Silent Man* (1917), Wm. S. Hart. Wm. S. Hart. F. LoC, UCLA.
*Silk Hosiery* (1920), Fred Niblo. Enid Bennett. F. LoC.
*The Sinews of War* (1913), Chas. Giblyn. Chas. Ray. S. GEH.
*Snowball and His Pal* (1912), Thos. H. Ince. Leo Maloney. S. GEH
(has abridged print).
*Son of His Father* (1918), Victor Schertzinger. Chas. Ray. S. LoC.
*The Square Deal Man* (1917), Wm. S. Hart. Wm. S. Hart. F. GEH,
LoC.
*Square Deal Sanderson* (1919), Wm. S. Hart and Lambert Hillyer.
Wm. S. Hart. F. LoC.
*The Struggle* (1913), Thos. H. Ince. J. Barney Sherry. S. MoMA.
*The Taking of Luke McVane* (1915), Wm. S. Hart. Wm. S. Hart.
S. GEH, MoMA.
*The Ten of Diamonds* (1917), Raymond B. West. Dorothy Dalton.
F. GEH.
*The Tide of Fortune* (1915), Jay Hunt. J. Barney Sherry. S. GEH.
*Tiger Man* (1918), Wm. S. Hart. Wm. S. Hart. F. MoMA.
*A Tour of the Thomas H. Ince Studio* (1922), Hunt Stromberg. Ince
contract players. S. MoMA.
*Truthful Tulliver* (1917), Wm. S. Hart. Wm. S. Hart. F. GEH. LoC.
*'Tween Two Loves* (1911), Thos. H. Ince. Mary Pickford. S. GEH,
LoC.
*The Typhoon* (1914), Reginald Barker. Sessue Hayakawa. F. GEH.
*Tyrant Fear* (1918), R.W. Neill. Dorothy Dalton. F. *LoC.
*Vengeance of Fate* (1912), Thos. H. Ince. Francis Ford. UCLA
(fragment).
*A Village Sleuth* (1920), Jerome Storm. Chas. Ray. F. LoC, UCLA.
*Wagon Tracks* (1919), Wm. S. Hart and Lambert Hillyer. Wm. S.
Hart. F. LoC, UCLA.
*War on the Plains* (1911), Thos. H. Ince. Francis Ford. UCLA
(fragment).
*What's Your Husband Doing?* (1919), Lloyd Ingraham. Douglas
MacLean. F. *LoC.
*With Lee in Virginia* (1913), Chas. O. Baumann. Joe King. S. LoC,
*GEH.
*Wolf Lowry* (1917), Wm. S. Hart. Wm. S. Hart. F. LoC, *GEH.
*The Woman in the Suitcase* (1920), Fred Niblo. Enid Bennett. UCLA.
*LoC.
*The Wrath of the Gods* (1914), Reginald Barker. Sessue Hayakawa.
F. GEH.

# Appendix C
# Feature Length Films Directed by D.W. Griffith

For Biograph:

*Judith of Bethulia* (March 1914, six months after Griffith's departure from Biograph) 4 reels, based on the Bible Apocrypha and a story by Grace A. Pierce. Main cast: Blanche Sweet, Henry Walthall. Story: In the midst of a military siege, a great lady of Bethulia travels incognito to the Assyrian camp and manages to seduce their leader, Holofernes. Just before she kills him, she realizes that she could have loved him.

For Mutual release:

*The Battle of the Sexes* (April 1914) 5 reels, based on *The Single Standard*, a novel by Daniel Carson Goodman. Main cast: Mary Alden as a wronged wife, Owen Moore the husband, Fay Tincher the temptress. Lillian Gish the daughter. Only a fragment remains. Remade in 1928.

*Home Sweet Home* (May 1914) 6 reels, four episodes, with large cast of Griffith regulars. Frame story about composer John Howard Payne, others about people moved by thoughts of home.

*The Escape* (June 1914) 7 reels, based on a play by Paul Armstrong. Main cast: Blanche Sweet, Mae Marsh, Robert Harron, Donald Crisp in sociological study of crime. No prints survive.

*The Avenging Conscience* (July 1914) 6 reels, based in part on Edgar Allan Poe's "The Telltale Heart." Main cast: Henry B. Walthall, Blanche Sweet, Spottiswoode Aiken. With many technical devices, a man's imagination of committing a murder is presented: his uncle has tried to prevent his marriage.

Epoch Producing Corporation, distributor (Aitken/Griffith):

*The Birth of a Nation* (February 1915, Los Angeles; March 1915, N.Y.) 12 reels, script by Griffith, assisted by Frank Woods, based on Thomas Dixon's novel and play *The Clansman*, with additional material from his *The Leopard's Spots*. Main cast: Lillian Gish, Mae Marsh, Henry Walthall, Miriam Cooper, Ralph Lewis, George Seigmann, Wallace Reid, Joseph Henabery, Josephine Crowell, Raoul

Walsh. Story: The Camerons, in South Carolina, are visited by Ben's friends from the north, the Stoneman brothers, who are attracted by his sisters and share a picture of their sister with Ben. War comes and the men go off to fight each other. Elsie Stoneman finds the wounded Ben Cameron in a hospital and after the war visits South Carolina with her father, leader of the House of Representatives, who promotes the idea of Negro domination of the state. Elsie is threatened by a black leader, and the younger Cameron sister, in fear of rape by a black renegade, jumps from a cliff. Ben gets the idea for Ku Klux Klan white-sheeted riders from some small children at play and rides to the rescue of Northern and Southern whites.

Wark Producing Corporation,distributor (Griffith,Aitken,etc.):

*Intolerance* (September 1916) 14 reels in Museum of Modern Art print, but seen in various lengths and versions re-edited by Griffith himself. Separate films made from modern story, *The Mother and the Law*, and *The Fall of Babylon*. Main cast: In the modern story, Mae Marsh, Robert Harron, Miriam Cooper, Walter Long. In the Babylon story, Constance Talmadge, Seena Owen, Tully Marshall, Alfred Paget, George Seigmann. In the story of Jesus, Howard Gaye. In the story of the French Huguenots, Margery Wilson, Eugene Pallette, Josephine Crowell. Four stories from different historic eras intercut to illustrate the effects of social and religious hatred. The Babylonian story: In an internal religious dispute, the reactionary high priest conspires with Babylon's enemy, Cyrus the Persian, to capture the city and depose the tolerant Belshazzar. The first attack is repulsed and victory is celebrated, but the invaders return and the priest opens the gate. The modern story: A rich factory owner cuts wages in order to give his sister more money for her charity work. The resulting strike is put down with troops and bloodshed. The Boy is put in jail because he tries to get rid of his underworld connections, and his Dear One has her child taken away by the chari-ty women, who call her an unfit mother. The Friendless One kills the Musketeer of the Slums but blames the Boy. Only an hour before his hanging, she confesses, and the Dear One rushes to save him with the governor's reprieve.

Special for British War Office Cinematograph Committee distribu-tion in British empire and for Paramount in U.S:

*Hearts of the World* (April 1918) 12 reels for first release before the end of the war, 8 reels thereafter. Scenario by D.W. Griffith (under assumed name). Main cast: Lillian Gish, Robert Harron, Dorothy Gish, George Siegmann. Story: A romance between expatriate Americans living in a French village is interrupted by events of World War I. The final climax of the film is an attempted rape by a German officer.

Artcraft productions for Paramount release:

*The Great Love* (August 1918) 7 reels, scenario by Griffith and S.E.V. Taylor. Main cast: Robert Harron, Henry Walthall, Lillian Gish, and certain ladies of British high society. Story: A love affair in London between a young Australian girl and a young American who has enlisted in the British army before the United States has entered the war. Society debutantes become war workers. No print of this film survives.

*The Greatest Thing in Life* (December 1918) 7 reels. Scenario by Griffith and S.E.V. Taylor. Main cast: Lillian Gish, Robert Harron. Story: Intolerant young man learns from wartime comradeship that love is important. A famous moment in this lost film: with a black man dying in his arms and calling for his mother, the white man gives him the kiss he asks for. No print of this film is known to exist.

*A Romance of Happy Valley* (January 1919) 6 reels. Scenario by Griffith (under assumed name). Main cast: Robert Harron, Lillian Gish. Story: Kentucky farm boy returns from New York success to take care of his family and marry the girl who waits.

*The Girl Who Stayed at Home* (March 1919) 7 reels. Scenario by S.E.V. Taylor. Main cast: Carol Dempster, Richard Barthelmess, Robert Harron, Clarine Seymour. Story: One brother welcomes the draft, the other doesn't. Intended as a fourth contribution to the war effort, the film was completed after the armistice and had in it a "good" German as a contribution to the peace.

*True Heart Susie* (June 1919) 6 reels, scenario by Marion Fremont. Main cast: Lillian Gish, Robert Harron, Clarine Seymour, Carol Dempster. Story: Susie sells her favorite cow so that she can secretly pay for her promising schoolmate's college career. He marries a more modern girl who, as a title suggests, "dies, as she had lived — a little bit unfaithful." Later he discovers the truth and returns to Susie.

*Scarlet Days* (November 1919) 7 reels, scenario by S.E.V. Taylor. Main cast: Richard Barthelmess, Carol Dempster, Clarine Seymour, Ralph Graves, Walter Long. A western in the period of California's gold rush. Though well reviewed, the film is lost.

Special for United Artists release (production costs advanced by
Zukor and Griffith):

*Broken Blossoms* (May 1919) 6 reels. Scenario by Griffith, based
on "The Chink and the Child," a story in Thomas Burke's *Limehouse
Nights*. Main cast: Lillian Gish, Richard Barthelmess, Donald Crisp.
Story: From China to London comes a young man hopeful of bringing the peaceful maxims of Buddha to the violent West. As a
shopkeeper in the sordid Limehouse district, he finds one day cower-
ing by his door an abused waif, daughter of a brutal prizefighter.
He takes her in and tries to comfort her, but while he is away, the
father finds her and drags her home for a fatal beating. The young
man comes, is forced to shoot the prizefighter, and returns with her
lifeless form to his shop, where he kills himself.

For First National release:

*The Greatest Question* (December 1919) 6 reels. Story by William
Hale, scenario by S.E.V. Taylor. Main cast: Lillian Gish, Robert
Harron. Appealing to audiences interested in spiritualism, this
"potboiler" ends with an attempted rape.
*The Idol Dancer* (March 1920) 7 reels. Scenario by S.E.V. Taylor,
ased on story by Gordon Ray Young. Main cast: Richard Barthelmess, Clarine Seymour, Creighton Hale. Exotic story of the South
Seas (with production headquarters at Fort Lauderdale) involving
a half-breed girl, a drunken beachcomber, and the nephew of a
missionary.
*The Love Flower* (August 1920) 7 reels. Scenario by Griffith, based
on story "The Black Beach" by Ralph Stock. Main cast: Carol
Dempster, Richard Barthelmess, George MacQuarrie, Anders
Randolf. Story: Rich youth in a sailboat unwittingly brings detective to island where the criminal he seeks is the father of the girl
he loves.

For United Artists release:

*Way Down East* (September 1920) 13 reels. Scenario by Anthony
Paul Kelly from play by Lottie Blair Parker. Main cast: Lillian Gish,
Richard Barthelmess, Lowell Sherman, Burr McIntosh. Story: Poor
country girl visiting rich relatives is seduced into fake marriage by
city slicker, leaving her with a child, which later dies. She wanders
into the country, is accepted as a servant by the Bartlett family, then
ordered to leave when her indiscretion is discovered. The son, who

has fallen in love with her, rescues her from a blizzard on the broken ice of the river.

*Dream Street* (April 1921) 10 reels. Scenario by Griffith (under assumed name). Based on two stories by Thomas Burke. Main cast: Carol Dempster, Ralph Graves, Charles Emmett Mack. Story: An attempt to follow up the critical success of *Broken Blossoms* with more poetic atmosphere, this time with an evil Chinaman plus a street musician and preacher who also represent evil forces in life. Two suitors compete for the hand of a music hall dancer: one finally wins her.

*Orphans of the Storm* (December 1921) 12 reels. Scenario by Griffith (under assumed name). Based on the play *The Two Orphans* by Adolph d'Ennery and Eugene Cormon. Main cast: Lillian Gish, Dorothy Gish, Joseph Schildkraut, Monte Blue. Story: A personal drama against the background of the French revolution: Henriette seeks a cure for her adopted sister's blindness, but they are separated in Paris and after many desperate adventures including a sentence to the guillotine, there is a ride to the rescue by Danton and friends. Parallels are drawn in the explanatory titles between the bloodthirsty Jacobins and the Bolsheviks in Russia.

*One Exciting Night* (October 1922) 11 reels. Scenario by D.W. Griffith (under assumed name). Main cast: Carol Dempster, Henry Hull, Porter Strong (playing a blackface comedy role). Story: A haunted house murder mystery written by Griffith to compete with stage successes like *The Bat*. A costly stormy night finale was added at Dempster's request.

*The White Rose* (May 1923) 10 reels. Scenario by Griffith, influenced by press stories about clergymen involved in sex crimes. Main cast: Mae Marsh, Ivor Novello, Neil Hamilton, Carol Dempster. Story: Divinity student meets and impregnates a simple orphan who is pretending to be a flapper in order to catch a man. She and her child are taken in by compassionate blacks, while he, all unknowing, preaches hypocritical sermons and pursues another woman — but finally accepts his child.

*America* (February 1924) 12 reels. Scenario by Robert Chambers, based on his revolutionary war novel, *The Reckoning*. Main cast: Neil Hamilton, Carol Dempster, and Lionel Barrymore as a villainous Indian agent for the British. Story: A romance between a dispatch rider for the Americans and the daughter of a Tory, played against the events of Paul Revere's ride, the battles of Concord, Lexington, Bunker Hill, and the Mohawk Valley, and the camp at Valley Forge.

For United Artists release, initial production for Paramount:

*Isn't Life Wonderful* (December 1924) 9 reels. Scenario by D.W. Griffith from story in *Defeat*, a book about life in postwar Germany, by Major Geoffrey Moss. Main cast: Carol Dempster, Neil Hamilton. Story: Young couple, part of a larger destitute family, raise potatoes on a tiny piece of land. Their first crop is stolen, but they are thankful to be alive.

*Sally of the Sawdust* (August 1925) 10 reels. Scenario by Forrest Halsey, based on *Poppy*, a play by Dorothy Donnelly. Main cast: W.C. Fields, Carol Dempster, Alfred Lunt. Story: On the road with a juggler and other carnival acts. Fields is guardian for rejected orphan, trying to get her rich grandparents to take her back.

For Paramount release:

*That Royle Girl* (January 1926) 11 reels. Scenario by Paul Schofield, from serial and novel by Edwin Balmer. Main cast: Carol Dempster, James Kirkwood, Harrison Ford, W.C. Fields. Story: Modiste in love with bandleader finds evidence that will save him from execution for murder, then falls instead for the prosecutor. No prints of the film are believed to have survived.

*The Sorrows of Satan* (October 1926) 9 reels. Scenario by Forrest Halsey, adapted by John Russell and George Hull, from an 1895 novel by Marie Corelli. A project originally intended for Cecil DeMille, who left Paramount; re-edited by Julian Johnson. Main cast: Adolphe Menjou, Ricardo Cortez, Lya de Putti, Carol Dempster. Story: Struggling author is tempted with devil's money and a beautiful woman, but the woman he loves finally helps him refuse the deal.

For United Artists release:

*Drums of Love* (January 1928) 9 reels. Scenario by Gerrit Lloyd. Main cast: Mary Philbin, Don Alvarado, Lionel Barrymore. Story: A 19th century version, set in Latin America, of Dante's Paolo and Francesca romance. The duke, an aging hunchback, sends his handsome younger brother to claim the princess who has been betrothed to the duke for political reasons. When the two young people are later discovered together, the sorrowful duke finds it necessary to kill them.

*The Battle of the Sexes* (October 1928) 10 reels. Scenario by Gerrit Lloyd, based on novel, *The Single Standard*, by Daniel Carson

Goodman. Remake of 1913 film; synchonized music. Main cast: Jean Hersholt, Phyllis Haver, Don Alvarado, Sally O'Neil. Story: A gold digger seduces a married man, but before she and her boy friend can profit from his compromised situation, his daughter confronts them and her father, who asks forgiveness.

*Lady of the Pavements* (January 1929) 9 reels. Scenario by Sam Taylor, based on a story by Karl Volmoeller; songs recorded on discs. Main cast: Lupe Velez, William Boyd, Jetta Goudal. Story: A countess in Paris in 1868 decides to have revenge upon the nobleman who rejected her. Because he said he would rather marry "a woman of the streets," she trains a cabaret performer to act like a lady, only to find the count does fall for her.

*Abraham Lincoln* (October 1930) 10 reels, sound. Scenario by Stephen Vincent Benet, with changes by Gerrit Lloyd and Griffith; final editing by John Considine, Jr. Main cast: Walter Huston, Una Merkel, Kay Hammond, Jason Robards. Personal and historic episodes in Lincoln's life.

*The Struggle* (December 1931) 9 reels, sound. Screenplay by Anita Loos, John Emerson. Main cast: Hal Skelly, Zita Johann, Evelyn Baldwin. Story: An alcoholic, slipping gradually into degradation and violence, threatens his daughter's life, but his wife helps him fight back to normalcy. (One proposed reason for his attraction to drink is the excitement of evading the law of Prohibition.) Because of negative reviews and audience reaction, the film was shown only in New York and Philadelphia.

Sources, stars, and stories summarized from: Iris Barry and Eileen Bowser, *D.W. Griffith, American Film Master* and Richard Schickel, *D.W. Griffith: An American Life.*

# Appendix D
# Feature Length Films Directed
# by Erich von Stroheim

For Universal release:

*Blind Husbands* (December 1919) 8000 feet. Scenario by Stroheim, from his story "The Pinnacle." Main cast: Erich von Stroheim, Sam de Grasse, Francilla Billington, Gibson Gowland. Story:A chance encounter at a hotel in the Italian Alps: a young Austrian lieutenant on leave meets an American surgeon and his wife on holiday. The wife feels neglected and much inclined to go off with him while her husband is mountain climbing, but she finally writes a note rejecting the idea. The note is discovered at the top of a mountain the lieutenant and the doctor are climbing together. The rope is cut and the would-be seducer, forced to come down by himself, falls to his death.

*The Devil's Passkey* (August 1920) 12,000 feet; no copy is known to exist. Scenario by Erich von Stroheim, from story by Baroness de Meyer, "Clothes and Treachery." Main cast: Sam de Grasse, Una Trevelyn, Maude George, Mae Busch, Clyde Fillmore. Story: In post-armistice Paris, an American playwright's wife is badly in debt to a famous modiste and seems willing to accept "charity" from a young American officer. He refuses, after all, to compromise her, but the lurid story becomes known. The playwright, unaware it is his own story, writes it up for all Paris to see. He finally learns the truth, but is told by his wife and the officer that he must believe that nothing happened.

*Foolish Wives* (January 1922) 21,000 feet, reduced to 14,120 for New York premiere, and to about 10,000 for national release. Original scenario by Stroheim. Main cast: Erich von Stroheim, Maude George, Mae Busch, Dale Fuller, Rudolph Christians (replaced in several scenes after his death by Robert Edeson), Patsy Hannen (a.k.a. Miss DuPont). Story: Supposedly a former Russian count and army officer, living in Monaco with his princess cousins, Karamzin is actually keeping up his villa with counterfeit money. He hopes to make real money by seducing and blackmailing the wife of the new American ambassador, but after one suspenseful effort of this sort does not work out, he is driven to begging from her on the pretext that he is in danger. His jealous maid overhears this and sets fire to the house, as both escape in full view of firemen and citizens. Karamzin ends up, after one more attempted seduction, stuffed in the sewer.

*Merry Go Round* (July 1923) 12,000 feet, reduced to 10,000. Scenario by Erich von Stroheim. Film completed by Rupert Julian supervised by Irving Thalberg. Main cast: Norman Kerry, Mary Philbin, Dorothy Wallace. Story: The Austrian emperor's favorite is required to marry a certain countess but is attracted instead by the daughter of the puppeteer at the amusement park, who is in turn menaced by her boss, who runs the carousel. After the war, the nobleman is penniless but comes back to find the girl.

For Metro-Goldwyn release:

*Greed* (December 1924) 24,000 feet reduced to 18,000 by Grant Whytock under Rex Ingram's supervision, to 16,000 by June Mathis, to 10,212 by Joe Farnham under supervision of Harry Rapf and Irving Thalberg. Scenario by Erich von Stroheim, from the Frank Norris novel, *McTeague*. Main cast: Gibson Gowland, ZaSu Pitts, Jean Hersholt. Story: McTeague, strong and slow-witted, gets away from the gold mines by apprenticing to an unlicensed traveling dentist. In San Francisco, his new friend Marcus brings Trina to have a tooth fixed. McTeague falls for her and Marcus agrees to give her up. But it now develops that she has also won $5000 in the lottery. This really angers Marcus, who gets back at McTeague by bringing down on his amateur status the wrath of the health department. He cannot get another job. Trina has transferred her affections to her gold pieces and won't spend a nickel of her winnings. They fight, he goes away, comes back, beats her to death, finds the money, starts running and ends up in Death Valley, where Marcus catches up with him and they die together.

*The Merry Widow* (August, 1925) 14,000 feet reduced by MGM to 10,027. Scenario by Erich von Stroheim and Benjamin Glazer from operetta libretto by Victor Leon and Leo Stein, famous for music by Franz Lehar. Main cast: Mae Murray, John Gilbert, Roy D'Arcy, Tully Marshall. Story: Two princes are in love with a dancer, who is so disillusioned by both of them that she agrees to marry an aged, crippled, wealthy baron. He collapses on their wedding night, and she takes his millions to Paris. After a duel between the princes, the death of the king, and the death of the crown prince, she ends up on the throne with the one she loves.

For Paramount release (P.A. Powers/Celebrity production):

*The Wedding March* (October 1928) 25,795 feet reduced to 17,993 by Josef von Sternberg, to 11,147 by Julian Johnston, and for release 10,400 by Stroheim and Sternberg. Part II, given the title of *The Honeymoon*, ultimately cut down from 22,484 to 6000 feet, was shown only in Europe. Scenario by Stroheim and Harry Carr. Main cast: Erich von Stroheim, Fay Wray, ZaSu Pitts, Matthew Betz, George Fawcett, George Nichols. Story: In Vienna, the emperor's impoverished captain of the guards plans his son Nicki's marriage to the daughter of a wealthy corn-plaster magnate: in fact, the two fathers agree on it while they are both in the local bordello. Meanwhile, Nicki has encountered lovely Mitzi, "harpist at the wine-garden." He rebels against taking a wealthy bride who seems to "limp on both legs," but is forced by his parents to go through the grand church ceremony. [Second half: Nicki has refused to consummate the marriage. He is alone in his mountain lodge with three people trying to reach him: his wife, determined to join him, Mitzi's unloved suitor on his way to kill him, Mitzi coming to warn him. The bullet intended for Nicki hits his wife. Mitzi, though she still loves him, goes to a convent to find peace. War comes and her cruel husband is killed. Nicki and Mitzi are married before he goes off to fight.]

For United Artists (Kennedy/Swanson production):

*Queen Kelly* (1928) 10 reels completed of 30 planned, of which 8 were released only in South America and Europe. Scenario by Erich von Stroheim, from his story, "The Swamp." Suspended after nearly three months of production. Main cast: Gloria Swanson, Walter Byron, Seena Owen. Story: In one of the tiny states of prewar Germany, the prince is about to marry his cousin, the queen. On patrol with some of his guards, he watches a group of convent girls go by, laughs when Kitty Kelly's panties slip down to the ground, then receives them in his face. He is so charmed that he starts a fire in the convent, kidnaps Kitty, and takes her to his apartment. This annoys the queen, who whips her out of the palace. [Script: Kitty is called by telegram to Africa, where her aunt, who has been paying for her education, causes her to be married, just before she dies, to a grisly old rich man. She doesn't live with him but inherits the income from her aunt's houses of prostitution and puts on airs as "Queen Kelly." Her husband dies and back home in Germany the queen dies. So Kitty marries her prince and becomes a real queen.]

For Fox release:

*Walking Down Broadway/Hello Sister* (May 1933) 14,000 feet by Stroheim, most of which was thrown out and replaced with 5800 feet directed by Alfred Werker and Edwin Burke, supervised by Sol Wurtzel; a sound film. Scenario by Erich von Stroheim and Leonard Spigelgass from play by Dawn Powell. Main cast: Boots Mallory, ZaSu Pitts, James Dunn, Terence Ray, Minna Gombell. Story: Millie, scared and possessive, and Peggy, who is beautiful, are picked up on Broadway by Smart Alec Mac and Nice Guy Jimmy. Millie gets paired with Jimmy, who really goes for Peggy, and this first mistake leads to tragedy when Millie realizes she is not wanted and decides to commit suicide on Christmas eve. She gets her name in the papers, but confesses on her deathbed that she had tried to keep Peggy and Jimmy apart.

[Sources, stars, and stories summarized from Herman Weinberg, *Stroheim: A Pictorial Record of His Nine Films* (1975), Thomas Quinn Curtiss, *Von Stroheim*, (1971), and Richard Koszarski, *The Man You Loved to Hate*.]

# Appendix E
# Twenty Notable Directors

*The following twenty directors began their careers during the period 1912-1919. They were therefore working at their craft in the United States during the same years that Ince, Griffith, and Stroheim were making movies. Most observers, then and now, would agree that these three film makers — given primary attention in this book — were of great importance and influence, receiving praise from critics and response from the public. But firm comparative evaluations are of course impossible to make in any measurable or even any widely acceptable way. Probably a good many silent film scholars would want to have Maurice Tourneur and Cecil B. DeMille, for example, included in any grouping of "important" film makers during the period of the teens.*

*It can only be said that the original plan included these men and others, but once the desirable Griffith and Stroheim selections were in place, further additions would have resulted in a much longer volume. Accepting the rationale that the major weight of their work in the silent era was in the 1920s, these other directors could reasonably be postponed to the fifth volume, to be titled* Films of the 1920s. *Of course this could as well be said of Stroheim, but his link to Griffith historically — and his difference from Griffith thematically — suggested his placement here.*

*Most of the names which follow may also be expected to turn up in the fifth volume, some represented by a single film review, others requiring broader perspective. All of them, except possibly for Marshall Neilan, did most of their work — or their best work — during the 1920s or later. Of this list only Brenon, William deMille, Ingram, Niblo, and Tourneur seem to belong specifically to the 1920s (in the U.S.). A few, like Borzage, Browning, Crosland, Cruze, and St. Clair, worked in the 1920s and with less success in the 1930s. The others — Cecil DeMille, Ford, King, Lloyd, Seiter, Seitz, Van Dyke, Vidor, and Walsh — belong to the 30s and 40s more than to the silent period, although some critics might say that Vidor's best pictures were silent.*

*For now, it is useful to note (borrowing Lewis Jacobs' phrase) 'a throng of directors,' unknown perhaps to readers unacquainted with the period, but rich in the qualifications of art and entertainment which we ask of movie makers. If only we had access to more of their films today!*

1912

Herbert Brenon (1880-1958). Born in Dublin. To U.S. at 16. Actor in stock. Writer for IMP (Laemmle). Director 1912. Best known for *Peter Pan* (1924) and *Dancing Mothers* (1926). Last film 1940, in England. Last in U.S. 1933.

1914

Alan Crosland (1894-1936). Born in New York City. Actor at 15. Edison Company 1912. Director of shorts 1914, features 1917. Directed earliest sound features at Warners, *Don Juan* (1926) and *The Jazz Singer* (1927). Last film 1935.

Cecil B. DeMille (1881-1959). Actor on Broadway 1900. Also playwright in collaboration with brother William. Partner with Jesse Lasky and Samuel Goldwyn in production of *The Squaw Man:* Co-director (with Oscar Apfel) 1914. Noted for spectacular and popular films, but in earlier silent period especially for stories exploiting sexual relationships in the light of Victorian morality. Of his 70 films *Male and Female* (1919) and *The Ten Commandments* (1923, 1956) may represent those types. Last film 1956.

Marshall Neilan (1891-1958). Born in San Bernardino, California. Actor in stock companies as teen-ager, later at Kalem. Director 1914; features 1916. Credited with 67 films, many of them in the teens; most famous for several silents starring Mary Pickford. Last film 1937.

Maurice Tourneur (1876-1961). Born in Paris. Assistant in Rodin's sculpture studio. Actor, assistant director, Eclair, 1911. Director 1912. Director, U.S. 1914. Credited with 56 films, which he often wrote or produced as well. Noted for pictorial quality, ranging from *The Wishing Ring* (1914) to *The Poor Little Rich Girl* with Mary Pickford (1917), and *The Last of the Mohicans.* Films in France 1928-1948. Last film in U.S. 1926.

Raoul Walsh (1887-1980). Born in New York City. Stage actor. Actor and assistant director for Griffith. Director 1914. A long career emphasizing outdoor action dramas, ranging from *The Thief of Bagdad* (1924) with Douglas Fairbanks to *High Sierra* (1941) with Humphrey Bogart. Last film 1964.

1915

Henry King (1888-1982). Born in Christiansburg, Virginia. Actor; in films 1912. Director 1915. Perhaps most praised for *Tol'able David* (1921) and *The Gunfighter* (1950). Prolific director at 20th Century-

Fox in sound period, working on many Darryl Zanuck productions. Last film 1962.

Frank Lloyd (1888-1960). Born in Glasgow. Actor at 15. To Canada 1910, U.S. 1913. Director 1915. Credited with some 100 films at various major studios (ten of them in 1919) including *Cavalcade* (1933) and *Mutiny on the Bounty* (1935). Producer of works of others and some of his own films. Wrote many of his silent scripts. Last film 1955.

## 1916

Frank Borzage (1893-1962). Born in Salt Lake City, Utah. Actor in Ince films 1912. Director at Universal 1916. Best known for such romantic stories in silent era as *Seventh Heaven* (1927) but made occasional films through the sound era to 1949. Last film 1959.

William C. deMille (1878-1955). Born in Washington, D.C. Elder brother of Cecil; playwright. To Hollywood, 1914. Director 1916. Interested in the quieter intricacies of human relations, he made fewer films than his brother, and *Nice People* (1922) perhaps epitomizes the tone of his plots, along with *What Every Woman Knows* and *Miss Lulu Bett* (1921). Writer for others, including Cecil. Last film as director 1934.

Rex Ingram (1892-1950). Born in Dublin. To U.S. 1911, studying sculpture. Actor-writer-set designer at Edison 1913. Director at Universal 1916. To Metro 1920. Credited with 27 films, often also as writer or producer; praised for pictorial sense. Most famous for *The Four Horsemen of the Apocalypse* (1921). Set up studio in Nice (1924) releasing through MGM. Last film also his first sound picture (1933).

George B. Seitz (1888-1944). Actor, writer for Pathé 1913. Writer and actor (1914-1916) for Pearl White serials. Director 1916, features 1925. Many action films divided between silent and sound periods; also most of the Andy Hardy series at MGM. Last film 1944.

## 1917

Tod Browning (1882-1962). Born in Louisville, Kentucky. At 16 a circus performer. About 1915 at Biograph, later assisting Griffith on *Intolerance*. Director 1917. Credited with 48 films including 7 in 1918, often based on his own stories. Most famous for *The Unholy Three* (1925), other pictures starring Lon Chaney at MGM, and for *Freaks* (1932). Last film 1939.

John Ford (1895-1973). Born in Cape Elizabeth, Maine. To

Hollywood 1913; propman, stuntman, assistant at Universal. Director 1917. Maker of a long line of distinguished American films ranging from *The Iron Horse* (1924) to *Stagecoach* (1939), *The Grapes of Wrath* (1940), *The Man Who Shot Liberty Valance* (1962). Last film 1966.

Fred Niblo (1874-1948). Born in York, Nebraska. Vaudeville performer and stage director. Director 1917 for Ince, especially films starring his wife, Enid Bennett. Credited with 46 films, almost all silent. Most famous for Douglas Fairbanks costume pictures and MGM's *Ben-Hur* (1926). Last film 1932.

W.S. Van Dyke (1889-1943). Born Seattle,Washington. Actor in stock as a child. Assistant to Griffith on *Intolerance*. Director 1917. Credited with four serials and 79 films, most of them at MGM, including *Tarzan the Ape Man* (1932), *The Thin Man* (1934) and successors, and *Naughty Marietta* (1935). Last film 1942.

## 1918

James Cruze (1884-1942). Born in Ogden, Utah. Actor at 16, in films 1908, at Lasky Co. 1916. Director 1918. Credited with 73 films, about a third of them in sound. Most famous for *The Covered Wagon* (1923) and *Beggar on Horseback* (1925). Last film 1938.

William A. Seiter (1892-1964). Born in New York City. Actor and writer for Sennett. Director 1918. Many light romantic dramas divided between silent and sound periods. Last film 1954.

## 1919

Malcolm St. Clair (1897-1952). Born in Los Angeles. Newspaper cartoonist, player and gag writer for Mack Sennett 1915. Director 1919. Features 1924. Co-directed two shorts with Buster Keaton, *The Goat* (1921) and *The Blacksmith* (1922). Noted in silent era for light social comedies like *The Grand Duchess and the Waiter* (1926). Last film 1948.

King Vidor (1894-1982). Born in Galveston, Texas. Hollywood 1915. Director 1919. Credited with 27 silent, 24 sound features. Best known for *The Big Parade* (1925), *The Crowd* (1928), and *Hallelujah* (1929). Last film 1959.

David Wark Griffith (1875-1948). Born in LaGrange, Kentucky. Stage actor 1897. Film director 1908; features 1914. Last film 1931.

William S. Hart (1870-1946). Born Newburgh, New York. Stage actor 1889. Film actor and director 1914. Last film 1925.

Erich von Stroheim (1885-1957). Born in Vienna. Film actor, Hollywood, 1914; director 1919. Last film as director in U.S., 1932.

[Information drawn from the following sources: David Robinson, *Hollywood in the Twenties* (1968); Lewis Jacobs, *The Rise of the American Film* (1929); William Everson, *American Silent Film* (1978); Ephraim Katz, *The Film Encyclopedia* (1979). Also Cecil B. DeMille, *Autobiography* (1959); Herman G. Weinberg, *The Lubitsch Touch* (1968); King Vidor, *A Tree Is a Tree* (1952).]

# Appendix F
# Bibliography

By and large, we have a respectable range of biographical materials now available on Thomas Ince, William S. Hart, D.W. Griffith, and Erich von Stroheim.

Richard Schickel, a veteran critic who has worked for both *Life* and *Time*, has given us, after years of devoted preparation, a truly extraordinary Griffith biography, weaving skilfully together in chronology the life, the films, the finances, the human and corporate relationships: *D.W. Griffith: An American Life* (1984).

Richard Koszarski, a younger scholar, has drawn from his dissertation the first relatively objective and nearly definitive account of Stroheim's life and films: *The Man You Loved to Hate: Erich von Stroheim and Hollywood* (1983).

These are gifts of exceptional value, adding distinction to film studies. Soon we shall have a much-needed biography of Ince from Steven Higgins (based on his dissertation). And not far off is Russell Merritt's long-awaited expansion of his earlier dissertation (1970) relating Griffith to American culture.

The autobiographies we have are fragmentary. They are in every case revealing. But they are lacking in those qualities of self-awareness and reader appeal so notable in memoirs by the actors, actresses, and comedians of the silent screen.

The best of the lot is Hart's *My Life East and West* (1929) primarily because of its engaging directness and emotional commitment. He was of course the chief performer of the films he directed. If we place beside it on the shelf Diane Kaiser Koszarski's paperback, *The Complete Films of William S. Hart: A Pictorial Record*, with its thoughtful brief introductory chapter, we have a rewarding package.

The Ince memoirs, as published in the *Exhibitors Herald* (1924-25), reflect well enough his blunt, efficient personality, and give a clear picture of how his studio fitted into the film industry from his own point of view, but it shares none of the human factors which would most interest us. The stirring final section (reprinted here) does make us wonder what he was like when he struggled to maintain those high standards.

There is no Stroheim autobiography, except for the lofty fictions he always maintained about his origins and the various public statements he made about the need for autonomy in film directing. His own version of his life is probably well served by the Peter Noble (1950) and Thomas Quinn Curtiss (1971) biographies, and his films have been given pictorial highlights in the books by Herman Weinberg.

Although Griffith, like Stroheim, had plenty of time during his last years to prepare a statement of his views and his memories, his brief attempt to do so does not encourage us to wish for more. What we have in the material he worked up with James Hart for publication in Louisville ("The Hollywood Gold Rush," in *The Man Who Invented Hollywood,* 1972) is like the spiel of a sports figure making jokes for the locker room, dropping famous names (David Lloyd George, Warren G. Harding) and only briefly shining with those youthful recollections we have chosen to reproduce here. Griffith was always in public. He does not spell out for us any long-held secrets. And the quality of his writing here, as in some of his film titles, leaves much to be desired. Perhaps it is true, as Linda Arvidson claimed in the alimony court proceedings, that she herself wrote his published poem and his play *A Fool and a Girl* (James Hart, p. 7).

Griffith needs to be understood as a maker of films, and he has benefited from a few interpreters who shared this obsession with him. His first wife remembers it all as an adventure: *When the Movies Were Young* (1925). Lillian Gish steadfastly thinks of him as a great man: *The Movies, Mr. Griffith and Me* (1969). Karl Brown looks upon him as a teacher and master editor: *Adventures With D.W. Griffith* (1973). Roy Aitken remembers him as a financial problem and a challenge: *The Birth of a Nation Story* (1956).

There are at least two indispensable outside observers: (1) Lewis Jacobs, whose enthusiasm and keen critical (as well as technical) understanding have given us a history of permanent value, *The Rise of the American Film* (1939). (2) Eileen Bowser, whose measured and perceptive brief summations of the films and their historical connections added so much in 1965 to the original Iris Barry monograph, *D.W. Griffith: American Film Master.*

Again, as in the previous volume, certain source books and reference works should be given special mention:

Kenneth Munden, *The American Film Institute Catalogue of Motion Pictures Produced in the U.S.: Feature Films 1921-1930* (1971). Annotated in first volume chronologically as to stories, themes, credits. Indexed in second volume according to these elements. Volume on teen years is promised.

Kevin Brownlow, *The Parade's Gone By* (1968). Lively interviews with survivors of the silent era in Hollywood, plus much connecting historical material by the author.

Richard Griffith, Arthur Mayer, and Eileen Bowser, *The Movies* (1984). A superior picture book on U.S. films, first published in 1957: a good first reader, half of it on the silent era.

Ephraim Katz, *The Film Encyclopedia* (1979). First-rate biographies and country histories: dependable, lucid, sometimes pungent, and more complete than one has a right to expect.

*Magill's Survey of Cinema: Silent Films* (1982). Uniquely valuable individual reviews since they are (1) rather lengthy (2) story-oriented (3) with some historical data (sources, authorial connections, awards, reviews, boxoffice, etc.).

**Books from which extracts are reprinted in this volume:**

Ball, Robert Hamilton. *Shakespeare on Silent Film.* N.Y., Theatre Arts Books, 1968.

Balshofer, Fred and Arthur Miller. *One Reel a Week.* Berkeley, University of California Press, 1967.

Bowser, Eileen. *Film Notes.* N.Y., Museum of Modern Art, 1969.

Brown, Karl. *Adventures With D.W. Griffith.* N.Y., Farrar, Straus, Giroux, 1973. Billy Bitzer's assistant cameraman.

Casty, Alan. *Development of the Film.* N.Y., Harcourt Brace Jovanovich, 1973.

Cripps, Thomas. *Slow Fade to Black: The Negro in American Film 1900-1942.* N.Y., Oxford University Press, 1977.

Eisenstein, Sergei. *Film Form.* N.Y.,Harcourt Brace 1949; Meridian books 1957.

Everson, William K. *American Silent Film.* N.Y., Oxford University Press, 1978.

Finler, Joel W. *Stroheim.* Berkeley, University of California Press, 1968.

Franklin, Joe. *Classics of the Silent Screen.* N.Y., Citadel Press, 1959.

Fulton, A.R. *Motion Pictures.* Norman, University of Oklahoma Press, 1960 and 1980.

Gish, Lillian. *The Movies, Mr. Griffith, and Me.* N.Y., Prentice-Hall, 1969.

Hart, James (ed.). *The Man Who Invented Hollywood.* Louisville, Ky., Touchstone Publishing Co., 1972. Sketchy biographical information plus D.W. Griffith's draft of an autobiography up to 1915, "The Hollywood Gold Rush."

Hart, William S. *My Life East and West.* Boston, Houghton Mifflin, 1929.

Jacobs, Lewis. *The Rise of the American Film.* N.Y., Harcourt Brace, 1939.

Knight, Arthur. *The Liveliest Art.* N.Y., Macmillan, 1957, 1978.

Koszarski, Diane Kaiser. *The Complete Films of William S. Hart: A Pictorial Record.* N.Y., Dover, 1980.

Lennig, Arthur. *The Silent Voice: A Text.* Lennig, 1969.

*Magill's Survey of Cinema: Silent Films.* Englewood Cliffs, N.J., Salem Press, 1982.

Perelman, S.J. *The Road to Miltown, or Under the Spreading Atrophy,* N.Y., Simon and Schuster, 1957. Original essay on *Foolish Wives* in *New Yorker* September 20, 1952.

Ramsaye, Terry. *A Million and One Nights.* N.Y., Simon & Schuster, 1926.

Schickel, Richard. *D.W. Griffith: An American Life.* N.Y., Simon & Schuster, 1984.

Silva, Fred (ed.). *Focus on The Birth of a Nation.* Englewood Cliffs, N.J., Prentice-Hall, 1971.

Slide, Anthony. *Early Women Directors..* Cranbury, N.J., A.S. Barnes & Co., 1977.

Weinberg, Herman G. *Stroheim: A Pictorial Record of His Nine Films.* N.Y., Dover Publications, 1975.

**Articles reprinted in this volume:**

Cobleigh, Rolfe. Boston branch, National Association for the Advancement of Colored People, *Fighting a Vicious Film.* Reprinted in Fred Silva, *Focus on Birth of a Nation.*

Corliss, Richard. "Writing in Silence," *Film Comment,* July-August 1985. Earliest scenario writers.

Firestone, Bruce. "A Man Named Sioux," *Film and History,* December 1977. William S. Hart.

Griffith, D.W. "The Hollywood Gold Rush," autobiography up to 1915, in James Hart, *op.cit., The Man Who Invented Hollywood.*

Gunning, Tom. "Weaving a Narrative: Style and Economic

Background in Griffith's Biograph Films," *Quarterly Review of Film Studies* 6 (No. 1, Winter 1981).

Hackett, Francis. "Brotherly Love," *New Republic*, March 20, 1915. Review of *The Birth of a Nation*.

Higgins, Steven. "Thomas H. Ince." *Field of Vision*, Number 14 (1987), reprint of introduction to program notes for retrospective showing of Ince films, Museum of Modern Art, October 1986.

Huff, Theodore. "Hollywood's Predecessor: Fort Lee, N.J." *Films in Review*, February 1951.

Ince, Thomas H. "Memoirs of Thomas H. Ince." *Exhibitors Herald*, December 13, 20, 27, 1924; January 3, 10, 1925,

Lambert, Gavin. "Stroheim Revisited: The Missing Third in the American Cinema," *Sight and Sound*, April 1953.

Lennig, Arthur. "D.W. Griffith and the Making of an Unconventional Masterpiece," *The Film Journal*, Vol.1 (No.3-4, Fall-Winter 1972).

Lucas, Blake. "A Directorial History of Silent Films," and *"Lady of the Pavements,"* in *Magill's Survey of Cinema: Silent Films, op.cit.*

Merritt, Russell. *"Intolerance."* In Christopher Lyon (ed.) *The International Dictionary of Films and Filmmakers: Volume I, Films.* Chicago, St. James Press/Macmillan, 1984.

Mitry, Jean. "Thomas H. Ince: His Esthetic, His Films, His Legacy," *Cinema Journal*, Winter 1983. Translation by Martin Sopocy with Paul Attalah of portions of a monograph in *Anthologie du Cinéma*, November 9, 1965.

Quirk, James R. "An Open Letter to D.W. Griffith," *Photoplay*, December 1924.

Stroheim, Erich von. "The Seamy Side of Directing," *Theatre Magazine*, November 1927. Reprinted in Richard Koszarski, *Hollywood Directors 1914-1940*, (N.Y., Oxford University Press, 1976).

Wing, W.E. "Tom Ince of Inceville," *New York Dramatic Mirror* December 24, 1913. Reprinted in George Pratt, *Spellbound in Darkness*, Rochester N.Y., University of Rochester, 1966.

**Other useful books:**

Agee, James. *Agee on Film*, Vol. 1. N.Y., McDowell Obolensky, 1958. Reviews from *Time, The Nation, etc.*

Aitken, Roy. *The Birth of a Nation Story*. Middleburg, Va., William Denlingers, 1956. As told to Al P. Nelson.

Altman, Rick (guest editor). *Quarterly Review of Film Studies* 6 (No. 1, Winter 1981) Special Griffith issue.

Altomara, Rita Ecke. *Hollywood on the Palisades: A Filmography of Silent Features Made in Fort Lee, New Jersey, 1903-1927.* N.Y.,Garland Publishing, 1985.

Arvidson, Linda (Mrs. D.W. Griffith). *When the Movies Were Young.* N.Y., E.P. Dutton, 1925. Reprint, Benjamin Blom,1968; Dover paperback, 1969.

Bardèche, Maurice and Robert Brasillach. *History of the Film.* London, Allen & Unwin, 1938. Reprinted N.Y., Arno Press, 1970. Translated and edited by Iris Barry, who notes her objections to the section on Ince.

Barry, Iris. *D.W. Griffith, American Film Master.* N.Y., Museum of Modern Art, 1940. Enlarged edition edited by Eileen Bowser, for the Museum and Doubleday, 1965.

Bitzer, G.W. *Billy Bitzer: His Story.* N.Y., Farrar, Straus, Giroux, 1973. Griffith's cameraman.

Blaché, Alice Guy. *The Memoirs of Alice Guy Blaché.* Translated by Roberta and Simone Blaché. Edited by Anthony Slide. Metuchen, N.J., Scarecrow Press, 1986.

Cooper, Miriam (with Bonnie Herndon). *Dark Lady of the Silents: My Life in Early Hollywood.* Indianapolis, Bobbs-Merrill, 1973. A Griffith actress.

Curtiss, Thomas Quinn, *et al. Film Culture,* special issue on Stroheim, Volume 4, Number 3, April 1958. Articles also by Herman Weinberg, Richard Watts Jr., Lotte H. Eisner, Rudolf Arnheim, and Erich von Stroheim.

Curtiss, Thomas Quinn. *Von Stroheim.* N.Y., Farrar, Straus and Giroux, 1971.

Deutelbaum, Marshall. *"Image" on the Art and Evolution of the Film.* N.Y.,Dover Publications, 1979.

Dixon Jr., Thomas. *The Clansman: An Historical Romance of the Ku Klux Klan.* N.Y., Doubleday Page, 1905. Reprint on microfilm by 3M International Microfilm Press, 1970.

Drew, William M. *D.W. Griffith's Intolerance: Its Genesis and Its Vision.* Jefferson, North Carolina, McFarland, 1986. Evidences of progressivism and anti-imperialism in his thought.

Fell, John. *Film Before Griffith.* Berkeley, University of California, 1983.

Geduld, Harry M. *Focus on D.W. Griffith.* N.Y., Prentice-Hall, 1971. Includes a number of his articles and interviews.

Goodman, Ezra. *The Fifty Year Decline and Fall of Hollywood.* N.Y., Simon & Schuster, 1961/Macfadden Books 1962. Chapter I is the depressing last interview with Griffith.

Graham, Cooper C., Steven Higgins, Elaine Mancini, and Joao Luiz Vieira. *D.W. Griffith and the Biograph Company.* Metuchen, N.J., Scarecrow Press, 1985. Credits for the films.

Griffith, D.W. *D.W. Griffith Papers 1897-1954: A Guide to the Microfilm Edition.* Museum of Modern Art/University of Louisville, 1982.

———. *The Birth of a Nation.* N.Y., Museum of Modern Art, 1961. Shot-by-shot analysis by Theodore Huff.

———. *Intolerance.* N.Y., Museum of Modern Art, 1966. Shot-by-shot analysis by Theodore Huff.

———. *The Rise and Fall of Free Speech in America.* Printed by the author, 1916. Pamphlet, 45 pages.

Hartz, Louis. *The Liberal Tradition in America.* N.Y., Harcourt, Brace & Co., 1955.

Hastings, Charles Edward. *D.W. Griffith: A Biography and Brief History of the Motion Picture in America,* N.Y., Exhibitors Trade Review, 1920.

Henderson, Robert. *D.W.Griffith: The Years at Biograph.* N.Y., Farrar, Straus, Giroux, 1970.

———. *D.W. Griffith: His Life and Work.* N.Y., Oxford University Press, 1972.

Higgins, Steven. *Thomas H. Ince: American Film Maker.* Ph.D. dissertation, School of the Arts, New York University, 1988.

Kauffman, Stanley. *Living Images.* N.Y., Harper and Row, 1975. Analysis of *Way Down East.*

Koszarski, Richard (ed.). *The Rivals of D.W. Griffith: Alternate Auteurs 1913-1918.* Minneapolis, Minn., Walker Art Center, 1976. Notes on 20 films in a program series.

Koszarski, Richard. *The Man You Loved to Hate: Erich von Stroheim and Hollywood.* N.Y., Oxford University Press, 1983.

Lindsay, Vachel. *The Art of the Moving Picture.* MacMillan 1915; Liveright 1970.

Lloyd, Ann (ed.). *Movies of the Silent Years.* London, Orbis, 1984. David Robinson, consultant editor.

Lounsbury, Myron. *The Origins of American Film Criticism, 1909-1939.* N.Y., Arno Press, 1973.

MacMahon, Henry. *Orphans of the Storm,* N.Y., Grosset and Dunlap, 1922. The film novelized.

Merritt, Russell. *The Impact of D.W. Griffith's Motion Pictures from 1908 to 1914 on Contemporary American Culture.* Doctoral dissertation, Harvard University, 1970.

Niver, Kemp R. *Motion Pictures from the Library of Congress Paper Print Collection 1894-1912.* Edited by Bebe Bergsten. Berkeley, University of California, 1967.

Noble, Peter. *Hollywood Scapegoat: The Biography of Erich von Stroheim*. London, Fortune Press, 1950. Appendix has comments by 13 critics.

Norris, Frank. *McTeague: A Story of San Francisco*. Donald Pizer, ed. N.Y., W.W. Norton & Co., 1977. With backgrounds, sources, and critical articles.

Petrie, Graham. *Hollywood Destinies: European Directors in America 1921-1930*. London,Routledge & Kegan Paul, 1985.

Pizer, Donald. *The Literary Criticism of Frank Norris*. Austin, University of Texas, 1964.

Renoir, Jean. *My Life and My Films*. N.Y., Atheneum,1974.

Rosen, Marjorie. *Popcorn Venus: Women, Movies, and the American Dream*. N.Y., Coward, McCann, & Geoghegan, 1973; Avon paperback 1974.

Rotha, Paul. *The Film Till Now*. N.Y., Funk and Wagnalls, 1949.

Sarris, Andrew. *The American Cinema: Directors and Directions*. N.Y., E.P. Dutton, 1968.

St. Johns, Adela Rogers. *Love, Laughter, and Tears: My Hollywood Story*. Garden City, N.Y., Doubleday & Co., 1978.

Sklar, Robert. *Movie-Made America: A Cultural History of American Movies*. N.Y., Random House, 1975.

Stern, Seymour. *Griffith: I — The Birth of a Nation. Film Culture* (special issue) Spring-Summer 1965.

Vardac, Nicholas. *Stage to Screen: Theatrical Method from Garrick to Griffith*. Cambridge, Harvard University, 1949.

Wagenknecht, Edward. *The Movies in the Age of Innocence*. Norman, Univeristy of Oklahoma, 1962. Chapter on Griffith.

Wagenknecht, Edward and Anthony Slide. *The Films of D.W. Griffith*. N.Y., Crown Publishers Inc., 1975.

Wasko, Janet. *Movies and Money: Financing the American Film Industry*. Norwood, N.J., Ablex Publishing, 1982. Valuable chapter on Griffith.

Weinberg, Herman. *The Complete Greed*. N.Y., Arno Press, 1972. Reconstruction of the Stroheim film in 348 still photos following the original screenplay.

**Other useful articles:**

Adams Jr., Robert L. "D.W. Griffith and the Use of Off-Screen Space," *Cinema Journal* 15 (No. 2, Spring 1976).

Agee, James. "David Wark Griffith," *Nation* 167 (Sept. 4, 1948).

Arthur, Charlotte. "In the Old Days," *Close Up* 6 (No. 4 & No. 5, 1930). Acting experiences at Inceville.

Belton, John. "The Art of the Melodramatic Style: D.W. Griffith and *Orphans of the Storm*," in *Cinema Stylists* (Metuchen, N.J., Scarecrow Press, 1983).

Berquist, Goodwin and James Greenwood. "Protest Against Racism: *The Birth of a Nation* in Ohio," *Journal of the University Film Association* 26 (No. 3, 1974).

Bowser, Eileen. "The Reconstitution of *A Corner in Wheat*," *Cinema Journal* 15 (No. 2, Spring 1976).

————. "Silent Fiction: Reframing Early Cinema," in Museum of Modern Art, *Circulating Film Library Catalog*, 1984.

Cadbury, William. "Theme, Felt Life, and the Last-Minute Rescue in Griffith after *Intolerance*," *Film Quarterly* Fall 1974.

Card, James. "Influences of the Danish Film," *Image* 5 (No. 3, March 1956). August Blom's *Atlantis* (1913) came before *The Birth of a Nation* (1915).

Carter, Everett. "Cultural History Written With Lightning: The Significance of *The Birth of a Nation*," *American Quarterly* 12 (Fall 1960).

Cripps, Thomas. "The Reaction of the Negro to the Motion Picture *Birth of a Nation*," *The Historian*, 26 (May 1963).

Dorr, John. "The Griffith Tradition," *Film Comment* 10 (No. 2, March-April 1974).

Everson, William K. "Erich von Stroheim, 1885-1957," *Films in Review*, August-September 1957.

Gartenberg, Jon. "From the D.W. Griffith Collection at the Museum of Modern Art," *Films in Review*, February, 1981. Refers also to past tributes: 1940, 1965, 1975.

Goldbeck, Willis. "Von Stroheim, Man and Superman." [Motion Picture] *Classic*, September 1922.

Gunning, Tom. "The Movies, Mr. Griffith, and Us," *American Film* 9 (No. 8, June 1984). Review of Richard Schickel's *D.W. Griffith:An American Life*.

Ince, Elinor. "Thomas Ince," *Silent Picture* (No. 6, Spring 1970). A letter explaining her husband's death was not murder.

Ince, Thomas. "The Early Days at Kay-Bee," *Photoplay*, March 1919, reprinted in Richard Koszarski, *Hollywood Directors 1914-1940* (N.Y., Oxford, 1976).

————. "What Does the Public Want?" *Photoplay* 11 (No. 2, January 1919).

————. "Your Opportunity in Motion Pictures," *Opportunities in the Motion Picture Industry*, (Photoplay Research Society, 1922).

Johnson, William. "Early Griffith: A Wider View," *Film Quarterly*, Spring 1976.

Kepley Jr., Vance. "*The Musketeers of Pig Alley* and the Well-Made Sausage," *Literature/Film Quarterly* 6 (No. 3, Summer 1978).

_____. "*Intolerance* and the Soviets: A Historical Investigation," *Wide Angle*, No.1, 1979.

Kozloff, Sarah R. "Where Wessex Meets New England: Griffith's *Way Down East* and Hardy's *Tess of the D'Urbervilles*," *Literature/Film Quarterly* 13 (No. 1, 1985).

Lounsbury, Myron O. "Flashes of Lightning: The Moving Picture in the Progressive Era," *Journal of Popular Culture*, Volume 3, No. 4 (1970).

Merritt, Russell. "Dixon, Griffith, and the Southern Legend: A Cultural Analysis of *The Birth of a Nation*," in Richard Dyer MacCann and Jack C. Ellis, *Cinema Examined*, N.Y., E.P. Dutton, 1982. Reprint substantially from *Cinema Journal* Volume XII No. 1, Fall 1972.

_____. "D.W. Griffith Directs the Great War: The Making of *Hearts of the World*," *Quarterly Review of Film Studies* 6 (No. 1, 1981).

Mitchell, George. "Thomas H. Ince," *Films in Review* 11 (No. 8, Oct 1960). Biography, personal recollections.

Mottram, Ron. "Influences Between National Cinemas: Denmark and the United States," *Cinema Journal* 14 (No. 2, Winter 1974-75). Nordisk was two doors away from Biograph in N.Y.

Pratt, George C. "In the Nick of Time: D.W. Griffith and the Last-Minute Rescue," *Image*, 6 (No. 3, March 1957).

_____. "See Mr. Ince...," *Image*, 5 (No. 5, May 1956). Notes written on Ince scripts in a Paris archive. Reprint of this and above article in Marshall Deutelbaum, *op. cit.*

Rosenbaum, Jonathan. "Second Thoughts on Stroheim," *Film Comment*, May 1974. Analysis of eight films.

Salt, Barry. '*The Physician of the Castle.*' *Sight and Sound*, Autumn 1985. A Pathé film of 1908 which anticipates Griffith cross-cut chase films.

Shepard, David. "Thomas Ince," in Tom Shales *et al.*, *The American Film Heritage* (Washington, D.C., American Film Institute/Acropolis Books, 1972). Tracking down 26 filing cabinets containing Ince business records and scripts.

*The Silent Picture*, Spring 1973. Special Issue on Griffith.

Sochen, June, "The New Woman and Twenties America: *Way Down East* (1920)." *American History/American Film*. N.Y., Frederick Ungar, 1979.

Staiger, Janet. "Tame Authors and the Corporate Laboratory: Stories, Writers, and Scenarios in Hollywood," *Quarterly Review of Film Studies*, Fall 1983. Silent era economics.

Stern, Seymour. "D.W. Griffith and the Movies," *American Mercury*, March 1949.

———. "Griffith and Poe," *Films in Review*, November 1951.

———. "The Soviet Directors' Debt to Griffith," *Films in Review*, May 1956.

Stroheim, Erich von. "Tribute to the Master," in Peter Noble, *Hollywood Scapegoat, op.cit.* Also in Harry Geduld, *Focus on D.W. Griffith, op.cit.* A Paris radio broadcast, 30 December 1948.

Wanamaker, Marc. "Alice Guy Blaché," *Cinema* (Calif.) No. 5 (1976).

Wolfe, Charles. "Resurrecting *Greed.*" *Sight and Sound*, 44 (1975), 170-174. A fuller examination of the nonrealistic aspects of the film suggested by Joel Finler.

# Filmography

## General

*Before the Nickelodeon: The Early Cinema of Edwin Porter.* Charles Musser, director-editor. Blanche Sweet, narrator. 60 min. A Film For Thought Production, Box 820, Times Square Station, N.Y. 10108.

*D.W. Griffith: An American Genius.* Walt Lowe, producer. Richard Schickel, writer-narrator. 56 min. Blackhawk Films.

*The Great Director: The Life and Work of D.W. Griffith.* John Boorman, producer. 52 min. BBC-TV.

*The Man You Loved to Hate.* Richard Koszarski, writer; Patrick Montgomery, producer. Film Profiles, 1979.

*A Tour of the Thomas H. Ince Studio.* Hunt Stromberg, director. 2 reels. Released through First National, 1922. Museum of Modern Art, not for circulation.

Available from the Museum of Modern Art:

(See Circulating Film Library Catalog for many other films of great interest, especially those directed by Griffith. Times below are calculated on the basis of 18 frames per second.)

Films of the 1890s. 1894-1899, 18 min.

Edison Program. 1903-1904, 8 min.

Edwin S. Porter Program I. 1903-1908, 33 min. Includes *The Great Train Robbery*, 1903, 11 min.

Griffith Biograph Program. 1909-1912, 69 min. Includes *The Lonely Villa*, 1909, 11 min.; *A Corner in Wheat*, 1909, 14 min.; *The Lonedale Operator*, 1911, 14 min.; *The Musketeers of Pig Alley*, 1912, 15 min.; *The New York Hat*, 1912, 15 min.

*The Battle at Elderbush Gulch.* Griffith, 1914, 27 min.

*Judith of Bethulia.* Griffith, 1914, 68 min.

*The Birth of a Nation.* Griffith, 1915, 180 min. Color version, 167 min.

*The Coward.* Ince/Barker, 1915, 74 min.

*The Taking of Luke McVane (The Fugitive).* Ince/Hart, 1915, 29 min.

*Civilization.* Ince/West,Willat, 1916, 95 min.

*Intolerance.* Griffith, 1916,170 min. Also color version.

*Hearts of the World.* Griffith, 1918, 147 min.

*Blind Husbands.* Stroheim, 1919, 98 min.

*Broken Blossoms.* Griffith, 1919, 92 min. Also color. Also color and orchestral sound requiring 18 fps projection.

*The Mother and the Law.* Griffith, 1919, 104 min. The modern story from *Intolerance*.

*True Heart Susie.* Griffith, 1919, 86 min.

*The Toll Gate.* Hillyer/Hart, 1920, 77 min.

*Way Down East.* Griffith, 1920, 154 min. Music version 104 min. at 24 fps.

*Orphans of the Storm.* Griffith, 1921, 176 min.

*Foolish Wives.* Stroheim, 1922, 118 min.

*The White Rose.* Griffith, 1923, 136 min.

*America.* Griffith, 1924, 173 min.

*Isn't Life Wonderful.* Griffith, 1924, 135 min.

*The Sorrows of Satan.* Griffith, 1926, 84 min,24 fps.

The searcher for good viewing copies of silent movies *on videocassettes*, whether VHS or Beta, has no easy task. One way to begin is with a local video rental/sales store, where a copy of the *Video Source Book* should be available. This hefty volume is published by National Video Clearinghouse Inc., 100 Lafayette Drive, Syosset, N.Y. 11791. It may also be at the public library. According to the 1987 (9th) edition:

*The Bargain* (Ince/Hart) (50 min) may be purchased or rented from Discount Video Tapes, Burbank CA.

*Hell's Hinges* (Ince/Hart) (65 min) may be purchased from Video Yesteryears, Sandy Hook CT.

*Intolerance* (Griffith) (120 min) can be purchased from five sources: Video Yesteryears; Hollywood Home Theater, Hollywood CA;

Blackhawk Films (Republic Pictures Home Video, Los Angeles CA); Discount Video Tapes (Burbank CA), and Western Film and Video Inc.(Westlake Village CA).

*Broken Blossoms* (Griffith) (102 min) can be purchased from four sources: Hollywood Home Theater; Western Film and Video Inc.; Festival Films (Minneapolis MN); and Movie Buff Video (New York, N.Y.).

*Way Down East* (Griffith) (107 min) is for sale by five sources: Video Yesteryears, Western Film and Video Inc., Blackhawk Films, Discount Video Tapes, and Kartes Video Communications (Indianapolis IN).

Other Griffith films available: *The Birth of a Nation* in four different lengths (106 to 175 min) from a dozen sources; *True Heart Susie* (87 min) from two sources; *Orphans of the Storm* from Blackhawk Films; *Abraham Lincoln* (93 min sound) from eight sources.

*The Short Films of D.W. Griffith: The Battle, The Female of the Species,* and *The New York Hat* (45 min); *The Avenging Conscience* (78 min); *Home Sweet Home* (62 min); *Dream Street* (138 min); and *The Babylon Story* from *Intolerance* (25 min) are all available from Video Yesteryears (Sandy Hook CT).

*Blind Husbands* (Stroheim) (98 min) is for sale by Video Yesteryears.

*Foolish Wives* (Stroheim) in a 75-minute version is for sale by Hollywood Home Theater, and in a 107-minute version by Blackhawk Films.

*The Wedding March* (Stroheim) (113 min) can be bought from Paramount Home Video, Hollywood, CA.

The following were available *in videotape form* in 1985, according to James Limbacher, *Feature Films: A Directory* (N.Y., Bowker, 1985). His annual directory has been based since 1966 on 16mm sources and the companies he cites duplicate in only a few instances those in the *Video Source Book*. Changes occur every year but most of these libraries still operate.

*The Return of Draw Egan.* (Ince/Hart) Rental, Video Communications Inc., Tulsa OK.

*Blind Husbands.* (Stroheim) Sale, Tamarelle's French Film House, Chico CA. Rental, Video Communications Inc.

*Foolish Wives.* (Stroheim) Same as above.

*The Birth of a Nation.* (Griffith) Sale, Blackhawk Films (Republic Pictures Home Video, Los Angeles CA); Cinema Concepts, Newington CT; EmGee Film Library, Reseda CA; National Film & Video Center, Eldersburg MD; Pyramid Films, Santa Monica CA;

Video Communications Inc. Tinted version: Cinema Concepts; Festival Films, Minneapolis, MN.

*Intolerance* (Griffith) Rental, Ivy Films, New York, NY; Video Communications Inc. Sale, Festival Films; Images Film Archive, Mamaroneck NY.

*Broken Blossoms.* (Griffith) Sale, Festival Films.

*Way Down East.* (Griffith) Sale, Cinema Concepts; EmGee Film Library; Festival Films; Ivy Films; Morcraft Films, Los Angeles CA; Video Communications Inc.; Images Film Archive.

*Orphans of the Storm.* (Griffith) Sale, Blackhawk Films.

*Abraham Lincoln.* (Griffith) Sale, EmGee Film Library.

Both reference works recommended here have full addresses and phone numbers of the companies listed, and intrepid home or school programmers can only hope to find the company that is nearest, least expensive, or boasting the best reproductions. Some will offer tinted versions. Others will have music sound tracks similar to the organ, piano, or orchestral background offered in silent film theaters.

Of course the problem of film speed has been decided, for good or ill — and sometimes with loving skill — by those who have transferred the images from film to the electronic form. Naturally, too, the degree of definition achieved on a TV screen is nothing like the rich black and white photography experienced by silent era audiences.

The following films starring William S. Hart and produced by Thomas H. Ince were available in 1985 *on 16 millimeter film* from the sources indicated according to Limbacher.

*The Bargain.* Rental, EmGee Film Library, Reseda CA; Film Images, Oak Park IL. Sale, Film Images.

*Hell's Hinges.* Rental, Budget Films, Los Angeles CA; EmGee Film Library; Film Images; Films Inc., Wilmette IL; Mogulls Films, Plainfield NJ; Westcoast Films, San Francisco CA. Sale, Edward Finney, Hollywood CA.

*On the Night Stage.* Rental, Budget Films; EmGee Film Library; Images Film, Mamaroneck NY; Kit Parker Films, Monterey CA. Sale, Blackhawk Films (Republic Pictures Home Video, Los Angeles CA).

*The Return of Draw Egan.* Rental, Budget Films; EmGee Film Library; Film Images; Films Inc.; Video Communications Inc., Tulsa OK; Wholesome Film Center, Boston MA. Sale, Glenn Photo Supply, Reseda CA; National Cinema Service, Hohokus NJ.

The following films directed by Erich von Stroheim were available in 1985 on 16 millimeter film from the sources indicated according to Limbacher.

*Merry-Go-Round.* Rental, Alan Twyman Presents; Creative Film, Northridge CA; Film Images, Oak Park IL.
*Greed.* Rental, Films Inc., Wilmette IL; MGM-United, New York NY
*The Merry Widow.* Rental, MGM United.
*Queen Kelly.* Rental, Kino International Corp., New York NY
*Hello Sister [Walking Down Broadway.]* Rental, Films Inc.

The following films directed by D.W. Griffith were available in 1985 in 16mm from various sources according to Limbacher.

*Abraham Lincoln; America; The Avenging Conscience; The Birth of a Nation; Broken Blossoms; Dream Street; The Fall of Babylon; The Girl Who Stayed at Home; Hearts of the World; Home Sweet Home; The Idol Dancer; Intolerance; Isn't Life Wonderful; Judith of Bethulia; The Mother and the Law; Orphans of the Storm; The Romance of Happy Valley, Sally of the Sawdust; The Struggle; True Heart Susie; The Unknown Soldier; Way Down East; The White Rose.*

Of special interest to Griffith scholars and fans are the following films available as of 1988 on *videocassettes* for home use by Killiam Shows Inc., 6 East 39th Street, New York, N.Y. 10016, "successors to the estate of D.W. Griffith." They are described by Paul Killiam as "restorations with custom scores."

*Judith of Bethulia* (1914) 45 min.
*The Birth of a Nation* (1915) 125 min.
*Intolerance* (1916) 123 min.
*Hearts of the World* (1918) 122 min.
*Broken Blossoms* (1919) 76 min.
*Way Down East* (1920) 119 min.
*Orphans of the Storm* (1921) 126 min.
*America* (1924) 95 min. (historical titles rendered vocally)
*Sally of the Sawdust* (1925) 92 min.
*Abraham Lincoln* (1930) 93 min. (a sound film)

# INDEX

**Names**

Adler, Mortimer 244-245
Adolfi, John G. 45
Aeschylus 26, 82
Agee, James xii, 26
Aiken, Spottiswoode 147
Aitken, Harry 16-20, 65, 72, 98
Aitken, Roy 16-18, 18n, 289
Aldrich, Thomas Bailey 145
Allen, E. H. 100
Altman, Rick xii
Anderson, G.M. (Broncho Billy) 34, 61n, 92, 266
Arbuckle, Fatty 48
Archainbaud, George 47
Aronson, Max 34
Arvidson, Linda 15n, 25, 40, 117, 124, 180, 289
Atkinson, Josephine 45
Attalah, Paul 82
August, Joseph 109
Baker, Hetty Gray 265
Baldwin, Evelyn 25
Ball, Robert Hamilton 40
Balshofer, Fred 36, 66-67
Balzac, Honoré de 182
Bankhead, Tallulah 49
Banzhaf, Albert 20
Bara, Theda 48
Bardèche, Maurice 82
Barker, Reginald 63, 76, 91, 100
Barnes, George 34
Barrington, Berkeley 53
Barriscale, Bessie 79, 81
Barry, Iris xii, 18n, 62, 82
Barrymore, Ethel 49
Barrymore, John 208
Barrymore, Lionel 46, 125, 266
Barrymore, Maurice 46
Barthelmess, Richard 9, 21, 119, 194, 196, 205, 214
Bauman, Charles 37, 48, 67, 70, 94, 98
Bazin, André xii, 221, 234, 249
Beban, George 76-77
Beethoven, Ludwig van 153, 160

Beggs, Lee 52
Belasco, David 116, 187
Bennett, Enid 71, 79
Beranger, Clara 265
Bergère, Ouida 265
Bernhardt, Sarah 208
Billy (Anderson), Broncho 34
Bitzer, Billy 3, 5n, 14, 20, 116, 128-129, 150, 152, 172
Blaché, Alice Guy 47, 49-55
Blaché, Herbert 47, 49, 51, 53-54
Blaché, Simone 53
Blackton, J. Stuart 32, 43-44
Blackwell, Carlyle 47
Blinn, Holbrook 47
Blue, Monte 130n
Boggs, Francis 66
Bordwell, David 179
Borzage, Frank 62, 286
Bowser, Eileen xii, 18n, 20, 117, 197, 217, 289-290
Boyd, William 213-214
Brady, Alice 47-48
Brady, William 47, 203
Brasillach, Robert 82
Breil, Joseph Carl 153, 157
Brenon, Herbert 265, 285
Brown, Clarence 48
Brown, Karl 4, 6, 126, 137, 152, 172, 289
Browning, Robert 4
Browning, Tod 130n, 286
Brownlow, Kevin 20, 55, 116, 126, 130n, 290
Brulatour, Jules 47
Bunuel, Luis 193, 233-235
Burke, Billie 47
Burke, J. Frank 100
Burke, Thomas 197
Burns, Vinnie 51
Busch, Mae 239, 241
Bush, Stephan 102
Bushman, Francis X. 26
Cadbury, William xii, 191
Capellani, Albert 47
Capra, Frank 26, 117

Carey, Gary 263, 265
Caruso, Enrico 177
Casty, Alan 4, 117
Celine, Louis 235
Chaplin, Charlie 1, 14, 16,
  20-21, 210, 249, 260-262, 266
Chapman, Charles 45
Chautard, Emile 47
Christ, Jesus 189
Clair, René 176
Clarke, Marguerite 49
Clayton, Ethel 47
Clifford, William H. 100
Clifton, Elmer 130n, 148
Clune, William H. 17n, 18n
Cobleigh, Rolfe 164, 168
Cochrane, Tom 68-69
Cocteau, Jean 82
Cody, Buffalo Bill 104
Cody, Lew 237
Coffee, Lenore 266
Colette 86
Colton, Wendell P. 33
Considine Jr., John 80-81
Conti, Albert 213
Cook, David 62
Cooke, Thomas Coffin 120
Cooper, James Fenimore 104
Cooper, Miriam 22, 148, 194,
  214
Corelli, Marie 184
Corliss, Richard 263
Cornwall, Blanche 52-53
Cowl, Jane 49
Crane, William H. 60
Cripps, Thomas 169
Crisp, Donald 80, 200
Crosland, Alan 285
Crowther, Bosley 251
Cruze, James 287
Curley, Mayor James 169-170
Curtiss, Thomas Quinn 226n,
  289
Cushman, Charlotte 45
Dalton, Dorothy 71, 79
Darkfeather, Mona 67
DaVinci, Leonardo 128
Davis, Bob 152
Dawley, J. Searle 123

Day, Richard 227
Dean, Thomas 222
DeCasseres, Ben 152
DeLacey, Ralph 127-128
Delluc, Louis 62, 82
DeMille, Cecil B. 5, 13, 65,
  80-81, 85, 115, 146, 210-211,
  230, 285
DeMille, William C. 286
Dempster, Carol 24, 217
Dickens, Charles 4, 179-184,
  186-187
Dillon, Edward 130n
Dintenfass, Mark 47
Dion, Hector 43
Dix, Beulah Marie 265
Dixon, Thomas 6, 17, 147-148,
  150-151, 160-168
Dorr, John xii, 191
Dostoevsky, Feodor 236, 241
Doublier, Francis 47
Dovzhenko, Aleksandr 250
Dowling, James 100
Dressler, Marie 47, 26
Dumas, Alexander 182
Duse, Eleonora 208
Dwan, Allan 55-60, 65, 71, 80,
  115, 211
Earp, Wyatt 104
Edison, Thomas 29
Edwards, Walter 79
Eisenstein, Sergei xii, 91, 117,
  137, 175-176, 178, 250
Eliot, George 182
Elliot, Maxine 49
Ellis, Havelock 256
Ellis, Jack 62
Elvidge, June 47
Emerson, John 62, 266
Epping, J.C. 20, 216
Esselman, Katherine 103
Etulain, Richard 103
Evans, Madge 47
Everson, William 63, 75, 103,
  220, 226, 229
Fairbanks, Douglas 20, 48, 57,
  62, 177, 197, 263, 266
Farnum, Dustin 79

Farnum, William 48
Farrar, Geraldine 49
Fellini, Federico 117
Fellowes, Rockliffe 237
Fenin, George 103
Ferdinand, Count 86
Ferguson, Elsie 49
Feuillade, Louis 47, 51
Fielding, Romaine 265
Fields, W.C. 123
Fife, Shannon 265
Fildew, Billy 129
Firestone, Bruce 102
Flaubert, Gustave 253
Fleming, Victor 58
Flynn, Errol 266
Ford, John 10, 62, 109, 115,
   117, 286
Fox, William 48
Foy, Magda 51
Franklin, Joe 108
Fraunholz, Fraunie 52
Frederick, Pauline 49
Freuler, John 16
Fuentes, Carlos 235
Gable, Clark 266
Gance, Abel 250
Garbo, Greta 225
Garden, Mary 49
Gardner, Helen 144
Gasnier, Louis 47
Gaumont, Leon 50-51
Geduld, Harry 5
Gephart, Fred 67
George, David Lloyd 289
George, Maude 239, 241
Germonprez, Valerie
   (Mrs. Stroheim) 227
Germonprez, Louis 227
Gershwin, George 26
Gilbert, John 224, 251
Gilbert, W.S. 126, 265
Gilmore, W.E. 32
Gish, Dorothy 11, 19, 23, 125, 206
Gish, Lillian 1, 9-12, 17n, 20-25,
   119, 125, 147, 157, 174,
   193-197, 199-200, 204-205,
   207-208, 226, 263, 289
Glaum, Louise 79, 109

Glyn, Elinor 211
Goldwyn, Samuel 18, 21, 49
Goodman, Ezra 26
Gordon, Kitty 47
Gosha, Hideo 193
Goudal, Jetta 213-214
Goya, Francisco 231
Graham, Ethel 67
Gregory, Thomas B. 165
Grey, Albert 20
Griffith, David Wark xi, xii,
   xiii, 1-25, 29-31, 33, 36, 40,
   42, 47, 58-60, 62, 64, 67-68,
   72, 79, 82-83, 90-91, 98,
   115-118, 123-137, 139-154,
   156-160, 164-165, 171-172,
   174-217, 220-221, 221, 224,
   226-227, 231, 249-250,
   252-254, 259-263, 274-280,
   288-289
Griffith, Evelyn Baldwin
   (see Baldwin)
Griffith, Jacob Wark 118
Griffith, Linda Arvidson
   (see Arvidson)
Griffith, Richard 218, 223, 225, 290
Gunning, Tom 12, 130
Hackett, Francis 160
Haggard, H. Rider 203
Hall, Emmett Campbell 265
Hammerstein, Elaine 49
Hanaway, Frank 34
Harding, Warren G. 25n, 289
Hardy, Thomas 182
Harlow, Jean 267
Harrison, Louis Reeves 188
Harron, Robert 9, 21, 23, 125,
   148, 174, 178, 194-195
Hart, James 22, 118, 289
Hart, William S. xi, 64, 68, 71,
   78-80, 84, 88, 91-92, 98, 100,
   102, 103-109, 268-273, 288
Harte, Bret 88
Hartz, Louis 218
Hearst, William Randolph 71
Henabery, Joseph 20, 130n, 171,
   175
Henderson, Robert 4
Henry, O. 152

Hepworth, Cecil 32
Hergesheimer, Joseph 203
Higgins, Steven 69, 288
Hillyer, Lambert 79
Hitchens, Robert 235
Hoadley, C.B. "Pop" 265
Hobbes, Thomas 219-220
Hoffner, Cal 95
Hogarth, William 231
Hollingsworth, Alfred 109
Hopkins, Arthur 49, 99
Howard, William K. 80
Huff, Theodore 46
Hull, Henry 47
Ibsen, Henrik 116
Ince, John and Emma 70, 80
Ince, Ralph 80
Ince, Thomas H. xi, xii, 18, 21,
  62-65, 68-75, 78-80, 82-87,
  90-92, 94-96, 98, 100, 110,
  116, 203, 231, 263, 267-273, 288
Ingram, Rex 235, 286
Irving, Henry 187
Ives, Charles 177
Jacobs, Lewis xii, 9, 29-30, 62,
  139, 249-250, 289
James, Gladden 53
Janis, Elsie 49
Jasset, Victorin 51
Jennings, Al 104
Johnson, Arthur 46, 125
Johnson, Christine 265
Joplin, Scott 177
Jordan, Michael 170
Jones, May (Mrs. Stroheim) 227
Joyce, Alice 46
Julian, Rupert 80, 222
Justice, Maybelle Heikes 265
Kael, Pauline 176
Kane, Gail 47
Katterjohn, Monte 80
Katz, Ephraim 290
Keaton, Buster 53, 62
Keenan, Frank 79
Kelly, Anthony Paul 204
Kennedy, Jeremiah 15
Kennedy, Joseph 81, 225
Kennedy, Madge 49
Kent, Charles 45

Kenyon, Doris 47
Kepley, Vance 176, 179
Kerrigan, J. Warren 58
Kershaw, Elinor 70
Kershaw, Willette 70
Kessel, Adam 36-38, 48, 70, 94, 98
Killiam, Paul 17n
King, Henry 81, 285
Knight, Arthur 62, 123, 150
Knox, Margaret (Mrs. Stroheim)
  227
Kolle, Herman 36-40
Koszarski, Diane 77, 100, 288
Koszarski, Richard 62, 220n,
  223n, 225-226, 231, 288
Kuleshov, Lev 176
Laemmle, Carl 43, 47, 67, 69-70,
  228, 237
Lackaye, Wilton 47-48
Lambert, Gavin 259
Lang, Fritz 217, 230
Lapierre, Marcel 234
Lasky, Jesse 21, 72
Lawrence, Florence 45, 134, 137
Lebedeff, Ivan 237
Lee, Lila 80
Lehar, Franz 224
Lenin, V.I. 12
Lennig, Arthur 197, 255
Leprohon, Pierre 234
Lewis, Ralph 158
Lewis, W. H. 170
Lincoln, Abraham 5, 13, 166-167
Lindsay, Vachel 6, 176, 188
Livingston, Margaret 80
Lloyd, Frank 286
Lloyd, Harold 266
Loew, Marcus 2, 98
Long, Walter 148, 158
Loos, Anita 263, 266-267
Lorraine, Lillian 47
Lounsbury, Myron 186
Love, Montagu 47
Lovett, Josephine 265
Lubin, Sigmund 36, 40
Lubitsch, Ernst 212-213, 230
Lucas, Blake 9, 117, 191, 212
Lucas, Wilfred 132
Lumiere, Louis & Auguste 27, 116

Mack, Hayward 69
MacKaye, Scott 187
MacPherson, Jeanie 266
Magill, Frank N. 290
Mansfield, Martha 49
Marinoff, Fania 47
Marion, Frances 265
Marsh, Mae 21-22, 49, 125, 135, 148, 158, 178, 190-191, 195, 214
Marshall, Tully 221, 251
Martin, Vivian 47-48
Martinette, Billy 33
Marvin, Arthur 14, 141
Marvin, Henry Norton 14
Mast, Gerald 62, 137
Masterson, Bat 104
Mathis, June 265
Maupassant, Guy de 253
Mayer, Arthur 218, 223, 225, 290
Mayer, Louis B. 18n, 224, 226, 229
McCardell, Roy L. 263-264
McCoy, Al 38-40
Meeks, Kate 60
Meighan, Thomas 49
Melies, Georges 116
Menzies, William Cameron 214
Meredith, George 182
Meredyth, Bess 81, 266
Merritt, Russell 8n, 175, 288
Metz, Christian 131
Meyerbeer, Giacomo 177
Miller, Arthur 36, 40
Miller, Joe 94
Miller, Walter 135-136
Mitry, Jean xi, xii
Mix, Tom 92
Moore, Owen 49, 125
Moore, Tom 49
Mottram, Ron 116, 130
Mozart, Wolfgang Amadeus 20
Mugnier-Serand, Yvonne 50
Munden, Kenneth 290
Murfin, Jane 265
Murphy, Eddie 266
Murray, Marie 33, 35
Murray, Mae 224, 25
Musser, Charles 30, 62
Napoleon 5

Nazimova 49
Neilan, Marshall 58, 80, 211, 285
Neill, William 79
Newhard, Robert 100
Niblo, Fred 79-80, 287
Nielsen, Asta 144
Niver, Kemp 29-30
Noble, Peter 218-219, 227, 289
Normand, Mabel 48-49, 125
Norris, Frank 192, 219n, 222, 242-249, 253-254
O'Brien, Eugene 49, 237
Obrock, Herman 37, 39
Oland, Warner 47
Olcott, Sidney 46
O'Neill, Eugene 81, 203
O'Neill, James 15
O'Sullivan, Tony 67
Ott, Fred 29
Pabst, G.W. 116, 217
Pangborn, Franklin 214
Panzer, Paul 43, 45
Parker, Lottie Blair 203
Parkhurst, Charles H. 164-165
Parsons, Louella 264-265
Peacock, Leslie T. 265
Pearson, Virginia 48
Perelman, S.J. 237
Perret, Leonce 47
Persons, Thomas 66
Petrova, Olga 49, 50
Pickford, Jack 67
Pickford, Mary 1, 4, 20, 24, 46, 48, 62, 64, 67, 135, 192, 197, 237, 265-266
Pitts, ZaSu 224-225
Poe, Edgar Allan 4
Porter, Edwin S. 3, 30-32, 103-104, 124
Powell, Frank 65
Pratt, George 72, 160n
Printzlau, Olga 276
Pudovkin, Vsevelod 176, 179
Quirk, Billie 52
Quirk, James R. 210
Ramsaye, Terry 27, 30-31, 66, 264
Ranous, William 40, 42-43, 45
Ray, Charles 71, 79-80, 91
Read, J. Parker 80, 98

Reed, Florence 47
Rejane, Madame 144
Renoir, Jean 26, 117, 225, 250, 253
Resnais, Alain 193
Reynolds, Burt 266
Roach, Hal 26
Rockefeller Jr., John D. 175-176
Rodin, Auguste 82
Rohauer, Raymond 62
Rommel, Field Marshal Erwin 226
Roosevelt, Theodore 188
Rosenbaum, Jonathan 222
Rotha, Paul xii
Russell, Lillian 47
Sabatini, Rafael 202
Sabine, George H. 220n
Sadoul, Georges 82, 176, 219n
Salt, Barry 116
Salter, Harry 134
Sanderson, Richard 29
Sardou, Victorien 116
Sargent, Epes Winthrop 263-265
Sarris, Andrew xii, 26, 249
Schallert, Edwin 222
Schenck, Joseph 13, 20, 25,
    80-81
Schertzinger, Victor 49, 79
Schickel, Richard xii, 12-13,
    19-20, 22, 65, 118, 202, 288
Schulberg, B.P. 265
Seiter, William A. 287
Seitz, George B. 286
Selznick, David O. 72
Selznick, Lewis J. 47
Sennett, Mack 4, 18, 36, 46, 71,
    79-80, 98, 100, 125
Seymour, Clarine 21, 194-195
Shakespeare, William 40-45
Shea, William 45
Shepard, David 17n, 62
Sherman, General William
    Tecumseh 151
Sherman, Harry 18n
Sherman, Lowell 47, 204
Sherry, J. Barney 67, 100
Siegmann, George 127, 148-149,
    158, 173
Sills, Milton 47
Sinclair, Upton 54

Sissle, Noble 266
Sklar, Robert 8n, 11n
Slide, Anthony 50
Sloane, Paul 80
Smith, Albert 32
Smith, Clifford S. 88, 96, 109
Smith, Frank Leon 52
Snow, Phoebe 33
Sopocy, Martin 63, 82
Spencer, Richard 75
Spoor, George K. 57
Stebbins, Emma 45
Steck, H. Tipton 265
Sternberg, Josef von 48
Stevens, Thaddeus 166
St. Clair, Malcolm 287
St. Johns, Adela Rogers 24, 60
Stoneham, Daniel 18n
Storey, Moorfield 169
Storm, Jerome 79
Stroheim, Erich von xi, xii, xiii,
    62, 75, 115, 130n, 218-231,
    233-262, 280-283, 288-289
Stroheim, Erich von (son) 227
Stroheim, Joseph Erich (son) 227
Stroheim, Margaret Knox
    (see Knox)
Stroheim, May Jones (see Jones)
Stroheim, Valerie Germonprez
    (see Germonprez)
Sudermann, Hermann 116
Sullivan, Sir Arthur 265
Sullivan, C. Gardner 65, 77-81,
    98, 107, 109, 263
Sunshine, Marion 134
Swanson, Gloria 57, 81,
    225-226, 251
Swayne, Marian 52
Sweet, Blanche 21, 49, 116, 125,
    135-136, 148-149, 194, 203
Sweetser, Lillian 265
Talmadge, Constance 267
Talmadge, Norma 49
Talmadge sisters 80
Teague, George 129
Thackeray, William 182
Thalberg, Irving 224, 228-229, 251
Thaw, Evelyn Nesbit 48
Thomas, Olive 49

Tilghman, William M. 104
Toscanini, Arturo 177
Tourneur, Maurice 47-48, 62, 71, 75, 285
Trollope, Anthony 182
Trotter, William Monroe 169
Tucker, George Loane 49, 234
Turner, Florence 43
Turner, Frederick Jackson 103
Ulric, Lenore 47
Unsell, Grace 265
Van Dyke, W.S. 26, 115, 130n, 287
Vardac, Nicholas 186
Velez, Lupe 212-215
Vernac, Denise 227n
Vertov, Dziga 179
Vidor, King 12, 71, 115, 117, 287
Vignola, Robert 46
Wagenknecht, Edward 176
Walkley, A.B. 181
Wallace, Lew 41, 203
Walsh, Governor David I. 170
Walsh, George 48
Walsh, Raoul 81, 115, 285
Walthall, Henry B. 46, 67, 125, 131-132, 136, 147, 155, 157, 194
Warner, H.B. 79
Warren, Edward 52
Warwick, Granville (pseud. for Griffith) 18
Warwick, Robert 48
Washington, Booker T. 170-171
Weber, Joe 99
Weber, Lois 265
Weinberg, Herman 227n, 233
West, Roland 81
White, James H. 32
White, Pearl 48
Whitman, Walt 26
Whitney, Claire 52
Wilder, Billy 226, 230
Willat, "Doc" (C.A. Willatowski) 48
Williams, Clara 100
Wilson, Woodrow 25n, 148, 162
Wing, W.E. 72
Wise, Rabbi 169
Wister, Owen 104
Woods, Frank 4, 20, 117, 137, 148, 152-154, 175

Wortman, Frank ("Huck") 127
Wray, Fay 224
Wray, John Griffith 71, 80
Wren, P.C. 202
Wright, Frank Lloyd 26
Wyler, William 233
Young, Clara Kimball 47-48
Zanuck, Darryl 72
Zecca, Ferdinand 51
Zola, Emile 222-223, 253-254
Zukor, Adolph 2, 13, 15, 18-20, 31, 64, 66, 79, 99, 144, 146
Zweig, Stefan 182

**Film Titles**

*Abraham Lincoln* 25, 210, 280
*Adventurer, The* 54
*Adventures of Dollie, The* 116, 192
*After Many Years* 133, 180
*Alibi, The* 81
*America* 5, 210, 278
*American Aristocracy* 48
*Anna Christie* 71, 203
*Apple Pie Mary (Home Sweet Home)* 128
*Around the World in 80 Days* 237
*Aryan, The* 88, 91
*As It Is in Life* 133, 141
*Asphalt Jungle, The* 260
*As You Desire Me* 225
*Atonement of Gosta Berling, The* 108
*Avenging Conscience, The* 274
*Bachelor Brides* 81
*Ballet Dancer* 28
*Bank Robbery, The* 104
*Bargain, The* 95-96, 100
*Battle, The* 46
*Battle of Elderbush Gulch, The* 14, 192
*Battle of Gettysburg, The* 65, 69, 84-85
*Battle of the Sexes, The* 274, 279
*Ben Hur* 41, 203, 229
*Betsy Ross* 48

Birth of a Nation, The 4, 6-8,
    11, 13, 16-17, 19, 24, 83, 85,
    92, 119, 136, 160-169, 171,
    173-174, 176-178, 184, 187,
    192, 194, 197-198, 208, 212,
    259, 260, 264, 274
Blind Husbands 221, 228, 234,
    237, 255, 257, 259, 280
Bluebird, The 48
Boy and Fruit Peddler 28
Branding Cattle 29
Broken Blossoms 9-10, 20, 83,
    92, 116, 184, 193, 196-198,
    207, 220. 224, 234, 252, 255,
    260-261, 277
Broken Locket, The 133
Bull Fight No.2 29
Burglar on the Roof, The 32
Cabiria 6
Call to Arms, The 141
Camille 48, 144
Canned Harmony 53
Carrie 261
Cheap Kisses 80
Cheat, The 85
Child of the Ghetto, A 141
Citizen Kane 177, 261
Civilization 85-86
Civilization's Child 78
Clansman, The 6, 8, 152-153,
    160, 168
Cleopatra 144
Clinging Vine, The 80
Comedy of Errors 43
Connecticut Yankee in King
    Arthur's Court, A 55
Converts, The 141
Corner, The 87
Corner in Wheat, A 11, 13, 192,
    254, 259, 260
Corporal Kate 80
Count of Monte Cristo, The 15
Coward, The 89, 91
Crossing the American Prairies
    in the Early Fifties 142
Cup of Life, The 78
Curtain Pole, The 46
Custer's Last Fight 84-85, 95
Daddy Long Legs 202

David Harum 59
Death's Marathon 135-136
Despoiler, The 85
Detective's Dog, The 53
Devil's Passkey, The 228, 234,
    259, 281
Diamond From the Sky, The 264
Diary of a Chambermaid 235
Dream Street 278
Dr. Jekyll and Mr. Hyde 202
Drive for Life, The 130
Drums of Love 279
Drunks in the Snow 28
Dynamite Smith 80
Enoch Arden 143
Escape, The 198, 274
Eternal Magdalene, The 49
Feeding the Baby 27
Female of the Species, The 192
Fighting Eagle, The 80
Five Graves to Cairo 226
Flood at Lyons 28
Foolish Wives 220-221, 227-228,
    233-234, 237-238, 241, 252,
    255, 257, 259, 281
Fugitive, The 133
Fury 261
Garden of Allah 235
Gigolo 80
Girl Climbing Apple Tree 28
Girl in the Armchair, The 53
Girl Who Stayed at Home, The 276
Girls in a Dormitory 28
Gold Is Not All 131, 141
Gold Rush, The 261
Gold Seekers, The 141
Gone With the Wind 214
Grand Illusion 225, 253
Grapes of Wrath, The 260-261
Gray Shadow, The 181
Great Adventure, The 54
Great Bank Robbery, The 35
Great Love, The 276
Greater Love Hath No Man 53
Greatest Question, The 277
Greatest Thing in Life, The 11, 276
Great Train Robbery, The
    30-31, 34-35, 104

Greed 220, 222-224, 229, 233,
  235, 242-248, 250, 252-257,
  259-261, 265, 282
Gypsy Blood 144
Hallelujah! 261
Hateful God, The 87
Heart of a Hero 48
Heart of a Painted Woman, The 54
Hearts of the World 206,
  208-209, 216, 275
Hello Sister (Walking Down
  Broadway) 225, 230, 259, 283
Hell's Hinges 108-10
Her Man O'War 80
Her Polished Family 77
His New Lid 65
His Picture in the Papers 266
His Trust 46, 265
His Trust Fulfilled 265
Home Sweet Home (Apple Pie
  Mary) 130, 274
Horsefeathers 237
House Divided, A 53
House of Hate, The 181
House With the Closed Shutters,
  The 141
Human Wreckage 71, 80
Hunchback of Notre Dame, The
  202
Husband and Stenographer 28
Idol Dancer, The 277
If Marriage Fails 80
In Life's Cycle 133
In Old California 141
In the Sage Brush Country 78
In the Season of Buds 141
Intolerance 4, 8, 10-13, 19, 22,
  83, 116, 136, 171, 175-180,
  184-185, 187, 189-190, 194,
  197-198, 208, 212, 237, 253,
  264, 275
Iron Strain, The 79
Isn't Life Wonderful 13, 20, 24,
  116, 184, 197, 210, 217-218,
  220, 235, 260, 279
Italian, The 63, 75
Joyless Street, The 116, 217
Judith of Bethulia 15, 145-146
Kameradschaft 116

King Lear 44
King's Row 214
Lady Eve, The 261
Lady of the Pavements 212-215,
  280
Lamb, The 52
Lassoing Steer 29
Last Deal, The 133
Last Drop of Water, The 142
Last Frontier, The 71
Les Miserables 47
Life of an American Fireman,
  The 30, 32-34
Little Foxes, The 261
Little Lord Fauntleroy 202
Little Nell's Tobacco 69
Locked Door, The 81
Lonedale Operator, The 142, 192
Lonely Villa, The 46, 125
Lorna Doone 71
Lost Squadron, The 225
Love Among the Roses 141
Love Flower, The 206, 277
Macbeth 43
Madame Sans Gene 144
Magnificent Ambersons, The 261
Man's Genesis 143
Mark of Zorro, The 181
Marriage Circle, The 212
Massacre, The 144
Matrimony's Speed Limit 53
Merry Go Round 221-222, 228,
  234, 253, 259, 281
Merry Widow, The 220-222,
  224, 226, 229, 248-249,
  251-252, 259, 282
Military Review, Hungary 27
Miracle Man, The 234
Monkey Business 237
Monsieur Verdoux 261
Moral Fabric, The 84
Mother and the Law, The 8,
  118, 176, 198
Mothering Heart, The 193
Mother Love 145
Musketeers of Pig Alley, The
  118, 260
Narrow Trail, The 99, 108
New York Hat, The 46, 266

One Exciting Night 260, 278
One Is Business, the Other
    Crime 12, 131
On the Midnight Stage 95
Orphans of the Storm 5, 21, 23,
    278
Othello 43
Over Silent Paths 141
Paddy O'Hara 84
Painted Soul, The 84, 86
Palace of the Arabian Nights,
    The 28
Palm Beach Story, The 261
Passing of Two-Gun Hicks, The
    78, 88
Payment, The 79
Peggy 78, 84
Peg O'My Heart 202
Perils of Pauline, The 43
Peter Pan 265
Phantom of the Opera, The 202
Pinto Ben 97
Pippa Passes 46, 146
Plain Jane 79, 84
Plain Song, A 135
Pollyanna 202
Polly of the Circus 49
Poor Little Rich Girl, The 48
Prisoner of Zenda, The 202
Prunella 48
Pueblo Legend, A 133
Queen Elizabeth 15, 144
Queen Kelly 221, 225, 234, 251,
    253, 259, 261, 283
Quo Vadis 116, 146
Rain 108
Ramona 141
Rescued by Rover 32
Rescued from an Eagle's Nest
    125
Restless Breed 56
Richard the Third 43
Rich Revenge, A 141
Riders of the Purple Sage 108
Rip's Sleep 28
River's Edge, The 56
Robin Hood 56, 177
Rogues of Paris, The 53
Romance 203, 206

Romance of Happy Valley, A 4,
    19, 118, 197, 276
Romance of the Western Hills,
    The 141
Romeo and Juliet 43
Romola 202
Rose of Salem Town 133
Sadie Thompson 81
Sally of the Sawdust 279
Salvation Army Lass, A 134
Sands O'Dee, The 135, 193
Sands of Iwo Jima 56
Scarlet Days 276
Seven Chances 53
Silver Lode 56
Skate on Skates, A 38
Song of the Shirt, The 12, 131
Sons of Toil 87
Sorrows of Love 87
Sorrows of Satan, The 184, 210,
    279
Sorrows of the Unfaithful, The 141
Spreading Dawn, The 49
Strange Interlude, 81
Struggle, The 26, 184, 212, 280
Sunrise 92
Sunset Boulevard 226, 261
Sunshine Sue 134
Taking of Luke McVane, The 88
Tarnished Reputations 54
Tarzan of the Apes 54
Teasing the Gardener 28
Tempest, The 81
Thais 49
That Royle Girl 210, 279
Thirty a Week 49
Those Who Pay 84, 87
Thread of Destiny, The 140
Three Faces East 80
Three Musketeers, The 202
Tigress, The 54
Tol'able David 203
Toll Gate, The 108
Trail of the Lonesome Pine, The
    202
Treasure Island 202
Treasure of the Sierra Madre
    261
Trilby 48

*Trip to the Moon, A* 28
*Troublesome Baby* 38
*True Heart Susie* 4, 9, 19, 83,
    118, 195-197, 212, 276
*Turkish Delight* 81
*Two Brothers, The* 141
*Two Men in the Desert* 253
*Typhoon, The* 85
*Unexpected Help* 141
*U.S. Battleship at Sea* 28
*Usurer, The* 12, 131, 141
*Vanity* 80
*Violin Maker of Nuremburg,
    The* 53
*Virginian, The* 105
*Walking Down Broadway (Hello
    Sister)* 225, 230, 283
*Wandering Husbands* 80
*Way Down East* 10-11, 13, 21,
    23, 84, 119, 184, 202-204,
    206-209, 277
*Way of the World, The* 141
*Wedding March, The* 221-222,
    224, 234, 248-249, 255-256,
    258-259, 261, 283
*What the Daisy Said* 141
*What Price Glory?* 246
*White Gold* 80
*White Rose, The* 197, 278
*White Rose of the Wilds, The* 142
*Wind, The* 92
*Wishing Ring, The* 48, 75
*Woman Disputed, The* 81
*Woman Scorned, A* 132
*Workers Leaving the Lumiere
    Factory* 27
*Wrath of the Gods, The* 84
*Yankee Clipper* 80
*Young Heroes of the West* 38